22-54

D. T. Suzuki

On Indian Mahayana Buddhism

D. T. Suzuki

On Indian Mahayana Buddhism

Edited with an Introduction by
EDWARD CONZE

Harper Torchbooks
Harper & Row, Publishers
New York, Evanston, and London

D. T. SUZUKI ON INDIAN MAHAYANA BUDDHISM

Printed in the United States of America.

First Edition: HARPER TORCHBOOKS, 1968
Harper & Row, Publishers, Incorporated,
New York, N.Y. 10016.

Library of Congress Catalog Card Number: 68-26896.

Contents

Abbreviations

BI	*Bibliotheca Indica*
EB	*The Eastern Buddhist*
EZB	*Essays in Zen Buddhism*
GOS	Gaekwad's Oriental Series
IIJ	Indo-Iranian Journal
JPTS	*Journal of the Pali Text Society*
LS	*Laṅkāvatāra Sūtra*
MChrB	*Mysticism: Christian and Buddhist*
MMG	Mimeograph copy (1928) of Professor H. Idzumi's copy of a Nepalese manuscript of the *Gaṇḍavyūha,* collated with another Nepalese manuscript in Kyoto
SBE	Sacred Books of the East
SOR	Serie Orientale Roma
St.	*Studies in the Laṅkāvatār Sūtra*
ZJB	*Zen and Japanese Buddhism* (Tokyo, Japan Travel Bureau, 1958)

Introduction

EDWARD CONZE

Zen and the Mahayana

DR. SUZUKI's vast and notable literary output over sixty years is devoted to two main themes, which, though fairly distinct, are nevertheless closely interrelated. While the bulk of his work deals with the "Zen" of China and Japan, a large section of it concerns itself with the Indian Mahayana. But whereas his exposition of Zen has had a remarkable effect on Europeans and Americans, his writings on the Indian Mahayana have so far had little influence.

As a direct result of Suzuki's books on Zen there is now a flourishing Zen movement all over the world, and this movement has caused an immense interest in those aspects of Zen not covered by Suzuki. Dozens of books are being published annually, nearly all of them by commercial publishers, who would soon desist if there were not an avid public to buy their wares. Nothing of the same kind has happened with Suzuki's Mahayana studies, which have aroused no great curiosity about those numerous aspects of the Mahayana on which he has not touched. The publications in this field are still of a purely scholarly and specialized character, heavily subsidized by various foundations and learned societies, and ignored by the general public.

First of all we must consider the question *why,* when Suzuki's teachings on Zen have had such an immense success, there should have been almost no response to his work on the Mahayana. To him there was no essential difference between the two. He saw the early Mahayana as a form of the Buddha's teaching suited to Hindu mentality, and Zen as a form of the same teaching suited to the mentality of the Far East.[1] But, though closely united in his own work, they seem to have drifted apart as soon as they left his hands and moved to the West. This drifting apart has no basis in Suzuki's own sayings or teachings and must therefore be due to some factors in the mentality of his American and European followers. It cannot spring from what he himself has said, but must come from the social position and cultural assumptions of his adherents. Five points will, I think, have to be considered in this context.

1. Zen may seem to be something immediately practical which can be done by anyone who has the will to do it, whereas the Mahayana Sutras appear to consist of a long series of rather inconsequential musings. Worse, they are reserved for people who call themselves "sons and daughters of good family," thereby affronting the democratic sentiments of our age. Moreover, a perusal of the Mahayana Sutras cannot leave us in any doubt that there is nothing we can do immediately about them. The reason is that our present condition is infinitely removed from the level on which they operate. They show us the universe as it appears to those whose self is completely extinct. But when we emerge from their study and observe how we behave in daily life, we cannot help noticing that our own self is far from being completely or even partially extinct. They hold out to us a vision of the world which corresponds to perhaps the sixth or seventh stage of a Bodhisattva, whereas even the great Nāgārjuna had only reached the first stage, and the rest of us, even such teachers as Āryadeva,[2] flounder about on the level of what are so politely called "the foolish common people." It was just this discrepancy between the sublimity of the teachings and the attainments of its students which led at a later time, when the traditional methods of meditation seem to have somewhat lost their regenerating power, to the development of new methods by which the gap might be bridged.

[1] Zen is "one of the Mahayana schools of Buddhism shorn of its Indian garb" (*EZB*, I, 37); it "is no doubt the native product of the Chinese mind" (*ibid.*, p. 36); a creation of "the practical imagination of the Chinese people" (*ibid.*, p. 164). See also pp. 159, 197 and pp. 3–4.

[2] Buston, *History of Buddhism*, trans. E. Obermiller, Heidelberg, O. Harrassowitz, 1932, II, 131.

On Indian soil they were the Tantras, in China and Japan Ch'an and Zen. If and when European Buddhism after about five centuries reaches its full maturity, it will also evolve its own indigenous methods of realizing these transcendental doctrines.

On the other hand it is often forgotten that the Mahayana Sutras can still promote spiritual regeneration in their own subtle and elusive ways. If we take the *Prajñāpāramitā,* all the study of it and all the talk about it can never result in anything which can be formulated with any degree of precision. But over the years the ardent devotion to its teachings and the reflection or meditation on its formulations seem to imperceptibly work some kind of spiritual transformation. This leads to an increasingly wisdom-led attitude to the problems of life, which proves its worth by greatly easing the burdens of existence and which is appreciated with some astonishment even by outsiders. To some extent this discipline operates through repetition,[3] and therefore great value is attached to the recitation of the *Heart Sutra,* or to the reading of large sections of the Sutras just for its own sake. This kind of thing does not, I know, accord any too well with modern ideas on education—but then those do not aim at anything which could reasonably be called spiritual growth.

2. Zen may seem to be empirical and a mere matter of direct experience, whereas the Mahayana Sutras at first sight seem to be replete with philosophical and even "metaphysical" speculations. E. Frauwallner, for instance, says that the *Prajñāpāramitā Sūtras,* "like the Mahayana Sutras in general, are concerned with the career of a Bodhisattva, i.e., of a future Buddha. But the philosophical sections take up a considerable part of the space and form their real core."[4]

This is often to their great disadvantage, particularly in England. In this connection it is quite interesting to note that no Englishman has ever contributed much to the elucidation of the Mahayana, and that all the more prominent Mahayana scholars came from countries where "philosophy" is not yet a dirty word. They were Frenchmen like Burnouf, S. Lévi, and

[3] See p. 97.
[4] *Die Philosophie des Buddhismus,* Berlin, Akademie Verlag, 1956, p. 147.

Demiéville, Belgians like de la Vallée-Poussin and Lamotte, Italians like Tucci, and, of course, Germans like M. Walleser in Heidelberg, Max Mueller and myself in England, J. Schmidt and E. Obermiller in Russia. In 1884 H. Kern, a Dutchman, translated at the request of Max Mueller *The Lotus of the Good Law* in its entirety for the "Sacred Books of the East." In 1930 an Englishman, W. E. Soothill, severely abbreviated his own translation on the strange ground that a full translation would be "unavoidably cumbrous and inspirationally innocuous."[5]

Arguments based on national character can, however, be overdone. At times indeed the national differences between various Buddhist commentators are most striking and must seem quite incommensurable. Kamalaśīla's extremely scholastic elaboration of Vasubandhu's commentary on the *Diamond Sutra*[6] is totally unlike Han Shan's intuitive meanderings on the same commentary ten centuries later,[7] and likewise the same Kamalaśīla's rigid scholasticism clashed in a fury of mutual incomprehension with the quietism of the Ch'an followers when the interpretation of the Mahayana Sutras was debated at the "Council of Lhasa"[8] about A.D. 800. Likewise only a practical Englishman could have written the books of Christmas Humphreys, only a metaphysical German those of I. J. Schmidt, and only a rational Frenchman those of E. Burnouf. But this is not all, because, when the whole national field is surveyed, a law of compensation is seen to be at work. The Chinese may be practical and matter-of-fact,[9] but it were Chinese who prized the *Prajñāpāramitā Sūtras* above all others[10] and who, as a counterbalance to the extreme rationalism of their normal approach, developed Taoism and the T'ien-t'ai. Likewise, hardheaded Englishmen are often drawn to the occult, the

5 *The Lotus of the Wonderful Law,* Oxford, Clarendon Press, p. viii.

6 G. Tucci, *Minor Buddhist Texts,* I, Rome, Ismeo, 1956, pp. 131–71.

7 Ch. Luk, *Ch'an and Zen Teaching,* I, London, Rider, 1960, pp. 149–206.

8 P. Demiéville, *Le concile de Lhasa,* I, Paris, Presses Universitaires, 1952; G. Tucci, *Minor Buddhist Texts, II, Rome,* Ismeo, 1958; E. Conze, *Buddhist Scriptures,* Harmondsworth, Penguin, 1959, pp. 214–17.

9 See, e.g., p. 31.

10 For the facts see E. Zuercher, *The Buddhist Conquest of China,* Leiden, E. J. Brill, 1959.

admiring inventor of Sherlock Holmes became a spiritualist, Victorian Englishmen kept astrology alive, and in the same period British universities were strongholds of Hegelianism. A revulsion against the arid sobrieties of its empiricism may one day impel even the Anglo-Saxon mind to take an interest in Mahayana thought.

3. Zen sayings, as rendered by Suzuki, are brief, succinct, and witty, and often may seem immediately intelligible. In their unexpurgated form the Mahayana Sutras are the very reverse, and to the average modern European they must appear verbose, repetitive, tedious, and full of ridiculous exaggerations. To take just one instance, a simile in the version of the *Prajñāpāramitā in 8,000 Lines* speaks of "a mother who has many children—five, or ten, or twenty, or thirty, or forty, or fifty, or one hundred, or one thousand."[11] As though one thousand children were not yet enough for one woman, other recensions attribute to her up to "one hundred thousand children." Such wild exaggerations occur all the time. A fine example of tediousness is the long passage from the *Gaṇḍavyūha* about the *bodhicitta,* or desire for enlightenment, which Suzuki translated so patiently[12] and which I have deliberately omitted from Chapter VII of this anthology. Here no fewer than 224 similes are piled one upon the other, without really telling us anything at all. We can well understand that, as Suzuki puts it,[13] "the Bodhisattva Maitreya is far from being satisfied with these endless varieties of metaphors" and need not be ashamed to share his view. As for the repetitions, in the "Large Sutra on Perfect Wisdom" hundreds of pages are at times given over to repeating one and the same formula with slight variations, so that the reader is almost bound to lose the thread of the argument. And Suzuki himself has commented on the "literary shortcomings" of the *Laṅkāvatāra.*[14]

Nevertheless it must be remembered that spiritual classics are rarely particularly entertaining or amusing. When seen

11 XII, 253. Suzuki on p. 36 sensibly sums this up as "a woman who has a large number of children."

12 *EZB,* III, 181–204.

13 *Ibid.,* p. 194.

14 *St.,* pp. 60–61.

in their totality, Zen writings are just as "tedious" as the Mahayana Sutras, or as the Abhidharma, or as all those Buddhist writings which are designed as technical treatises to be studied for their contents alone, like textbooks of thermodynamics or crystallography. A good example is Luk's translation of the *Stories of the Founders of the Five Ch'an Sects*,[15] which manages to envelop the teaching of the Dharma in a fog of total incomprehension. As a stranger to the Zen lineage I must confess that these stories told me precisely nothing, that I understood not one of them, and that I soon laid the book aside with a yawn and a shrug. And yet how these stories used to charm us when we found Dr. Suzuki adding a few at a time as a kind of seasoning to his masterly discourses on the spiritual life!

The Sung masters, of course, never intended these collections of quaint sayings and incidents to be used as "books" read by all and sundry entirely divorced from their proper context of spiritual discipline. These are "esoteric" works. Esoteric literature has a definite place in Buddhism, but it should never be forgotten that it loses all meaning when severed from the living tradition which sustains it. As subjects of meditation under an acknowledged Zen master these stories should be invaluable. When read by outsiders they are incomprehensible, just as are remarks made in a private language current in a closely knit family when told to those who do not belong to it. The language used by lovers, intimates, and initiates is indeed quite different from the language of the general public.[16]

15 *Ch'an and Zen Teaching*, II, London, Rider, 1961.

16 May I be permitted to illustrate this difference between a "private" and a "public" language with at least one extremely simple example. If the word "seagull" occurs in a public document, then its meaning, if unknown, can be ascertained from a dictionary, where it is found to be "a sea bird in the family *Leridae*." In the private language of my family "seagull" is a synonym for the idle reiteration of futile statements which may just as well be left unsaid. It goes back to the time when my wife used to say on our daily walks in the Eton playing fields with feminine persistence "It must be stormy on the coast—just look at the many seagulls!" After a few months of this I learned to anticipate her remark by saying "seagulls," and we rejoiced at how well we understood one another. The meaning of "seagulls" in this context is known only to the two of us, and unless we tell others they cannot possibly guess it. Now I can well imagine that the secret meaning of the "cypress tree," "the three pounds

In the first five centuries of Buddhist history the tradition was entirely oral, and nothing was ever written down. In the second five hundred years there was a profusion of public documents, written down and available to anyone sufficiently interested to get hold of them.[17] A large part of the writing of the third five hundred years, i.e., that of the Tantra and Zen, was couched in a secret and esoteric language, which could be understood only when explained by an initiated master (as in the case of the Tantra), or became luminously clear when the disciple had reached the level of *satori,* or "enlightened living" (as in the case of Zen). In consequence, while those who are initiated or those who have attained *satori* may well derive an immense benefit from the cryptic sayings of the masters, those who are not initiated and who are not in contact with a fully qualified teacher may just as well seek for the meaning of Buddhism in public documents, like the Mahayana Sutras. These may, in fact, be more rewarding than the often self-defeating attempts to listen to what the sages whispered to one another in a particularly obscure form of the Chinese language a thousand years ago. Experience has shown that many of those whose interest in Buddhism was first aroused by books on Zen have formed the impression that it is very difficult to understand Zen without a knowledge of the earlier tradition.

4. Few people at present realize that spirituality, as soon as it goes beyond the stage of a raw beginner, is a matter of definite traditions and lineages, and cannot be comprehended outside them. Many of those who regard Zen as a kind of "do it yourself" affair feel a perpetual urge to sever it from the traditions of the Mahayana. Suzuki, on the other hand, points out "that Zen is most intimately connected historically and doctrinally with the Prajñā teaching"[18] and that "the

---

of flax," and so on has either been faithfully transmitted from one generation of initiates to the next, or can be grasped by those who have won *satori.* But what I cannot imagine is how anyone outside this chain of initiates or adepts could ever possibly divine the true meaning of these sayings.

17 P. H. L. Eggermont (*IIJ,* II, 225–28) has shown the close connection between the traditions about the writing down of the scriptures and the traditions about the decline of the Dharma after the first 500 years.

18 P. 33.

sutras and Zen are not antagonistic, nor are they contradictory."[19] They "both agree in spirit," and "the one will prove complementary to the other when we endeavor to study Buddhism comprehensively."[20]

Far from rejecting the Sutras, the early Ch'an masters were saturated in them, and many of their sayings are either direct quotations from the Sutras or contain allusions to them. Translators or readers who do not know the Sutras or believe them to be irrelevant will miss many points. What, for instance, can they make of Tsung-chih's reply to Bodhidharma's query about her achievement if they have never read Chapter 28 of *The Perfection of Wisdom in 8,000 Lines*?[21] On a deeper level, although Zen as an essentially non-discursive response to reality has never set out to formulate a philosophy of its own, it nevertheless everywhere presupposes and takes for granted the philosophy formulated by the Mahayana Sutras.[22] That is an "absolute monism,"[23] and "like other monisms" it maintains "the idea of absolute oneness."[24] But whereas the Sutras just teach this oneness by various devices, Zen is an "*exercise* in oneness."[25] It is surely tempting for us at the present period of history to seek for an immediately verifiable religious experience, free from the outmoded "superstitious" and dubious assumptions which keep so many educated people away from the traditional religions of mankind. But it still

[19] P. 159.

[20] In describing the intentions of *The Eastern Buddhist*, Suzuki specifically stated that "the Mahayana ought to be considered one whole indivisible thing and no sects, especially no sectarian prejudices, to be recognized in it." I, 156.

[21] Pp. 192–93 of my translation, Calcutta, The Asiatic Society, 1958. The nun Soji said: "As I understand it, it [i.e., the truth] is like Ananda's viewing the Buddha land of Akshobhya: it is seen once and never again." Suzuki in *The Essentials of Zen Buddhism*, ed. B. Phillips, London, Rider, 1963, p. 119.

[22] Those who want to treat Zen as a detachable technique can, however, find encouragement in some of the master's sayings: e.g., "Strictly speaking, Zen has no philosophy of its own. Its teaching is concentrated in an intuitive experience, and the intellectual content of this experience can be supplied by a system of thought not necessarily Buddhistic." *Zen and Japanese Culture*, London, Routledge and Kegan Paul, 1959, p. 44.

[23] *EZB*, I, 297.

[24] *EZB*, I, 270.

[25] *ZJB*, p. 27. My italics.

remains to be shown how far one can get in one's knowledge of the heavenly kingdom if one dispenses with faith and a collectively imposed self-discipline.

The Mahayana Sutras in their turn are but a stage in a spiritual tradition which begins with the teaching of the Lord Buddha himself, corrects the views of the Disciples and Pratyekabuddhas, and is enshrined in Sutras which are incomplete without the commentaries. To appreciate their background requires more study than the average busy person can afford without neglecting his worldly pursuits, and without giving up one's whole life to them one will never get to the bottom of these Sutras. But is Zen really any different? How can one grasp the koans without a qualified teacher? How can one practice Zen with any success without thinking of it all the time, and rarely of anything else?

Though fully aware of its debt to tradition, Zen has, of course, its anti-traditionalist elements. The nature of this anti-traditionalism is, however, often misunderstood by the wild men to whom Zen is a matter of tearing up Sutras, killing cats, and burning images of the Buddha. The intention is not to reject tradition altogether, but to put it into its place. Suzuki is often blamed for the misunderstandings which his work has aroused.[26] If he is to be blamed for anything, it is an insufficient awareness of the aridity of the desert into which he transplanted his lovely azalea tree. For what he unsuspectingly did was to feed an Eastern form of spirituality into a predominantly ex-Protestant environment which, having lost touch with spiritual tradition, gravitated inevitably toward a self-assertive nihilism.

Zen was designed to operate within emptiness. On its journey West it has been transferred into a vacuum. Let us just recollect what Zen in the East took for granted as its antecedents, basis, and continuing background:[27] a long and unbroken tradition

[26] E.g., Chen-chi Chang, "The Nature of Ch'an (Zen) Buddhism," *Philosophy East and West,* VI, 4, 1958. Though it makes some telling points against the vulgarizers, this article makes the essential soundness of Suzuki's own work quite apparent.

[27] All this has been very well explained by J. Evola in "Zen and the West," *The Middle Way,* XXX, 108–13, 123. Reprinted from *East and West* (Rome), July 1955.

of spiritual "know-how"; firm and unquestioned metaphysical beliefs,[28] and not just a disbelief in everything: a superabundance of scriptures and images; a definite discipline supervised by authoritative persons; insistence on right livelihood and an austere life for all exponents of the Dharma; and a strong Sangha, composed of thousands of mature and experienced monks housed in thousands of temples, who could keep deviations from Buddhist principles within narrow bounds. As I have said elsewhere, the Ch'an sect "found a situation in which the fervor of the faithful had so multiplied the means of salvation, in the form of Sutras, commentaries, philosophical subtleties, images and rites, that the goal itself was apt to be lost sight of, and the spiritual life was in danger of being choked by the very things which were designed to foster it. In their reaction against the overgrown apparatus of piety they advocated a radical simplification of the approach to enlightenment. They never tired of denouncing the misuse of this apparatus, which could so easily become an end in itself."[29]

It is a fundamental error if these denunciations are mistaken for a desire to altogether abolish traditional spiritual practices. Suzuki in faraway Japan could not possibly have foreseen it. Likewise, when he condemned the intellect as inhibiting our original spontaneity, Suzuki took it for granted that once the intellect is eliminated the Tao will take over. He was relatively unfamiliar with Western irrationalist philosophy,[30] where the elimination of the intellect makes room for nothing more sublime than the uninhibited assertion of self-willed instincts,[31] and where everything is left as it was before. When he spoke of spontaneity he meant the spontaneity of sages, and not that of unreformed worldlings.

5. One main source of the success of Zen has been that it

[28] "Zen is steeped in metaphysics and in transcendentalism" (*MChrB* 107).

[29] E. Conze, *A Short History of Buddhism*, Bombay, Chetana Ltd., 1960, pp. 74–75.

[30] But see pp. 69–70 about the difference between irrationality and what is actually seen with the Prajña eye.

[31] I have said more about the insidious similarity between spiritual nihilism and the teachings of the Mahayana in "The Development of Prajñāpāramitā Thought" in *Buddhism and Culture*, ed. S. Yamagucchi, Kyoto, 1960, pp. 38–39.

is often welcomed (quite wrongly, I think) as a therapeutic method on a level with psychoanalysis,[32] capable of removing mental conflicts, of curing marital maladjustments, and of allowing people to function efficiently in whatever they may set out to do. I have no doubt that, like many other procedures, it can do all these things to some extent. On the other hand, someone under constant pressure from his own mental conflicts is hardly the kind of person who would be much interested in the Mahayana Sutras. They can be appreciated only to the extent that neurosis is left behind. A neurosis is always about the self imprisoned in itself and constantly concerned with itself, whereas the Mahayana Sutras show us the world as it reveals itself when that self is gone. They contain endless instructions about layers of the mind and facets of the cosmos which escape the ken of people struggling to free themselves from their own preoccupations with themselves, and which have in the West been splendidly described with much loving care by St. Thomas in the *secunda secundae* of his *Summa Theologica* and by Dante in his *Paradiso*: "Oceans as yet undared my vessel dares."[33] For those meant to appreciate the Sutras, the statement that "all is one and the same" is not a flat abstract proposition, but the starting point for a long and thrilling voyage of discovery.

> Not that the living light I looked on wore
> More semblances than one, which cannot be,
> For it is always what it was before;
> But as my sight by seeing learned to see,
> The transformation which in me took place
> Transformed the single changeless form for me.[34]

The Mahayana Sutras, just like Zen in its unadulterated form, pour forth veritable torrents of spirituality which have no meaning whatever for anyone who has not reached a fairly high degree of self-effacement. Those outpourings *(niṣyanda)*

[32] See, e.g., D. T. Suzuki, E. Fromm, and R. de Martino, *Zen Buddhism and Psychoanalysis*, London, Allen and Unwin, 1960.

[33] Dante, *The Paradise*, II:7, trans. D. L. Sayers and B. Reynolds, Harmondsworth, Penguin, 1962.

[34] *Ibid.*, XXXIII:109–14. *Satori* is "to experience the suchness or is-ness of things" (*ZJB*, p. 37), but "the principle of Suchness is not static, it is full of dynamic forces" (p. 250).

of the Tathagata's grace, as the scriptures call them, cannot possibly interest the average worldling battling desperately to maintain his own miserable self against adverse circumstances. They describe the fruits of the spirit when this self has to some extent quieted itself down, and speak eloquently about such unworldly subjects as disinterested goodness, self-sacrificing generosity and compassion, the ability to transcend the limitations of the body, sheer emptiness and the translucent light of the Dharma. No neurotic can want to learn about these topics, except for reasons of academic self-advancement. Such themes are reserved for people who have no greatly urgent personal problems, who habitually treat all worldly concerns as utterly trivial, and who are not bored but positively fascinated by the prospect of spending long ages in Amitabha's paradise, where, seated on lotuses, they do nothing but gaze upon His shining form and listen to the sound of His holy Dharma.

Suzuki's Contributions to the Knowledge of the Mahayana

We must now consider the range and value of Suzuki's work on the Mahayana. In mere bulk alone this side of the teaching is quite considerable. It began in 1907 with the publication of the *Outlines of Mahāyāna Buddhism.*[35] This massive book of 420 pages is still, over half a century later, substantially sound, though at times somewhat old-fashioned, and the English diction is surprisingly idiosyncratic. There is also a strong leaning toward socialist views, which seems to have dropped out later on.[35a] Its main shortcoming is a distortion of the historical perspective which results from Suzuki placing the complications of *The Awakening of Faith in the Mahāyāna,*[36] which he attributes to Aśvaghosha, at the beginning of the Indian Mahayana development;[37] whereas meanwhile it has

[35] Reprinted 1963, New York, Schocken Books, with a prefatory essay by Alan Watts.

[35a] E.g. pp. 187–91.

[36] Which he had himself translated in 1960. Chicago, Open Court Publishing Company.

[37] I.e., to "the first century before Christ" (p. 246). He also calls him "the first Mahāyāna philosopher."

been shown to be a Chinese work belonging to the very end of this development.[38] Still, in 1968 there are only two comprehensive surveys of the Mahayana, the one being Suzuki's based on Chinese sources, and the other that of N. Dutt[39] based on Sanskrit sources. At the relatively early age of thirty-seven Suzuki already revealed himself as a profound and subtle thinker, with manifold interests also in non-Mahayana thought. The book, in fact, contains, at least by way of hints, the majority of his later ideas, except that there is in it almost nothing about Zen.[40] It was never brought up to date,[41] and his wife's much shorter book[42] to some extent replaced it in 1938.

After a pause of fourteen years there came, at first in articles in *The Eastern Buddhist*,[43] the extensive studies of Indian Sutras which had at one time or other influenced Chinese Ch'an. The year 1932 saw the translation of the *Lankāvatāra Sūtra*, preceded in 1930 by *Studies* in that Sutra and followed in 1933 and 1934 by an *Index*. Then in 1934 almost the entire third series of *Essays in Zen Buddhism* was devoted to the *Prajñāpāramitā*, and to the *Gaṇḍavyūha* which Dr. Suzuki with the help of H. Idzumi edited in the original Sanskrit between 1934 and 1936. For many years afterward he planned a translation of the *Gaṇḍavyūha*, which he believed to require the collaboration of a number of scholars, but his efforts in this direction always came to nought. The next year brought, in the *Manual of Zen Buddhism*, some fine translations from the *Diamond Sutra*, and 1939 a study of the *Sukhāvatīvyūha*.[43] Then there was another pause of nearly twenty years. In 1957 Suzuki published "The Basis of Buddhist Philosophy" (as seen by a Mahayanist!) (our Chapter VIII) and his famous essay on Meister Eckhart (our Chapter IX). They represent a new phase

38 For the latest survey of this question see W. Liebenthal, "New Light on the Mahāyāna-Śraddhotpāda Śāstra," *T'oung Pao*, XLVI, 155–216. Leiden, E. J. Brill, 1959.

39 *Aspects of Mahāyāna Buddhism and Its Relation to Hīnayāna*. London, 1930.

40 Although in 1907 he wrote "The Zen Sect of Buddhism" for *JPTS*!

41 For Suzuki's own comments (1934) see p. 211.

42 B. L. Suzuki, *Mahāyāna Buddhism*, 170 pp., London, The Buddhist Lodge, with a valuable introduction by D. T. Suzuki. Reprinted in 1948 by David Marlowe Ltd. and in 1959 by Allen and Unwin.

43 For a list see the bibliography.

of Dr. Suzuki's thought, which for a time became quite saturated with Meister Eckhart.[44, 45]

All this taken together would by itself make the reputation of a scholar anywhere. Nor must the originality of Suzuki's work be forgotten. Almost everywhere he broke new ground. While some of the shorter texts had been previously translated, before 1930 nothing, or next to nothing, was known of the *Large Prajñāpāramitā* or of the *Laṅkāvatāra* and *Gaṇḍavyūha*.

How then have scholars reacted to the quality of Suzuki's work? On the negative side we must note that the grammarians have found fault with his translation of the *Laṅkāvatāra*, and Franklin Edgerton in his *Buddhist Hybrid Sanskrit Dictionary* (1953) adduces numerous occasions on which Suzuki departed from the Sanskrit text. In nearly all cases Edgerton is probably right. His strictures do not, however, testify against the value of Suzuki's translation, because Suzuki tells us expressly that "when difficulties were encountered in the course of my English translation of the Sanskrit text, I have frequently followed the T'ang reading" of the Chinese translation, on the ground that "the Sanskrit text itself as we have it is still far from being perfect, and there is no doubt that Nanjo's edition requires many corrections in order to yield a more intelligible reading."[46] It is, after all, the sense and not the grammar which matters in philosophical works, and as a first attempt Suzuki's translation has carried the meaning of the Sutra to an almost miraculous extent into a language quite unprepared to receive it.

[margin note: true, but who has understand]

Nevertheless, thirty years later there can be no doubt that this translation of the *Laṅkāvatāra* is now in need of revision, and it is a great pity that the master himself is unable to undertake it. In the introduction to his translation he speaks of "its many imperfections";[47] in the preface to the "Studies"

---

44 *EB*, VII, 227–46.

45 In consequence I could not, as originally intended, place Chapter VIII at the beginning of these selections. At first sight it seemed logical to have the more general precede the more particular. But to do so would have meant to place works written in the 1950's before works written in the 1930's, and in view of the constant growth of Suzuki's thought the result would have been unconvincing as well as bewildering.

46 *LS*, pp. xlix, xlviii.

47 *LS*, p. xlvii.

he said that "the results he has gained so far in his study . . . are no doubt short of being quite satisfactory from a strictly scholarly point of view";[48] and in a note appended in 1957 he speaks of his wish to improve parts of his work and regrets that he cannot find the time to do so. In 1932 he had to invent a new terminology in an alien language,[49] and some improvements are now possible.[50] This is a fate which must overtake all pioneer translations. Much of the technical vocabulary of the Mahayana is still unexplored, and even accomplished scholars are often forced to guess where they do not know. The only serious objection that can be made is that Suzuki, bored with the scholasticism of the later Hinayana and unimpressed by the discoveries of Rosenberg and the "Leningrad school," never paid attention to the radical difference between "dharmas" and "things."[51] Also in some details he can be somewhat misleading. A reader will, for instance, be greatly puzzled when he reads that "gold, vajra and the relics of the Buddha, owing to their specific character, are never destroyed but remain the same until the end of time." The text actually says that they last for an aeon *(kalpa-sthitāḥ)*, and an aeon is but a very small part of the whole of time.[52]

It cannot be easy for outsiders to realize fully the immense difficulties involved in translating Mahayana Sutras. These teachings are so utterly sublime, unworldly, and transcendental that no individual can at the first attempt do justice to them. The few older translations that we possess of extensive texts, like Kern's *Lotus of the Good Law* (1884) or Bendall-Rouse's *Śikshā-Samuccaya* (1922), are, when checked against the originals,

48 P. v.

49 "It is a bold attempt on the part of the translator to try to render some of the deepest thoughts that have been nourished in the East into a language to which he was not born." *LS*, p. xlvii.

50 In the glossary I have proposed occasional alternative renderings which seem to me preferable. These have been placed in parentheses.

51 See my *Buddhist Thought in India*, London, Allen and Unwin, 1962, pp. 92–106. In this context it is interesting to read the extremely cool unsigned review of Stcherbatsky's "Central Conception of Buddhism" in *EB*, III, 84–85.

52 *LS*, p. 204. For further details the reader must be referred to my *Buddhist Texts*, nos. 178–80, 182–83. By comparing my rendering with Suzuki's he will see what modifications I believed to be necessary in 1954.

obviously now quite inadequate and frequently distinctly misleading on doctrinal matters. "As it is illustrated in the long history of the Chinese translation of the Buddhist texts, there must be several attempts before the work assumes something of finality."[53] In Tibet also multitudes of scholars had to struggle for centuries before the true meaning of these writings could be brought out.

While admitting Suzuki's deficiencies on points of detail, I must, however, emphasize that he is still unsurpassed in his grasp of the spirit of the doctrine. A few years ago I read through everything that had so far been published on Mahayana philosophy. Somewhat to my surprise I found that the *Studies in the Laṅkāvatāra Sūtra* were still the most illuminating work in existence. The reason was that Suzuki alone did not treat Buddhist philosophical statements as exercises in philosophical ingenuity or disputatiousness, but as expressions of Buddhist life and meditational experience. As he himself puts it, "we must keep one thing always before our minds, which is, that Buddhist thought is always the outcome of Buddhist life; that its logic, or psychology, or metaphysics cannot be understood adequately unless we realize that facts of Buddhist experience are at its basis, and, therefore, that pure logic is not the key to the understanding of Buddhist philosophy. . . .[54] "The one most important thing that students of Buddhism have to realize at the very outset of their study is that Buddhism is not a system of philosophy, has nothing to do with speculations as such, has no intention to present a logically coherent formula of thought. . . . What the Mahayana Sutras contain are plain statements of facts experienced by the Indian Buddhist minds, that is, they are most direct statements based upon the intuitive knowledge these minds have gained regarding the religious life. Their statements may be logically untenable or impossible, but they have not lost sight of the facts or experiences that have flashed through their minds. All their paradoxes, contradictions, incomprehensibilities, and even all their apparently nonsensical utterances must be reduced first of all to their intuitions. . . ."[55] "In

[53] *LS*, p. lxviii.
[54] *St.*, pp. 162–63; cf. also p. 169.
[55] *St.*, p. 285.

matters religious, life and experience count for more than analysis."[56]

Suzuki's basic thesis is somewhat unexpectedly confirmed by a quite unbiased source, an Austrian scholar who is not a believing Buddhist and was brought up in the German tradition of "pure scholarship." According to E. Frauwallner, "the Buddha had no use for purely philosophical questions. He occupied himself with theoretical questions only to the extent that they were needed for providing a foundation for his doctrine of salvation. Whatever went beyond that he rejected as superfluous and misleading. He maintained this attitude throughout his entire life, and for a long time after his death it must have been respected by his followers."[57]

While therefore the theoretical statements can only be properly understood as the incidental by-products of spiritual intuitions, there has been throughout the whole of Buddhist history a tendency among lesser minds to treat them as dogmatic formulations valid on logical grounds. This trend was constantly combated by the central tradition of Buddhism. In early times it took the form of condemning people who held "views."

> The partisan who hugs
>   the creed he fancies most
> Brands rival creeds as "stuff."
>   And so strife dogs his days.
> Adepts dismiss as "clogs"
>   this claim and arrogance.
> So, Almsman, do not build
>   on works and things of sense;
> Nor rear on lore or works
>   a speculative view;
> Nor claim to be "as good,"
>   or "worse" or "better far."
> Unprejudiced and free,
>   not based on learning's stores,
> Owning no sect or school,
>   holding no theories.[58]

[56] *EZB*, III 155. See also pp. 41, 55–6, 159, 171–2 below.
[57] *Die Philosophie des Buddhismus*, Berlin, Akademie-Verlag, 1956, p. 61.
[58] *Suttanipāta*, vv. 796, 789–800. This is Lord Chalmer's free but racy translation, *Buddha's Teachings*, Cambridge, Harvard Univ. Press, 1932. A more literal translation can be found in E. M. Hare, *Woven Cadences*, London, Oxford Univ. Press, 1944.

In later times it led to polemics against "logicians" and "philosophers." Suzuki's books afford many examples from a Zen angle. In the Tantra, which is to some extent the Indian equivalent of Zen, we find the same. The whole Chapter 34 of *The Hundred Thousand Songs of Milarepa*[59] is devoted to this theme. To be fully appreciated it must be read in its entirety. It combats those people who say that "all human knowledge should be examined and evaluated through logic *(pramāṇa)*. Logic is the most important science of all learning. If one knows logic all other studies become secondary."[60]

Milarepa replies that "the fact that one knows or knows not the Dharma, can easily be detected by whether or not he can conquer his own ego-clinging desires. . . . One may be very eloquent in talking about the Dharma, and win all the debates, but if he cannot subdue even a fraction of his own ego-clinging desires, but merely indulges himself in words and talk, his victories in debate will never bring him any profit but will only increase his egotism and pride.[61] . . . My 'logic' has brought me happiness and peace. Therefore it is very helpful and important."[62] And the converted opponent concedes that "we logicians have little sincerity, faith, or devotion; nor do we have the pure thoughts and spirit of renunciation. I am now really skeptical about the usefulness of our knowledge. Truly, I do not know whether his knowledge is helpful or obstructive to the course of Liberation."[63]

There are two alternative ways of dealing with Buddhist thought. The one assumes that somebody says something because somebody else has said the opposite. For instance, the assertion that all dharmas are the same may be explained as a rebuke to those who held that they are different, or the thesis that all dharmas are unreal as a retort to the theory that they are real. This is a quite childish way of looking at serious things, and it is greatly influenced by the observation of what has happened in Europe in recent times. There the Oedipus complex has been the chief guide of several genera-

59 Trans. C. C. Chang, New York, University Books, 1962.
60 *Ibid*, p. 389.
61 *Ibid.*, p. 384.
62 *Ibid.*, p. 390.
63 *Ibid.*, p. 395.

tions of philosophers. In England the universities for some time preached the Absolute as the only true reality, and without fail the next generation (of Ayer and his contemporaries) assumed it to have no reality at all. In Germany, H. Cohen was an absolute idealist, and N. Hartmann, his most cherished disciple, soon after his death published a huge volume in defense of "realism." Likewise, Heidegger's whole conception of philosophy "seems to arise in opposition to his teacher Husserl."[64] And so on.

Each generation feeds on its hate for the one that precedes it. Some historians describe the development of Buddhist thinking as though it had been governed by animosities of this kind. D. T. Suzuki believes them to be wrong. He thinks that one set of philosophers had one spiritual experience, and that another set of philosophers had another spiritual experience. Each formulated just their own experiences, and the clash arose later on when the theoretical formulations were compared. Let us illustrate Suzuki's attitude with two examples:

1. The Void, when regarded as a theoretical proposition, i.e., that "all things are empty," seems to result in *nothingness.* When the same proposition is viewed as a spiritual statement, it is seen to result in *skill in means.*[65] The theoretical proposition can be made by any worldling who has read Jeans and has learned from him that in one atom the solid matter occupies about as much space as seven wasps in Waterloo station, the rest being "emptiness." The spiritual statement can be made only by someone who has reached the sixth stage of a Bodhisattva, i.e., who had previously fulfilled in himself the perfections of giving, morality, patience, vigor, meditation, and wisdom. His benevolence, etc., is a vital factor in his ability to see all things as unsubstantial and then he does not just sit down and do nothing, but his compassion takes over, and he manipulates those unsubstantial things to serve the ends of his compassion. Manifold miraculous spiritual fruits result from his "emptiness" just because he is that kind of person.[66]

64 F. H. Heinemann, *Existentialism and the Modern Predicament*, London, A. & C. Black, 1958, p. 95.

65 See pp. 74 ff. below.

66 See p. 109 below.

2. The Mahayanists claim that all dharmas are "unproduced." This may be interpreted as a reaction against the Hinayanist theory, according to which all conditioned dharmas are produced and stopped, whereas only the unconditioned Dharma has neither been produced nor stopped. Nothing of the kind is intended. The Hinayanist, intent on understanding the impermanency of things, watched their rise and fall and noted that one dharma, the Unconditioned, was not subject to it. The thinkers of the Mahayana, in their turn, were interested in a totally different problem. In Europe born metaphysicians have often been defined as men who are genuinely surprised that there should be anything at all, and who therefore devote their lives to finding out in what sense anything can be said "to be." In answer to this basic metaphysical problem the Mahayanists tell us that "dharmas do not exist in such a way as the foolish common people are wont to suppose,"[67] that these people "have constructed dharmas out of their ignorance and craving,"[68] though in fact they do not exist, and that nothing has ever been made or "produced." In consequence there is no need to worry, because spiritual freedom, in the absence of anything to obstruct it, can never be impeded, and therefore is always sovereign and complete. "If we go along in life with nothing in mind, who can harm us?"[69] The Mahayana doctrine of "non-production" was therefore never designed to produce a theoretical antithesis to the Hinayana, but aimed at fostering a state of spiritual quietude, akin to the *apatheia* and *ataraxia* of the Greek Stoics, Epicureans, and Sceptics.

The Literature of the Mahayana

The word "Mahayana" is unfortunately used in two different senses. (1) In a wider sense it was used by European scholars of the nineteenth century to denote the "northern" Buddhism of Tibet, Mongolia, China, and Japan. The opposite here is "Theravāda," the doctrine prevalent in the "southern" Bud-

[67] *The Large Sutra on Perfect Wisdom*, trans. E. Conze, London, Luzac, 1961, I, 84.
[68] *Ibid.*
[69] *ZJB*, p. 60.

dhism of Ceylon, Burma, and so on. (2) In a more narrow sense it is used in Indian works on Buddhism written between about 100 B.C and A.D. 650. The opposite there are the teachings of "the Disciples and Pratyekabuddhas."[70] This two-fold usage has led to a great deal of confusion. In the first case Zen and Tantra form part of the "Mahayana," whereas with the second they follow upon it and grow out of it. It is very difficult to know what to do about this. The best thing would be to abolish the first meaning altogether and to replace it by "northern Buddhism." Or, if this is not done, one must be careful to speak of the second as "the early Indian Mahayana." In this book the word "Mahayana" is always employed in the sense which it had with those who first coined it, i.e., in sense two.

Little can be said here about the literature of the Mahayana, except that it is vast and still largely unexplored, and that it is written in a special kind of Sanskrit, though often preserved only in Chinese and Tibetan translations. It falls into two groups, (1) "Sūtras" and (2) "Śāstras," i.e., scholastic treatises, chiefly by Mādhyamikas and Yogācārins. The first are anonymous works which claim, without much historical justification, to be sayings of the Buddha himself, and are either brief or extensive *(vaipulya)*. These extensive Sutras are the real glory of the Mahayana, but few have so far been translated into European languages. What Suzuki has to say about them constitutes our fifth extract (pp. 118–28). In conformity with the general trend of the Chinese, as distinct from the Indian and Tibetan tradition, Suzuki greatly prefers the Sūtras to the Śāstras, and pays little attention to the latter. "I recommend the study of the Sūtras themselves and not that of the Śāstras or philosophical treatises of Mahāyāna Buddhism—that

70 We do not clearly know who these opponents were. They were certainly not the Ceylonese Theravādins, who, in the words of Professor Murti (*The Central Philosophy of Buddhism*, London, Allen and Unwin, 1955, p. 69), "had little or no direct influence on the development of Buddhist schools in India." In the later stages of scholastic elaborations some of the formulations of Mahayana beliefs arose from controversies with Sarvāstivādins and Sautrāntikas, but rarely if ever with Theravādins. We do not in fact know what degree of doctrinal development had been reached by the Hinayana opponents whom the Mahayana encountered at its inception.

is, if students really wish to grasp the spirit, or share in the experiences of the Mahāyāna."[71] This option accounts for the strength of his work, as well as for its occasional weaknesses.

The Teachings of the Mahayana

It will assist most readers of this anthology if I now tabulate in a more or less logical order the distinctive teachings of the early Indian Mahayana. They are not always of the same age, and for an understanding of Suzuki's work it seems to me important to distinguish between two stages, the one codified about A.D. 150, the other by about A.D. 350. It is impossible for us at present to decide whether these were innovations made by Mahayanists, or continuations of much older trends which now received a new emphasis. To Suzuki they were all authentic expressions of the Buddha's own doctrine.

1. The first phase, completed by about A.D. 150, corresponds to what is traditionally known as "the second turning of the wheel of the Dharma" (the sermon of Benares being the first). It consists of three main points, originally perhaps fairly independent, which in the course of time were wrought into a convincing synthesis.[72]

A. *The Bodhisattva ideal.* As a result of prolonged reflections on the nature of enlightenment *(bodhi)*, a section of the Buddhist community became at one point very interested in the differences between three kinds of "enlightenment"—that of the "Disciples" *(Śrāvaka)*, that of the Pratyekabuddhas, and that of the Buddhas. It is difficult for us to recapture the enthusiasm with which these issues were then debated, and we cannot even speak with any certainty of the circumstances in which this problem became so prominent. Suffice it to say that the "Mahayanists" solved it by contrasting the achievement of the Disciples and Pratyekabuddhas to its disadvantage with

71 *EZB*, III, 155.

72 These three points have been explained in greater detail in my article on "Buddhism: The Mahayana," in R. C. Zaehner, ed., *The Concise Encyclopedia of Living Faiths*, London, Hutchinson, 1959, pp. 298–320.

that of the Buddhas.[73] What the "Disciple" (or Arhat) achieves through his enlighenment is the severance of all fetters that bind him personally to this world. The Pratyekabuddha in addition achieves a deeper insight into the workings of causality, while the Buddha attains omniscience, i.e., nothing less than the knowledge of everything, both in general and in detail. This is obviously quite a late development of the doctrine, and on the surface seems to be rather arid and of no great practical consequence.

But something great and precious came out of this debate, a new conception of the perfect man which has had great influence in the Far East and still can appeal to many of us today. Before he has won full enlightenment, the Buddha is called a "Bodhisattva," a "Buddha-to-be." Roughly speaking, in the first period of Buddhist history the ideal man was an Arhat, in the second the Bodhisattva, in the third the Tantric *siddha* or the Zen *roshi.* All I can do here is to give a painfully bald outline of the main features of a Bodhisattva's life:

a. It begins when he has a desire to win a Buddha's enlightenment *(bodhicitta,* literally "the thought of enlightenment").

b. Thereafter he practices for aeons and aeons the six transcendental virtues known as "perfections" *(pāramitā),* i.e., giving, morality, patience, vigor, concentration, and wisdom.

c. Instead of the motives which normally influence human beings the Bodhisattva is impelled by two equally strong forces, wisdom and compassion. The first induces him to realize the emptiness of all that is, the second to serve all beings.

d. Once the climax of wisdom has been reached and the emptiness of everything has been realized, compassion becomes the only motive power that keeps a Bodhisattva going. Now a "celestial" Bodhisattva, for aeons he showers his benefits upon beings, whether primitive or advanced, and gives each one according to his needs, although he knows that the beings are illusory, their troubles are illusory, and his help is illusory.

e. The advance of a Bodhisattva is divided into ten stages *(bhūmi).* The first six are devoted to the "perfections," on the

73 See pp. 78–81, 88–9 below.

seventh he begins the "effortless life" of a celestial Bodhisattva, and on the tenth he becomes a Tathagata.

f. In achieving Buddhahood the Bodhisattva realizes the triple body of a Tathagata, i.e., (1) the Dharmabody, (2) the Enjoyment Body, and (3) the Transformation Body.

The career of a Bodhisattva is known as "the great vehicle" *(mahā-yāna),* in contrast to the "inferior vehicle" of the Disciples and Pratyekabuddhas. Because it seemed self-evident that, since the enlightenment of a Buddha is so much superior to that of the Disciples and Pratyekabuddhas, the path which leads to it must also be superior.

B. *Mythological doctrines.* Here again I must be content to note the main facts without going into the reasons behind them. The objects of worship were greatly increased by the Mahayana, in three ways:

a. In addition to the Buddhas who have appeared on earth much was now said about the Buddhas who reside in the stars outside this rather puny satellite of the sun. So we have Akshobhya in the east, Amitābha in the west, and so on.

b. The celestial Bodhisattvas also became objects of a religious cult. So we have Avalokiteśvara, governed by compassion, Mañjuśrī, the embodiment of wisdom, and so on.

Suzuki himself[74] seems to place this development within three centuries of the Buddha's Nirvana. Few scholars would at present agree with him. The great majority would expect it to have taken place about *five* centuries after the Buddha's death, and would attribute much of it to contact with non-Indian cultures.[75]

c. A number of these celestial Bodhisattvas were female, something unheard of in the rather patriarchal Hinayana. By about A.D. 400 quite a number of them had made their appearance, the first being the *Prajñāpāramitā,* "the mother of the Buddhas,"[76] and the *Tārā,* or "savioresses," who are "the mothers of the world, born of the power of Avalokiteśvara's

[74] P. 129 below.

[75] *The Concise Encyclopedia of Living Faiths,* ed. R. C. Zaehner, London, Hutchinson 1959, pp. 304–6.

[76] See pp. 36–7 below.

vow and understanding," and who protect, reassure and "fulfill all our hopes."

Suzuki has something to say about *a* and *b*, but very little about *c*, and on the whole his Zen mentality is inclined to minimize this side of the Mahayana, with its devotional fervor and almost feminine self-abandonment.

C. *Ontological doctrines.* By contrast, he takes great interest in the ontology of the Mahayana. For beginners its tenets can be stated in the form of four propositions:

a. All things are "empty." Not only are persons empty of a "self" but all dharmas are also empty of an "own-being."[77] Each dharma is nothing in and by itself, ultimately non-existent and indistinguishable from any other dharma.

b. If all is the same, then also the Unconditioned will be identical with the conditioned,[78] and nothing will separate Nirvana from the world of birth-and-death.

c. The "Emptiness" of things is also called their "Suchness." What we must learn is to take everything "such as it is," without adding anything to the actual fact or subtracting anything from it.[79]

d. All duality and multiplicity is a mistake, or illusion,[80] and true knowledge must rise above them.

Nobody can be expected to understand these four propositions by merely reading them, unless he has understood them before. They nevertheless give the substance of the new message, and Suzuki has amply explained it in the pages which follow.

2. Next, we consider the second phase, completed by about A.D. 350, and which corresponds to the third "turning of the wheel of the Dharma." The points mentioned in the first phase had dealt with man's attitude to the outer world, whereas those of the second deal with his inwardness. They are again three:

A. *Thought-only.* When carried to any length philosophical

77 See pp. 49, 54, 58–61 below.
78 See p. 20.
79 See pp. 41–3, 50, 53–5, 61, 69–71, 105–6 below.
80 See pp. 50–5.

reflection is almost bound to distinguish between subjective and objective factors, and to ask itself what weight can be assigned respectively to either of these. In a karmic action, whenever we do something that affects our happiness, how much is due to the objective circumstances and how much to our own mind? The Buddhist answer has always been quite unequivocal: "It is thought which guides the world and drags it about. All dharmas are under the sway of this one dharma, i.e., of thought."[81] "Beings are defiled through the defilement of thought, and through the purification of thought they are purified."[82] A clear "mentalist" bias is also expressed in the famous first verse of the Pali *Dhammapada*, which assures us that "dharmas are mind-controlled; mind is pre-eminent among them; they are mind-made" *(manomayā)*.[83]

Furthermore, what is the role of mind in the presentation of an object? When I see a tree before me, how much of its appearance can be attributed to the tree as an objective fact, and how much to my mental elaboration of the fact? The Buddhist answer again was quite unequivocal: nearly the whole appearance is a fabrication due to subjective factors.[84]

But this is not all. What we would call the "visions" experienced in trance have no objective sensory correlate. Buddhists, as distinct from modern Europeans, assume that transic experiences are more "true" than those of ordinary people, "because he who is in a trance sees what really is." Transic visions cannot be reflections of objects because there are none. In consequence they are mere modifications of consciousness. And so are ordinary perceptions also, because otherwise they would have a greater cognitive value than transic concentration.[85]

From ancient days there had been handed down the saying

[81] For the sources see E. Lamotte, *L'enseignement de Vimalakīrti*, Louvain, Publications Universitaires, 1962.

[82] *Ibid.*, p. 53.

[83] It is interesting to note that other recensions have *mano-javā*, i.e., "have the speed of mind," in the sense that they are momentary (J. Brough, *The Gandhari Dharmapada*, London, Oxford Univ. Press, 1962, p. 243). Before he became a Yogācārin, Asanga had been a Mahīśāsaka, and for some time Mahīśāsakas and Theravādins were one and the same sect. See my remarks in *IIJ*, VII, 1963, 74.

[84] Conze, *Buddhist Thought in India*, pp. 186–91.

[85] *Ibid.*, pp. 253–56.

that "self-luminous is this thought, though sometimes defiled by adventitious defilements, and sometimes freed from them."[86] The Hinayana schools tended to push aside this aspect of the doctrine as incompatible with their dharma theory, but the Yogācārins developed the latent idealism of Buddhism into a full-fledged idealism, according to which Mind or Thought alone is real, and everything else is "mere representation." This doctrine plays a big part in the *Laṅkāvatāra.*

B. *The embryonic Tathagata.* Later Sutras, like the *Tathāgatagarbha* and the *Śrīmaladevī,*[87] interpreted the absolute self-luminous thought as the "embryo of the Tathagata," pure, eternal, immanent in all beings and only accidentally defiled by adventitious passions. The introduction of this concept had a bearing on the explanation of the process of salvation. The older schools had thought that at first there was a series of conditioned dharmas dominated by an imaginary self, and altogether without the unconditioned dharma; with the attainment of Nirvana that series was miraculously transformed into another series in which the self was altogether absent and which was instead dominated by the Unconditioned.

The change seemed rather abrupt and in need of a connecting link. To solve this problem it was assumed that every worldling already contained within himself an embryonic Tathagata who would be set free in due course if and when the defiling layers which had overlaid him were removed. A special book, Sāramati's *Ratnagotravibhāga*[88] (*ca.* A.D. 250), was devoted to this theory, though at the time when Suzuki wrote his "Essays" it had not yet been published. He treats of it only in the occasional statements which found their way into the *Laṅkāvatāra,* and the reader who is interested in this aspect of the doctrine is advised to study Sāramati's "Treatise

86 Lamotte, *L'enseignement de Vimalakīrti,* p. 52; Conze, *Buddhist Thought in India,* pp. 133, 196.

87 Lamotte, *L'enseignement de Vimalakīrti,* pp. 55–56.

88 Ed. E. H. Johnston, T. Chowdhury, *Journal of the Bihar Research Society* (Patna), XXXVI:1 (1950); translated from the Tibetan by E. Obermiller, *Acta Orientalia,* IX, 1931, 81–306. Some parts have been translated from the Sanskrit by myself in E. Conze, *Buddhist Texts,* Oxford, Cassirer, 1954, nos. 126, 169, 185; and by E. Frauwallner in *Die Philosophie des Buddhismus,* pp. 255–64.

about the Lineage of the Tathagata." Once this conception had been developed, but not before, it became possible to say that the only purpose of meditation is to discover the "Buddha-self" within one's own mind. It also could dominate the interpretation of Sutras, as in the case of Han Shan, who treated the *Diamond Sutra* as a progressive series of statements intent on laying bare our own "original nature."[89]

C. *The store-consciousness*. The *Laṅkāvatāra,* as well as Asanga further on, identify the embryonic Tathagata with one of the facets of the *ālaya-vijñāna.*[90] This theory of the "store-consciousness" is one of the most abstruse and controversial which the Mahayana has produced, and I personally cannot claim to have understood it. In fact I feel great sympathy with Vasubandhu's remark when he said that "Alas, Asanga has founded a system, so difficult and burdensome, / That it can be carried only by an elephant!"[91] Luckily my obtuseness with regard to this topic is of no great consequence. Although it plays a prominent part in the *Laṅkāvatāra Sūtra* and in Suzuki's *Studies* of it, this anthology practically never mentions it. Those who know French or Tibetan will find all the additional information they require in Asanga's *Mahāyānasaṃgraha.*[92]

Editorial Principles

Everywhere I have printed the text exactly as I found it, except at pages 228, 234–6, where I have introduced slight corrections at Dr. Suzuki's request. In addition I have made a few very slight editorial adjustments which do not in the least affect the sense in any way, but were made necessary by the new context in which these writings are printed here. In general it seemed to me best to give lengthy essays in their totality, though I have made some cuts here and there, which can be seen in the bibliography. But where Suzuki has inter-

89 See p. 4.
90 See p. 159 below.
91 Buston, *History of Buddhism,* II, 143.
92 E. Lamotte, *La somme du grand véhicule d'Asanga,* Louvain, Bureaux du Muséon, 1938–39, II, 12–86.

spersed his exposition of the Indian Mahayana with explanations of Zen, I have in most cases removed the latter as not belonging to the theme of this book. A number of misprints in the Sanskrit words have been tacitly corrected. The diacritical marks appear as they did in the original edition, and are therefore not always consistent with each other. I have also added in square brackets a few bibliographical notes about scholarly publications which have appeared since Suzuki wrote. In the Glossary I have given the chief Sanskrit technical terms which Dr. Suzuki often left untranslated.

Even where later research seems to have disproved some of Suzuki's statements, I have scrupulously refrained from excising the offending sentences. On page 212, for instance, he assures us that the Tantra "must be regarded as a degeneration of pure Mahāyāna Buddhism." Now by 1934, when this sentence was written, apart from some ugly rumors nothing whatsoever was known about the Tantras. It has only been since 1949 that some of the documents have been studied by competent scholars. Far from being a degeneration of Buddhism the Indian Tantra has turned out to be a logical continuation of it,[93] and because Zen and the "Whispered Lineage" arose at about the same time and from the same motives,[94] their attitudes are often remarkably alike.[95]

One last point. The extracts from Suzuki have in this anthology been arranged into some kind of logical sequence, and the reader is advised to read them in the order in which they are given.

[93] This is made quite clear in D. L. Snellgrove's introduction to *The Hevajra Tantra,* London, Oxford Univ. Press, 1959.

[94] For instance, the fear of ossification obsesses them both.

[95] Quite at random I quote just one of Milarepa's replies to the logicians: "I attain all my knowledge through studying my mind within, thus all my thoughts become the teachings of Dharma. So long as I do not become separated from my own mind, I am always accompanied by sūtras. I have realized that all manifestations are Mind, and the mind itself is the illumination. These are my Gurus." Trans. C. C. Chang, New York, University Books, 1962, p. 378.

I

The Philosophy and Religion of the Prajñāpāramitā

PRELIMINARY

THE *Prajñāpāramitā*[1] is one of the oldest Buddhist canonical books translated into Chinese. The first *Prajñāpāramitā,* known as the *Tao-hsing* ("The Practicing of the Way"), appeared in A.D. 172. *The Sūtra of Forty-two Chapters* is supposed to have been translated by the first Indian missionaries who came to China in A.D. 69, but we are not quite sure of its historical authenticity. An Shih-kao, who came from Parthia to China in A.D. 148, worked for twenty-two years on converting the Buddhist texts into Chinese, but they were all Hīnayāna. This being the case, the *Tao-hsing Prajñāpāramitā,* which was translated by Lokaraksha of Yüeh-chih (then known as the kingdom of Kuṣana), must be said to be really the first Mahāyāna text of all the Buddhist sūtras ever introduced into China. It is wonderful to notice that the Buddhist teaching which declares all things "empty" and as having "no self-nature" was the first really important work to be propagated among a people who are deeply imbued with the pragmatic, utilitarian spirit. Decidedly, the followers of "Emptiness" did not think this kind of missionary activity to be a work of "empty" significance.

In the third century A.D. two sūtras belonging to the Prajñāpāramitā were translated into Chinese, and in the fourth

1 Italicized when it means the sūtra.

century still another appeared. Kumārajīva's were finished early in the fifth century. It was in the latter half of the seventh century that Hsüan-chuang completed his grand translation of the *Mahāprajñāpāramitā* in six hundred fascicles. This is an encyclopedic compilation including most sūtras pertaining to the Prajñāpāramitā group of the Mahāyāna sūtras.

In Sanskrit the largest collection consists of 125,000 slokas or stanzas of thirty-two syllables. The four shorter ones contain 100,000, 25,000, 10,000 and 8,000 slokas respectively. The shortest one was published in 1888 by the Indian pundit Rājendralāla Mitra, and the 100,000 one was edited by Pratāpacandra Ghosha in 1902, but as far as I know a complete edition of it has not yet seen the light. The oldest of these various *Prajñāpāramitā* compilations seems to have been the shortest of them, the 8,000-sloka one known as *Aṣṭasāhasrikā.* The longer ones are all later amplifications. The *Aṣṭasāhasrikā* corresponds to Lokaraksha's *Tao-hsing,* Kumārajīva's *Shorter Prajñāpāramitā* known as *Hsiao-p'in,* Hsüan-chuang's *Mahāprajñāpāramitā,* Fas. 538–555, and Shih-hu's *Fomu Prajñāpāramitā.*[2] As all the essential ideas, philosophically and religiously considered, of the *Prajñāpāramitā* are contained in it, my thesis will be mainly based on this sūtra in Sanskrit and its corresponding Chinese versions, though occasional quotations are taken from the other *Prajñāpāramitās.* Readers interested in the *Prajñāpāramitā* literature may consult Dr. Tokumyō Matsumoto's brochure on *Die Prajñāpāramitā-literatur.*[3]

But as the Sanskrit *Aṣṭasāhasrikā* as well as the several Chinese *Prajñāpāramitās* here mentioned are not easily accessible to the reader, the *Vajracchedikā,* or *Diamond Cutter* in English translations by Max Müller and William Gemmel, may be recom-

2 These different versions of the *Prajñāpāramitā* are in this article abbreviated as follows: *Aṣṭa for Aṣṭaṣāhasrikā, Hsiao-p'in* or Kumārajīva for Kumārajīva's *Shorter Prajñāpāramitā, Mahā* or Hsüan-chuang for Hsüan-chuang's *Mahāprajñāpāramitā, Fo-mu* for Shih-hu's translation, *Tao-hsing* for Lokaraksha's. The Kōkyō-shoin edition of the Tripitaka popularly known as "Shuku-satsu" (*so-shua*) which means "in smaller print" is used throughout this article. [English translation of the *Aṣṭa* by E. Conze, The Asiatic Society, Calcutta, 1958, BI 284.]

3 Verlag W. Kohlhammer, Stuttgart, 1932. [E. Conze, *The Prajñāpāramitā Literature,* Mouton & Co., The Hague, 1960.]

mended for his perusal.[4] The chief defect, however, with the *Diamond Cutter* is that it emphasizes the Śūnyatā aspect of the Prajñāpāramitā teaching too strongly, giving to the general reader the impression that this is the Alpha and Omega of the Mahāyāna. Dr. Max Walleser of Heidelberg translated into German some chapters of *Aṣṭasāhasrikā*.[5]

The object of this essay is to state that the teaching of the *Prajñāpāramitā* consists in defining the essence of Bodhisattvahood. This is what is known in all the Mahāyāna texts as Bodhisattvacaryā. *Caryā* means "life," and the Bodhisattvacaryā is what distinguishes the Bodhisattva as such from other beings; in Mahāyāna Buddhism especially from the Śrāvaka and the Pratyekabuddha. The *Prajñāpāramitā* finds this life in the understanding of Prajñā with all its implications, intellectual, moral, and spiritual. In the following pages, therefore, we shall see first what is meant by Prajñā and then proceed to discover its practical contents. When this is done, the essence of Bodhisattvahood will naturally come to light. That Zen is most intimately connected historically and doctrinally with the Prajñā teaching is, I believe, already well known to the reader.

Prajñā will then be described from the various points of view in which it is generally observed in the *Prajñāpāramitā Sūtras*.

I

The Philosophy of the Prajñāpāramitā

1. *Prajñā as the Directing Principle*

Prajñā is one of the six virtues of perfection *(pāramitā)* especially designed for the Mahāyāna Buddhists or Bodhisattvas. When they are satisfactorily disciplined in each of these six virtues they are assured of finally attaining enlightenment. But the sūtras of the Prajñāpāramitā group regard the Prajñā as

4 [New edition and translation by E. Conze, *Vajracchedikā Prajñāpāramitā*, SOR XIII, Ismeo, Rome, 1957.]

5 *Prajñāpāramitā, die Vollkommenheit der Erkenntnis*, Vandenhoeck und Ruprecht, Göttingen, 1914.

the directing principle of the other five virtues; for without the Prajñā the other Pāramitās are unable to know by themselves where they are bound, or what they are meant for. They are, when left alone, lost like a company of blind men in the wilderness. They cannot enter into the final abode of Reality. They are without any eye, they cannot recognize all-knowledge, and all their efforts are in vain without the leadership of the Prajñā. The Prajñā is the eye that surveys with perfect clearness the entire field of the Buddhist life and determines where and how the Bodhisattva's steps are to be guided. The five Pāramitās—charity, morality, humanity (or patience), strenuousness, and meditation—are called Pāramitās[6] because of the Prajñā which is their eye.[7]

Again, the Prajñā is like the earth which makes possible the growth of vegetation. All the other conditions may be there for a seed to grow, but without the earth it will never grow. So without the Prajñā the other Pāramitās will altogether lose their potentiality; there will be no life in them.[8] Again, it is by virtue of the Prajñā that all the other Pāramitās are guarded, taken hold of, gathered together, and systematically practiced. As all the sixty-two heretical views issue from the notion that there is a real individual substance (*satkāyadristi*), so all the five Pāramitās issue from the Prajnā. As all the bodily organs enjoy their vitality when "life" continues, so all the five Pāramitās are very much alive when the Prajñā embraces them under her protective wings.[9]

2. *The Prajñā Compared to the Bird's Wings and the Jar*

The Bodhisattvas are like those heavenly birds whose wings may stretch out to the extent of one yojana, or even to five yojana. When they are not fully developed they cannot fly. They may wish to fly from their heavenly abodes down to this world, or they may change their minds in the meanwhile and want to go back to the heavens. In the first case can they come on earth without hurting themselves? In the second case can they

6 *Pāram* = the other shore, *itā* = reached.
7 *Aṣṭa*, pp. 172–3. 8 *Ibid.*, p. 81. 9 *Ibid.*, pp. 431–2.

fly back safely to their home? No, they can do neither, but they are doomed to self-destruction because they are still fledglings, they are not yet qualified for such flights. In like manner, the Bodhisattva may have the desire already fully awakened for enlightenment, he may have accumulated all kinds of virtues in the form of charity, morality, patience, strenuousness, and tranquilization; and yet if he has not Prajñā and its Upāya (skillful means) all his desires and efforts will come to naught, and he will fall back to the state of Śrāvakahood and Pratyekabuddhahood.[10]

Again, the Bodhisattva without the Prajñā may be likened to an earthenware jar which has not been perfectly baked. A man may use such a jar half-baked for carrying water from the well or the river, but he will certainly find it broken before he reaches home. Why? Because the jar had been taken out of the kiln before it was fully baked and dry. In a similar manner, the Bodhisattva may have faith in the enlightenment, and the desire for it, and also patience, joy, understanding, reverence, diligence, pure thought, etc.; but if he has not Prajñā and its Upāya (skillful means) wherewith he is properly guarded in the course of his Bodhisattva life, he will surely retrogress and, falling back to the state of Śrāvakahood and Pratyekabuddhahood, will not be able to attain Sarvajñatā.[11]

By these appraisals of the Prajñā the sūtra strongly impresses us with the extraordinary importance of this Pāramitā virtue. Before the development of this idea, the six Pāramitās were treated as equally significant in the life of the Bodhisattva. The rise of the Mahāyāna has altered this relative position. The Prajñā is now singled out and given the highest prominence. Without this the rest of the Pāramitās are like a boat which has lost her compass and her captain. This is remarkable phase in the evolution of Buddhist thought. When we know that Buddhism derives its vitality from the doctrine of Enlightenment, the all-importance of the Prajñā is inevitably asserted. But it is

10 *Fo-mu*, 43b–44a.

11 *Ibid.*, 40a. *Sarvajñatā* = all knowledge. When the Prajñā is perfected, this is attained. "All-knowledge" belongs to Buddhahood, it is what constitutes the essential nature of the Buddha. "All-knowledge" and "Enlightenment" (*sambodhi*) are interchangeable terms in *the Prajñāpāramitā Sūtras,* and also in the *Gaṇḍavyūha.*

possible that the author of the *Prajñāpāramitā* had some apprehension about his teaching being immediately and unreservedly accepted by the Buddhists. For this reason I believe the sūtra makes so many references to not being frightened or depressed over the theory of Prajñāpāramitā. The sūtra says that it is of rare occurrence indeed for one to listen to the doctrine of Prajñā in his life and yet not to become frightened about it. To embrace it and not to waver in following its dictates requires the accumulation of merit for many lives.

3. *The Prajñā as Mother of Buddhas and Bodhisattvas*

That the Prajñā is the directing principle of the Pāramitās comes from the fact that it is conceived by the Mahāyānists to constitute all-knowledge *(sarvajñatā),* that is, the perfect knowledge which is in the possession of the all-knowing one. Therefore the Prajñā is an all-illuminating light which demands our respect. It stands above all the contaminating influence of worldly objects. It eradicates all the darkness there is in this world of dualities, thus giving peace and comfort to all beings. It supplies a light to the blind who can thereby walk safely through the dark night of ignorance. It leads those who have gone astray to the right path. It reveals to us the truth of all things, which is all-knowledge. It is the refuge of all beings, it bestows on them perfect fearlessness, it is the five-eyed one who illuminates the entire world. It is the truth that is above birth and death, above all doings and hankerings. It is Emptiness itself. It is the treasure house of all truth (*dharmakośa*). It is the mother of all the Buddhas and Bodhisattvas.[12]

Since Prajñā is the mother and progenitor *(janayitrī)* of all the Buddhas and Bodhisattvas, they are always quite anxious over her health and well-being and prosperity. The sūtra says:[13] "It is like a woman who has a large number of children. If she should be ill, all her sons and daughters would see to it that she soon recovers her health. For the one thought they have is that she is their mother who has brought them up with care

[12] *Aṣṭa,* pp. 170–1, 253, 272, 396–7, etc.
[13] *Ibid.,* p. 253. Chapter XII, "Viewing the World."

and love, that everything they claim now to be their own is her gift of wisdom and tenderness. She cannot be neglected, she must be well looked after, and all medical care must be given her so that she will be well again, free from suffering and annoyance of all kinds. Thus she will be cherished by all her children." In the same manner, the Buddhas and Bodhisattvas are deeply concerned with the well-being of Prajñā as their own mother, they make use of every contrivance to guard her from the interferences of evil spirits and to help her to be firmly established in the world. Hence their missionary activities of seeing the Prajñāpāramitā copied, studied, recited, memorized, meditated upon, and preached until the end of time.

4. *Prajñā = Saṁbodhi = Sarvajñatā*

The Prajñā was said in the beginning to be the means of attaining enlightenment, the highest end of the Buddhist discipline. But it has now come to be identified with the end itself—Prajñā is enlightenment (*saṁbodhi*); for in the Buddhist experience the working of the Prajñā in its original purity is possible only when there is enlightenment. When it is conceived as possessing an end which lies outside, it is not yet itself, it is not in its pure state; it comes back to itself only when it is identified with enlightenment. As long as enlightenment is considered something to be sought after by means of Prajñā, not only is enlightenment far away from you but Prajñā fails to function in its native activity. Prajñā to be Prajñā must be identified with enlightenment. We can say, therefore, that Prajñā finds itself, recognizes its own undisguised, unspoiled figure in enlightenment. When the practice of the Prajñāpāramitā is to be brought to its judicious culmination, the identification of Prajñā and enlightenment must be achieved, must become fact.

Conceptually, Prajñā makes its first movements toward the apprehension of what it supposes its object. When it is actually taken hold of, however, the seizer and the seized become one; dualism ceases and there is a state of perfect identity which is known as enlightenment, and also all-knowledge. This experience may be described in this way too: Prajñā first divides or contradicts itself in order to see itself, starting a state of duality such as means and end, subject and object, this and that, the seer and the seen. When the work of seeing itself is accomplished, in Prajñā there is no more duality, Prajñā is seen in enlightenment, and enlightenment in Prajñā. It sees everywhere its own names, only differently spelt; Prajñā is one name, enlightenment is another, Nirvāna is a third, and so on. That is to say, all these names are only conceptual, they are discriminated as such for the convenience of our intellection. What really and truly is, is the identity of these names, and nothing more.

Prajñā is then Saṁbodhi (enlightenment), Prajñā is Sarvajñatā (all-knowledge), Prajñā is Nirvāṇa, Prajñā is Tathatā (suchness), Prajñā is Citta (mind), Prajñā is Buddhatā (Buddhahood); Prajñā taken in itself then is preeminently the Unattainable *(anupalabdha)* and the Unthinkable *(acintya)*. And this Unattainable and Unthinkable is the basis of all realities and thoughts. Quite naturally, therefore, the writers of the *Prajñāpāramitā Sūtras* extol the Prajñā as a worker of miracles, almost personifying Prajñāpāramitā as an object of worship and finally urging its devotees to pay the highest homage even to all the texts containing the teaching of the Prajñāpāramitā as if the texts themselves were active living embodiments of the agency that achieves wonders. Not only their study *(paryavāpti)*, recitation *(vācana)*, memorizing *(dhāraṇa)*, and copying *(lekhana)* are recommended, but the reverence *(satkāra)* and worship *(gurakāra)* of them are encouraged, by means of offerings *(pūjā)* of flowers, wreaths, incense, ointment, lamps, flags, banners, canopies, and robes. As to the spiritual merit that accrues from believing *(abhiśraddhā)* and trusting *(adhimukti)* with the utmost sincerity *(adhyāśayata)* in the Prajñāpāramitā, no one can begin to estimate it accurately. The devotional side of the Prajñāpāramitā is curiously blended with its most high-soaring metaphysics.

The subject of the *Prajñāpāramitā Sūtras* is, however, properly speaking, the Bodhisattva life which consists in the practice of the Prajñā whereby one comes to the realization of supreme enlightenment. The question how to practice the Prajñā is constantly raised and answered—this indeed being the most absorbing topic of all the *Prajñāpāramitā Sūtras*. When it is successfully carried out the Buddhist discipline comes to an end. But as was said before, the practicing of the Prajñā is not something heterogeneous in nature with what makes up enlightenment itself. Enlightenment grows out of this practicing as the flower grows out of the plant; there is a continuity of life between the two terms, and continuity is no less than a form of identity. Thus, the following logic holds good: the Prajñā takes form in its being practiced, and this practicing is the content of enlightenment; therefore, the Prajñā is enlightenment. Prajñā = Saṁbodhi may be ascertained also from the practical side of the question. As these terms are constantly used interchangeably in all the *Prajñāpāramitā Sūtras,* what characterizes the one is equally applicable to the other. In fact the trinity Prajñā = Saṁbodhi = Sarvajñatā is the thread linking the various chains of teaching in them. You pick up one of the links and the rest follow. But if we wish to make a differentiation here we can define Prajñā as an epistemological instrument with which Sarvajñatā is attained, while Saṁbodhi (enlightenment) is more or less psychological in the sense that it connotes a state of spiritual awakening. Prajñā is shared by all beings without distinction, although it may not be found in them functioning in its absolute purity. In the Buddha, Prajñā is Sarvajñatā because he is in the state of perfect enlightenment.

Enlightenment is described in the *Mahāprajñāpāramitā* in the following terms:[14] "By enlightenment *(bodhi)* is meant emptiness *(śūnyatā),* suchness *(tathatā),* reality limit *(bhūtakoṭi),* spiritual realm *(dharmadhātu),* and essence *(dharmatā).* These are, however, names, words, provisional connotations. Enlightenment itself is the highest truth and ultimate reality; it is the norm not subject to change; it is indestructible, beyond discrimination; it is the true, pure, and all-pervading knowledge possessed by all the Buddhas; it is the most fundamental perfection whereby the Buddhas gain an insight into the nature of all realities, of all forms; it is beyond every mode of expression, beyond all thought-constructions created by the mind."

When the Bodhi, enlightenment, is thus described with further identifications the result may appear somewhat confusing,

[14] Fas. 526, Division III, Chapter 26 (4), "On Skillful Means," 29a.

and further remarks will be made on these later on. As far as the characterization itself is concerned, it is bodily transferable to Prajñā, and we can say this: that the Prajñā is seeing into the essence of things as they are *(yathābhūtam);* that the Prajñā is seeing things as in their nature empty; that thus seeing things is to reach the limit of reality, i.e. to pass beyond the realm of the human understanding; that, therefore, the Prajñā is grasping the ungraspable, attaining the unattainable, comprehending the incomprehensible; that when this intellectual description of the working of the Prajñā is translated into psychological terms, it is not becoming attached to anything whether it is an idea or a feeling.

We read in the "Devaparivarta" of the *Aṣṭasāhasrikāprajñāpāramitā:* "Those who have first taken up the practice of the Prajñā should practice all the six Pāramitās in such a way as to turn all the merit thereby gained to the realization of enlightenment. To do this, however, they should never cling *(parāmṛikṣa)* to enlightenment as the goal of their exercises nor to the five Skandhas a irreducible individual realities. For all-knowledge is something beyond grasp *(aparāmṛiṣṭā).*[15]

"Beyond grasp" means "not being attached." The Unattainable and the Unthinkable being the nature of the Prajñā, the Bodhisattva who has regained its original function will naturally have no attachment even to Prajñā, Sarvajñatā, or Saṁbodhi. This is an important phase in the life of the Bodhisattva, to which I may later have occasions to make further reference.

5. *Prajñā as Seeing Things Yathābhūtam*

Because of this virtue of non-attachment we can say that Prajñā is able to see the world as it is, to see things in their aspect of suchness *(yathābhūtatā).* This is the most characteristic function of the Prajñā, which is gained by the Bodhisattva when he realizes that he comes, such as he is, from the Prajñā itself, and, therefore, that the latter is the begetter of him as well as of all the Buddhas. Once his eyes are open to this truth, he surveys the world and all its multiplicities in the state they truly are. That is to say, as far as our senses go, the world is seen

[15] *Ibid.*, p. 292.

to be all the time changing, undergoing various forms of combination and decomposition. But the Bodhisattva whose Prajñā is fully awakened perceives that the five Skandhas which make up this world, in spite of their superficial transformations, are in their self-nature *(svabhāva)* never destroyed, show no signs of destruction, are never subject to vicissitudes, to birth and death, to taking forms, to cherishing desires or passions.

The *Prajñāpāramitā* being at once a philosophy and a religion, its teaching is always a mixture of ontology and psychology. In fact, it is not concerned with being as such, but with its human implications. To know the world is to know the human spirit and its workings. There are no metaphysical questions which are not at the same time questions of salvation and enlightenment. Therefore, when the Bodhisattva perceives the world as *yathābhūtam,* he also perceives human minds as they are; he is thus prepared to work out his skillful means *(upāya).* So, says the sūtra, the Bodhisattva perceives by means of his Prajñā-eye the minds of all sentient beings, and he knows how inexhaustibly varied they are in character, in function, in response, in moral value, in spirituality, and so on. Yet his perception *yathābhūtam* penetrates through these superficialities and recognizes that whether their minds are pure or impure, collected or scattered, greedy or not greedy, they are all devoid of self-substance, of attachment, of discrimination. This is known as seeing all beings in their aspect of suchness, where pluralities in all forms vanish, revealing themselves such as they are in the light of the Prajñā.[16]

It is evident, therefore, that the seeing things *yathābhūtam* in the *Prajñāpāramitā* means to see them through the veil of multiplicity which obscures our sight, and to grasp them with Prajñā in their state of suchness. Suchness *(tathatā)* is an uncouth term, but in Buddhist phraseology one of the most expressive terms. To understand exactly what it means is to understand the whole system of Buddhist thought. Suchness is not to be confounded with the sameness or oneness of things. When "the vanishing of pluralities" is talked of, one may imagine that they are ignored or annihilated in order to reveal their aspect of

16 *Fo-mu,* 35b; *Aṣṭa,* p. 259 ff.

oneness. But what the Prajñā devotees mean is that they are understood in their true relations, not only to one another but to that which makes up their reason of being.

There is a section[17] in the *Prajñāpāramitā* devoted to the discussion of Subhūti's being an Anujāta of the Tathāgata. *Anujāta* means "to be born after" or "to be born in accordance with." That Subhūti who is the expounder of the philosophy of the Prajñāpāramitā is born after the Tathāgata, i.e. his younger brother, or better, that he is born in accordance with what makes the Tathāgata such as he is, is one of the most significant statements in the *Prajñāpāramitā,* especially when this is considered in relation to the teaching of Suchness.

Tathāgata, which is generally regarded as another title of the Buddha, literally means either "one who has thus come" or "one who is thus gone." What is important here is the meaning of *tathā* rather than *āgata* or *gata;* and apparently the author of the *Prajñāpāramitā* places great stress on *tathā* as the key to the understanding of the doctrine of Tathatā or Yathābhūtatā (suchness). When he refers to the suchness of Tathāgatahood *(tathāgata-tathatā),* he means the reason, or cause, or ground principle that makes possible the appearance of the Tathāgata on earth. Therefore, Subhūti's being born after *(anujāta)* the suchness of Tathāgatahood means that Subhūti and Tathāgata come from the same cosmic womb, which is called, in the *Laṅkāvatāra* and other Buddhist texts, *tathāgatagarbha* or the "Womb of Tathāgatahood." With this preliminary explanation the following passage on Anujāta and Tathatā will become more intelligible.

"When it is said that Subhūti is born after the Tathāgata, it means this: that the suchness of the Tathāgata is the suchness of Subhūti, that there is no difference between the two suchnesses, for suchness is one in all sentient beings and here is no dualism, no separation, no twofoldness; that in all suchness there is neither coming nor going as they have never been born; that they have no abiding place where they can be located as particularities; that they are non-doing, by which it is meant that they are not to be perceived as functioning in a certain

17 *Aṣṭa,* Chap. XVI, "On Tathatā."

definite manner so as to reveal their specific characteristics which are their limitations; and yet that they are not to be taken as remaining for ever quiescent and doing nothing; that they retain their suchness in all places, at all times, under all circumstances, in all causal combinations; that in them there is neither past nor present nor future though sentient beings themselves are reckoned as coming into existence, abiding, and passing away; they are not subject to discrimination, do not take particular forms, are beyond attainability; and finally that in spite of all these qualifications they appear as realities, capable of being named and defined and discriminated, though when they are thus treated they are no more of suchness. For these reasons Subhūti's suchness is the Tathāgata's suchness, and the Tathāgata's suchness is the suchness of all beings, and between these no division is conceivable. One uniform suchness prevails here, but as soon as this definite statement is made of suchness, suchness ceases to be suchness. It is the most elusive thought, yet without this thought there are no Tathāgatas, no Subhūtis, no Buddhas, no Arhats, no sentient beings. To understand this is the Tathāgata; no other beings can grasp this truth. Subhūti, since he understands, can expound the deep mysteries of the Prajñāpāramitā, and for this reason he is the Anujāta of the Tathāgata."

Further, we read in Chapter XVII, "On the Special Features of the Avinivarta Stage of Bodhisattvahood": "There are varieties of spiritual stages in the Buddhist life, but they are all one as regards their aspect of suchness, and no discrimination is to be made among them. For it is through this oneness of suchness that the Bodhisattva can enter into the Dharmatā (briefly, Truth). Thus entering into the Dharmatā, he does not therein cherish any discrimination. Even when he listens to other teachings he refrains from criticizing them, for he knows how to get into the Dharmatā through various avenues of approach. Even when he listens to all forms of verbal and conceptual argumentations, he entertains no doubts as to the absolute validity of suchness which he embraces within himself."

One of the functions of the Prajñā is then seen as perceiving things *yathābhūtam* or in their aspect of suchness *(tathatā)*. In this suchness, all beings are found to be free from defilement, and therefore to be one with the Buddhas who may in this especial respect be called Tathāgatas. As they are thus all one, they are brothers *(anujāta)* to one another, including Buddhas and Bodhisattvas. The motherly womb from which all these brothers issue is truly known as "Tathāgata-garbha." The motherhood of the Prajñā becomes more convincing than ever, and the meaning of the reverence paid to the Prajñāpāramitā more natural.

6. *Prajñā and Sūnyatā*

The *Prajñāpāramitā* is generally regarded as exclusively teaching the philosophy of Emptiness *(śūnyatā)*. Most people, including scholars of Buddhism, subscribe to this view, but as to what is really meant by Emptiness they do not seem to have a very clear conception. Since the study of the Prajñāpāramitā means viewing all things in their aspect of suchness or emptiness, let me make a few remarks here about the doctrine of Emptiness.

In Hsüan-chuang's version of the *Mahāprajñāpāramitā* eighteen[18] forms of emptiness are enumerated, and they are explained in detail in Nāgārjuna's commentary on the sūtra. This enumeration is in fact concerned with so many ways of definitely arriving at the idea of emptiness. The eighteen ways of describing it are: (1) Adhyātmā-śūnyatā, emptiness of the inner things, (2) Bahirdhā-śūnyata, emptiness of the outer things, (3) Adhyātmā-bahirdhā-śūnyata, emptiness of the inner-and-outer things, (4) Śūnyatā-śūnyatā, emptiness of emptiness, (5) Mahā-śūnyatā, great emptiness, (6) Paramārtha-śūnyatā, emptiness of the ultimate truth, (7) Saṁskṛita-śūnyatā, emptiness of things created, (8) Asaṁskṛita-śūnyatā, emptiness of things uncreated, (9) Atyanta-śūnyatā, ultimate emptiness, (10) Anavarāgra-śūnyatā, emptiness of limitlessness, (11) Anavakāra-śūnyatā, emptiness of dispersion, (12) Prakṛiti-śūnyatā, emptiness of primary nature, (13) Svalakṣaṇa-śūnyatā, emptiness of selfhood, (14) Sarvadharma-śūnyatā, emptiness of things, (15) Anupalambha-śūnyatā, emptiness of unattainability, (16) Abhāva-śūnyatā, emptiness of the non-being, (17) Svabhāva-śūnyatā, emptiness of self-nature, and (18)

[18] Twenty in the *Śatasāhasrikā*, but no such reckoning in the *Aṣṭasāhasrikā*.

Abhāva-svabhāva-śūnyatā, emptiness of the non-being of self-nature.

1. By "the inner things" are meant the six consciousnesses *(vijñāna)*. When they are said to be "empty" it means that all our psychological activities have no ego-soul behind them, as is commonly imagined by us. This is another way of upholding the doctrine of Anātman or Anattā.

2. "The outer things" are objects of the six Vijñānas, and their emptiness means that there are no self-governing substances behind them. As there is no Ātman at the back of the psychological phenomena, so there is no Ātman at the back of the external world. This is technically known as the "egolessness of things." Primitive Buddhism taught the theory of Anātman in us, but it was by the Mahāyānists, it is said, that the theory was applied to external objects also.

3. We generally distinguish between the inner and the outer, but since there is no reality in this distinction it is here negated; the distinction is no more than a form of thought construction, the relation can be reversed at any moment, there is no permanent stability here. Change the position, and what is inner is outer, and what it outer is inner. This relativity is called here emptiness.

4. When things outside and inside are all declared empty we are led to think that the idea of emptiness remains real or that this alone is something objectively attainable. The emptiness of emptiness is designed to destroy this attachment. To maintain the idea of emptiness means to leave a speck of dust when all has been swept clean.[19]

5. The "great emptiness" means the unreality of space. Space was conceived in olden days to be something objectively real, but this is regarded by the Mahāyāna as empty. Things in space are subject to the laws of birth and death, that is, governed by causation,—this all Buddhists recognize; but space itself is thought by them to be eternally there. The Mahāyānists teach that this vast vacuity also has no objective reality, that the idea of space or extension is mere fiction.

6. The "ultimate truth" means the true being of all things,

19 Cf. Jōshu's remark on nothingness. *Zen Essays,* Series I, p. 175.

the state in which they truly are, apart from all form of subjectivity. This is something not subject to destruction, not to be held up as this or that, to which nothing can be affixed. Therefore, this ultimate truth is empty. If real, it is one of those objects that are conditioned and chained to the law of causation. Nirvāṇa is but another name. When Nirvāṇa has something attachable to it, it will no more be Nirvāṇa. It will be seen that "emptiness" is here used in a somewhat different sense from number 3, when objects inner or outer are declared "empty."

7, 8. These may be treated together. *Saṁskṛita* means things that have come to existence owing to conditions of causation. In this sense they are "created." *Asaṁskṛita* are things not subject to causation, such as space. To say that the Saṁskṛita are empty is another way of saying that the world external as well as internal is empty. Existence is sometimes divided into Saṁskṛita and Asaṁskṛita, sometimes into inner and outer, sometimes into the five Skandhas, etc., according to points of view necessitated by the course of reasoning. All these distinctions are, however, only relative and have no corresponding objectivity, and are, therefore, all empty. The Asaṁskṛita exist because of their being contrasted to the Saṁskṛita. When the latter have no reality, the former are also no more. They both are mere names, and empty.

9. This emphasizes the idea of all "things" being absolutely empty. "Ultimate" means "absolute." The denial of objective reality to all things is here unconditionally upheld. The "emptiness of emptiness" means practically the same thing. The room is swept clean by the aid of a broom; but when the broom is retained it is not absolute emptiness. Nay, the broom, together with the sweeper, ought to be thrown aside in order to reach the idea of Atyanta-śūnyatā. As long as there is even one dharma left, a thing or a person or a thought, there is a point of attachment from which a world of pluralities, and, therefore, of woes and sorrows, can be fabricated. Emptiness beyond every possible qualification, beyond an infinite chain of dependence—this is Nirvāṇa.

10. When existence is said to be beginningless, people think that there is such a thing as beginninglessness, and cling to the idea. In order to do away with this attachment, its emptiness is

forcing intellect to free all
graspings

pronounced. The human intellect oscillates between opposites. When the idea of a beginning is exploded, the idea of beginninglessness replaces it, while in truth these are merely relative. The great truth of Śūnyatā must be above those opposites, and yet not outside of them. Therefore, the *Prajñāpāramitā* takes pains to strike the middle way and yet not to stand by it; for when this is done it ceases to be the middle way. The theory of Emptiness is thus to be elucidated from every possible point of view.

11. There is nothing perfectly simple in this world. Everything is doomed to final decomposition. It seems to exist as a unit, to retain its form, to be itself, but there is nothing here that cannot be reduced to its component parts. It is sure to be dispersed. Things belonging to the world of thought may seem not to be subject to dissolution. But here change takes place in another form. Time works, no permanency prevails. The four Skandhas—Vedanā, Saṁjñā, Saṁskāra, and Vijñāna—are also meant for ultimate dispersion and annihilation. They are in any way empty.

12. Prakṛti is what makes fire hot and water cold, it is the primary nature of each individual object. When it is declared to be empty, it means that there is no Ātman in it, which constitutes its primary nature, and that the very idea of primary nature is an empty one. That there is no individual selfhood at the back of what we consider a particular object has already been noted, because all things are products of various causes and conditions, and there is nothing that can be called an independent, solitary, self-originating primary nature. All is ultimately empty, and if there is such a thing as primary nature, it cannot be otherwise than empty.

13. Lakshaṇa is the intelligible aspect of each individual object. In some cases Lakshaṇa is not distinguishable from primary nature, they are inseparably related. The nature of fire is intelligible through its heat, that of water through its coolness. The Buddhist monk finds his primary nature in his observance of the rules of morality, while the shaven head and patched garment are his characteristic appearance. The *Prajñāpāramitā* tells us that these outside, perceptible aspects of things are empty, because they are mere appearances resulting from various

combinations of causes and conditions; being relative they have no reality. By the emptiness of self-aspect or self-character *(svalakṣaṇa)*, therefore, is meant that each particular object has no permanent and irreducible characteristics to be known as its own.

14. The assertion that all things *(sarvadharmā)* are empty is the most comprehensive one, for the term *dharma* denotes not only an object of sense but also an object of thought. When all these are declared empty, no further detailed commentaries are needed. But the *Prajñāpāramitā* evidently designs to leave no stone unturned in order to impress its students in a most thoroughgoing manner with the doctrine of Emptiness. According to Nāgārjuna, all dharmas are endowed with these characters: existentiality, intelligibility, perceptibility, objectivity, efficiency, causality, dependence, mutuality, duality, multiplicity, generality, individuality, etc. But all these characterizations have no permanence, no stability; they are all relative and phenomenal. The ignorant fail to see into the true nature of things, and become attached thereby to the idea of a reality which is eternal, blissful, self-governing, and devoid of defilements. To be wise simply means to be free from these false views, for there is nothing in them to be taken hold of as not empty.

15. This kind of emptiness is known as unattainable *(anupalambha)*. It is not that the mind is incapable of laying its hand on it, but that there is really nothing to be objectively comprehensible. Emptiness suggests nothingness, but when it is qualified as unattainable, it ceases to be merely negative. It is unattainable just because it cannot be an object of relative thought cherished by the Vijñāna. When the latter is elevated to the higher plane of the Prajñā, the "emptiness unattainable" is understood. The *Prajñāpāramitā* is afraid of frightening away its followers when it makes its bold assertion that all is empty, and therefore it proceeds to add that the absence of all these ideas born of relativity does not mean bald emptiness, but simply an emptiness unattainable.

With the wise this emptiness is a reality. When the lion roars, the other animals are terrified, imagining this roaring to be something altogether extraordinary, something in a most specific sense "attained" by the king of beasts. But to the lion the roaring is nothing, nothing specifically acquired by or added to him. So with the wise, there is no "emptiness" in them which is to be regarded as specifically attained as an object of thought. Their attainment is really no-attainment.

16, 17, 18. These may be treated together. Existence is viewed here from the point of being (*astitva*) and non-being (*nāstitva*), and these two views, whether taken individually or relatively, are said to be empty. *Abhāva* is the negation of being, which is one sense of emptiness; *svabhāva* means "to be by itself," but as there is no such being it is also empty. Is then the opposition of being and non-being real? No, it is also empty, because each term of the opposition is empty.

What "emptiness" really means I believe has been made clear by these detailed explanations. Emptiness is not to be confounded with nothingness; nor is one to imagine that there is an object of thought to be designated as emptiness, for this idea goes directly contrary to the nature of emptiness itself. Nor is it to be defined as relativity, as is done by some scholars. It is true that the *Prajñāpāramitā* teaches that things exist mutually related as results of causal combinations and therefore they are empty. But for this reason we cannot state that relativity and emptiness are synonymous. In fact, it is one thing to say that things are relative, but quite another to say that they are empty. Emptiness is the result of an intuition and not the outcome of reasoning, though the use here of the particle of inference, "therefore," gives this effect. The idea of Emptiness grows out of experience, and in order to give it a logical foundation the premise is found in relativity. But, speaking strictly logically, there is a gap between relativity and Emptiness. Relativity does not make us jump over the gap; as long as we stay with relativity we are within a circle; to realize that we are in a circle and that therefore we must get out of it in order to see its entire aspect presupposes our once having gone beyond it. The experience of Emptiness has been there all the time when we began to talk about relativity. From Emptiness we can pass to relativity, but not conversely. This analysis is important in the understanding of the *Prajñāpāramitā* philosophy. It is the Prajñā that sees into all the implications of Emptiness, and not the intellect of Vijñāna, and they are wise who have opened their Prajñā-eye to the truth of Emptiness. If the Mahāyāna system were built upon the idea of relativity, its message would never have called out such responses as we see in its history in India, China, and Japan. That the teaching of Emptiness has actually achieved wonders in the spiritual life of the Far Eastern peoples is the irrevocable proof of its deep insight into the abyss of human consciousness.

Emptiness, for these reasons, is called the unattainable *(anupaladha)* or the unthinkable *(acintya)*, showing that it is not a notion to be subsumed in any categories of logic. It is synonymous with suchness *(tathatā)*. Tathatā or Śūnyatā is thus truly the object of study for the Bodhisattvas.

7. *Prajñā and Māyā*

One of the favorite analogies used by the Prajñā philosophers when they wish to impress us with the doctrine of Emptiness is that of Māyā, and they are frequently called by other teachers the Māyāvādins. What is the meaning of this Māyā simile? Let me quote a few passages and see what Māyā means.

"The Buddha asked Subhūti: O Subhūti, do you think Māyā to be different from Rūpam[20] and Rūpam from Māyā? Do you think, again, Māyā to be different from Vedanā, Saṁjñā, Saṁskāra and Vijñāna; and Vedanā, Saṁjñā, Saṁskāra and Vijñāna from Māyā?

"Subhūti said: No, Blessed One, they are not different. If Rūpam is different from Māyā, it is not Rūpam; if Māyā is different from Rūpam, it is not Māyā. Māyā is Rūpam and Rūpam is Māyā. The same can be said of Vedanā, Saṁjñā, Saṁskāra and Vijñāna.

"The Buddha: O Subhūti, do you think the five clinging Skandhas constitute Bodhisattvahood, or not?

[20] Rūpam (form), Vedanā (sensation), Saṁjñā (thought), Saṁskāra (conformation), and Vijñāna (consciousness)—these five are technically known by Buddhists as the Five Aggregates (*pañcaskandhāḥ*), that is, the five ultimate constituents of existence. Therefore, when reference is made to these Five Aggregates, we may regard them as meaning this world of matter and thought in its entirety. They are "clinging" when we regard them as final realities, and are unable to extricate ourselves from their tyrannical hold on us.

"Subhūti: O Blessed One, they do.

"The Buddha: O Subhūti, and you should know that these five clinging Skandhas are no more than Māyā itself. Why? Because Rūpam is like Māyā, and Vedanā, Saṁjñā, Saṁskāra and Vijñāna are like Māyā; and these five Skandhas and six senses are what constitutes Bodhisattvahood, and, therefore, the Bodhisattva too is like Māyā. Those who wish to discipline themselves in the Prajñāpāramitā should do so as if disciplining themselves in Māyā. . . . But those Bodhisattvas who have first started in their disciplining exercises may be terribly frightened and led astray, if they are not properly guided by good spiritual teachers."[21]

Such a discourse as this, indeed, if the hearer is not properly instructed by a great competent master of the Prajñāpāramitā, will lead us to the follies of libertinism. Listen further to this:

"The Buddha: It is like a magician *(māyākāra)* conjuring up by his magical art a large crowd of beings at a crossroad. As soon as they are seen to come into existence they vanish. O Subhūti, what do you think? Do they really come from some definite locality? Are they real realities? Do they really pass away somewhere? Are they really destroyed?

"Subhūti: O no, Blessed One.

"The Buddha: It is the same with the Bodhisattva. Although he leads innumerable sentient beings to Nirvāna, in reality there are no sentient beings to be led to Nirvāna. Those who are not frightened at all, even when listening to such discourses as this, are true Bodhisattvas well fortified in the Mahāyāna armor."[22]

"Subhūti said to Pūrna: The Rūpam of the magical creation is neither in bondage nor released from it; so with his Vedanā, Saṁjñā, Saṁskāra, and Vijñāna—they are neither in bondage nor released from it. The same is to be said of the suchness of his Rūpam and the other four Skandhas. Nothing of him has ever been in bondage, and he is therefore never released from anything. Why? Because of non-actuality *(asadbhūtatvāt)*, there is for him neither bondage nor emancipation; because of detachment *(viviktatvāt)*, there is for him neither

21 *Aṣṭa*, pp. 16–17 (Fo-mu, 3b). 22 *Ibid.*, p. 21 (*Fo-mu*, 4a).

bondage nor emancipation; because of no-birth *(anutpannatvāt)*, there is for him neither bondage nor emancipation. Those Bodhisattvas who realize this are really abiding in the Mahāyāna and are well furnished with the Mahāyāna armor."[23]

"Then the Devaputras asked Subhūti: Are all beings like Māyā, or are they not?

"Subhūti said: O Devaputras, they are all like Māyā; again, they are like a dream *(svapna)*. Why? Because no distinction is to be made between all beings and Māyā or a dream; there is indeed between them no dualistic contrast. Therefore, all beings are like Māyā and a dream. The four orders of Śrāvakahood as well as Pratyekabuddhahood, they are like Māyā and a dream; supreme enlightenment itself is like Māyā and a dream.

"The Devaputras: If this is so, is Nirvāṇa, too, Māyā and a dream?

"Subhūti: Nirvāṇa is indeed like Māyā and a dream, and how much more the rest of things!

"The Devaputras: Why so?

"Subhūti: Even when you declare that there is something superior to Nirvāṇa, I tell you that this something too is no more than Māyā and a dream; for there is between them no difference, no dualistic contrast to be made out."[24]

From this point of view it is natural for followers of the Prajñāpāramitā to conclude that "Buddha is mere name[25] *(nāmadheya-mātram)*; Bodhisattva is mere name; Prajñāpāramitā is mere name; and these names have no real origination *(anabhinirvṛitta)*."[26]

Names that have never known their real origination are like a void space *(ākāśa)* whose whence and whither are in no way indicable, and which is thus altogether beyond all forms of predictability. In other words, this void is Śūnyatā. "The Buddha's teaching is in accordance with the nature of all beings, which is beyond attainability. This truth knows no hindrances anywhere. It is like a vacuity of space which is not hindered by

[23] *Ibid.*, pp. 22–3 (*Fo-mu*, 4b).

[24] *Ibid.*, p. 39 (*Fo-mu*, 6b).

[25] Name here means concept or thought construction. Name only, therefore, is the same as Prajñaptimātra. This is where the teaching of Śūnyatā comes in contact with the idealism of the Yogācāra.

[26] *Ibid.*, p. 25 (*Fo-mu*, 5a).

anything, it refuses to take any predicates. As it is beyond all forms of dualism, in it there are no contrasts, no characterization is possible of it. As there is in it no opposition, it knows nothing that goes beyond it. As there is in it no origination, it leaves no traces behind it. As there is in it no birth and death, it is unborn. As there are in it no pathways to mark its transformation, it is pathless."[27]

From these quotations one may feel like drawing the conclusion that the Dharma of the *Prajñāpāramitā* is after all quite a visionary, dreamy, ungraspable something almost equal to a nonentity. If to view all things in accordance with the Prajñāpāramitā is to view them in accordance with Sarvajñatā (all-knowledge) and if to view all things in accordance with Sarvajñatā is to view them in accordance with the nature of a void space (*ākāśa*), the teaching of the *Prajñāpāramitā* may be regarded after all as the teaching of nothingness, fairly termed as "Māyāvada," the doctrine of the unrealness of all things.[28] No wonder, we may say, that the sūtra repeatedly warns its readers not to become alarmed, or terrified, or horrified out of their senses when they listen to the philosophy of the deepest Prajñāpāramitā (*gambhīrā-prajñāpāramitā*).[29] Can we then for these reasons declare that the Prajñā is Māyā and a dream and a mere name and that the Mahāyāna is an edifice constructed on sand? Is it no more than a conceptual plaything consisting of bubbles and echoes? This has decidedly been the conclusion of some scholars, especially of the West. It is very difficult to rise above the notion of the unreality of things and to take them for what they are—that is, in their aspect of suchness. To understand the Māyā theory is to perceive the suchness of things.

The Indians are noted for being clever in magic, and it is natural for the Buddhist philosophers to illustrate the fleeting nature of all existence by means of magical creations. But we must not take their rhetoric in its literal sense. We must try to get at its true meaning. As has repeatedly been stated, the force

27 *Ibid.*, p. 306 (*Fo-mu,* 43a).

28 *Ibid.*, p. 302 (*Fo-mu,* 42b).

29 This warning is given throughout all the sūtras on Prajñāpāramitā, and it is said that the true test of Bodhisattvahood consists in boldly accepting this doctrine and feeling really cheerful about it.

of argument adopted in the *Prajñāpāramitā* is directed against the fundamental error we all have in regard to the world generally—that is, naïve realism. The chief feature of this realism is to take the world as a reality eternally fixed and externally existing against what is conceived to be an inner world of thoughts, feelings, and sensations, while the latter is governed by an ego-soul individually isolated from others and warring against them. One of the best weapons for destroying the stronghold of naïve realism is to declare all is Māyā and that there is no permanently fixed order in the world, that the dualistic conception of existence, inner and outer, being and non-being, etc., is visionary, and that to reach the real basis of existence it is necessary to awaken the Prajñā which takes hold of the unattainable. For it is only by means of the Prajñā that all kinds of clinging and attachment, whether intellectual or affectional, can be rightly corrected, and that the suchness of existence can be truthfully perceived and acted upon. The *Prajñāpāramitā* has always in view this pragmatic consideration of its philosophy in spite of its soaring flights of imagination and its ever vanishing mysticism.

The Buddhist idea of having any system of philosophy at all is thereby to uproot the evil passions *(kleśa)* which clog the harmonious unobstructed activity of the Prajñā. The passions are always one-sided and create all forms of clinging, and by means of these passions and clingings evil deeds are committed in three ways, by body, mouth, and mind, and these lead further on to endless repetitions of the same. So we are told that the pleasures and pains with which we are affected have no permanent nature as such; and likewise with objects of pleasure and pain, they are transitory and changeable like Māyā. They all have no substantial reality. They are mere appearances and to be regarded as such and of no further value. As far as appearances go, they are there, and this fact will not be ignored; but as for clinging to them thus as finalities, the wise know much better, for their Prajñā-eye has penetrated into the rockbed itself of reality. According to Nāgārjuna,[30] the child sees the moon in the water, the desire is stirred in him to scoop it out, he extends his arm into the water. Not, however, being able to

[30] His commentary on the *Prajñāpāramitā,* Fas. XXXII.

take hold of it, he is very much grieved. A wise man now tells him that what he sees there in the water is not to be handled. In the same way, a world of appearances is not denied, only its seizability or attainability is denied. A world of pluralities is there before the wise as well as the ignorant; the difference between the two is that the former see it with a mind free from attachments while the latter have not yet gone far enough into the realm of Śūnyatā. The veil of Māyā is recognized as such by the Bodhisattvas, but those who are still in bondage take it for reality.

The Māyā teaching is, therefore, to be understood against the background of Śūnyatā or Tathatā. Without this, the Māyā remains forever as such, and the Buddhists will never be able to find their foothold, although this foothold ought not to be reckoned as belonging to the realm of discriminations. When this commentary is not given, the Māyā will entirely lose its significance in the teaching of the *Prajñāpāramitā*. The statement "even Nirvāṇa is Māyā and a dream" will be no more than gibberish. The Māyā is a pointer. Those who follow it intelligently will see behind the screen a world of inexpressible mysteries and "unattainable" realities.

8. *Prajñā and Intuitions*

To understand the position of the Prajñāpāramitā as a philosophical teaching, it is necessary to ascertain where its foundation lies. When this is not properly done, the critic may take the shadow for the substance. Where, then, is the foundation of the Prajñāpāramitā? As the Mahāyānists take it, it is not based on logic as the latter is commonly interpreted; but it is based on intuitions. The Prajñāpāramitā is a system of intuitions. Its thorough understanding requires a leap from logic to the other shore. When one tries to unravel it without this experience, the system becomes all the more a mass of confusion or an unintelligible jargon. Most writers approach the Mahāyāna without this indispensable preliminary. They must discard conceptual arguments.

What is the meaning of this discarding in the doctrine of the Prajñāpāramitā?

According to the Mahāyānists, logic so called or our ordinary human way of thinking is the outgrowth of a dualistic interpretation of existence—*astitva* and *nāstitva,* being and non-being. This dualism goes on throughout our thinking. We can never get away from this so long as we stay with the conditions of thinking. The opposition of "A" and "not-A" is fundamental, is the warp and woof of human understanding. But, singularly, our heart or spirit never rests quietly so long as we do not transcend this apparently logically essential position. Ordinary logic is the most useful implement in our practical life, for without it we can never expect to rise above the animal plane of existence. It is due to our faculty of forming concepts that we can go, as it were, out of ourselves, out of our immediate experiences. It is the greatest weapon we have over our brother animals. Unfortunately, we have become so enamored with our concept-forming power that we have gradually detached ourselves from the sources of our being—the sources that enabled us to construct ideas and carry out abstract reasoning. The result of this is that we have begun to feel somehow uneasy about ourselves. Even when we are convinced of the accuracy and perspicuity of our logic, we seem to cherish somewhere a sense of inner vacancy, we are not able to locate it in our logic, but the logic itself as a whole seems to lack a certain fundamental convincing power. In any event we are dissatisfied with ourselves and with the whole world so long as we cling to the dualism of *asti* and *nāsti,* "A" and "not-A."

Perhaps our so-called logic is only the ultimate utilitarian instrument wherewith we handle things belonging to the superficialities of life. The spirit or that which occupies the deepest part of our being requires something thoroughly non-conceptual, i.e., something immediate and far more penetrating than mere intellection. The latter draws its materials from concepts. The spirit demands immediate perceptions. Evidently, what may be designated an inner or a higher perception, which expresses itself through the ordinary senses, but which is not bound by them, must be awakened, if the spirit is to be satisfied with itself.

The final goal of all the Buddhist disciplines is the awakening of this inner sense. So with the Prajñāpāramita, the awakening is the one thing that is most needful here. All the teachings expounded in the sūtras, all the bold statements at which the student is warned not to become terrified, are the views extended before the awakened sense of the Bodhisattva. They are his intuitions, they are the dialectic of his immediate experiences, and not that of his concepts. This is the reason why the sūtra so repeatedly refers to seeing things *yathābhūtam,* i.e. as they are. It must be remembered that "seeing" and not "reasoning" or "arguing" logically is here the topic. *Yathābhūtam* is the term applicable only to the act of seeing or viewing, and not to the process of inference.

The Mahāyānists uphold this new point of view acquired by the awakening of the inner sense which is the Prajñā or Sarvajñatā, and declare it to be something more fundamental than mere logic. However logically impossible or full of contradictions a statement which is made by the Prajñāpāramitā may be, it is utterly satisfying to the spirit, inasmuch as it is a statement made *yathābhūtam* in perfect accord with the inner sense, which functions in a realm beyond the dualism of *astitva* and *nāstitva.* Such statements are then said to be characterized with *yathābhūtatā,* or simply they are statements of Tathatā (suchness). That they are not at all logical does not mean that they are untrue. As far as truth is concerned, there is more of it in them. *Truth* means "it is so"; *yathābhūtatā* means no less.

Statements of immediate perception in a realm beyond *astitva* and *nāstitva* cannot fail to be most frightening to those whose eyes have never been raised above the utilitarian dualism of the sense world. To announce that all is Māyā, all is a dream, is surely horrifying. But let us here rise above the dualistic interpretation of existence, and we realize that what is is because of what is not, and that what is not is not because of what is. We cannot single out one thing and declare it to be final. But this is what we are practicing in our daily life and in our ordinary logic. When the *Prajñāpāramitā* says that all is Māyā, it simply describes what it sees *yathābhūtam* in this sense world. Māyā, more exactly stated, is "to exist as if not existing."[31] This is not denying the world in a wholesale manner. Superficially, it is a denial, but at the same time it is asserting something

[31] *Yathā na saṁvidyante tathā saṁvidyante. Aṣṭa,* p. 15.

behind. It is at once a negation and an affirmation. Logic cannot uphold this position, but the Prajñā intuition does. Students of the Mahāyāna sūtras are always advised to keep this in mind.

9. *The Prajñā as Unattainable, and Relativity*

This position of the Prajñāpāramitā attained by the awakening of the inner sense is called *anupalabdha,* "unattainable." Paradoxes are here unavoidable. The Hegelian dialectic may explain them as being also in accordance with the law of logic. But in the Prajñāpāramita there is no need to go through the process of thesis, antithesis, and synthesis because there is no room in the Mahāyāna world of intuitions to admit such a roundabout process of moving from one idea to another. Once beyond a world dualistically constructed, the unattainable is the attainable, and the attainable is the unattainable. This may be called the transcendental viewpoint of the Prajñāpāramitā.

We can now see why those scholars are in the wrong who want to identify the doctrine of Emptiness *(śūnyatā)* with that of relativity. According to them, all things are empty because their existence is thoroughly conditioned by the principle of relativity, which is the same as saying that all things are bound up by the law of causation. If Buddhist philosophy is based on causation and karma, this means relativity; and if all things are what they are because of the causal net pervading the entire range of existence, and if they are thus characterized as Emptiness, Emptiness is relativity. But this identification of Emptiness and relativity is untenable; the so-called identification is confusion. The scholars have not fully grasped the purpose of the Mahāyāna teaching; they are still holding to their former position, that is, the position we generally have prior to the awakening of the inner sense to which allusion has already been made.

To understand truthfully *yathābhūtam,* what Emptiness is, the awakening *(saṁbodhi)* is indispensable. The awakening is the turning up *(parāvṛitti),* so repeatedly mentioned in the Mahāyāna sūtras such as the *Laṅkāvatāra.* This turning up or turning back means reversing the order of one's mental outlook. What used to be dualistic is now to be seen from the "wrong side" of it. The inside which was hitherto hidden out of sight now stands revealed in full view. Things are now surveyed from this newly discovered position. Naturally, one's view of the world must change; things seen from the outside cannot be the same as things seen from the inside. A tree was observed as expressed in color and with its branches swaying in the wind; but now there is no more a tree distinct from its fellow trees, from its surroundings; the leaves are no more green; there are no swaying branches; no flowers are in bloom; and all these have vanished; what has apeared to the senses and been constructed by thought is all gone. Here lies a new world. All that has been "attainable" remains here; but this is changed—though not to a state of nothingness, for nothingness still savors of somethingness. Lacking in all forms of expression, the *Prajñāpāramitā* calls this "the unattainable," "the empty," "the unobstructed," etc.

There is no room here for relativity to design its machinery. Relativity is one of the notions we have formed while observing existence from the point of *astitva* and *nāstitva,* where everything has its second, where every "A" is accompanied by its "not-A." From this position it is impossible to penetrate into a realm of Emptiness; the position must once for all be quitted; as long as the philosopher clings to this, his relativity dogs his every step; he cannot draw anything else out of it; it never transforms itself into Emptiness. In order to get into the world of Emptiness, existence itself must be made to turn a somersault. One must once experience sitting at the center of existence and viewing things from this hub. Let one remain at this side of dualism and the gap between relativity and Emptiness can never be bridged. Things of this world are relative because of their being empty by nature; and not conversely. Śūnyatā is realized only after the awakening of the inner sense, after the turning over *(parāvṛitti)* in the Ālayavijñāna. It is only after this "turning" which is also a leaping that we can make such statements as these: "All is bound up in the chain of origination, and therefore all is empty"; or "All is Māyā, all is Śūnyatā"; or "All is such as it is *(yathābhūtam),* and yet all is not."

When the Buddhists refer to the chain of origination *(hetu-pratyaya* or *kāraṇasamutpāda),* in order to explain the making up of a fleet or the production of a Buddha-image,[32] and say that nothing is produced without the combination of various

[32] See *Zen Essays,* Series II, pp. 299–300 ff.

causes and conditions, and further that they do not come from any definite quarters, nor do they disappear into any definite quarters, the idea may seem to point toward the identification of relativity and Emptiness. In one of the Chinese versions of the *Prajñāpāramitā Sūtra,* known as the *Tao-hsing Pan-jê,*[33] we have the following:[34]

"It is like those heavenly mansions which are inhabited by beings of the Akanishṭa Heaven. Their glowing beauty surpasses everything we on earth can think of. But they have been made by themselves; they have not been brought over here from anywhere else, nor is there any creator who has created them out of nothing, nor is their whence and whither known to anybody. Their coming into existence is due to the law of causation; when those celestial beings were matured on account of their previous deeds to enjoy such radiantly shining celestial palaces, the latter came into existence. In like manner, when various causes and conditions are matured, sentient beings are able to see the Buddha-body. They first conceive the desire to see the Buddha; they then accumulate all kinds of merit by practicing good deeds; they avoid being born in the eight undesirable habitations; being intelligent they have full faith in the Buddha. When these several conditions are fulfilled, they will interview the Buddha. As to the Buddha-body itself, it has no whence and whither; it knows no creator; there is no one who has brought it over here for the benefit of the devotees, it has no form; it is not attached to anything; like the palaces of the Akanishṭa, it just manifests itself there in order to make all sentient beings attain final emancipation. . . ."

The doctrine of causation *(kāraṇasamutpāda)* as upheld here is only applicable to a world of dualities and combinations. Where there are no such happenings, the doctrine at once loses its significance. As long as we are bound to a world of particulars we see causation and relativity everywhere, because this is the place for them to function. But since we are never satisfied

33 *Tao-hsing* is the title of the first chapter. This was translated by Louchio-sh'an (Lokarakṣa), of the Eastern Han dynasty (A.D. 25–220), and is the earliest *Prajñāpāramitā* done into the Chinese language. In the Kumārajīva and the Hsüan-chuang "Tao-hsing" is "Miao-hsing," and in the Sanskrit *Aṣṭasāhasrikā* "Sarvākārajñatācaryā."

34 This part is missing in Kumārajīva, and also in Shih-hu.

with this state of affairs, not only spiritually but logically in the deeper sense of the word, we leap for life or death over the bottomless abyss gaping before us. The leap lands us in the realm of Emptiness, and we realize that it is after all this Emptiness that lies underneath the world of causes and conditions.

Emptiness is that which makes the work of causation possible, it is a form of canvas on which causation paints its most variegated pictures. Emptiness thus comes first though not in time, for time presupposes a chain of causation; the coming first means being fundamental. When causation or relativity is made at all thinkable, there is already in it Emptiness. This distinction is most vital in all our religious experience and, I should think, also in all our clear philosophical thinking. The *Prajñāpāramitā* philosophers, therefore, insist that Emptiness is the most fundamental idea when their intuitions strive to express themselves through the medium of the intellect. It is not a negative notion but decidedly positive. It sounds negative only to those who have not gone to the other side of the screen. When penetration is imperfect the intellect becomes muddled, and wrong inferences are many.

Scholars unfortunately slur over the fact that in the *Prajñāpāramitā* and other Mahāyāna texts Śūnyatā (emptiness) and Tathatā or Yathābhūtatā (suchness) are synonymously used as expressing an identical thought. If Emptiness is a negative term and connotes nothing of affirmation, it can never be made to build up the grand edifice of the religion known as Mahāyāna Buddhism. It is really astonishing to see how prejudiced and superficial some of the critics are who fail to see the needs of the human sense for something really affirmative and therefore soul-supporting. The Oriental mind, generally speaking, is more inner and intuitive, working outwardly, as it were, from the center of its being. It may not be so logical and system-loving as the Western mind, and for this reason it is capable of more deeply grasping the fundamental facts of life. Those who start from a dualistically constructed world are unable to destroy this construction and to return to its source which really is no-source. Thesis *(astitva)* and antithesis *(nāstitva)* may be raised to a synthesis, but this after all remains an idea, a concept, and never becomes an experience; and, therefore, when they are asked

"Where does the One return?" they are at a loss where to find the way out.[35]

Intuition may be despised by the philosopher, but there are grades of intuition. The deepest are those experienced by religio-philosophical minds belonging to the order of the Prajñāpāramitā. But when their intuitions are translated into terms of relative knowledge, how insipid, negative, and nonsensical! The understanding of the Prajñāpāramitā becomes an impossibility. Hence its repeated warnings not to hide oneself under a cover, not to cherish a shadow of doubt, not to feel dejected or frightened or threatened.

10. *The Prajñā and Irrationalities*

Seeing thus where the Prajñāpāramitā stands, we can realize why it abounds with negative phrases and irrational assertions. Its intuitions could not be conveyed in any other way if they were to be expressed at all. In fact, we can say that all the deep soul-stirring truths are paradoxically stated, so much, indeed, that we are almost led to imagine that the authors are incorrigibly and deliberately enigmatic. The following quotations supply examples:

"Subhūti asked: How does the Bodhisattva come to the knowledge of the five Skandhas when he disciplines himself in the deep Prajñāpāramitā?

"Buddha said: He comes to the knowledge of the five Skandhas when he disciplines himself in the deep Prajñāpāramitā by perceiving *yathābhūtam* (1) what the characteristic marks *(lakṣaṇa)* of the Skandhas are, (2) whence they come and whither they go, and (3) what is meant by their suchness.

"(1) Rūpam (form) has no ultimate solidity; it is full of cracks and holes; it is like a bubble. Vedanā is like a boil; it is like an arrow, quickly rising and quickly disappearing; it is like a foam, deceiving and fleeting; it takes its rise when there is a triple combination of conditions. Saṁjñā is like a mirage, there are no real fountains in it; because of thirst of desire it rises, and expresses itself in words though there is nothing substantial in it. Saṁskāra is like a plantain tree; when each leaf is peeled off,

[35] See *Zen Essays,* Series I, p. 283.

nothing remains. Vijñāna is like a Māyā creation; it is there when causes and conditions are variously combined. It is a provisionary construction; the magically created soldiers are seen marching through the streets; though they look real they are in fact without substantiality.

"(2) As regards the whence and whither of the five Skandhas, the Bodhisattva knows *yathābhūtam* that they come from nowhere although they seem to manifest themselves actually before him; that they depart nowhere although they seem to disappear altogether out of sight, and yet that there is in the Skandhas a happening known as their rise or their disappearance.

"(3) Lastly, the Bodhisattva perceives *yathābhūtam* that there is what is to be known as the suchness of the five Skandhas, which is neither born nor dead, neither comes nor departs, is neither pure nor tainted, neither loses nor gains; which for ever remains in the state of suchness free from all falsehood, from all forms of change."[36]

The position of the Prajñāpāramitā is not necessarily to deny the so-called phenomenal world; it gives the world its judicious claim as a stage of birth and death, of being and non-being. But at the same time it never forgets to assert that what we see here displayed or performed are passing shadows of something behind, and that when the latter is not finally grasped by our experience the meaning of the passing shadows will never be properly recognized and appraised. Therefore, the Mahāyānists are always meticulously careful about distinguishing between "the attainable" and "the unattainable," technically so called. "The attainable" belongs to this world dualistically constructed and "the unattainable" to a world beyond that. Wherever the contrast between *astitva* (being) and *nāstiva* (non-being) is possible, there is attainability and, therefore, attachment which is the enemy of enlightenment and emancipation.

"The Buddha says to Subhūti: Wherever there is a form of duality, this is attainability; wherever there is no duality in whatever form, this is non-attainability. When the eye stands against form *(rūpam)*, or the mind against ideas *(dharma)*, there

36 Abstract from Hsüan-chuang's translation of the *Mahāprajñāpāramitā*, Fas. 532, Chapter 29 (1) 55 ff. [For an alternative translation by Arthur Waley see *Buddhist Texts*, ed. E. Conze, 1954, B. Cassirer, Oxford, pp. 154–8.]

is a duality. When there is what is known as supreme enlightenment set against the Buddha who is regarded as having attained it, this is again a duality. Any teaching that is based on dualism is incorrect, it belongs to a realm of the attainables.

"Let the duality of eye and form, ear and sound, mind and thought be altogether done away with; likewise with that of the enlightened and enlightenment let us have nothing to do; and then there will be a state of non-duality, free from all false teachings and illegitimate speculations. The unattainable is thus attained.

"Subhūti asks: 'Is it the unattainable because of depending on the attainable? Or because of depending on the unattainable?

"The Buddha: It is the unattainable because of depending on neither the attainable nor the unattainable. It is termed 'unattainable' when the attainable and the unattainable are regarded as one. The discipline of the Bodhisattva in the Prajñāpāramitā consists in realizing this oneness of the attainable and the unattainable. Let him be freed both from the idea of the attainable and that of the unattainable; he will then be free from all faulty entanglements.

"O Subhūti, you may ask: if the attainable and the unatttainable are one, how does the Bodhisattva, who is defined as progressively going through from one stage to another, finally reach the enlightenment of the all-knowing one? O Subhūti, the Bodhisattva's life is a series of unattainables. He has nothing attained while going through the various stages of Bodhisattvahood; for in the Prajñāpāramitā there is nothing attainable, nor is there any in the enlightenment of the all-knowing one. When the Bodhisattva is disciplining himself in the Prajñāpāramitā, there is in his discipline nothing to be recognized as attained, and in this non-attainment there is also really nothing attained in any time and at any place.[37]

This sounds nonsensical when we confine ourselves to the relativity aspect of existence, or to the discursive understanding of the human mind. But let us reverse the order of things; let us see the world of pluralities from the other side which reveals itself to the inner eye now opened by a process known as Parā-

[37] *Ibid.*, Fas. 525, Chapter 26 (3) 23a.

vṛitti, and we shall realize that all these irrationalities are possible. Irrationalities are such because of our position. The question is whether we can abandon this position, whether we can adopt an altogether new one where things are surveyed from their aspect of suchness. As we have already seen, the acquirement of this is made possible by the supreme efforts we put forward when impelled by a certain inner urge. The new position is open only to our will power and not to the intellect. Logic halts here; ideas are unable to array themselves in regular sequence of cognition and analysis. The intellect surrenders itself to the dictates of the will. The door is forced to open, and we see a realm of unattainables extending itself before the eye. It is in this realm that we attain an unattainability by not really attaining it. Critics may declare: "By this we have not gained anything, for we stand where we were before the Parāvṛitti. If this is so, what is the use of exercising ourselves so much over the so-called situation? When we have a thing as if not having it, it is practically the same as not having it at all from the first." The reasoning is sound as far as intellection is concerned. But we may remember that we have already gone over to the other side of intellection, and that whatever statements we make are made after the leap. There is the history of an experience intervening; this is a great event which creates an unsurpassable gap between philosophy and the teaching of the *Prajñāpāramitā*.

11. *The Unattainable and the Unattached*

"Unattainable" *(anupalabdha)*, otherwise expressed, is "not-seized" or "unattached" *(apāramṛiṣṭa)*. "Unattainable" has still an intellectual ring, while "unseizable" or "unattached" belongs to the terminology of emotion. The assertion that "All-knowledge is indeed unattached" *(aparāmṛiṣṭā hi sarvajñatā)* is in fact one of the refrains we constantly come across in the *Prajñāpāramitā Sūtra*. In this we are made to be strongly convinced that the Mahāyāna text is a document describing the views of the other side of existence where the dualism of *astitva* and *nāstitva* ceases to hold good. In the following passages, *apāramṛiṣṭa* is replaced by *aśleṣa* and *asaṁga*, which denote the same idea; our author tries hard to impress us with the importance of this teaching of non-attachment.

"When the Bodhisattva attains enlightenment, he teaches all beings with the doctrine of non-attachment *(aśleṣa)*. By non-attachment is meant not to be bound by Rūpam *(rūpasyāsaṁbandhā)*, by Vedanā, Saṁjñā, Saṁskāra, and Vijñāna. When a person is not bound by them, he is unconcerned with their rise and disappearance. Being unattached to these happenings, he is neither in bondage nor emancipated."[38]

"This teaching of the *Prajñāpāramitā* is difficult to understand, difficult to believe. Because form itself *(rūpam)* is neither bound nor emanicapted. Why? Because form has no self-nature *(asvabhāva)*. The same may be said of the rest of the Skandhas. There is no self-nature in any one of them, neither in the beginning, nor in the midway, nor at the end. As this having no self-nature is its self-nature, there is nothing bound, nothing emancipated. The Prajñāpāramitā is, therefore, difficult to grasp."[39]

"But as soon as we cling to name *(nāma)* and appearance *(nimitta)*, there is attachment *(saṁga)*. Name and appearance are products of discrimination *(vikalpa)*. Discrimination takes place when the Prajñāpāramitā is clung to as such." Discrimination, attachment, and the losing sight of the Prajñāpāramita are synonymous and interchangeable in the lexicon of Mahāyāna Buddhism. Form is empty *(rūpam śūnyam)*, but when it is so asserted there is clinging *(saṁga)*, and the clinging separates us from the Prajñāpāramitā.

"Here is a novitiate Bohisattva who has awakened the desire for enlightenment; he has gone through with a disciplinary course in the life of Bodhisattvahood; and he may have conceived the idea that he has thereby accumulated a certain amount of merit. But no sooner is this idea stirred in him than he commits a deed of clinging, he is no more in the Prajñāpāramitā. Wherever there is discrimination, this leads to clinging; or we may reverse it and state that wherever there is clinging there is discrimination. Enlightenment is attained only when there is no clinging, no conscious striving, no dualism of *astitva*

[38] *Aṣṭa*, p. 294 (*Fo-mu*, 41a).
[39] *Ibid.*, pp. 185–6; Hsüan-chuang, Fas. 545, Chapter 8, 19b.

and *nāstitva;* for enlightenment is non-attainment, and its self-nature consists in not having self-nature."[40]

This being free from discrimination, from clinging or attachment, and having no self-nature is sometimes called a state of "absolute purity" *(atyantaviśuddhi).* And it is said that because of this absolute purity the Prajñāpāramitā is unfathomably deep, glowingly brilliant, a perfect unit, unattainable, unseizable, unknowable, unborn, indestructible, abiding nowhere, etc.[41]

To illustrate further the philosophy of the unattainable or of absolute solitude as described in the *Prajñāpāramitā,* I quote another passage from the sūtra where a chapter is devoted to the treatment of Māyā.[42]

"Subhūti then said: How can the mind which is like Māyā attain supreme enlightenment?

"The Buddha: Do you see the mind which is like Māyā?

"Subhūti: No, I do not.

"Buddha: Do you see Māyā?

"Subhūti: No, I do not.

"Buddha: When you do not see Māyā, nor the mind which is like Māyā, do you think there is an existence *(dharma)*—other than the Māyā or the Māyā-like mind—which attains supreme enlightenment?

"Subhūti: No, I do not see any such existence *(dharma).* If there is any existence apart from the mind which is like Māyā, nothing can be predicated of it, for it is neither a being *(asti)* nor a non-being *(nāsti).* All is absolutely solitary *(atyantavivikta),* and in this absolute solitude there is nothing which we can assert either as being or as not being; there is nothing in which discipline is possible, or of which attainment is to be avouched. For this reason, the Prajñāpāramitā is absolutely solitary. So is supreme enlightenment. Between these two absolutely solitary terms there cannot be any relationship; we cannot describe the one as the means of attaining the other, nor the other as something attainable. The Bodhisattva is spoken of as attaining supreme enlightenment because of the Prajñāpāramitā. But the Bodhisattva himself is also an absolutely solitary being *(dharma),*

40 *Ibid.,* p. 190 *(Fo-mu,* 25 b).
41 *Ibid.,* pp. 186 et seq. *(Fo-mu,* 25b).
42 *Ibid.,* Chapter XXVI, "On the Simile of Māyā."

and we cannot make any assertion about his attaining anything, even enlightenment.

"Buddha: Well done, Subhūti. It is just as you state. Absolutely solitary are all things *(dharma)*—the Bodhisattva, the Prajñāpāramitā, and supreme enlightenment. And yet amid those absolutely solitary dharmas the Bodhisattva is awakened to the true nature of the Prajñāpāramitā and attains the knowledge that the Prajñāpāramitā is absolutely solitary, and that what is known as Prajñāpāramitā is not Prajñāpāramita. There is really the attainment by the Bodhisattva of supreme enlightenment, and yet in this attainment there is really nothing that can be held out as something attained, something seized; and all things *(dharma)* remain absolutely solitary as if nothing [had] ever happened."[43]

12. *Reality as Seen from the Other Side*

"Absolutely solitary" *(atyantavivikta)*, "absolutely pure" *(atyantaviśuddhi)*, "unattainable" *(anupalabdha)*, "unattached" *(aśleṣa,* or *asaṁga,* or *aparāmṛiṣṭa)*, "neither bound nor emancipated" *(abaddhāmukta)*, "neither born nor extinguished" *(anutpādānirodha)*, "not abiding anywhere" *(asthita)*, "not depending on anything" *(anāśrāya)*, "not exhausted" *(akṣaya)*, "pathless" *(apatha)*, "trackless" *(apada)*, etc.—all these belong to the terminology to be met with in the *Prajñāpāramitā Sūtra,* and come from the realm of Emptiness. When we try to understand them from our ordinary logical point of view, which deals with the relativity aspect of existence, they do not seem to convey much sense; they are too negative or too obscure in meaning for us to locate the definite quarters where they intend to lead us. As soon, however, as we abandon our dualistically built up relativity standpoint, and enter into the inner life of things, we seem to understand those obscure terms; we even come to think that this inner world is only describable by means of this kind of mystical phraseology. The religious life is after all a life to live and experience and not a concept to think about, yet the human mind is so constructed that it cannot avoid giving expression to

[43] *Aṣṭa,* pp 438 ff; *Fo-mu,* 61; *Māhā,* Fas. 553, 60a; Kumārajīva, 78b.

the life. The expressions in the *Prajñāpāramitā* are thus the more or less intellectual outpourings of the Mahāyāna genius.

To study or discipline oneself in the Prajñāpāramitā is, therefore, to approach this realm of absolute solitude or absolute emptiness. The Prajñā generally lies obscured in the deepest recesses of consciousness. Unless this is successfully awakened and made to see the other side of reality, which is to see reality *yathābhūtam,* there is no escape from the bondage of ignorance and suffering. This release is called attaining supreme enlightenment or all-knowledge *(sarvajñatā).*

The Prajñāpāramitā is the objective of all the Buddhist discipline. But when this is attained there is really nothing of which one can say that one has attained it. This is the meaning of such phrases: "There is no perception of Suchness in Suchness"; "Not by means of absolute solitude is absolute solitude realized"; "There is something accomplished, and yet no discrimination *(avikalpa)* we have, because of the Prajñāpāramitā's being non-discriminative"; etc. Some may call these phrases mystical in the sense that they are irrational and beyond syllogistic reasoning. This may be right, for "incomprehensible" *(acintya)* is one of the terms most frequently used in all Mahāyāna literature. But from the standpoint of the Prajñā philosophers they are far from talking irrationalities; they are simply giving expression to what they actually see with their own Prajñā-eye.

In the beginning, not being satisfied with themselves and their so-called objective world, they had everywhere searched for Reality in or with which they could peacefully live. The Parāvṛitti took place somewhere in their mind. The order of things is reversed. The universe *(sarvadharma)* is no more observed from the point of view with which they have hitherto been so deeply, so inextricably involved. This is now completely abandoned. Things are seen, as it were, from the reverse side. A world of Rūpam, Vedanā, Saṁjñā, Saṁskāra, and Vijñāna is there as before, but it is seen lined with the silver lining of Tathatā (suchness) and no more indeed as an isolated event cut off from its roots. Without the roots, which are, however, no roots, we merely drifted like a dead leaf before the autumn wind, and the drifting had no meaning whatever, which was, to use Buddhist terminology, ignorance and transmigration and torture. The scene has changed, and to describe this change simply, and in a most unsophisticated manner, the *Prajñāpāramitā* writers now exhaust their literary power. The "irrationalities" so called belong to the philosopher and logician, and not to the Prajñā devotee.

Teachers of the Prajñāpāramitā have their foothold or dwelling *(sthāna)* always on the other side *(pāram)* of this world of relativity. They thus seem to be negating the latter, regarding it as Māyā, as a dream, as an echo, and so on. Even when reference is made to their own quarters of Śūnyatā, this Śūnyatā is also empty and has no fixed abode. Because theirs is an absolute Śūnyatā and allows nothing to oppose it, it is absolutely without predicates of any sort whatever. Suchness has thus come to be one of the most favorite terms they use to designate Śūnyatā. "Absolute emptiness" or "absolute solitude" is indeed difficult for dualistically minded beings to comprehend. This is the reason why the *Prajñāpāramitā* repeatedly warns its readers not to become frightened or depressed when they hear of the doctrine of Emptiness; it must sound to them as trumpeting a universal annihilation. And those who would embrace the teaching at once without the least hesitation are praised as being those who have listened to it for many times in their past existences. The warning and the assurance prove that the Prajñā is something most extraordinary; and most extraordinary indeed it is, seeing that the ordinary order of things is completely reversed in the Prajñāpāramitā. Is it not shocking to know that the Mount Hiei which we people of Kyoto see every day in the northeastern part of the city is no more a reality; more than that, all the heavens including all the luminaries whose lights are measured to reach this earth after millions of years are said to be mere bubbles in the ocean of eternal Emptiness? Who would not be terrified before this audacious proclamation? But this is the proclamation that rings through the *Prajñāpāramitā*. What a grand, thoroughly penetrating intuition it must be that would blow out this entire cosmos like a soap bubble into the immensity of absolute Emptiness *(atyanta-śūnyatā)!*

Emptiness is absolute when it stands alone, rejecting all predicability. As long as reference is made to inner or outer, created or uncreated, substance or appearance, Emptiness is not yet absolute, it remains still relative and predicated. All must be set aside, Emptiness must stand shorn of all its trappings when its true features will strike us with their primeval awfulness. Primeval awfulness I say because Emptiness itself is now vanished; it is as if this physical body were left in mid-air, with nothing covering its head, nothing supporting its feet. It is awful to imagine such a situation. But the *Prajñāpāramitā* unmistakably contrives to create it for us. No wonder it gives us warnings constantly on this point.

"All is empty" *(sarvaṁ śūnyam)*—by this one of the legs is broken off. "Emptiness itself is empty" *(śūnyatā-śūnyatā)*—by this the remaining one departs; and at the same time the entire earth vanishes from beneath one. I am like Hsiang-yen's man up in a tree,[44] and even the teeth are now letting go the hold. Out of this great negation there is the awakening of the Prajñā, and the great affirmation takes place, which is Sarvajñatā and Saṁbodhi, all-knowledge and enlightenment. Śūnyata seems to have changed into Tathatā, but in reality Śūnyatā is Tathatā, and Tathatā Śūnyatā. The solid earth has not vanished. Mount Hiei stands before one even more solemnly than before, and the starry heavens are an ever-inspiring wonder not only for the philosopher but for all of us. We now really know what is meant by seeing *yathābhūtam*. The world is revealed as thoroughly pure, detached, unattainable, free from an ego thought, and therefore the home of peace and happiness. The Mahāyāna sūtras talk so much of embellishing[45] the world. When the Bodhisattva is awakened in Tathatā, he is the embellisher.

II

THE RELIGION OF THE PRAJÑĀPĀRAMITĀ

1. *Where the Prajñā Functions*

The Prajñāpāramitā may be said to be standing on the line which divides the absolute aspect of existence from its relative

44 *Zen Essays,* Series I, pp. 277–8.
45 [*Alaṃkāra, vyūha.*]

aspect, and this line is a geometrical one just marking the boundary and having no dimension. Even then we must not conceive the Prajñā as looking this way or that way when it wants to survey the two realms of existence. If the Prajñā were to take Śūnyatā alone without its Aśūnyatā, or Aśūnyatā alone without its Śūnyatā, it would no more be Prajñā. To symbolize this, the Indian gods are furnished with one extra eye cut straight up between the two ordinary ones. This is the Prajñā-eye. By means of this third eye the enlightened are enabled to perceive Reality *yathābhūtam,* without splitting it into two and then unifying them, for this splitting and unifying is the work of abstract thinking. The Prajñā-eye, placing itself on the boundary line of Oneness and Manyness, of Śūnyatā and Aśūnyatā, of Bodhi and Kleśa, of Prajñā and Karuṇā, Buddha and Sarvasattva, Enlightenment and Ignorance, Samādhi and Karma, takes in these two worlds at a glance as one Reality. "Prajñā is not on this side, nor on that side, nor in the middle; when it is subjected to discrimination, it is lost, it is no more there." [46]

The intellect represents the Prajñā as sitting astride of the two realms of existence, but as far as the Prajñā itself is concerned it is not conscious of such a division, it goes on with its own experience. Śūnyatā is not felt to be something separate from a world of Saṁsāra, and the latter from Śūnyatā. When the Prajñā asserts itself, the two, Śūnyatā and Saṁsāra, are drawn up in one string. Hitherto, we have given ourselves up too much to abstraction, the Prajñā has been colored too pale, and as the result the entire universe has come to assume too indifferent an aspect—probably not satisfying enough to the needs of our heart. When the landscape is painted with one daub of Śūnyatā, there is no room for mountains, rivers, rocks, chrysanthemums, etc. in the canvas called the universe. If this be the case, the fault is our own and not the Prajñā's.

When we wish to make ideas more comprehensible, we generally translate them into spatial relations. And then we take these relations for realities, forgetting that the spatial representations are symbols. The manipulation of symbols is not the same as grasping the original. The Prajñā ought to be released from

[46] *Hsiao-p'in,* 58b.

Gladiola bulbs

these static complications. The realm of Śūnyatā ought not to be severed from the world of particulars; for the severance is merely to facilitate the analytical intellect. When it has served its utility the sooner it is put aside the better. One of the reasons why the *Prajñāpāramitā* is so tiresomely repetitive is to impress the reader with the fact that Śūnyatā is not an abstraction but an experience, or a deed enacted where there is neither space nor time. When Śūnyatā and everything else is declared to be merely a name, it is to be so understood.

Further, all human activities, mental and physical, are carried on in time; or, at least, when we try to describe them they are set in the frame of time. Even when we talk of eternity or beginninglessness, the idea has the background of time. It is very difficult to get rid of this form of thinking, and especially is this the case when the Prajñā is to be properly understood. The following question undoubtedly comes from the notion that Prajñā or Saṁbodhi is a child of time, while the fact is that time starts from the awakening of Prajñā, and Prajñā is where there is yet neither time nor space.

"Subhūti: Is Saṁbodhi to be attained by the awakening of a preceding thought or by the awakening of a succeeding thought? If it is by the preceding one, this does not concord with the succeeding one. If it is by the succeeding one, this does not concord with the preceding one. And when there is no concordance between the two, how can a stock of merit be increased? [And also how is the attainment of Saṁbodhi possible?]"[47]

According to Subhūti, what we call mind is a succession of thoughts, it can be cut up into so many thoughts and arranged in time form, i.e., in terms of priority and posteriority. When thoughts are supposed to succeed one another in time sequence, what is it that links two thoughts together, as their concordance *(samanvahita)* is otherwise not possible? In the absence of such concordance, how can one single thought of enlightenment be construed to pervade a whole series of thoughts, which by definition is a mind? This is the central point in Subhūti's question.

The Buddha illustrates this by means of a flame and says: The

[47] *Aṣṭa,* p. 352; *Fo-mu,* 49b.

burning takes place not by a preceding flame, nor by a succeeding one; yet it is not separated from either. It goes on through the succession of flames. When it is taken by itself, there is no burning. When it is cut up into flames, it is difficult to conceive its successive burning. But in point of fact there is a suchness of burning. When experience is described in terms of birth-and death, coming-to-exist and passing-away, going-ahead and following-after, it is no more there, the suchness of things slips out of one's grasp.

The Prajñā thus escapes all our intellectual efforts to pin it down in the loom of time. The process must be reversed if it is to be judiciously orientated. Instead of placing it somewhere in our scheme of thought constructions, let us begin with the Prajñā itself as the starting point of all our activities and thoughts, and the whole text of the *Prajñāpāramitā* becomes intelligible. Time and space complications rise from the Prajñā in which there is yet neither time nor space. With its awakening we really live, and a world of particulars reveals itself before us with its problems. These preliminary remarks will probably help us to pass on to the second part of this essay, in which what the Mahāyāna philosophers technically termed Upāya ("skillful means") will be discussed.

2. *Upāya ("Skillful Means")*

As long as our point of view is confined to the absolute aspect of the Prajñāpāramitā, we stop there and no room is left for us to make further advances. In this case there will be no more of Mahāyāna Buddhism, or of Bodhisattvahood. If all things are like a vision *(māyā),* one may reason, and if there is no reality whatever in them, how can a Bodhisattva make progress towards the attainment of Sarvajñatā (all-knowledge)? How can the nature of Sarvajñatā itself be established? How can there be any turning over of merit to the realization of Sarvajñatā? These are the questions naturally asked by one whose understanding of the Prajñāpāramitā is made to fit into the scheme of time-concept. Śāriputra's answer is as follows:[48]

"If all things were not like a vision but had something of

[48] *The Mahāprajñāpāramitā,* Hsüan-chuang, Fas. 587.

reality in them, it would be impossible for the Bodhisattva to turn his merit toward the attainment of Sarvajñatā, or to make progress toward its realization. It is just because there is nothing real in all things, which are like a vision, that the Bodhisattva can turn his merit over to the attainment of Sarvajñatā and advance toward realization; it is just because he perceives the unreality and the vision-like character of all things that he endures and untiringly practices the virtue of strenuousness.

"What is the reason of this endurance, of this untiring strenuousness?

"It is owing to the operation of 'skillful means' *(upāyakauśalya)* which is born of the Bodhisattva's great compassionate heart for all sentient beings. Because of this skillful means he is told that all things are empty; and also because of this skillful means he does not attempt to realize in himself the truth of absolute solitude. It is like a man who, firmly holding a huge umbrella in his hands, stands at the top of a high mountain. He may bend himself and look down into the gaping abyss at the foot of the precipice, but he cherishes no fears, does not tremble at the thought of being swallowed up in the bowels of the earth; for he is supported by the umbrella, which, by the aid of the wind, keeps him from falling. In like manner, by virtue of Prajñā which sees into the nature of all things, by virtue of a compassionate heart which keeps him among his fellow beings in this world of tribulations, the Bodhisattva disciplines himself in all the Pāramitās, by degrees making his progress toward Sarvajñatā, so that he is finally enabled to mature all beings, to benefit and bestow happiness on all beings, and to establish a Buddha land."

Skillful means *(upāyakauśalya),* or simply means *(upāya),* has a technical sense in the teaching of the Mahāyāna. It is the creation of the great compassionate heart which the Bodhisattva has. When he perceives his fellow beings drowning in the ocean of birth and death because of their ignorance and passionate clinging to a world of particulars, he awakens his great heart of love and compassion for them and contrives all kinds of means to save them, to enlighten them, to mature their consciousness for the reception of the ultimate truth. The means grows out of the Bodhisattva's clear perception of the truth of Śūnyatā (emptiness), though not out of Śūnyatā itself. The truth as such remains powerless, it must go through the consciousness of the Bodhisattva; for beings of the two vehicles, the Śrāvaka and the Pratyekabuddha, are unconcerned with the welfare of their fellow beings. They are content with the intellectual understanding of the truth, they abide with the truth of absolute solitude, they do not venture out of their cell of self-sufficiency. Therefore, there is no skillful means with them. The means cohabits with the intuition (*prajñā*) in the mind of the Bodhisattva. It is his intellectual insight, as it were, into the nature of things when he sees that they are not real, they are like Māyā, they are "empty"; but his is more than this insight, more than the intellect, more than a cold indifferent surveying of a world of turmoil and suffering from the viewpoint of absolute solitariness or of eternal serenity. As he perceives that a world of particularities is like Māyā, he is not attached to it; but he knows that this world is right before him, because it is the stage where all his activities are performed, that is to say, where all his ignorant and egoistic fellow beings are actually suffering and harassed to the extreme. Hence the Upāya growing out of the Prajñā.

The chain linked with Prajñā, Karuṇā, and Upāya goes through all the systems of Mahāyāna Buddhism. This linking is the most characteristic feature of it. So says the *Prajñāpāramitā:*[49] "The Mahāyāna consists in the practice of the six Pāramitās, and this practice is characterized with the raising of mind in conformity with Sarvajñatā (all-knowledge). This raising is headed with a great compassionate heart, which creates means; and the means is characterized with non-attainment (*anupalambha*) [that is, with non-attachment]. All things inside and outside are given up for the sake of directing all beings toward Sarvajñatā. And this merit of giving up is performed not only by oneself but by others. . . ."

The thesis of the *Prajñāpāramitā* is that the realization of the Prajñā comes foremost in thoroughly comprehending the spirit of the Mahāyāna, which constitutes the life of the Bodhisattva (*bodhisattvacaryā*). When his mind (*citta* or *manasikāra*) is

[49] Hsüan-chuang, Fas. 413, Chapter "On Samādhi."

abiding in perfect conformity *(pratiyukta)* day and night with the Prajñāpāramitā, he becomes the benefactor *(dakṣiṇīya)* of all beings; for it is then that a great compassionate heart *(maitrīsahagatam cittam)* is awakened in him toward all beings. With his penetrating insight into the nature of Prajñā, he perceives that all beings are held in leash and far from being free masters of themselves. He is seized with a great feeling of pity *(mahākaruṇā)*. Being also endowed with a spiritual eyesight, he perceives beings suffering from the evil karma they have committed or entangling themselves in the net of falsehood. He is intensely agitated over these facts and firmly makes up his mind to the effect that he will be a protector of and a refuge *(nātha)* for the world and release it from the bondage of ignorance and passion.[50]

We can thus see that there is an inevitable relationship between Sarvajñatā, Prajñā, Karuṇā, Upāya, and Saṁbodhi or Moksha. Theoretically stated, Sarvajñatā is the outcome or content of Saṁbodhi which is realizable by Prajñā; but Prajñā in itself is unable to achieve any practical result, it operates through Upāya and this Upāya is born of Karuṇā. The *Prajnāpāramitā* illustrates these relations with the following similes:[51]

"Subhūti, it is like a man taking himself out on the sea; after a while his boat is wrecked; if he does not take hold of a life buoy or a piece of board or wood, he is sure to be drowned in the water before he reaches his destination. Subhūti, in like manner a Bodhisattva may have faith in the supreme enlightenment *(anuttara-samyak-saṁbodhi)*, may accept it whole-heartedly, may have a strong longing for it, may have an understanding of it, may be pleased with it, may find great joy in it, may aspire earnestly for it, may have confidence, resignation, assiduity, vigilance, pure thought regarding it. In spite of these virtues on his part, the Bodhisattva is unable to attain Sarvajñatā unless he is taken care of by Prajñā and Upāya. For he is sure to retrogress in the middle of his career. By 'the middle of his career' is meant the stage of Śrāvakahood and Pratyekabuddhahood; by 'retrogression' is meant the losing sight of Sarvajñatā.

50 Abstract from *Fo-mu*, Fas. 20, Chapter "On Good Friends."

51 *Fo-mu*, Fas. 14, Chapter "On Similes" *(aupamya)*. Generally, four similies are given, but only two of them are quoted here.

"It is otherwise with the man who takes hold of a life buoy or a piece of board when his boat is wrecked, for he can safely attain the other shore; and also with the Bodhisattva who, with all his virtues of faith, understanding, etc., in the supreme enlightenment, is taken care of by Prajñā and Upāya; for he attains Sarvajñatā without stopping in the middle of his career at the stage of Śrāvakahood and Pratyekabuddhahood."

To give another simile: Here is an old man one hundred and twenty years old; being assailed by all forms of illness, he is kept to his bed and patiently endures his pain; as to his getting up and walking a few miles, not to say anything of a very much longer distance, he is unable even to dream of such an undertaking. Here to him come two strong men and tell him to get up, for they will support him and carry him along the road to whatever end he wishes to reach. He follows their advice. Weak as he is, he finally attains his destination.

In a similar way, whatever confidence, delight, resignation, etc., a Bodhisattva may have in the supreme enlightenment, he cannot reach the other shore of Sarvajñatā unless he is helped by the two strong men, Prajñā and Upāya; for these are the supporters of the Bodhisattva in his progressive career toward the goal of his life, and without them he will assuredly break down in the midst of his progress and sink into the level of Śrāvakahood and Pratyekabuddhahood. Why? Because this is the suchness of things.

3. *The Bodhisattva and the Śrāvaka*

As was stated elsewhere, what characteristically distinguishes the Bodhisattva from the Śrāvaka and the Pratyekabuddha is that while the former is concerned with the welfare, spiritual and material, of all beings, the latter are content with their own enlightenment or deliverance; they keep up their meditation undisturbed and do not go out of their cell, so that they can do something to relieve other fellow beings of their karma, ignorance, and suffering. This spiritual egotism stands in great contrast to the self-sacrificing impulses of the Bodhisattva. As far as the enlightenment goes, both the Bodhisattva and the Śrāvaka may be on the same level, but the former is ready whenever necessary to come down from his supreme position and mix himself with his unenlightened, bespotted, karma-bound fellow beings, and live their life too if there are opportunities to benefit them in one way or another. The Bodhisattva would therefore very frequently abandon the life of an ascetic, or a monk, or a hermit, in order to be in the world, to live with the world, to suffer its sufferings, and thereby to bring it to a state of final enlightenment. To be thus in a world of particulars and passions and to follow the laws that govern it (that is to say, "not to obscure cause and effect")—this is the Bodhisattva's way of living, this is the "being taken care of by Prajñā and Upāya." Sarvajñatā comes out of that.

For this reason, we read throughout the *Prajñāpāramitā* that the motive which prompts the Bodhisattva to realize within himself the supreme enlightenment is not for his own benefit but for all beings; he wishes to raise them from the bondage of karma and ignorance so that they are finally established in Parinirvāṇa. This is the most difficult achievement, especially for the Bodhisattva who lives in the realm of birth-and-death *(saṁsāra)*. He is thus warned not to relax in his vigilance, not to become frightened.

The Bodhisattva's desire is to benefit the world *(lokahita)*, to give happiness to the world *(lokasukha)*, to stir within himself a compassionate heart for the world *(lokānukampā)*.

Therefore, when he realizes in himself the supreme enlightenment, he vows to become the world's great benefactor, protector, refuge, dwelling house, ultimate path, isle of retreat, illumination, leader, and passageway.[52]

Thus the Bodhisattva is no retiring, negative soul always wishing to flee from the world for his own perfection and enlightenment; but he is a most aggressive rescuer of the world; he positively works upon it to yield the result he wishes from his active contact with it. His self-assertion consists in cherishing the thoughts of sameness *(samam cittam utpadya)* and not the thoughts of discrimination *(viṣamacittam)* toward all beings, in holding thoughts of compassion *(maitracittam)*, of benevolence *(hita)*, of good friendship *(kalyāṇa)*, of not hurting

[52] *Ibid.*, Fas. 14, Chapter "On Wise Men."

(nihatamāna), of non-resistance *(apratihata)*, of not-injuring *(avihiṁsā)*, of not-harming *(aviheṭhanā)*. The Bodhisattva will also regard all beings as his mother, father, sons, or daughters.[53] Maitrī (friendliness), Karuṇā (compassion), Anukampā (sympathy), and others are terms we most frequently come across in all the Mahāyāna sūtras; for to regard all beings with these thoughts is the one desire *(praṇidhāna)* all the Bodhisattvas most heartily cherish.

The following dialogue between Pūrṇamaitrāyaṇīputra and Śāriputra quoted from the *Mahāprajñāpāramitā*[54] gives us an idea as to the reason why the Bodhisattva feels compassionate toward his fellow beings who are not fully enlightened. In the feeling of fellow love there is no thought of superiority, no thought of separation or of exclusiveness, which keeps one from another as distinct in some fundamental and irreconcilable manner. The Bodhisattva, even when he is distinguishable from the Śrāvaka and the Pratyekbuddha and their discipline, motive, morality, attainment, and wisdom, entertains no sense of superiority; he is not at all inclined to think slightingly of others; he maintains his attitude of reverence toward all beings as possible Buddhas and Tathāgatas.

Oath of Bodhisat

"Pūrṇamaitrāyaṇīputra asks Śāriputra: Should the Bodhisattva pay respect only to other Bodhisattvas and not to all beings generally?

"Śāriputra answers: The Bodhisattva should respect all beings just as much as he does the Tathāgata. He should respect all the Bodhisattvas and all sentient beings without making any distinction between them. For it is for the Bodhisattva to cultivate toward all beings the feeling of humility and reverence and not to look upon them with arrogance. He should in fact revere them with the same feeling of self-abnegation as he does the Tathāgatas.

"The Bodhisattva is to think in this way: When I attain enlightenment I will instruct all sentient beings in the essence of the Dharma in order to make them cut off their evil passions and realize Nirvāṇa, or attain enlightenment and rest in peace

[53] *Ibid.*, Fas. 16, Chapter "On Tathatā"; *Aṣṭa*, p. 321.
[54] Hsüan-chuang, Fas. 387, Chapter 12 "On Morality."

and happiness, or become fully emancipated from the pain of the evil paths.

"The Bodhisattva should thus awaken a great compassionate feeling toward all beings and keep his mind completely free from arrogance and self-conceit, and let him feel in this wise: I will practice all the skillful means *(upāya)* in order to make all sentient beings realize that which is the foremost in themselves, i.e. their Buddha nature *(buddhatā)*. By realizing this they all become Buddhas, and I will by virtue of the skillful means lead them to this final realization which entitles them to the rank of Dharmarāja. The Dharmarāja is the highest and most honorable position, for here one becomes master of all things *(dharma)*.

"Therefore, let the Bodhisattva respect all sentient beings, let his compassionate feeling pervade all around, irrespective of its objects; for the Dharmakāya of the Tathāgata pervades all things. . . ."

4. *Śūnyatā Seen but Not Realized*

compassion

We know now that the complex of Prajñā, Karuṇā, and Upāya constitutes the career of the Bodhisattva, but here lies the fundamental mystery of human life which is too deep for the intellect to fathom. By this I mean that the mystery involves contradictions which philosophers have failed to reconcile. What the author of the *Prajñāpāramitā* attempts, therefore, is not to give a logical account of his experiences but to narrate them in the plainest words he can command. If there is anything incoherent about his accounts, it is due to the inherent nature of the experience, and it is our duty to endeavor to comprehend them by looking into the inmost recesses of our own consciousness. This means that the *Prajñāpāramitā* is to be read through our own life and experience and not by means of the intellect. When we watch earnestly, deeply, and with patience the workings of our soul, we see the sūtra unroll its contents before our own eyes. Whatever difficulties we formerly had will now be thoroughly dissolved. Logical entanglements and intellectual incomprehensibilities exist no more. It is like seeing an apple as apple. The fruit lies before us, we see it, we handle it, we can eat it and taste it sweet, we find it in every way satisfactory. The chemist, the botanist, the medical scientist, the agricultural expert, etc., may find in the apple many questions still unsolved and go on discussing them and experimenting with it; but the practical man of the world is satisfied with the actuality of things of which he is assured of himself, not depending on anybody else or on some process of analysis and abstraction which always interferes with the immediacy of perception and feeling.

The following passages quoted from the chapter entitled "Skillful Means" in the *Aṣṭasāhasrikā* are full of difficulties and complexities, and our imagination is charged to the utmost to unravel them successfully. But as they make up the very essence of the Bodhisattva's life, they are given below.

"If," says the Buddha, "the Bodhisattva wishes to practice Prajñāpāramitā, he should regard *(pratyavekṣitavyam)* all things[55] as empty by seeing into their nature with a steady, uninterrupted mind *(avikṣiptayā cittasantatyā)*; but at the same time he may not realize Emptiness within himself."[56]

In our ordinary way of thinking, this is an impossible situation: to see things as empty, to abide in the Samādhi of Emptiness, and yet not to realize Emptiness in oneself. How can this be possible?

To this, the Buddha replies: "While the Bodhisattva sees *(pratyavekṣate)* that all things thoroughly contain within themselves the reason of Emptiness, he refuses to follow this reason up to its practical conclusion; for he knows that the time is for him to discipline himself in Emptiness and not to realize it in himself."[57] Thus he stops short before he reaps the legitimate fruit of the Samādhi, does not unreservedly abandon himself into the midst of Emptiness. Being guarded by the virtue of Prajñāpāramitā, he, while not realizing Emptiness, does not neglect the practice of the factors of enlightenment, nor does he sink, by destroying all his passions, into the abode of absolute extinction. It is for this reason that the Bodhisattva, in his prac-

[55] That is, the five Skandhas: *Rūpam, Vedanā, Samjñā, Samskāra,* and *Vijñāna.*

[56] *Na śūnyatām sākṣātkaroti.*

[57] *Parijayasyāyam kālo nāyam kālaḥ sākṣātkriyāyā.* P. 370.

tice of the Samādhi of Emptiness which leads to final emancipation, does not give himself up to the unconditioned realization of Emptiness; and that, while abiding in the Samādhi of no-form *(animitta),* he does not give himself up to the unconditioned realization of no-form, nor does he abide in form. His knowledge is deep, and his accumulation of merit is perfect, and, being under the protection of the Prajñāpāramitā, he perceives this his life here now is meant for maturing himself and not for realization. Thus he keeps himself from stepping into the reality limit *(bhūtakoṭi).*

This explanation does not seem to be quite sufficient and is therefore not quite convincing as far as the unenlightened are concerned. Hence the following parable in which the Bodhisattva's will and insight are illustrated:

Here is a man handsome in features and strong in prowess; he is active and strenuous; as a soldier he is well versed in all the arts of fighting; as a gentleman he is intelligent, virtuous, and an expert in various fields of life; he is thus highly revered by all who know him. One day he has business to transact in a distant region; to reach there he has to travel through wild mountainous districts inhabited by bandits and outlaws. His parents, wife, children, and others accompanying him are afraid of an assault from these villainous brigands. But the man full of valor and wisdom tells them not to cherish any anxieties over their journey, because he knows how to outwit these highwaymen and to carry his party safely and comfortably over the mountains and across the wilderness. They feel at ease with his assurances. They finish the trip unmolested and are comfortably settled at their destination. This is altogether due to the man's intelligence, wisdom, dauntless courage, and unparalleled firmness of mind.

In like manner, the Bodhisattva's compassionate heart is ever bent on benefiting all beings; he is always ready to practice pity, compassion, loving kindness, joy, impartiality toward all beings; he is protected by the power of the Prajñāpāramitā *(prajñāpāramitayā parigṛihītaḥ);* he is furnished with the skillful means; he turns all his meritorious deeds over to the attainment of Sarvajñatā. For this reason, the Bodhisattva, while disciplining himself in emptiness, no-form *(animitta),* and no-desire *(apraṇi-*

hita), stops short of realizing Bhūtakoṭi[58] in himself. He is not in this respect like the Śrāvaka and the Pratyekabuddha.[59] For his mind is always occupied with the welfare of all beings, wishing to see them attain the supreme enlightenment of Buddhahood.

That the Bodhisattva does not realize in himself the actuality of Emptiness even while disciplining himself in it is like the bird flying in the air. It neither remains in the air nor does it fall on the ground. The Bodhisattva wishes to practice all the teachings of Buddhism for the sake of all beings, and as to the fruit of his life he waits for the proper time to enjoy it.

It is again like the shooting of one arrow after another into the air by a man whose mastery of archery has attained a very high degree. He is able to keep all the arrows in the air, making each arrow support the one immediately preceding. He does this as long as he wishes. The Bodhisattva seeks the supreme enlightenment, and, being protected by the power of Prajñāpāramitā, he does not retreat into the doing-nothingness of Bhūtakoṭi. He waits for it until all his works are accomplished, although his deep insight penetrates even into the emptiness of all things. His compassionate heart for all beings who are groping in the dark for the truth that will release them from ignorance and suffering, and his skillful means which is generated from this all-embracing love and sustains him throughout the long and arduous course of his Prajñāpāramitācaryā—these are the forces which determine Bodhisattvahood.

However this may be, there is no doubt that this is one of the greatest mysteries in the spiritual life of the Mahāyānist—to be living Emptiness, to be abiding in Emptiness, to be attaining the Samādhi of Emptiness, and yet not to realize the reality limit within himself. The Buddha himself acknowledges that it is an achievement of the greatest difficulty, of the most extraordinary nature.[60] The mystery indeed lies in the Bodhi-

58 *Na tv eva bhūtakoṭim sākṣātkaroṭi. Bhūtakoṭi* is used throughout the sūtra as a synonym of *śūnyatā.* It literally means "reality limit." It has quite a modern note.

59 Cf. the *Gaṇḍavyūha's* description of the two Yānas, as *bhūtakoṭīpratiṣṭhitā* and *atyantaśāntaniṣṭhāṁgatā.* See pp. 162 ff.

60 *The Aṣṭasāhasrikā,* p. 375. "The Buddha then said to Subhūti: So it is, so it is! It is difficult indeed; it is of the utmost difficulty that the

sattva's cherishing the most wonderful vows that he will not abandon all beings, that he will deliver them from ignorance and suffering. All the mysteries and incomprehensibilities of the Buddhist life are traceable to this awakening in us of the desire for universal emancipation. When this is firmly established in the mind of the Bodhisattva, he is said to be at the stage of Avinivartanīya (no turning back).

Incidentally, it may be interesting to see what are the specific qualities of the Bodhisattva who has attained this stage of the Buddhist discipline; for the psychology of the dream is brought in very much here in the determination of the Bodhisattva mentality. In fact, it is not the psychologist alone who will read deeply into one's unconscious. The spirit also works through it from the far deeper source.

"The Buddha said to Subhūti: If a Bodhisattva shows no desire whatever even in a dream for the position of the Śrāvaka and the Pratyekebuddha, or if he harbors no thought of being born in the worlds which they are inhabiting, he is said to be at the stage of Avinivartanīya. . . .

"If a Bodhisattva sees himself in a dream as sitting in the air and preaching to people, as emitting rays of light from his body and going around in the form of a Bhikshu in the other Buddha-

---

Bodhisattva Mahāsattva, training himself in Śūnyatā, abiding in Śūnyatā, and in the attainment of Śūnyatā-Samādhi, should not yet realize Reality Limit (*bhūtakoṭi*). Why? Because he has made most wonderful vows (*praṇidhānaviśesāḥ*) not to abandon all beings, but to lead them to final emancipation. Having made these vows, he enters upon the Samādhi of Emancipation as regards emptiness, formlessness, and desirelessness; but in the meantime he does not realize Reality Limit since he is fully equipped (*samanvāgata*) with Skillful Means. Protected by Skillful Means, he knows how far to go in the realization of Reality Limit before he fulfills all the Buddha-dharmas. His mind is firmly made up not to enjoy the fruit of his discipline in Śunyatā until all beings are delivered from attachment and suffering."

In another place (*ibid.*, p. 28) we have this: "Śāriputra asks Subhūti: If I understand you right, the Bodhisattva is unborn; being unborn how does he ever come to conceive and undertake such a hard thing as to benefit all beings? Subhūti answers: I should not like to have the Bodhisattva think this kind of work hard to achieve and hard to plan out. If he did, there are beings beyond calculation, and he will not be able to benefit them. Let him on the contrary consider the work easy and pleasant, thinking they were all his father and mother and children, for this is the way to benefit all beings whose number is beyond calculation."

lands in order to carry out works of Buddhism such as preaching, etc., he is said to be at the stage of Avinivartanīya. . . .

"If a Bodhisattva sees in a dream scenes of a hell where all beings are suffering all forms of pain, and having seen them, makes up his mind to attain supreme enlightenment, and by this attainment to keep the Buddha-land clean of all impurities and evil passions so that even the name of hell will be unheard of in his land, he is said to be at the stage of Avinivartanīya. . . ."[61]

The ever-recurring questions which rise while reading the *Prajñāpāramitā* are: How can the Prajñā which sees into the absolute aspect of all things known as Emptiness be made to generate out of itself Karuṇā and Upāyakauśalya, which have their meaning in a world of particulars only? How can the Bodhisattva whose wings are always soaring high up to the realm of Sarvajñatā be made to hover around this earth filled with sufferings, iniquities, follies? More than that, how can he come to suspend his final flight which brings him to the ultimate goal of his discipline because his heart is called back to the welfare of his fellow beings and he does not wish to abandon them to their own karma hindrances? How can his eyesight be made to look in two opposite directions? According to the *Prajñāpāramitā,* he accomplishes this mystery just because he is ever aspiring after Prajñā and Sarvajñatā and disciplining himself in it.

And "this is not difficult," according to Subhūti, although it has been so pronounced elsewhere. "What is most difficult is to lead all beings, in number beyond calculation, and to make them safely abide in Mahāparinirvāṇa. The Bodhisattva wears the armor of energy and strenuousness. But beings *(sarvasattva)* are characterized like space with solitude *(viviktatva)* and unattainability *(anupalabdhatā);* they are ultimately unknowable.[62] The Bodhisattva, however, is not frightened to learn it, he is not taken aback, he is by no means depressed or dejected; for he is disciplining himself in the Prajñāpāramitā. . . . For he who is in the practice of the Prajñā gives the evil spirits no opportunities to interfere with his work if he observes two things: (1)

[61] *Fo-mu,* 43ab.

[62] *Te ca sattvā atyantatayā na saṁvidyante.—The Aṣṭasāhasrikā,* p. 445.

Seeing into the truth that all things are empty, and (2) Never abandoning all beings." Evidently there is no way to reconcile this contradiction except by unflinchingly leaping down into the abyss of Śūnyatā itself.

5. *Some of the Significant Opposites*

The *Prajñāpāramitā* thus offers to us a set of opposites out of which we are to draw a higher synthesis, not by logical cleverness but by actually living the life of the Bodhisattva who walks the way to Sarvajñatā. Some of the significant opposites may be formulated as follows:

(*a*) *Prajñā or Sarvajñatā versus Karuṇā or Upāya.* This antithesis is fundamental in the *Prajñāpāramitā* and also in all the other teachings of Mahāyāna Buddhism. The contrast is, however, conceptual and, therefore, superficial, as in all other cases; for in the actual life of a Bodhisattva this opposition is not felt and offers no obstruction in the execution of all the Buddha works. Or we may say that one is a Bodhisattva when these apparently contradicting notions disappear from one's religious consciousness. For instance, we read in the sūtra:[63]

"To practice Prajñā means to practice Sarvajñatā, which in turn means realizing Tathatā. For the title 'Tathāgata' means one who has realized Tathatā, suchness of all things. And in this Suchness *(tathatā)* there is neither extinction *(kṣaya),* nor birth *(utpāda),* nor disappearance *(nirodha),* nor rising *(janaka),* nor manifesting *(vibhāvana),* nor defilement *(rajas),* nor freedom from defilement, nor existing like space, nor being in any state. And yet in practicing this Prajñā the Bodhisattva perfects his own virtues, affords a refuge for others, and performs all that comes forth from a loving compassionate heart, a joyous spirit, and a great charitable feeling toward all beings. Not only this, the Bodhisattva helps others to discipline themselves in the way of emancipation and keeps the family of the Tathāgata in continuous prosperity. . . ."

(*b*) *Practicing Dhyāna and yet Refusing Its Fruits.*[64] "Disciplin-

[63] *Fo-mu,* 59b (Hsüan-chuang, Fas. 552, 56b ff.; Kumārajīva, 77ab). Hsüan-chuang's version differs widely from the other two in that it negates what the latter affirm. I have drawn my own conclusion.

[64] Hsüan-chuang, Fas. 552, 57b (*Fo-mu,* 60a; *Hsiao-p'in,* 77b).

ing himself in the Prajñā, the Bodhisattva refuses to be born in the various heavens according to the various Dhyānas, in which he is a thorough adept. This is by virtue of the skillful means *(upāyakauśalya)* inborn of the Prajñā, for it is the Upāya that keeps him from giving himself up to the enjoyment of the heavenly pleasures. Adepts in the Dhyānas are destined to be born in the celestial abodes, where, free from worldly cares, they are recipients of all kinds of untainted pleasures. But the Bodhisattva has no desire to leave this world of suffering where his fellow beings are still kept in bondage. To be in the world, of the world, and yet not to be tainted by it—this is the Bodhisattva's discipline. In spite of his worldly life he is fully endowed with the purities.

"Subhūti asks: If all things are in their original nature pure and free from defilements—which is the Buddha's teaching—how does the Bodhisattva in any special sense attain the purities as if he were not by nature pure?

"The Buddha answers: Yes, all things, as you say, are primarily pure, and the Bodhisattva disciplining himself in this purity—which is the Prajñā—realizes all things pertaining to it. This is the Upāya inherent in and born of the Prajñā. He sees into this reality as it is, and is free from fright and despondency."

(c) The Bodhisattva versus the Śrāvaka. In all the Mahāyāna texts this opposition is made the most of, for the life of the Bodhisattva stands sharply against that of the Śrāvaka. The latter is ready to quit this world for his own enlightenment and emancipation, he is willing to lend his ear to the advice of Māra the Tempter who would tell him: "The heavenly pleasures are of the most exquisite and transcendent nature, and cannot be compared with those of this world which is characterized with transiency, suffering, emptiness, and dissolution. Train yourself so as to enjoy the fruits of the various religious disciplinary measures, so as not to suffer the karma of rebirth on this earth." The course of the Bodhisattva is, however, otherwise destined; he wants to remain with us, to do something for us. Disciplining himself in the Prajñā, he accepts every spiritual advantage accruing from the life of the Śrāvaka, but rejects the idea of forever abiding with its fruits. He knows that the Prajñā

is the mother of all the Buddhas and Bodhisattvas, and that what constitutes the reason of Buddhahood is Sarvajñatā, and further that Sarvajñatā is Prajñā and Prajñā is Sarvajñatā because each is born of the other.[65] Knowing this, he devotes himself to the study of the Prajñā. But he never thinks of himself as studying and disciplining himself in the Prajñā, nor does he think that his study and discipline will bring him to the realization of the Prajñā. His Prajñā-life consists in neither seeing, nor hearing, nor thinking of, nor being conscious of, the Prajñā; for this is truly practicing it, studying it, and disciplining himself in it.

Why? Because when you think, "This is my mind," "I am conscious of this," "I take hold of the mind," etc., the Prajñā is no more there, for the Prajñā is no-mind *(acitta.)*[66]

(d) Realities versus Māyā. Superficially, the Prajñāpāramitā seems to deny realities, declaring them to be Māyā-like existences; and Śūnya and Māyā are taken as synonymous. In the understanding of the sūtra this is perhaps one of the most difficult points, as has been repeatedly pointed out.

According to the Sūtra,[67] all things are Māyā, the five Skandhas are Māyā, since all things have no hindrances, i.e. no self-substance. Not only all things are Māyā, but the Buddha-dharmas are Māyā, Nirvāṇa is Māyā; even when there is something surpassing Nirvāṇa, it is Māyā; there is no distinction whatever between one thing and another *(sarvadharma)* including Nirvāṇa and Māyā. However this may be, Māyā is not to be understood in the sense of illusion or unreality as when we say that all is a dream. The Buddhist sense of Māyā is that the Prajñā is to be found neither in the five Skandhas nor away from it, that it is to be sought for "where Subhūti moves about." As long as the world is statically conceived, it has no reality behind it, it is Māyā; the world must be grasped as it "moves about," as it becomes, as it passes from one state of being to another. When this movement is arrested, there is a corpse. When movement is thought of as something distinct by itself

65 See Kumārajīva, 60b, 63b, 64b, 78b, etc.
66 *Ibid.*, 46b.
67 *Ibid.*, 47, 49a, and elsewhere.

and apart from the things in which it is conceived as manifested, it loses all its significance. To understand this, *yathābhūtam*, is Prajñā.

Most people are frightened when they are told that the world is illusion, and imagine that if it is so their life is of no value and they can do anything they like and are not responsible for their deeds. This is one of the greatest misinterpretations of the Māyā theory. When the Mahāyānists make this announcement, they do not mean to ignore certain laws regulating the Māyā. Even when all is Māyā there are laws in it, and nothing in it can escape them; all must conform to them. The Māyā does not release anybody in it from being controlled by them. Only those who have found a realm of reality in the Māyā, and yet are not conditioned by it, can be masters of it and its laws. That all is Māyā can be declared by such seers of the truth and by no others.

The Mahāyānists are, therefore, those who, in conformity with the truth of Śūnyatā, abide in the Prajñā, refusing to find their foothold in Rūpam, Vedanā, Saṁjñā, Saṁskāra, and Vijñāna, neither in a world of Saṁskritas nor in a world of Asaṁskritas. This abode is called an abode in which there is no abode. For this reason, abiding in the Prajñā must mean not abiding in it; to abide in the Prajñāpāramitā in any other sense means to have a fixed point of attachment, and this is to be avoided if one wishes to be the free master of oneself. When a point is fixed anywhere, even in the Prajñā, this has a binding effect on us, and we cease to be independent intellectually, morally, and spiritually. The *Prajñāpāramitā* thus teaches us to wipe off every possible point of fixture or reference in our consciousness. When a world of no references is obtained, this is a no-abode, or abiding in Śūnyatā. The Buddha or the Bodhisattva gives out his teaching from this abode of no references; therefore, in them there is nobody teaching, nothing taught, and no audience listening. This is the meaning of the Māyā.[68]

(e) Prajñā versus Discrimination. As soon as a thought that discriminates arises *(saṁjñāsyate)* we leave the Prajñā behind, we separate ourselves from the Prajñā.[69] Discrimination *(vikalpa)*

[69] *Aṣṭa*, pp. 189–190.
[69] *Aṣṭa*, pp. 189–190.

or the awakening of consciousness is the destroyer of the Prajñā, it puts a stop to the triumphant course of the latter. Discrimination is no doubt born of the Prajñā, for without it Saṁjñā itself is impossible. The only trouble with it is that it asserts itself at the expense of Prajñā. It takes no notice of Prajñā, in spite of the fact that its function prevails because of Prajñā. This one-sidedness is so characteristic of Saṁjñā that the latter always stands contrasted to Prajñā, and causes attachment *(saṁga)* to exercise its baneful influence over the entire field of consciousness. Discrimination itself is harmless, but when it it coupled with attachment—and this coupling takes place inevitably in all consciousness—it does a great deal of harm. So says the sūtra, "Because of name *(nāma)* there is attachment; because of form *(nimitta)* there is attachment." Naming is discrimination, so is recognizing form, and from this naming and recognizing there arises attachment. Intellection and conation always go hand in hand.

"When you declare Rūpam to be empty, this is attachment *(saṁga)*. When you declare Vedanā, Saṁjñā, Saṁskāra, and Vijñāna to be empty, this is attachment. When you declare dharmas of the past, present, and future as belonging to the past, present, and future, this is attachment. When you recognize yourself to be a Bodhisattva in whom the desire for enlightenment has for the first time been awakened and who thereby has succeeded in accumulating so much merit, this is attachment. When you recognize yourself to be a Bodhisattva of long standing in whom much more merit has already been stored up, this is attachment."[70]

Therefore, to practice the Prajñā means not to practice according to Rūpam, Vedanā, Saṁjñā, Saṁskāra, and Vijñāna, but to practice it as if practicing nothing. Practicing is doing something, and yet to be doing nothing—this is the Upāya born of Prajñā, this is the way the Mahāyānists describe the Bodhisattva's life as *sasaṁgata cāsaṁgata,* i.e., "attached and not attached." When this state of consciousness in which neither discrimination nor attachment obtains, the depths of Prajñāpāramitā are said to have been fully sounded.

For this reason it is inevitable that Prajñā has come to be

[70] *Ibid.,* p. 190; *Fo-mu,* 25b.

defined in self-contradicting terms, and finally declared to be beyond the sphere of relative knowledge. The following are some of the terms we encounter everywhere in the *Prajñāpāramitā,* all of which tend to show that there is a deep cleavage between the intellect and the Prajñā experience: (1) Incomprehensible *(acintyā);* (2) Difficult to understand *(duranubodhā);* (3) Isolated [from all knowledge] *(viviktā);* (4) Not at all intelligible *(na kaścid abhisambudhyate);* (5) Not to be known by the intellect, not accessible to the intellect *(na cittena jñātavyā, na cittagamanīyā);* (6) Not a thing made *(akṛtā),* because no maker is obtainable *(kārakānupalabdhitaḥ);* (7) What is regarded as the original nature *(prakṛti)* of all things, that is a no-nature *(aprakṛti),* and what is *aprakṛti* that is *prakṛti;* (8) All things are characterized with oneness *(ekalakṣaṇa),* which has the nature of no-character *(alakṣaṇa).*

A quotation from a chapter in the *Mahāprajñāpāramitā*[71] will conclude this part of the essay:

"Sāriputra asked Subhūti: When the Bodhisattva-Mahāsattvas practice the Prajñā, does this mean that they practice something which is firmly fixed *(sāra)* or something which is not firmly fixed?

"Subhūti said: They practice something which is not firmly fixed, and not something which is firmly fixed. Why? Because in the Prajñāpāramitā as well as in Sarvadharma (all things) there is nothing firmly fixed. Why? Because when the Bodhisattva-Mahāsattvas practice the deep Prajñāpāramitā, they do not perceive in it as well as in Sarvadharma even that which is not firmly fixed, much less anything that is firmly fixed and attainable.

"At that time there was a present a numberless crowd of the heavenly beings from the world of Kāma and from the world of Rūpa, and they thought: Those beings belonging to the Bodhisattva vehicle cherish the desire for supreme enlightenment, practice the Prajñāpāramitā whose deep signification is beyond measure. Yet they do not in themselves realize the reality limit *(bhūtakoṭi),* thereby keeping themselves away from the state of the Śrāvaka and the Pratyekabuddha. For this reason, those

71 Hsüan-chuang, Fas. 558, 61a.

Bodhisattvas are wonderful beings, they set for themselves a task most difficult to accomplish. Deep reverence is to be paid to them. Why? Because although they practice the truth of all things, they do not in themselves realize the reality limit.

"Knowing what thought was being cherished by those heavenly beings, Subhūti then said: That those beings of the Bodhisattva vehicle do not in themselves realize the reality limit so as not to fall into the state of the Śrāvaka and the Pratyekabuddha is not anything so wonderful and difficult to accomplish.

"What is most wonderful and difficult to accomplish with the Bodhisattvas is this: even though they fully know that all things and all sentient beings, in their ultimate nature, are not to be regarded as being and attainable, they raise the desire for supreme enlightenment for the sake of all beings, innumerable and immeasurable; and, putting on the armor of strenuousness *(vīrya),* they bend all their efforts toward the salvation of all beings so that the latter will all be led finally to Nirvāṇa.

"This is indeed like attempting to put vacuity of space under discipline. Why? Because vacuity of space is by nature transcendental *(vivikta),* empty *(śūnya),* and not firmly fixed *(asāra),* and to be regarded as not being *(na saṁvidyate);* and so are all sentient beings transcendental, empty, not firmly fixed, and to be regarded as not being. And yet the Bodhisattvas attempt to convert all beings and lead them to final Nirvāṇa.

"They put on the armor of great vows *(mahāpraṇidhāna)* in order to benefit all beings, to discipline all beings. And yet they are fully aware of the truth that all beings as well as their great vows are in their ultimate nature transcendental, empty, not firmly fixed, and to be regarded as not being. With this knowledge, they are not at all frightened, or depressed, or mortified. They thus practice the deep Prajñāpāramitā. . . ."

III

Recapitulation

We are now in a position to summarize what has been stated as constituting the principal teachings of the *Prajñāpāramitā:*

1. The object of the discourse is to exhort and extol the practice of the Prajñā.

2. The Prajñā is one of the six Pāramitās. Being the mother body from which all the Buddhas and the Bodhisattvas issue, it is the vivifying spirit of all the other Pāramitās. Without it the latter remain inactive, are not at all productive of meritorious works.

3. The Prajñā leads us to the attainment of all-knowledge or Sarvajñatā, which makes up the reason of Buddhahood. Sarvajñatā is used synonymously with Prajñā. For it is from the Prajñā that Buddhas of the past, present, and future are born, and it is from Sarvajñatā that the Prajñā is born.

4. By means of the Prajñā the Bodhisattva sees into the nature of all things which is empty *(śūnya)*.

5. Emptiness does not mean the state of mere nothingness. It has a positive meaning, or rather it is a positive term designating the suchness of things *(tathatā)*. In a sense Tathatā and Śūnyatā are interchangeable notions.

6. Bhūtakoṭi is one of the technical terms used in all the Mahāyāna texts. It is here translated "reality limit," *bhūṭa* = reality, and *koṭi* = limit or end. As it is often used synonymously with Śūnyatā, it means the ultimate end of all realities. If Śūnyatā is identified with the Absolute, Bhūtakoṭi is also another term for the Absolute. It has a cold intellectual ring. Śrāvakas and Pratyekabuddhas are supposed, according to the Mahāyānists, to be finally so absorbed into it as to find their eyes wholly closed to the sufferings of their fellow sentient beings. They realize Bhūtakoṭi. But the Bodhisattva refuses to identify himself with the Absolute, for the identification puts a stop to the pulsations of his heart which feels for a world of particulars and iniquities. In other words, with the eye of absolute purity he perceives the Tathatā (suchness) of all things, which is Śūnyatā, but keeps his other eye open, seeing into multiplicities, i.e. the world of ignorance and suffering. Technically, this is known as "not realizing Bhūtakoṭi (reality limit) within oneself."[72]

7. Why and how can the Bodhisattva achieve this wonder—

72 *Aṣṭa*, p. 373. *Na bhūtakoṭiṃ sākṣātkaroti.*

to be in it and yet not to be in it? This contradiction is inherent in the Prajñā, for the Prajñā is not only an intellectual seeing into the emptiness of things but an emotional plunging into realities as they appeal to the will. The Prajñā is thus found unifying in itself the seeing and the feeling. The feeling aspect is known as being "skillful in means" *(upāyakauśalya)*. The Prajñā harbors in it the Upāya that works out a complete scheme of salvation for all sentient beings. This logic of contradiction is what may be called the dialectics of Prajñā.

8. This Prajñā dialectics prevails through the entire system of Mahāyāna thought. The Bodhisattva being a living spirit lives this dialectics in his so-called Prajñāpāramitācaryā. This is his life *(caryā)*, not mere behavior conventionally regulated according to the logic of the philosopher. The two contradicting principles, Prajñā and Karuṇā, are found harmoniously living in the person of a Bodhisattva. This is the main teaching of the *Prajñāpāramitā*.

9. Readers are apt to make more of the philosophy of Śūnyatā or Tathatā than of the practical moral aspect of it. This in fact has been the case with some Buddhist scholars. But we must never close our eyes to the meaning of Praṇidhāna, the Bodhisattva's vow to enlighten and benefit all his fellow beings. The Praṇidhāna is frequently lost sight of because of the too startling nature of the Śūnyatā. The Śūnyatā, however, is the chief qualification of the Hīnayāna, and in this latter is, according to all the Mahāyāna texts, placed in diametrical opposition to the Bodhisattva ideal.

10. When Sarvadharma or existence generally is regarded as empty and unattainable, all the means and vows which are cherished by the Bodhisattva seem to be really "like waging war against the sky or vacuity of space *(ākāśa)*." This idea is quite frightening or at least very depressing. Frightening because all our moral strivings seem to come to naught; depressing because, in spite of the vows and means, all the ignorance and suffering in the world are Māyā-like phenomena and do not substantially yield to the Bodhisattva's skillful treatment. This is the mystery of the religious life, that is, of the Prajñā life.

11. The Bodhisattva lives this mystery, which is regarded in the *Prajñāpāramitā* as *āścaryam*, as marvelous. His eye turns in

two opposite directions, inwardly and outwardly; so does his life proceed in two opposite directions, that is, in the direction of Śūnyatā and in the direction of Sarvasattva (all beings). He does not immerse himself in the ocean of eternal tranquillity; if he does, he is no more a Bodhisattva; he somehow keeps himself on the wavy surface of the ocean, allowing himself to suffer the fate of an aspen leaf on the turbulent waters. He does not mind subjecting himself to the tyranny of birth-and-death *(saṁsāra)*; for he knows that thereby he can be a good friend to all his fellow beings who are also like him tormented and harassed to the extreme.

12. This Prajñāpāramitācaryā of the Bodhisattva corresponds to the Laṅkāvatāra's Anābhogacaryā.[73] In both there is no thought of accumulating merit for oneself, every good performed by the Bodhisattva is turned over *(pariṇāmana)* to the general attainment by all beings of Sarvajñatā or Anuttara-samyak-saṁbodhi; but even in this he has no conscious feeling of elation, he cherishes no thought of having achieved something praise-worthy. This is also known as the life of no-discrimination *(avikalpa)*, or, we may say, the life of the lilies of the field.

13. To understand the *Prajñāpāramitā* we must entirely abandon what may be called the "this side" view of things, and go over to the "other side" *(pāram)*. The "this side" view is where we generally are, that is, where a world of particulars and discrimination extends. The shifting of this position to the "other side" of Śūnyatā, Tathatā, Viviktatā, and Sarvajñatā is a revolution in its deepest sense. It is also a revelation. The *Prajñāpāramitā* reviews all things from this new position. No wonder that its expressions and demonstrations are full of paradoxes or irrationalities. Nothing else could be expected.

14. When this revolution is not complete, our position involves many complexities from which it is difficult to extricate ourselves. Because when we are imagining a complete about-facing, our legs are still carrying the ancient dust; each time we try to walk, the path of absolute purity *(atyantaviśuddhi)* is found bespotted. By this it is meant that the reasoning and wording we resort to are ever remindful of the "this side" view.

[73] [See pp. 113–7.]

We are caught in the net we have ourselves set up. The *Prajñāpāramitā,* therefore, uses every possible cleverness to keep us away from this self-working snare. The *Aṣṭasāhasrikā,* "the sūtra of 8,000 verses," has thus developed into the *Śatasāhasrikā,* "the sūtra of 100,000 verses."

15. One of the reasons why all these sūtras are so repetitious, so full of reiterations which are tiring to us modern readers, is due to the fact that all the Mahāyāna sūtras, especially the *Prajñāpāramitā,* are not meant to appeal to our reasoning faculties, that is, to our intellectual understanding, but to a different kind of understanding, which we may call intuition. When the *Prajñāpāramitā* is recited in Sanskrit or Chinese or Tibetan, without trying to extract its logical meaning, but with a devotional turn of mind and with the determination to go through masses of repetitions, the Prajñā-eye grows gradually more and more penetrating. Finally, it will see, through all the contradictions, obscurities, abstractions, and mystifications, something extraordinarily transparent which reveals the "other side" together with "this side." This is the awakening of the Prajñā and the study of the deep Prajñāpāramitā. Herein lies the secret of the sūtra recitation.

16. The mystery of "not realizing Bhūtakoṭi although deeply immersed in it" may thus become comprehensible. As long as we are on "this side," it is impossible to carry two diametrically opposed and mutually exclusive ideas; if we have a thing, we cannot not have it; if we do a thing, we cannot not do it; having and not having, doing and not doing, being and not being—they exclude each other. Between these two sets of thoughts there is an impassable chasm. The Bodhisattva, however, has crossed this chasm and is setting himself on the "other side," which is the realm of Tathatā. He finds here that things formerly impossible to accomplish are readily accomplished as if they were nothing extraordinary. There is a spade in his hands and yet the tilling of the ground is done by him empty-handed. He is riding on the back of a horse, and yet there is no rider in the saddle and no horse under it. He passes over the bridge, and it is not the water that flows, but the bridge. The Śrāvaka still stays in spite of his realization on "this side," and therefore his realization is something quite distinct from his experience. The

very idea of Śūnyatā hinders his really living it. With the Bodhisattva Śūnyatā ceases to be Śūnyatā. He is just living his life, and is no more troubled with Śūnyatā and Aśūnyatā, with Nirvāṇa and Saṁsāra, with Sambodhi and Avidyā. This is what is termed in the *Prajñāpāramitā* "not realizing Bhūtakoṭi although already in the Samādhi of Śūnyatā." And it is one of the most characteristic attitudes of the Bodhisattva toward existence.

17. That, by virtue of Upāya which is inherent in the Prajñā, the Bodhisattva suffers the miseries of birth and death with the rest of his fellow beings is the description of his actual life. And it is because of this actual suffering on the part of the Bodhisattva that he is able to know what life means and what pain means. If not for this actual living, all his "skillful means" would be no more than mere abstraction and productive of no effects whatever. His vows, too, could not go beyond mere earnest wishing. In this connection reference may be made to the "original vows" of the Bodhisattva Dharmākara, which constitute the foundations of the Pure Land teaching.[74] The main idea expressed in those vows is that the Bodhisattva would not attain supreme enlightenment until all beings were also ready to cross over to the "other side." As he has disciplined himself for so many kalpas in all the Buddhist disciplines, he is fully qualified for the final attainment. But he cannot make up his mind to leave all his suffering fellow beings behind. So he refrains in the meantime from enjoying the fruit of his work. This is exactly the position of the *Prajñāpāramitā* Bodhisattva, in fact of all the Bodhisattvas, as distinguished from the Śrāvakas and the Pratyekabuddhas.

18. The differentiation of Bodhisattvahood means that Buddhism has abandoned its ascetic monasticism. A religion which was perilously near to the point of appealing to the elite only has now been rescued from this exclusive aristocratic spirit, which is not at all in correspondence with the spirit of the founder. Although the teaching of Parināmana is not quite definitely formulated in the *Prajñāpāramitā,* the idea already has its distinctive note here; for it is something inseparable from

[74] [See pp. 138 ff.]

the secularization and democratization of so-called primitive Buddhism. The Bodhisattva ideal is most intimately connected with the social development of the religious consciousness. The possibility of one's merit being turned over to others presupposes the fellowship of all beings. The social nature of the Mahāyāna is thus strongly reflected in the doctrine of Pariṇāmana.

19. The *Prajñāpāramitā* points out in what the detached life *(viviktavihāra)* of the Bodhisattva really consists. With the Śrāvakas, to be detached means to keep themselves away from the world, from city life, from living in society with other fellow beings; so they fly away from the crowd, live in the wilderness where they think they are safe from worldly entanglements.[75] But the detached life of those who practice the Prajñāpāramitā means to practice a great compassionate heart and loving-kindness toward his fellow beings by living with them, among them, and for them. Mere physical detachment does not mean anything. The Bodhisattva is detached when he sees the Śūnyatā of all things. As far as his living is concerned, democratization sums up its essence.

20. With this spirit strenuously and persuasively inculcated by devotees of the Prajñāpāramitā, Mahāyāna Buddhism has spread all over Asia. It is doubtful if Buddhism in its so-called primitive form would have been able to accomplish this. The six Pāramitās are really the Mahāyāna categories of life, and followers of the Prajñāpāramitā have singled out this Prajñā category in order to give the six Pāramitās a directing unifying principle. Charity, morality, patience, strenuousness, and tranquillization have now come to have a definite meaning attached to their execution.

21. Mystic trends have no doubt been encouraged by the propagation of the Prajñāpāramitā teaching, especially in China. What is essential in religion is life and not philosophy, and this life—which means in Mahāyāna the life of the Bodhisattva *(bodhisattvacaryā* or *prajñāpāramitācaryā)*—is a great mystery. And when a man faces this mystery one day in his life, he is filled with the mystic sense which goes utterly beyond intellection.

[75] *Ibid.*, p. 394 (*Fo-mu*, 55a).

II

The Story of Ever-Weeping

I WISH to give especial consideration to one or two classical instances of *Kṣānti* and *Vīrya,* both of which I take to be closely connected with the life of passivity and the philosophy of Śūnyatā. We may think that *Kṣānti* (patience) may have something to do with passivity; but how about *Vīrya* (energy), which is apparently a quality opposite to meek suffering? How could energy be thought of as issuing from religious passivity and emptiness?

This is a significant point in the life of the Mahāyāna Buddhist and in the teaching of the *Prajñāpāramitā Sūtra.* For according to the latter, which is lived by the Bodhisattva, an inexhaustible mine of energy obtains just because of the emptiness of things; if there were something determinable at the back of our existence, we could not put forward such an energy exhibited by the Bodhisattva Sadāprarudita. And, owing to this energy, patience or humility is again made possible. To be patient or to practice *Kṣānti* does not mean merely to submit oneself to sufferings of all kinds which are brought upon him from external sources, but it means to exert the virtue of energy *(vīrya)* in the life of emptiness, which is no less than what is known in all the Mahāyāna sūtras as the life of a Bodhisattva *(bodhisattvacaryā).* So we read in the *Diamond Sūtra:*

"O Subhūti, at the time when Kalirāja cut my flesh from every limb, I had no idea of a self, of a person, of a being, or of a living being; I had neither an idea nor no-idea. And why? Because, O Subhūti, if I at that time had had an idea of a self, of a person, or a being, or of a living being, I should also have had an idea of malevolence. And why? Because, O Subhūti, I remember the past five hundred births when I was a Rishi Kṣāntivādin. At that time also I had no idea of a self, of a person, of a being, or of a living being. . . ."[1]

We can thus see that without a philosophical comprehension of emptiness there will be no real patience or passivity in the life of the Mahāyāna Buddhist, which, supported by energy, never grows weary of seeking for the highest good. *Śūnyatā, Kṣānti,* and *Vīrya* are inseparable. The story of the Bodhisattva Sadāprarudita is in this respect quite illuminating. The story runs as follows.[2]

The Buddha said to Subhūti: "If thou shouldst really desire Prajñāpāramitā, thou shouldst behave like the Bodhisattva Sadāprarudita who is at present living the life of a Bodhisattva under the Tathāgata Bhīshma-garjita-nirghoshasvara. When he was intently bent upon realizing Prajñāpāramitā, there was a voice from the sky, saying, "If thou goest eastward thou wilt have the chance of listening to Prajñāpāramitā. While proceeding there abandon all thy thoughts about growing tired, about sleep, eating and drinking, day and night, cold and heat; do not trouble thyself at all about such affairs, have no thought whatever about them; be done away with flattery; cherish no self-conceit, no arrogance; free thyself from the idea of a being, from the desire of making a name, of amassing wealth; free thyself from the five hindrances, from envy; assert no dualistic notions as to subject and object, inner and outer, etc.; while walking along, do not turn either side, left or right; do not think of the points of the compass, front or behind, above or below; do not be disturbed with thy form *(rūpa),* sensation *(vedanā),* thought *(saṁjñā),* conformation *(sanskāra),* and consciousness *(vijñāna).* Why? Because he who is disturbed in these, walks into birth-and-death and not into the Buddhist life, and will never attain Prajñāpāramitā."

When Sadāprarudita heard this voice from the sky, he said: "I will behave indeed in the way I am instructed. For my wish is to become a light for all sentient beings by storing up all the truths of Buddhism." The mysterious voice gives the

1 S.B.E., XLIX, pp. 127–8. [Ch. 14e.]

2 *The Aṣṭasāhasrikā-prajñāpāramitā-sūtra.* Chapter on the Bodhisattva Sadāprarudita.

Bodhisattva further advice regarding the Mahāyānistic view of the world, absolute confidence to be placed in the teacher of Prajñāpāramitā, the temptations of the Evil One which would appear in various forms to a serious seeker of truth, etc.

Sadāprarudita now following the advice starts on his eastern pilgrimage, but before he is very far off, he thinks again: "Why did I not ask the voice how far east I have to go and of whom to hear about Prajñāpāramitā?" When he was seized with this thought, he felt so grieved over his stupidity that he did not know what to do but gave himself up to intense grief and self-reproach. But he was determined to stay on the spot, no matter how long, if he could only have another advice from the sky. He felt like a person who had lost his only child, there was no other thought in his mind than wishing to know about his further procedure, when lo! a form looking like the Tathāgata appeared before him and said:

"Well done, Sadāprarudita! All the Buddhas in the past have behaved like thee when they were intently bent upon realizing Prajñāpāramitā. Go eastward for a distance of five hundred yojanas, where thou wilt come to a city known as Gandhavatī which is constructed of seven precious stones and most magnificently decorated in every way. In this city there is a high wide terrace on which stands a splendidly built palace belonging to a Bodhisattva called Dharmodgata. A large assemblage of gods and men is gathered here, who are desirous of listening to the discourses given by this Bodhisattva on Prajñāpāramitā.

"Sadāprarudita, he is thy teacher and it is through him that thou comest to the understanding of Prajñāpāramitā. Go, therefore, on thy eastward journey until thou reachest the city. Conduct thyself as if thou wert pierced with a poisonous arrow, have no other thoughts than having it withdrawn from thy flesh as the earliest possible opportunity; have no rest until thou comest into the presence of thy teacher, the Bodhisattva Dharmodgata."

When Sadāprarudita was listening to this voice, he entered upon a state of ecstasy whereby he could see more or less clearly into the spiritual conditions of all the Buddhas. When he came out of the Samādhi, all the Buddhas who were before him suddenly disappeared. He was now troubled with the new

Sadāprarudita – willing to sell himself

question: "Whence are these Buddhas? Whither did they go?" He was grieved but at the same time more determined than ever to reach the palace of Dharmodgata.

He had, however, to think, of the offerings[3] he had to make to his teacher. He was poor and did not know how to get the necessary offerings. But he was not to be daunted; he decided to sell himself, thinking, "I have gone through many a rebirth, but ever being haunted by selfish impulses I have never performed deeds of goodness and purity, which would save me from the tortures of purgatories."

When he came to a large town, he went up to the market calling out loudly for someone who would buy his person. The Evil One heard the cry and lost no time in keeping the inhabitants of the town away from him, for Māra was afraid of Sadāprarudita's attaining his object and later leading people to the realization of Prajñāpāramitā. There was, however, one maiden of a wealthy householder, whom Māra could not overshadow.

When there was no response, Sadāprarudita was exceedingly mortified. "How heavy my sin is! Even when I am ready to sacrifice myself for the sake of supreme enlightenment, nobody is forthcoming to help me out!" Śakradevendra, god of the gods, however, hearing him, conceived the idea of testing the sincerity of this truth-seeker. The god assumed the form of a Brahman and appeared before Sadāprarudita. Finding out what was

[3] Offerings are made by Buddhists to their object of devotion for their own spiritual development, which results from giving up all that is regarded as belonging to themselves. Offerings are therefore not meant to please the recipient, for what would the Buddhas do with all those material treasures, musical instruments, or celestial maidens? The practice of self-sacrifice is for the benefit of the donor himself. When this is done in the real spirit of selflessness, the Buddha accepts the offerings. A story is told of a noted Zen master who resided at Engakuji, Kamakura, early in the Tokugawa era, which illustrates the nature of Buddhist donation. When his temple required renovation, a wealthy merchant who was one of his admirers offered him a large sum of money for the work. The master received it nonchalantly, put it aside, and uttered not a word of thanks. The merchant was dissatisfied and explained how deeply the donation cut into his capital and that it was quite a sacrifice on his part, which perhaps deserved just one word of acknowledgment from the master. The master quietly said, "Why shall I have to thank you for the merit you are accumulating for yourself?" Offerings are thus self-sacrifice, part of the giving-up of selfhood.

the reason of his excessive lamentation, the Brahman said: "I do not want your person, but as I am going to conduct a certain religious ritual, I wish to have a human heart, human blood, and human marrow. Would you give them to me?" Sadāprarudita was overjoyed because of the opportunity of gaining some offerings for his teacher and thus enabling him to listen to his discourses on Prajñāpāramitā. He agreed at once to give up everything demanded by the Brahman for any price, he did not care how much it was.

The Brahman took out a sharp knife, and incising it into Sadāprarudita's right arm, he got enough blood needed for his purpose. When he was about to rip up the poor victim's right thigh in order to get the marrow, the maiden of a wealthy householder saw it from her apartment. She at once came down and interfered, "O sir, what is all this for?" Sadāprarudita explained. The maiden was struck with his unselfish motives and promised him that she would see to whatever offerings he needed for his visit to Dharmodgata.

The Brahman, then resuming his proper form, said to Sadāprarudita: "Well done, indeed, son of a good family! I am now convinced of your devotion to the Dharma. Such was also the devotion of all the Buddhas of the past when they were still seeking after Prajñāpāramitā. My only wish with you was to see how earnest you were in this. How can I recompense you?"

Said Sadāprarudita, "Give me supreme enlightenment."

The god confessed his inability to give him this kind of gift, whereupon Sadāprarudita wished to have his mutilated body restored. This was accomplished at once and Śakradevendra disappeared. The maiden of a wealthy householder then took him into her house, where he was introduced to her parents. They were also greatly moved and even permitted their daughter to go along with him. Rich offerings of all sorts were prepared, and, accompanied by five hundred attendant maidens, they proceeded further eastward to the city of Gandhavatī.

The city was finally reached, and they saw the Bodhisattva Dharmodgata discoursing on the Dharma. As the party of truth-seekers approached him, they were again accosted by Śakradevendra, who performed some miraculous deeds over a treasure casket. The casket was explained to contain Prajñāpāramitā, but nobody was allowed to open it, as it was sealed seven times by Dharmodgata himself. Some offerings were made to it.

At the palace of Dharmodgata, Sadāprarudita, the maiden of a wealthy householder and five hundred maiden attendants all paid him due respect; flowers, incense of various kinds, necklaces, banners, canopies, robes, gold, silver, precious stones and other things were offered, accompanied by music. Sadāprarudita informed him of his mission and the experiences which he had had on his way to Gandhavatī; then he expressed his desire to know whence all those Buddhas came who appeared before him and whither they disappear later, as he wished to be all the time in their presence. To this answered Dharmodgata:

"From nowhere the Buddhas come and to nowhere they go. Why? Because all things are of suchness and immovable, and this suchness is no less than the Tathāgata himself. In the Tathāgata there is no going, no coming, no birth, no death; for ultimate reality knows neither coming nor going, and this reality is the Tathāgata himself. Emptiness knows neither coming nor going, and this emptiness is the Tathāgata himself. The same can be said of suchness *(yathāvatta)* of detachment *(virāgatā),* of cessation *(nirodha),* and of space; and all these qualities also belong to the Tathāgata. O son of a good family, apart from all these dharmas, there is no Tathāgata. As they are of suchness, so is the Tathāgata; they are all of one suchness which is neither two nor three; it is above numbers and nowhere attainable.

"Toward the end of the spring, when it is warm, there appears a mirage on the fields, which is taken for a sheet of water by the ignorant. Son of a good family, whence thinkest thou this vapory appearance comes? From the eastern sea? or from the western sea? or from the northern sea? or from the southern sea?"

Replied Sadāprarudita: "In the mirage there is no real water, and how can one talk of its whence and whither? The ignorant take it for water where there is really none whatever."

"And so," continued Dharmodgata, "it is with the Tathāgata. If a man gets attached to his body, form, and voice, and begins to think about his whence and whither, he is an ignoramus who, altogether destitute of intelligence, imagines the presence of real water in a mirage. Why? Because no Buddhas are to be regarded as having the material body, they are the Dharma-body, and the Dharma in its essence knows no whence, no whither.

"Son of a good family, it is again like those magic-created figures—elephants, horses, carriages, foot soldiers; they come from nowhere, go nowhere. It is again like those Tathāgatas who appear to a man in a dream, one, two, ten, twenty, fifty, one hundred, or even over one hundred in number; when he awakes from the dream he sees not even one of them.

"All things are like a dream, they have no substantiality. But as the ignorant realize it not, they are attached to forms, names, physical bodies *(rūpakāya),* words, and phrases; they imagine various Buddhas to be coming into existence and going out of it. They comprehend not the true nature of things nor that of the Buddhas. Such will transmigrate through the six paths of existence, separated from Prajñāpāramitā, separated from all the teachings of Buddhism. It is only those who understand the nature of ultimate reality *(dharmatā)* who would cherish no discrimination as regards the whence and whither of the Tathāgata. They live Prajñāpāramitā, they attain supreme enlightenment, they are true followers of the Buddha, they are worthy of being revered by others, they are indeed the fountain of blessings to the world.

"Son of a good family, it is like those treasures in the sea which have not come from the east, from the west, from the south, or from the north, or again from above or below. They grow in the sea owing to the good meritorious deeds of sentient beings. They are there not independent of the chain of causation, but when they disappear they do not go east or west or anywhere. When conditions are so combined they come into existence; when they are dissolved things disappear.

"Son of a good family, it is even so with the Tathāgata body which is not a fixed existence. It does not come from any definite direction, nor does it exist outside the chain of causation, for it is the product of previous karma *(pūrvakarmavipāka).*

"Son of a good family, it is like the musical sound of a lute which issues from the combination of its frame, skin, strings, and stick as it is played by the human hand. The sound comes not from any one of these parts when they are disconnected. Their concordant action is needed to produce the sound. In a similar manner the Tathāgata is the outcome of numberless meritorious deeds of the past, apart from which his whence and whither cannot be conceived. From any one single cause nothing takes place; there must be several of them which when combined produce a result. When they discontinue to act conjointly the Tathāgata goes out of existence. This being the case the wise do not talk of his appearance and disappearance. Indeed, with all things, not only with the Tathāgata, there is no birth, no death, no coming, no going. This is the way to reach supreme enlightenment and also to realize Prajñāpāramitā."

When this discourse was finished the whole universe trembled violently, including the abodes of the gods and those of the evil ones. All the plants at once burst out in full bloom, and Śakradevendra with his four guardian kings showered a rain of flowers over the Bodhisattva Dharmodgata. It was explained that these miraculous phenomena took place owing to the fact that the discourse given by the Bodhisattva Dharmodgata on the whence and whither of the Tathāgata opened the spiritual eyes leading to supreme enlightenment of ever so many beings.

This pleased the Bodhisattva Sadāprarudita immensely, for he was now more than ever confirmed in his belief in Prajñāpāramitā and his destiny of attaining Buddhahood. More offerings were given to Dharmodgata, who, first accepting them in order to complete the meritorious deeds of the Sadāprarudita, returned them to him. He then retired into his own palace not to come out of it again before seven years elapsed; for it was his habit to enter upon a profound Samādhi for that space of time. But Sadāprarudita was determined to wait, how long it did not matter, by the palace of Dharmodgata, since he wished to listen again to his discourses on Prajñāpāramitā and its skillful means (*upāyakauśalya*). He was so devoted to his teacher that all the while he never laid himself in bed, never tasted any delicious food, never gave himself to his own sensuous pleasure, but anxiously waited for the rise of Dharmodgata from his deep meditation.

Dharmodgata finally awoke from his meditation. Sadāprarudita prepared the ground for his teacher's discourse by shedding his own blood, for he was again frustrated by the Evil One in his attempt to obtain water. But Śakradevendra came to his assistance once more, and all the due decorations and offerings were supplied. Dharmodgata then gave a further discourse on the identity of all things, and, therefore, of Prajñāpāramitā, in which there is neither birth nor death, being free from all sorts of logical predicates.

While listening to this profound discourse on the transcendental nature of Prajñāpāramitā, Sadāprarudita realized 6,000,000 Samādhis and came into the presence of the Buddhas numbering even more than the sands of the River Gangā, who, surrounded by a large assemblage of great Bhikshus, were discoursing on Prajñāpāramitā. After this the wisdom and learning of the Bodhisattva Sadāprarudita was beyond the conceivability of an ordinary mortal; it was like a boundless expanse of ocean, and wherever he went he was never separated from the Buddhas.

III

On Emptiness

EMPTINESS *(śūnyatā)* is the gospel of the *Prajñāpāramitā-sūtra* and also the fountainhead of all the Mahāyāna philosophies and practical disciplines. It is indeed owing to this Emptiness as the ground of existence that this universe is at all possible with its logic, ethics, philosophy, and religion. Emptiness does not mean relativity as it is sometimes interpreted by Buddhist scholars, it goes beyond that, it is what makes relativity possible. Emptiness is an intuitive truth whereby we can describe existence as related and multifarious. And the Buddhist life of passivity grows out of this intuition which is called Prajñāpāramitā in the *Prajñāpāramita-sūtra* and Pratyātmāryajñāna in the *Laṅkāvatāra-sūtra.* The intuition is enlightenment as the culmination of Buddhist discipline and as the beginning of the life of a Bodhisattva. Therefore, we read in the *Vimalakīrtinirdeśa-sūtra* that all things are established in "non-abiding," which is Emptiness, *apratishṭhiti* = *śūnyatā,* and in the *Vajracchedikā-sūtra* that *na kvacit pratishṭhitaṃ cittam utpādayitavyam,* "thoughts should be awakened without abiding anywhere."

When a thing is established *(pratishṭhita),* there is something fixed, definitely settled, and this determination is the beginning at once of order and confusion. If God is the ultimate ground of all things, he must be Emptiness itself.[1] When he is at all

[1] To quote from the *Theologia Germanica* (p. 184): "For God is One and must be One, and God is All and must be all. And now what is and is not One, is not God; and what is, and is not All and above All, is also not God, for God is One and above One, and All and above All. . . . And a man cannot find all satisfaction in God, unless all things are

determined in either way as good or bad, straight or crooked, pure or impure, he submits himself to the principle of relativity; that is, he ceases to be God, but a god who is like ourselves mortal and suffers. "To be established nowhere" thus means "to be empty," "to be unattached," "to be perfectly passive," "to be altogether given up to other-power," etc.

This Buddhist or Zen life of Emptiness may be illustrated in two ways, each of which has its own signification as it depicts a particular aspect of the life.

1. When Subhūti was sitting quietly in a cave, the gods praised him by showering celestial flowers. Said Subhūti, "Who are you that shower flowers from the sky?"

"We are the gods whose chief is Śakradevendra."."

"What are you praising?"

"We praise your discourse on Prajñāpāramitā."

"I have never uttered a word in the discourse of Prajñāpāramitā, and there is nothing for you to praise."

But the gods asserted, "You have not discoursed an anything, and we have not listened to anything; nothing discoursed, nothing heard indeed, and this is true Prajñāpāramitā" So saying they shook the earth again and showered more flowers.

To this Hsüeh-tou attaches his poem:

One to him, and One is All, and something and nothing are alike. But where it should be thus, there would be true satisfaction, and not else." This is fine, indeed, but why stop short with God? If God is "One and above One, All and above All," is this not Emptiness? God himself must be lodged in it. When we stop at God and refuse to go further, God himself loses his abode, he cannot stay even where he is placed. He is either to go with All or altogether part company with All, he cannot be "All and above All" as the theologians would like to have him, for he thus murders him. To save God from this perplexity he must be placed in Emptiness where he can be "All and above All." If he is placed anywhere else, he is no more himself, and the "true satisfaction" so fervently sought after by the Christians will no longer be obtainable. Inasmuch as Buddhist scholars fail to penetrate into the true signification of Śūnyatā and are contented with interpreting it as relativity or mere nothingness, they can never expect to understand the Mahāyāna. Again, it is only possible in Emptiness to see "something and nothing alike." "Something" here is Buddhist *asti* and "nothing" *nāsti*, and true Prajñā obtains only when the dualism of being and non-being is transcended. There is no doubt that in these respects Buddhist philosophy and experience go deeper.

The rain is over, the clouds are frozen, and day is about to break;
A few mountains, picture-like, make their appearance; how blue,
how imposing!
Subhūti, knowing nothing, in the rock cave quietly sits;
Lo, the heavenly flowers are pouring like rain with the earth
shaking!

This poem graphically depicts the inner life of Emptiness, from which one can see readily that Emptiness is not relativity, nor nothingness. In spite of, rather because of, Subhūti's "knowing nothing," there is a shower of celestial flowers, there tower the mountains huge and rugged, and they are all like a painting beautiful to look at and enjoyable to all who understand.

2. While Vimalakīrti was discoursing with Mañjuśrī and others, there was a heavenly maiden in the room who was intently listening to all that was going on among them. She now assumed her original form as a goddess and showered heavenly flowers over all the saintly figures assembled there. The flowers that fell on the Bodhisattvas did not stick to them, but those on the Srāvakas adhered and could not be shaken off though they tried to do so. The heavenly maiden asked Śāriputra, one of the foremost Śrāvakas in the group and well known for his dialectic ability:

"Why do you want to brush off the flowers?"

"They are not in accordance with the Dharma, hence my brushing," replied Śāriputra.

"O Śāriputra," said the maiden, "think not that the flowers are not in accordance with the Dharma. Why? Because they do not discriminate and it is yourself that does the discriminating. Those who lead the ascetic life after the teaching of the Buddha commit an unlawful deed by giving themselves up to discrimination. Such must abandon discrimination whereby their life will be in accord with the Dharma.

"Look at those Bodhisattvas, no flowers touch them, for they are above all thoughts of discrimination. It is a timid person that affords a chance for an evil spirit to take hold of him. So with the Śrāvakas, as they dread the cycle of birth and death they fall a prey to the senses. Those who have gone beyond fears and worries are not bound by the five desires. The flowers stick where there is yet no loosening of the knots, but they fall away when the loosening is complete." (That is to say, when Emptiness is realized by us, nothing can take hold of us, neither the flower nor dirt has a point to which it can attach itself.)

The life of Emptiness, thus we can see, is that of non-discrimination, where the sun is allowed to rise on the evil and on the good, and rain is sent on the just and on the unjust. Discrimination is meant for a world of particulars where our relative individual lives are passed, but when we wish to abide beyond it, where real peace obtains, we have to shake off all the dust of relativity and discrimination, which has been clinging to us and tormented us so long. Emptiness ought not to frighten us, as is repeatedly given warning in the *Prajñā-pāramitā-sūtra*.

> When all is done and said,
> In the end thus shall you find:
> He most of all doth bathe in bliss
> That hath a quiet mind.[2]

Where to find this quiet mind is the great religious problem, and the most decided Mahāyāna Buddhist answer is "In Emptiness."

[2] Lord Vaux Thomas, 1510–1566.

IV

The Effortless Life

WHEN their religious experience is matured, i.e. when it accompanies moral perfection, Buddhists will finally acquire what is technically known as *anābhogacaryā*,[1] and theirs will also be its wonderful achievements as most elaborately detailed in the *Daśabhūmika Sūtra* where they are said to take place in the life of a Bodhisattva, the ideal being of Mahāyāna Buddhism. We can say that the effortless life is the perfection of passivism.

According to the *Daśabhūmika Sūtra* the effortless life is attained when a Bodhisattva passes from the seventh to the eighth stage of spiritual life by realizing what is known as the "acceptance of all things as unborn" *(anutpattikadharma-kṣānti)*.[2] To quote the Sūtra:[3]

"The Bodhisattva Vajragarbha said, O son of the Buddha, when the Bodhisattva, while at the seventh stage, has thoroughly finished examining what is meant by cleansing the paths with transcendental wisdom and skillful means *(prajñopāya)*, has accumulated all the preparatory material *(sambhāra)*, has well-equipped himself with the vows, and is sustained by the power

[1] For the explanation of this important idea, see my *Zen Essays*, I, pp. 78 *fn.*, 93; *Studies in the Laṅkāvatāra Sūtra*, pp. 43, 378; *The Laṅkāvatāra-Sūtra*, p. 78; etc.

[2] This is one of the Mahāyāna terms quite frequently misinterpreted by Buddhist scholars of the West. The point is that they fail to grasp the central conception of the Mahāyāna according to which all things (*sarvadharma*) are unborn (*anutpanna*), unattainable (*anupalabdha*), and therefore empty *(śūnya)*.

[3] Edited by Rahder [J.-B. Istas Louvain, 1926], pp. 63 *et seq.* [Ed. R. Kondō, The Daijyō Bukkyō Kenyō-kai, Tokyo, 1936 (with the *gāthās*), pp. 134 *et seq.*]

of the Tathāgatas, procuring in himself the power produced from the stock of merit, attentively thinking of and in conformity with the powers, convictions, and unique characteristics of the Tathāgatas, thoroughly purified, sincere in heart, and thoughtful, elevated in virtue, knowledge and power, great in pity and compassion which leaves no sentient beings unnoticed, and in pursuit of the path of wisdom, that is beyond measurement; and, further, when he enters, truly as it is, upon the knowledge that all things are, in their nature, from the first, unborn *(anutpanna)*, unproduced *(ajāta)*, devoid of individualizing marks *(alakshaṇa)*, have never been combined *(asambhūta)*, are never dissolved *(avināśita)*, nor extinguished *(anishṭhita)*, nor changing *(apravṛitti)*, nor ceasing *(anabhinivṛitti)*, and are lacking in self-substance *(abhāvasvabhāva)*; when he enters upon the knowledge that all things remain the same in the beginning, in the middle, and in the end, are of suchness, non-discriminative, and entering into the knowledge of the all-knowing one; [and finally] when he thus enters upon the knowledge of all things as they really are; he is then completely emancipated from such individualizing ideas as are created by the mind *(citta)* and its agent *(manovijñāna)*; he is then as detached as the sky, and descends upon all objects as if upon an empty space; he is then said to have attained to the acceptance of all things as unborn *(anutpattika-dharmakṣānti)*.

"O son of the Buddha, as soon as a Bodhisattva attains this acceptance, he enters upon the eighth stage called immovable *(acalā)*. This is the inner abode of Bodhisattvahood, which is difficult to comprehend, which goes beyond discrimination, separated from all forms, all ideas, and all attachments; which transcends calculation and limitation, as it lies outside [the knowledge of] the Śrāvakas and Pratyekabuddhas and above all disturbances and ever in possession of tranquillity.

"As a Bhikshu, furnished with supernatural faculties and freedom of mind and gradually entering into the Samādhi of Cessation, has all his mental disturbances quieted and is free from discrimination, so the Bodhisattva now abides in the stage of immovability, that is, detached from all works of effort *(ābhoga)*; he has attained effortlessness, has put an end to strivings mental, verbal, and physical, and is beyond discrimination as he has put away all forms of vexation; he is now established in the Dharma itself which he enjoys as the fruit of his past work.

"It is like a man who, in a dream finding himself in a great river, attempts to go to the other side; he musters all his energy and strives hard with every possible means. And because of this effort and contrivance, he wakes from the dream, and being thus awakened all his strivings are set at rest. In like manner the Bodhisattva sees all beings drowning themselves in the four streams, and in his attempt to save them exerts himself vigorously, unflinchingly; and because of his vigorous and unflinching exertion he attains the stage of immovability. Once in this stage, all his strivings are dropped, he is relieved of all activity that issues from the notion of duality or from an attachment to appearance.

"O son of the Buddha, as when one is born in the Brahman world, no tormenting passions present themselves in his mind; so when the Bodhisattva comes to abide in the stage of immovability, his mind is entirely relieved of all effortful activities which grow out of a contriving consciousness. In the mind of this Bodhisattva there is indeed no conscious discrimination of a Bodhisattva, or a Buddha, or enlightenment, or Nirvāṇa; how much less the thought of things worldly.

"O son of the Buddha, on account of his original vows the Bodhisattva sees all the Buddhas, the Blessed ones personally presenting themselves before him in order to confer upon him the wisdom of Tathāgatahood whereby he is enabled to get into the stream of the Dharma. They would then declare: 'Well done, well done, O son of a good family, this is the Kṣānti (acceptance) of the first order which is in accordance with the teaching of the Buddhas. But, O son of a good family, thou hast not yet acquired the ten powers, the fourfold fearlessness, and the eighteen special qualities possessed by all the Buddhas. Thou shouldst yet work for the acquirement of these qualities, and never let go thy hold of this Kṣānti.

" 'O son of a good family, though thou art established in serenity and emancipation, there are ignorant beings who have not yet attained serenity, but are being harassed by evil passions and aggrieved by varieties of speculation. On such ones thou shouldst show thy compassion. O son of a good family, mindful of thy original vows, thou shouldst benefit all beings and have them all turn towards inconceivable wisdom.

" 'O son of a good family, the ultimate essence of all things is eternally such as it is, whether or not Tathāgatas have come to appear; they are called Tathāgatas not because of their realization of this ultimate essence of things; for all the Śrāvakas and Pratyekabuddhas, too, have indeed realized this essence of non-discrimination. Again, O son of a good family, thou shouldst look up to our body, knowledge, Buddhaland, halo of illumination, skillful means, and voice of purity, each of which is beyond measurement; and with these mayest thou too be completely equipped.

" 'Again, O son of a good family, thou has now one light, it is the light that sees into the real nature of all things as unborn and beyond discrimination. But the light of truth possessed by the Tathāgatas is as regards its infinite mobility, activity, and manifestation, beyond all measurement, calculation, comparison, and proportion. Thou shouldst raise thy intention towards it in order to realize it.

" 'O son of a good family, observing how boundlessly the lands extend, how numberless beings are, and how infinitely divided things are, thou shouldst know them all truthfully as they are.'

"In this manner, O son of the Buddha, all Buddhas bestow upon the Bodhisattva who has come up to this stage of immovability infinitude of knowledge and make him turn toward knowledge of differentiation and work issuing therefrom, both of which are beyond measurement.

"O son of the Buddha, if the Buddhas did not awake in this Bodhisattva a desire for the knowledge of the all-knowing one, he would have passed into Parinirvāṇa abandoning all the work that will benefit beings. As he was, however, given by the Buddhas infinitude of knowledge and work issuing therefrom, his knowledge and work that is carried on even for a space of one moment surpasses all the achievements that have been accomplished since his first awakening of the desire for enlightenment till his attainment of the seventh stage; the latter is not comparable even to one-hundredth part of the former, nor indeed even to one immeasurably infinitesimal part of it; no comparison whatever is possible between the two For what reason?

"Because, O son of the Buddha, the Bodhisattva who has now gained this eighth stage after starting first with his one body in his course of spiritual discipline is now provided with infinite bodies, infinite voices, infinite knowledge, infinite birth, and infinite pure lands; and has also brought infinite beings into maturity, made offerings to infinite Buddhas, comprehended infinite teachings of the Buddhas; is furnished with infinite supernatural powers, attends infinite assemblages and sessions; and, by means of infinite bodies, speeches, thoughts, and deeds, acquires perfect understanding of everything concerning the life of the Bodhisattva, because of his attainment of immovability.

"O son of the Buddha, it is like a man going into the great ocean in a boat; before he gets into the high sea he labors hard, but as soon as his boat is pulled out to sea he can leave it to the wind, and no further efforts are required of him. When he is thus at sea, what he can accomplish in one day would easily surpass what is done even after one hundred years' exertion in the shallows.

"In like manner, O son of the Buddha, when the Bodhisattva, accumulating a great stock of meritorious deeds and riding in the Mahāyāna boat, gets into the ocean of the life of a Bodhisattva, he enters in one moment and with effortless knowledge into the realm of knowledge gained by the omniscient. As long as he was dependent upon his previous achievements which were characterized with purposefulness *(sābhogakarma)*, he could not expect to accomplish it even after the elapsing of innumerable kalpas. . . ."[4]

[4] Rather freely done, for a literal translation would be to most readers quite unintelligible. The text goes on still further into details of the life of the Bodhisattva at the eighth stage of immovability. But the above may be sufficient to show what the spirituality of the Bodhisattva is like when he realizes a life of effortless activities.

V

The Breadth of Mahayana Buddhism and the Teaching of the Laṅkāvatāra

BUDDHISM, especially Mahayana Buddhism so called, is like a vast ocean where all kinds of living beings are allowed to thrive in a most generous manner, almost verging on a chaos. Students who lightly step into it generally find it too complicated and overwhelming for their logical comprehension. But the fact is that Mahayana Buddhism is the outcome of long years of development of a religious system among a people furnished with a most fertile imagination. The student has to be patient. The best method of study may probably be found by taking up one principal Mahayana sutra at a time, and examining its contents historically, philosophically, and psychologically. The Chinese scholars encountered the same difficulties centuries ago, and as in those days there was no lower or higher criticism of the sacred texts, every tradition was respected on its face value. The scholars exhausted their ingenuity to make a logical, humanly plausible arrangement among the vast treasure of literature brought over from India and all claiming to have been delivered by the Buddha himself. This untenable position is now abandoned, and each sutra has come to be studied historically, critically, and analytically.

Each principal sutra may now be regarded as marking a certain stage or phase of development in the history of Mahayana Buddhism, which is indeed too huge and unwieldy to be handled as one solid piece of work completed within a few decades.

What, then, does the *Laṅkāvatāra* signify in the composite system of Mahayana Buddhism? What phase does it represent in the long history of Buddhism? What in short is the message of the *Laṅkāvatāra* as we have it now? What function does it or did it perform in the conservation of Buddhist thought and experience?

Each principal sutra has had its special work to accomplish in the unfoldment of the religious consciousness of the Buddhists. For instance, the *Saddharmapuṇḍarīka* marks the epoch in the history of Buddhism when Śākyamuni ceased to be conceived of as a historical personage subject to the fate of all transient beings; for he is no more a human Buddha but one who lives through eternity for the benefit of all creatures. All that he is recorded to have done in history is no more than one of his "skillful means" *(upāya)* to save mankind. So we read:

"I show the place of extinction, I reveal to all beings a device *(upāya)* to educate them, albeit I do not become extinct at the time, and in this very place [that is, Mount Gṛidhrakuta] I continue preaching the Dharma. Here I rule myself as well as all beings. But men of perverted minds in their delusion do not see me standing here. In the opinion that my body is completely extinct, they pay worship in many ways to the relics, but me they see not. They feel, however, a certain aspiration by which their minds become right. When such upright, mild, and gentle creatures leave off their bodies, then I assemble the crowd of disciples and show myself here on the Gṛidhrakuta. And I speak thus to them in this very place: I was not completely extinct at the time; it was but a device of mine, monks; repeatedly am I born in the world of the living. . . . I see how the creatures are afflicted, but I do not show them my proper being. Let them first have an aspiration to see me; then I will reveal to them the true Dharma."[1]

[1] S.B.E., Vol. XXI, pp. 307–8 [Ch. 15].

The *Suvarṇaprabhāsa,* at least in part, belongs to the same period when it says: "Every drop in the oceans may be counted up, but the age of Sākyamuni is altogether beyond calculation. Mount Sumeru may be pulverized and every particle is countable, but the age of Sākyamuni is altogether beyond calculation. However innumerable, every particle of dust composing the great earth may be counted up, but not the age of the Victorious One. However boundless space is, its ends may be reached, but the age of Sākyamuni is altogether beyond calculation. However long one may live through hundreds of kotis of eons, he cannot count up the age of the Buddha. There are two deeds whereby a man's life is prolonged: not to kill others and to give away much food. For this reason the age of the Great Man cannot be measured, it is like the measure of kalpas which are incalculable. Therefore, harbor not any shadow of doubt as to the age of the Victorious One which is indeed beyond the reach of measurement."[2]

The *Sukhāvatīvyūha* represents a stage in the history of Buddhist experience which ceased to be wholly satisfied with the intellectual presentation of the doctrine of enlightenment, when Buddhists began to be oppressed with the idea of sin and doubt hanging over them too heavily and acutely. Read the following in which the destiny of those Bodhisattvas is described who have not yet come to have an absolute faith in the wisdom of the Buddha but who try to save themselves by amassing their own stock of merit:

"And, O Ajita, there might be a dungeon belonging to an anointed Kshatriya king, inlaid entirely with gold and beryl, in which cushions, garlands, wreaths, and strings are fixed, having canopies of different colors and kinds, covered with silk cushions, scattered over with various flowers and blossoms, scented with excellent scents, adorned with arches, courts, windows, pinnacles, fireplaces, and terraces, covered with nets of bells of the seven kinds of gems, having four angles, four pillars, four doors, four stairs; and the son of that king having been thrown into the dungeon for some misdeed is there, bound with a chain made of the Jambunada gold. And suppose

[2] Nanjo and Idzumi ed., pp. 9–10. [Ed. J. Nobel, pp. 10–12, O. Harrassowitz, Leipzig, 1937.]

there is a couch prepared for him, covered with many woollen cloths, spread over with cotton and feather cushions, having Kalinga coverings, and carpets, together with coverlids, red on both sides, beautiful and charming. There might be brought to him much food and drink, of various kinds, pure and well prepared. What do you think, O Ajita, would the enjoyment be great for that prince?

"Ajita said: Yes, it would be great, O Bhagavat.

"The Bhagavat said: What do you think, O Ajita, would he even taste it there and notice it, or would he feel any satisfaction from it?

"He said: No, indeed, O Bhagavat; but, on the contrary, when he had been led away by the king and thrown into the dungeon, he would only wish for deliverance from there. He would seek for the nobles, princes, ministers, women, elders, householders, and lords of castles, who might deliver him from that dungeon. Moreover O Bhagavat, there is no pleasure for that prince in that dungeon, nor is he liberated, until the king shows him favor.

"The Bhagavat said: Thus, O Ajita, it is with those Bodhisattvas who, having fallen into doubt, amass a stock of merit, but doubt the knowledge of the Buddha. . . ."[3]

It is very interesting to contrast these passages from the *Sukhāvatīvyūha* with the thought pervading the *Prajñāpāramitā-sūtra*. For the *Prajñāpāramitā* dwelling on the conception of unreality or emptiness *(śūnyatā)* seeks deliverance from the dungeon of existence, or rather interprets the Buddhist realization purely from a metaphysical point of view. The doctrine of Śūnyatā[4] constituting the keynote of the *Prajñāpāramitā* is really the foundation of all the Mahayana schools of Buddhism

[3] S.B.E. XLIX, *The Larger Sukhāvatīvyūha*, pp. 63–64.

[4] The theory of Sūnyatā (emptiness or void) is one of the best-known theories propounded by the Mahayana, but it is one of the least-understood especially by those whose thought has never run along the line of Mahayana ontology. But, even among Buddhist scholars, there are some who do not so fully comprehend the doctrine as one may expect of them, seeing that they must have been imbued with the idea since the beginning of their study. The reason is that the doctrine itself is quite liable to be wrongly or inadequately interpreted, owing to its subtlety or depth, or to its extreme simplicity, as it is variously approached and taken hold of. See also *St.*, 381 where the doctrine of "Anutpāda" (no-birth) is treated.

including even the Yogācāra. What is known as primitive Buddhism denied the existence of an ego-substance *(ātman)*, but its conception of the external world was that of the naïve realist. The *Prajñāpāramitā* philosopher insists on the non-existence of a particular body as such, that is, as an objective reality whose identity is absolute. Every being or every object, as he sees it, is relative, impermanent, and not worth attachment. This *Prajñāpāramitā* idea of unreality, or emptiness as the literal sense of the term *śūnyatā* is, is the foundation of the Buddhist theory of nature.

Thus, in the *Prajñāpāramitā,* supreme enlightenment is identified with the attainment of Śūnyatā. In other words, the object of the Buddhist life is to find an unattached abode in this realization. This abode is called *apratishṭhita,* not-abiding. Hence the noted phrase in the *Diamond Sūtra,* X: *na kvacit pratishṭhitaṁ cittam utpādayitavyam.*[5] The Tathagata has no dwelling place in the sense that all his thoughts and doings have no exterior or ulterior objects in view to which he desires to adapt himself, and therefore that he is like the sun that shines on everybody just and unjust, or like the lily in the field that blooms in its best even when there is nobody around to admire its supra-Solomonic array. So we have again in the *Ashṭasāhasrikā,* Chapter II, p. 34: "A Bodhisattva-Mahāsattva should abide himself in the perfection of Prajñā by abiding in emptiness. . . . The Tathagata is so called because he is not abiding anywhere, his mind has no abode neither in things created nor in things un-created, and yet it is not away from them." This is the message of all the sutras belonging to the *Prajñāpāramitā* class.

As to the *Avataṁsaka-sūtra,* it is really the consummation of Buddhist thought, Buddhist sentiment, and Buddhist experience. To my mind, no religious literature in the world can ever approach the grandeur of conception, the depths of feeling, and the gigantic scale of composition as attained by this sutra. It is the eternal fountain of life from which no religious mind will turn back athirst or only partially satisfied. It is a great pity that this magnificent literature still remains concealed in a language not so universally accessible. Here not only deeply

5 "A Bodhisattva should have his thoughts awakened without abiding in anything whatever."

speculative minds find satisfaction, but humble spirits and heavily oppressed hearts, too, will have their burdens lightened. Abstract truths are so concretely, so symbolically represented here that one will finally come to a realization of the truth that even in a particle of dust the whole universe is seen reflected—not this visible universe only, but a vast system of universes, conceivable by the highest minds only.

Where does the *Laṅkāvatāra* stand then? It may be classed in a way with the *Avataṁsaka* inasmuch as it teaches the absolute idealism of the latter and is the disclosure of the inner mind of the Buddha, but it has a special message to give to the Buddhist world in a manner characteristic of the sutra. It is devoid of all symbolism, quite different in this respect from *Avataṁsaka*. It is, instead, straightforward in expression and notes down in a somewhat sketchy style almost all the ideas belonging to the different schools of Mahayana Buddhism. It is partly for this reason that the sutra requires a great deal of learning as well as an insight to understand all the details thoroughly. The principal thesis of the *Laṅkāvatāra*, however, may be regarded as summarized in the following passage:[6]

"Again, O Mahāmati, there may be other Śramanas and Brahmans who hold the following views: that all things have no self-substance *(niḥsvabhāva)*, they are like a cloud, like a circle traced out by a revolving firebrand, or like the aircastle of the Gandharvas; that they are unborn *(anutpāda)*, that they are like māyā, or mirage, or the moon in water, or a dream; that external objects are manifestations of the mind erroneously perceived due to false discrimination *(vikalpa)* since time immemorial, that by thus viewing the world one ceases to be conditioned by the false discrimination worked out in one's own mind, one does away with the terminology belonging to such false discrimination and with the signification of words such as predicating and predicated; that when one understands that the body, property, and abiding place[7] are the particularizations of the Ālaya-vijñāna (or *citta*, mind), one is freed from

[6] This is done mainly from the T'ang version, the Kōkyōshoin edition of the Buddhist Tripitaka, *huang*, VI, 87*b* f. Cf. the Sanskrit text (pp. 42 ff.). [Ed. B. Nanjo, Otani University Press, Kyoto, 1923.].

[7] *Deha-bhoga-pratishṭha* is found generally in combination. It means this bodily existence with its material possessions and its physical surroundings; in short it stands for the world generally.

[ideas such as] perceived and perceiving, attains to a state of no-image, or shadowlessness *(nirābhāsa)*.[8] O Mahāmati, such a Bodhisattva-Mahāsattva will before long realize the sameness of Saṁsāra and Nirvāṇa.

"O Mahāmati, by deeds of great love *(mahākaruṇā)*, skillful mean *(upāya)*, and effortlessness *(anābhogacaryā)*,[9] a Bodhisattva reviews all beings and knows that they are like māyā, they resemble shadows, they are not produced by causes; and further, knowing that the world exists not outside the mind, he leads a life of formlessness *(animitta)*. As he gradually goes up the higher stages *(bhūmi)*, he will realize a state of Samādhi where he comes to the understanding that the triple world is Mind itself *(cittamātra)*. The Samādhi he attains is called Māyā-like *(māyopama)*. He will further free himself from all images, perfect his knowledge, and realize that things are unborn, and entering upon the Samādhi called Vajrabimbopama, will obtain the Buddha body. He will, always abiding in the suchness of things, manifest himself in transformed bodies, he will be endowed with the ten Powers, the six Psychic Faculties, and the tenfold Self-mastery. O Mahāmati, adorned with Upāya (skillful means), he will visit all the Buddha lands; and disengaged from the philosophical doctrines as well as from the Citta, Manas, and Vijñāna, he will experience a revulsion *(parāvṛitti)* within himself and by degrees will attain the Tathāgata-body.

"Therefore, O Mahāmati, if a Bodhisattva wishes to attain the Tathāgata-body, he should keep himself away from the Skandhas, Dhātus, Āyatanas, Cittam, causation, works, discipline, birth, staying and passing, and cease from discriminating, philosophizing, and abide in the thought of the "Mind-only" *(cittamātra)*.

"When the triple world is surveyed [by the Bodhisattva], he

[8] This is a spiritual state of absolute purity in which one finds no traces of dualism. It is a complete identification of the self with the suchness or thusness (*tathatā*) of things, and there is no thought of birth, abiding, and disappearance, seeing that all things start from the evolution of one's own mind (*svacitta*).

[9] Or purposelessness, a state of perfect adjustment, when one is not at all conscious of doing anything special for any particular individual. The sun is said to be effortless or purposeless in its work when it shines on the just and on the unjust.

perceives that this existence is due to memory *(vāsanā)* that has been accumulated since the beginningless past but wrongly interpreted. He recognizes that Buddhahood is a state imageless, unborn, and to be inwardly experienced by oneself, when the mind becomes fully controlled and purposeless deeds are accomplished. Like the Cintamani (wish-gem), he will now manifest himself in a variety of forms according to the needs of sentient beings and lead them to the view that only Mind is, and then gradually compel them to ascend the stages. Therefore, O Mahāmati, let the Bodhisattva discipline himself well in the work of self-realization *(svasiddhānta).*"

Being full of technical terms, the reader may find the import of the passage here quoted difficult to understand, but as we go on, it will, I hope, grow fully intelligible. In the meantime, the following paraphrase will help the reader to get a general idea of it.

The highest stage of Buddhist experience is reached when a man comes to realize that things are devoid of a self-substance, or that they are not after all final, irreducible realities, for they never have been created, they are what they are from beginningless past; if we say that they have come into existence, or that they exist as we perceive them through the senses, this will imply that individualization is ultimate fact, which, however, is contrary to the truth inwardly perceived by an enlightened mind.

Individualization is due to discrimination *(vikalpa),* which is falsely interpreted and adhered to by a heart blinded by desires and passions, and from this fact there issue all kinds of human tragedies and comedies. What really exists is mind, which is above all discrimination, that is, above logic and analysis. When this Mind which is designated in the sutra as the Ālaya or Ālayavijñāna is discriminated by an erroneously self-created and self-reflecting agent called Manas this world of particulars develops in its misleading fullness and richness.

Discrimination is the result of memory *(vāsanā)* accumulated from the unknown past. *Vāsanā* literally means "perfuming," or "fumigation," that is, it is a kind of energy that is left behind when an act is accomplished and has the power to rekindle the old and seek out new impressions. Through this "perfuming," reflection takes place which is the same thing as discrimination, and we have a world of opposites and contraries with all its practical consequences. The triple world, so called, is therefore the shadow of a self-reflecting and self-creating mind. Hence the doctrines of "Mind-only" *(cittamātra)*.

Reality as it is, or Mind in itself, is also called the suchness *(tathatā)* or sameness *(samatā)* of things, as herein are unified all forms of antithesis which constitute our actual world of sense and logic. The Bodhisattva abides in this suchness which transcends all our reasonings and discriminations. And because he abides in this transcendental realm, his all-loving heart works without the taint of selfishness and one-sided attachment, using all contrivances *(upāya)* whereby to save his fellow beings from pain and suffering. These works of his are called purposeless for the reason that they are not actuated by any egotistic interests or desires or motives. They are called out from the abundance of his inner goodness which now shines forth free from all defilements of intellection as well as of conation.

The world is like māyā, or mirage; as his intellect is no longer snared in the meshes of dualistic logic, he intuitively perceives that the world of particularization is no more than the reflection of his own mind. His life is thus designated as formless or imageless and his deeds effortless and purposeless. Yet he never relaxes his efforts to benefit all sentient beings. He knows from his transcendental position that Samsāra and Nirvāṇa are the same *(samatā)*, and yet he knows not when to stop working for the realization of the highest ideals and also for universal salvation. His inner mind is then said to be abiding in the Samādhi known as Māyopama (mirage-like).

This seems to be the highest state of spiritual attainment realizable by a mind encased in a human body; but there is still a higher state to be attained by the Buddhist. There is a higher body called Buddhakāya which is obtained when a man enters upon Vajrabimbopama Samādhi. When this is obtained one is endowed with the ten Powers, the six Psychic Faculties, and the tenfold Self-mastery. He is then able to transform himself into various forms in order to benefit sentient beings in accordance with their desires and circumstances. He is also able to visit all the Buddhalands and to perform all Buddha deeds.

The main object of the Buddhist life is thus seen to consist in having a certain spiritual revulsion, whereby we are able to leap from the dualistic shore of this individualistic world to the other shore of Nirvana, where there are no egoistic impulses and desires in evidence any longer, though this means not at all the death of a loving heart itself. To effect this revulsion, spiritual discipline is needed which finally leads up to a certain exalted inner condition. Enlightenment, self-realization, or the opening of an inner eye is the name given to it. The *Laṅkāvatāra* calls it Pratyātmāryajñānagocara, or Svasiddhānta, and the main object of its teaching is to acquaint us with the fact of an inner perception which causes a spiritual revolution in our whole life.

Another thing that the student of the *Laṅkāvatāra* notices is that the Buddha here tells Mahāmati to attain to a state of inner realization *(pratyātmagocara)* and not of enlightenment *(saṁbodhi)*. These two are psychologically the same process; when one has Pratyātmajñāna, one is enlightened. But in the *Lankāvatāra* the ultimate goal of the Buddhist life is generally stated in terms of experience *(gocara)* and not intellectually as illumining.[10] I am inclined to think that the *Laṅkāvatāra* is unique in this respect explaining perhaps the reason why Bodhidharma, the father of Zen Buddhism in China, recommended it to his mystic followers.

When the *Laṅkāvatāra* refers to Gocara or Gatigocara, instead of to Bodhi or Saṁbodhi, we realize that the main object of the sutra centers on the acquirement and cultivation of a certain general subjective attitude toward the world and life, which is not merely philosophical or conceptual, but which comes from the experience of some definite turning in the activity

[10] This does not mean that the *Laṅkāvatāra* never refers to the attainment of the Bodhi, for the Bodhi is the cardinal idea in every school of Buddhism, and the sutra frequently speaks of it; for instance, see pp. 70, 73, 79, 85, 89, 112, 114, 148. We cannot help noticing, however, and emphasizing the fact that the *Laṅkāvatāra* makes more frequent references to that higher state of consciousness in which is revealed the inmost truth of things than to the attainment of supreme enlightenment.

of the mind. Saṁbodhi or enlightenment looks more toward the cognitive aspect of the revulsion *(parāvṛitti)* one experiences. This is all well as far as it goes, which is indeed the basis of all Buddhism, be it Hinayana or Mahayana. The *Laṅkāvatāra,* however, has come to see that the whole of the Buddhist life is not in merely seeing into the truth, but in living it, experiencing it, so that there will be no dualism in one's life of seeing and living: seeing must be living, and living seeing, with no hiatus between them, except in language. Hence the *Laṅkāvatāra's* reference so much to living or experience, Gocara or Gatigocara, that is, Pratyātmagocara.

VI

The Buddhism of Faith in India

1

OF ALL the developments Mahayana Buddhism has achieved in the Far East, the most remarkable one is the Shin teaching of the Pure Land school. It is remarkable chiefly for this reason, that, geographically, its birthplace is Japan, and, historically, it is the latest evolution of Pure Land Mahayana and therefore the highest point it has reached.

The Pure Land idea first grew in India, and the Sutras devoted to its exposition were compiled probably about three hundred years after Buddha. The school bearing its name started in China toward the end of the fifth century when the White Lotus Society was organized by Hui-yüan (334–416) and his friends in 403. The idea of a Buddha land *(buddha-kṣetra)* which is presided over by a Buddha is as old as Buddhism, but a school based upon the desire to be born in such a land in order to attain the final end of the Buddhist life did not fully materialize until Buddhism began to flourish in China as a practical religion. It took the Japanese genius of the thirteenth century to mature it further into the teaching of the Shin school. Some may wonder how the Mahayana could have expanded itself into the doctrine of pure faith which apparently stands in direct contrast to the Buddha's supposedly original teaching of self-reliance and enlightenment by means of Prajñā.[1] The Shin is thus not infrequently considered altogether unbuddhistic.

What is then the teaching of the Shin?

Essentially, it is a teaching growing from the Original Vow *(pūrva-praṇidhāna)* of Amida, the Buddha of Infinite Light and Eternal Life. Amida has a Pure Land created out of his boundless love for all beings, and wills that whoever should cherish absolute faith in his "vows"[2] which are the expression of his Will would be born in his Land of Purity and Bliss. In this Land inequalities of all kinds are wiped out and those who enter are allowed equally to enjoy Enlightenment. There are thus three essential factors constituting the Shin teaching: Amida, his Vow, and Faith on the part of his devotees.

Amida is not one who enjoys quietly in his Land of Purity an infinite light and eternal life; he holds all these qualities on the condition that they are to be shared by all beings. And this sharing by all beings of his light and life is made possible by their cherishing an unconditioned faith in Amida. This faith is awakened in all beings who hear the Name *(nāmadheya)* of Amida, and sentient beings are bound to hear it sooner or later as he has made his vows to the effect that his Name be heard throughout the ten quarters of the world.

Some may ask, "How is it that Amida's vows are so effective as to cause us to turn toward him for salvation or enlightenment?" The Shin follower will answer: Amida is Infinite Light, and, therefore, there is no corner of the human heart where its rays do not penetrate: he is Eternal Life, and, therefore, there is not a moment in our lives when he is not urging us to rise above ourselves. His vows reflect his Will—the Will as illumined by Infinite Light and imbued with Eternal Life; they cannot be otherwise than the most efficient cause to lift us above ourselves who are limited individuals in time and space.

Amida's vows are expressions of his love for all beings, for Amida is love incarnate. Love is eternal life and emits infinite

[1] Transcendental wisdom or intuitive knowledge—one of the specifically Buddhist terms requiring a somewhat lengthy explanation.

[2] The Chinese version adopted by the Jōdo followers counts forty-eight, for which see below.

light. Each ray of light carries his Name to the farthest end of the universe, and those who have ears are sure to hear it. They are indeed recipients of Amida's love whereby they are at once transferred into his Land of Purity and Bliss, for hearing is receiving and receiving is believing and believing is the condition Amida requires of his devotees.

In short, the above makes up the principal teaching of the Shin sect.

2

The evolution of the Pure Land idea marks an epoch in the history of Mahayana Buddhism. While the latter itself is a phenomenal fact in the history of general Buddhism, the rise of the Pure Land idea illustrates the persistent and irrepressible assertion of certain aspects of our religious consciousness—the aspects somewhat neglected in the so-called primitive teaching of the Buddha.

Mahayana Buddhism is a religion which developed around the life and personality of the Buddha, rather than a religion based upon the words of his mouth. The person is greater and more real than his words; in fact words gain validity because of a person behind them; essentially is this the case with moral teachings and truths. Mere logicality has no spiritual force which will compel us to follow it. Intellectual acquiescence occupies a corner of our surface consciousness, it does not penetrate into the seat of one's inner personality. Words or letters are needed to communicate events detached partly or wholly from personality, and therefore they are more or less impersonal, and to that extent ineffective to move the spirit itself. Religion is nonsensical unless it comes in direct contact with the spirit. This contact is only possible when a real personality stands before you or when his image or memory lives for ever vividly and inspiringly in you. For this reason the Mahayana was bound to rise soon after the passing of the Buddha, and became a form of Buddhism in which the personality of the Buddha occupied the center, although this does not mean that his words were neglected or altogether set aside. Indeed his teachings were interpreted in the light of his life and personality and followed as containing the seeds which will eventually come to maturity in Buddhahood.

There is no doubt that Buddha was a wonderful personality; that is, there must have been something in him which was superhuman, impressing his immediate disciples with a supernaturally overwhelming and entirely irresistible power. While still walking among them, Buddha wielded this power over them with every syllable he uttered; in fact his mere presence was enough to inspire them to rise above themselves not only in the spiritual sense but even in the physical because some of his followers believed that his miraculous power was capable of driving away an evil spirit which would cause pestilence.

It is perfectly in accord with human nature to believe that the great personality has divine power known among the Mahayanists as Adhiṣṭhāna. This power goes out of its owner and moves the inmost hearts of those who came into its presence. It is a kind of personal magnetism raised to the *n*th power, we may say. The Buddha attained Enlightenment, that is to say, Siddhartha Gautama of the Śākya family became the Enlightened One after so many kalpas (eons) of moral and spiritual training. Enlightenment means perfected personality—one who is perfect in Prajñā ("transcendental or intuitive knowledge") and Karuṇā ("love"). Inasmuch as this perfection is the result of the accumulation of all kinds of spiritual merit, it cannot be something exclusively enjoyed by an individual being, that is, something which does not go out of himself in some way. When one is perfected the rest of the world must also to a certain extent share in its perfection, because the world is not a mere aggregate of units individually separated, but an organism whose units are in a most intimate way knitted together. This is the reason why the Enlightenment of the Buddha does not stay closed up in himself, in his individual personality, but is bound to step out of its spatial-temporal shell into a world encompassing all beings. The appearance of a Buddha therefore corresponds to the awakening of faith in universal enlightenment. The Buddha is creative life itself, he creates himself in innumerable forms with all the means native to him. This is called his *adhiṣṭhāna,* as it were, emanating from his personality.

The idea of Adhiṣṭhāna is one of the Mahayana landmarks in the history of Indian Buddhism and it is at the same time the beginning of the "other-power" *(tariki* in Japanese) school as distinguished from the "self-power" *(jiriki)*[3] The principle of the "self-power" school is one of the characteristics of the so-called Hinayana or the earlier school of Buddhism in India. "Self-power" means "to be a lamp to yourself," it is the spirit of self-reliance, and aims at achieving one's own salvation or enlightenment by the practice of the Eightfold Noble Path or of the Six Virtues of Perfection. If this is impossible in one life, the devotee of the self-power will not relax his efforts through many a life as was exemplified by the Buddha who underwent many a rebirth in order to perfect himself for his supreme enlightenment. Recruits for the self-power school must therefore be endowed with a strong will and a high degree of intelligence. Without intelligence he will not be able to grasp the full significance of the Fourfold Noble Truth, and an intelligent grasp of this truth is most necessary for the sustained exercise of the will power, which is essential for the performance of the various items of morality as prescribed by the Buddha.

The purport of the Fourfold Noble Truth is to acquaint us with the moral law of causation, i.e., the doctrine of karma. Karma means "What you sow, you reap," and the Noble Truth states it in a more formal way from the point of view of spiritual emancipation. The reason why Buddhists condemn Ignorance *(avidyā)* so persistently is that the being ignorant of the Noble Truth which is the spiritual law keeps one forever committing evil deeds. Evil in Buddhist terminology is to ignore the law of causation and the doctrine of karma, for this ignoring involves us in an endless transmigration. Self-power, karma, and causality thus are closely correlated terms in Buddhism, and as long as this correlation continued there was no need for the idea of Adhiṣṭhāna to develop among the Buddhists.

There is, however, an innate yearning in our hearts to break up this closely knitted correlation existing between Karma, causality, and self-power; there is something in the depths of our consciousness always craving to go beyond these terms of mutual

[3] *Ta* = other, *riki* = power, and *ji* = self.

limitation. This secret yearning is indeed the primal factor entering into the foundation of the Mahayana teachings. It may be regarded in a way as contradicting the views of the earlier Buddhists or even those of the Buddha. But it had already been on its way to a fuller development when the Mahayanists began to conceive the personality of the Buddha together with his teachings, as the basis of their religious life and thought.

In short, it is human desire to transcend karma, to break through the chain of causation, to take hold of a power absolutely other than "self-power." It may not be quite adequate to call this a desire; it is far stronger, more innate, more fundamental, and more enduring than any kind of desire the psychologist may analyze; it occupies the core of personality; it is awakened in the human heart with the awakening of consciousness, and really constitutes the grand paradox of human life. But it is here where we have the fundamental of the "other-power" *(tariki)* teaching.

Karma, the moral law of causation, is the principle governing human life as it endures in a world of relativity. As long as Buddhism moves in this world demanding the practice of the Eight Paths of Morality and of the Six Virtues of Perfection, the law of karma is to be most scrupulously followed, for without this law all our moral and ascetic endeavors will come to naught. But as our existence reaches out into a realm of the unconditioned, it never remains satisfied with the teachings based upon the rigid, inflexible law of karma, it demands teachings more pliable, adaptive, and mobile, that is to say, more living and creative. Such teachings are to be founded on things lying beyond the ken of karma or causality which is after all only applicable to the conditionality phase of existence.

Human life is rigorously karma-bound, there is no denying it, and when we disregard this fact we are a sore sight. But at the same time one of the human legs stands in a world where karma loses its domination. It may be better to describe this state of affairs thus: while our limited consciousness urges to conform ourselves to the working of karma, the Unconscious attracts us away to the Unknown beyond karma. The Unconscious and the Unknown are not terms to be found in the dictionary of our ordinary life, but they exercise a mysteriously irresistible power over us, before which logic and psychology are of no avail. This most fundamental contradiction which appears in every section of human life refuses to be reconciled in any other way than by the "other-power" teaching of Mahayana Buddhism.

To be living within the boundaries of karma and yet to transcend them—that is, to be and yet not to be—is the climax of irrationality as far as logic goes. "To be or not to be" is the question possible only within logic. Simultaneously to be and not to be means to occupy two contradicting points at once—and can there be anything more absurd, more nonsensical, more irrational than this?

The self-power is logical and therefore intelligible, appealing to ordinary minds, but the other-power is altogether irrational, and the fact is that this irrationality makes up human life. Hence the inevitability of Mahayana Buddhism.

We must, however, remember that the teaching of the other-power school does not mean to annihilate the karma phase of human life in order to make it absolutely transcend itself, to live altogether away from its own life. This is an impossibility inasmuch as we are what we are; if we try to deny the present life as we live it, that is surely suicidal, it is no transcending of the earthly life. What the other-power tries to do, indeed what all the schools of the Mahayana try to do, is to live this life of karma and relativity and yet to live at the same time a life of transcendence, a life of spiritual freedom, a life not tied down to the chain of causation. To use the Christian expression, immanence is conceivable only with transcendence and transcendence with immanence; when the one is made to mean anything without the other, neither becomes intelligible. But to have both at the same time is altogether illogical, and this is what we are trying to do, showing that logic somehow contrives to adjust itself to the fact.

The Mahayana philosophers have a theory to solve the question of immanence and transcendence or to explain the relationship between *karma* and *akarma*.[4] This theory, as systematically expounded in Aśvaghosha's *Awakening of Faith,* starts

[4] In Sanskrit *a* is a privative prefix and *akarma* means the negation of karma.

with the idea of Suchness *(tathatā* in Sanskrit). Suchness is the limit of thought, and human consciousness cannot go any further than that; expressed in another way, without the conception of Suchness there is no bridge or background whereby the two contradictory ideas, karma and akarma, could be linked. In Suchness or Thusness, affirmation and negation, that is, all forms of opposites find their place of reconciliation or interpenetration; for affirmation is negation and negation is affirmation, and this interpenetration is only possible in Suchness. Suchness may thus be said to be standing on two legs—birth and death which is the realm of karma, and no birth and death which is the realm of akarma beyond the reach of causality.

Suchness is also termed "Mind" *(citta)* from the psychological point of view, and again "Being-Body" *(dharmakāya)*. "Suchness" may sound too abstract and metaphysical, and the Mahayana doctors frequently substitute "Mind" for it; "Mind" is a more familiar and therefore more accessible and also acceptable term for general Buddhists, who can thus establish an intimate relation between their individual minds and Mind as final reality. When, however, even "Mind" is regarded to be too intellectual the Buddhists call it Dharmakāya "Being-Body." *Dharmakāya* is commonly rendered "Law-Body," but *dharma* really means in this case not "law" or "regulative principle," but any object of thought abstract or concrete, universal or particular, and *kāya* is "the body," more in the moral sense of "person" or "personality." The Dharmakāya is therefore a person whose bodily or organic or material expression is this universe, Dharma. The doctrine of the Triple Body *(trikāya)* has thus evolved from the notion of Dharmakāya.[5]

There is still another term for Suchness, considered principally characterizing the teaching of the *Mahāprajñāpāramitā Sūtra*. It is Emptiness or Void *(śūnyatā)*—one of the terms most frequently misinterpreted by Buddhist critics of the West who have never been able really to get into the Buddhist way of thinking. Emptiness is Suchness in which there is nothing empty. When we speak of Emptiness, we are apt to understand it in its relative sense, that is, in contrast to fullness, concreteness, or

[5] *Cf. Studies in the Lankāvatāra,* Pt. III, Ch. III, pp. 308 ff.

substantiality. But the Buddhist idea of Emptiness is not gathered from the negation of individual existences but from the transcendental point of view as it were, for Emptiness unites in itself both fullness and nothingness, both karma and akarma, both determination and freedom, both immanence and transcendence, both jiriki ("self-power") and tariki ("other-power").

3

The principal Sutra of the Shin sect of the Pure Land school is the *Sutra of Eternal Life* in Chinese translation. The Sanskrit text[6] still available is not in full agreement with the Chinese version which is used by Japanese and Chinese followers of the Pure Land school. The points of disagreement are of various nature, but as it is the Chinese text translated by Kōsōgai (K'ang Sêng-k'ai), that is, Sanghavarman of Khotan, of the third century, and not the Sanskrit text still extant, which forms the basis of the Pure Land teaching, here will be given a summary of the Chinese version.

The Sutra of Eternal Life consists roughly of 9,000 Chinese characters and is divided into two parts. Its interlocutors are Śākyamuni, Ānanda, and Maitreya or Ajita. The scene is placed on Mount Gṛidhrakūta, where the Buddha sits surrounded by a large number of Bhikshus and Mahayana Bodhisattvas. Ānanda, observing the Buddha's expression full of serenity, clear, and shining, asks for its reason, and the Buddha begins to tell the whole congregation the story of Dharmākara the Bhikshu who devoted himself to the work of establishing a land of happiness for all sentient beings.

It was a long time ago indeed, in an innumerable, immeasurable, incomprehensible kalpa before now, that Dharmākara studied and practiced the Dharma under the guidance of a Tathagata called Lokeśvararāja. His motive was to perfect a Buddha land in which every conceivable perfection could be brought together. He asked his teacher to explain and manifest for him the perfection of all the excellent qualities of hundreds of thousands of kotis of Buddha lands, and after seeing all these

6 *Sukhāvatī-vyūha-sūtra.*

excellently qualified Buddha lands he was absorbed in deep meditation for a period of five kalpas. When he arose from the meditation his mind was made up for the establishment of his own land of purity and happiness, in which all the inconceivable excellences he observed were to be integrated. He appeared before his teacher Lokeśvararāja and vowed in the presence not only of this Buddha but of all the celestial beings, evil spirits, Brahma, gods, and all other beings, that unless the following forty-eight conditions were not fulfilled he might not attain the highest enlightenment. These vows are what is known by Amida followers as his Original Vow.

After this, Dharmākara, the Bhikshu devoted himself for a space of innumerable, immeasurable, incomprehensible kalpas to the practice of innumerable good deeds which were characterized with the absence of the thoughts of greed, malevolence, and cruelty. In short, he completed all the virtues belonging to the life of a Bodhisattva, which consists of the realization of Love *(karuṇā)* and Wisdom *(prajñā)*. He is now residing in the Western quarter in the Buddha land called Sukhāvatī, Land of Happiness, far away from this world by a hundred thousand niyutas of kotis of Buddha lands. He is called Amitābha, Infinite Light, because of his light the limit of which is beyond measurement. He is again called Amitāyus, Eternal Life, because the length of his life is altogether incalculable. For instance, let all beings in this world collect their thoughts on measuring the length of Amida's life for hundreds of thousands of kotis of kalpas and yet they would fail to obtain a result.

The forty-eight vows enumerated in the Sutra are as follows:

1. If in my country after my obtaining Buddhahood there should be hell, a realm of hungry ghosts, or brute creatures, may I not attain the Highest Enlightenment.

2. If those who are born in my country after my obtaining Buddhahood, should return to the three evil paths of existence, may I not attain the Highest Enlightenment.

3. If those who are born in my country after my obtaining Buddhahood should not all shine in golden color, may I not attain the Highest Enlightenment.

4. If those who are born in my country after my obtaining Buddhahood should not all be of one form and color, showing

no difference in looks, may I not attain the Highest Enlightenment.

5. If those who are born in my country after my obtaining Buddhahood should not have the remembrance of their past lives, at least of things of hundreds of thousands of kotis of kalpas ago, may I not attain the Highest Enlightenment.

6. If those who are born in my country after my obtaining Buddhahood should not be endowed with the heavenly eye so as at least to be able to see hundreds of thousands of kotis of Buddha countries, may I not attain the Highest Enlightenment.

7. If those who are born in my country after my obtaining Buddhahood should not be endowed with the heavenly ear so as at least to be able to hear and retain in memory all the Buddhas' preaching in hundreds of thousands of kotis of Buddha countries, may I not attain the Highest Enlightenment.

8. If those who are born in my country after my obtaining Buddhahood should not be endowed with the mind-reading faculty so as at least to be able to perceive all the thoughts cherished by beings living in hundreds of thousands of kotis of Buddha countries, may I not attain the Highest Enlightenment.

9. If those who are born in my country after my obtaining Buddhahood should not be able to step over in the moment of one thought at least hundreds of thousands of kotis of Buddha countries, may I not attain the Highest Enlightenment.

10. If those who are born in my country after my obtaining Buddhahood should cherish any thought of the body and be attached to it, may I not attain the Highest Enlightenment.

11. If those who are born in my country after my obtaining Buddhahood should not be definitely settled in the group of the faithful before their entrance into Nirvana,[7] may I not attain the Highest Enlightenment.

12. If after my obtaining Buddhahood my light should be limited and not be able at least to illumine hundreds of thousands of kotis of Buddha countries, may I not attain the Highest Enlightenment.

[7] According to Shin, "entering into Nirvana" means "attaining enlightenment," and the attaining of enlightenment which takes place in the Pure Land is to be preceded by joining while here with the group of the faithful.

13. If after my obtaining Buddhahood the length of my life should be limited and not be able at least to last for hundreds of thousands of kotis of kalpas, may I not attain the Highest Enlightenment.

14. If after my obtaining Buddahood the number of Śrāvakas in my country should be measurable by all beings in three thousand chilicosms, who, becoming Pratyekabuddhas, should devote themselves to counting for hundreds of thousands of kotis of kalpas, may I not attain the Highest Enlightenment.

15. If those who are born in my country after my obtaining Buddhahood should be limited in the length of their life, except those who because of their original vows have their life shortened or lengthened, may I not attain the Highest Enlightenment.

16. If those who are born into my country after my obtaining Buddhahood should hear even the name of evil, may I not attain the Highest Enlightenment.

17. If after my obtaining Buddhahood all the immeasurable Buddhas in the ten quarters do not approvingly proclaim my name, may I not attain the Highest Enlightenment.

18. If after my obtaining Buddhahood all beings in the ten quarters should not desire in sincerity and trustfulness to be born in my country, and if they should not be born by only thinking of me for ten times, except those who have committed the five grave offenses and those who are abusive of the true Dharma, may I not attain the Highest Enlightenment.

19. If after my obtaining Buddhahood all beings in the ten quarters awakening their thoughts to enlightenment and practicing all deeds of merit should cherish the desire in sincerity to be born in my country and if I should not, surrounded by a large company, appear before them at the time of their death, may I not attain the Highest Enlightenment.

20. If after my obtaining Buddhahood all beings in the ten quarters hearing my name cherish the thought of my country and planting all the roots of merit and turn them in sincerity over to being born in my country, and if they should fail in obtaining the result of it, may I not attain the Highest Enlightenment.

21. If those who are born in my country after my obtaining Buddhahood should not be complete in the thirty-two marks of

a great personality, may I not attain the Highest Enlightenment.

22. If after my obtaining Buddhahood all the Bodhisattvas in other Buddha lands should desire to be born in my country and if they should not be all bound to one birth only, excepting indeed those Bodhisattvas who, because of their original vows to convert all beings, would, fortifying themselves with the armor of universal salvation, accumulate the stock of merit, deliver all beings from misery, visit all the Buddha countries, practice the discipline of Bodhisattvahood, pay homage to all the Buddha-Tathagatas in the ten quarters, and enlighten all beings as immeasurable as the sands of the Ganga so that all beings might establish themselves in true peerless enlightenment, and further be led on beyond the ordinary stages of Bodhisattvahood, even indeed to the virtues of Samantabhadra, may I not attain the Highest Enlightenment.

23. If after my obtaining Buddhahood all the Bodhisattvas born in my country should not by virtue of the Buddha's miraculous power pay homage to all the Buddhas, and even in one meal's duration visit all the Buddha countries numbering as many as hundreds of thousands of kotis, may I not attain the Highest Enlightenment.

24. If after my obtaining Buddhahood all the Bodhisattvas born in my country should desire to cultivate all the root of merit, and if they should not be able to obtain according to their wish every possible article of worship they may require, may I not attain the Highest Enlightenment.

25. If after my obtaining Buddhahood all the Bodhisattvas born in my country should not be able to preach the Dharma which is in harmony with all-knowledge, may I not attain the Highest Enlightenment.

26. If after my obtaining Buddhahood all the Bodhisattvas born in my country should not be endowed with the body of Nārāyana, may I not attain the Highest Enlightenment.

27. If after my obtaining Buddahood, all beings born in my country should not be able even with their heavenly eye to enumerate and describe precisely all the objects there which are shining in all splendor and purity in the most exquisite manner, may I not attain the Highest Enlightenment.

28. If after my obtaining Buddhahood the Bodhisattvas born

in my country, even those endowed with the least merit, should not perceive a Bodhi tree most exquisitely colored and four hundred yojanas in height, may I not attain the Highest Enlightenment.

29. If after my obtaining Buddhahood the Bodhisattvas in my country, who devote themselves to the reading, reciting, and expounding of the sutras, should not be in possession of perfect knowledge and eloquence, may I not attain the Highest Enlightenment.

30. If after my obtaining Buddhahood, the Bodhisattvas in my country should be in possession of eloquence and perfect knowledge the extent of which is measurable, may I not attain the Highest Enlightenment.

31. If after my obtaining Buddhahood my country should not be so pure and spotless as to illumine, like a bright mirror reflecting images before it, all the Buddha worlds in the ten quarters which are in number beyond description and calculability, may I not attain to the Highest Enlightenment.

32. If, after my obtaining Buddhahood, my country from the ground up to the sky should not be filled and ornamented most exquisitely with all kinds of vases made of jewels emitting an immeasurable variety of sweet perfume which, rising above gods and men, spreads over the ten quarters and if the Bodhisattvas smelling it should not be induced to practice the virtues of Buddhahood, may I not attain the Highest Enlightenment.

33. If, after my obtaining Buddhahood, all beings in all the immeasurable and inconceivable Buddha worlds in the ten quarters should not be enveloped in my light and if those coming in touch with it should not enjoy the softness of the body and mind beyond the reach of gods and men, may I not attain the Highest Enlightenment.

34. If, after my obtaining Buddhahood, all beings in all the innumerable and inconceivable Buddha worlds in the ten quarters hearing my name should not obtain the recognition of the unborn Dharma[8] and all the Dharanis belonging to Bodhisattvahood, may I not attain the Highest Enlightenment.

35. If, after my obtaining Buddhahood, women in all the

8 "The Unborn Dharma" means Reality in the absolute aspect, that is, the Dharma not affected by birth-and-death.

immeasurable and inconceivable Buddha worlds in the ten quarters should not, after hearing my name, be filled with joy and trust and awaken their thoughts to enlightenment and loathe their femininity, and if in another birth they should again assume the female body, may I not attain the Highest Enlightenment.

36. If, after my obtaining Buddhahood, all the Bodhisattvas in all the innumerable and inconceivable Buddha worlds in the ten quarters should not, after hearing my name, always devote themselves to the practice of the holy deeds, in order to perfect the Buddha truth, this even to the end of their lives, may I not attain the Highest Enlightenment.

37. If, after my obtaining Buddhahood, all beings in all the innumerable and inconceivable Buddha worlds in the ten quarters should not, hearing my name, prostrate themselves on the ground to worship me in joy and trust and devote themselves to the practice of the Bodhisattva discipline, thereby winning the reverence of all gods and men, may I not attain the Highest Enlightenment.

38. If, after my obtaining Buddhahood, beings born in my country should not acquire whatever exquisite cloaks they wish to have which are permitted by the Buddha, and if these cloaks should not be placed upon their bodies, which require neither cleaning, nor fulling, nor dyeing, nor washing, may I not attain the Highest Enlightenment.

39. If, after my obtaining Buddhahood, beings born in my country should not be recipients of joy as great as that enjoyed by Bhikshus thoroughly purged of their defilement, may I not attain the Highest Enlightenment.

40. If, after my obtaining Buddhahood, Bodhisattvas born in my country should not be able to see innumerable Buddha lands in the ten quarters produced from among the jewel trees in the land, according to their wish and at any moment desired and so transparently as one perceives one's image in a brightly burnished mirror, may I not attain the Highest Enlightenment.

41. If, after my obtaining Buddhahood, all the Bodhisattvas in other countries should, having heard my name, sustain any defects in their sense organs while pursuing the study of Buddhahood, may I not attain the Highest Enlightenment.

42. If, after my obtaining Buddhahood, all the Bodhisattvas in other countries should not realize the samadhi called "pure emancipation" by hearing my name and if they even while in this samadhi should not be able to awaken a thought and pay homage to all the innumerable and inconceivable Buddha-Tathagatas and yet all the time retain their samadhi, may I not attain the Highest Enlightenment.

43. If after my obtaining Buddhahood, all the Bodhisattvas in other lands having heard my name should not be born after death in noble families, may I not attain the Highest Enlightenment.

44. If, after my obtaining Buddhahood, all the Bodhisattvas in other lands should not, by hearing my name, leap with joy and devote themselves to the practice of the Bodhisattva discipline and perfect the stock of merit, may I not attain the Highest Enlightenment.

45. If, after my obtaining Buddhahood, all the Bodhisattvas in other lands should not by hearing my name realize the samadhi called "Samantānugata" (all-arrived) and if abiding in this samadhi they should not always see until their attainment of Buddhahood all the Buddhas beyond measure and thought, may I not attain the Highest Enlightenment.

46. If, after my obtaining Buddhahood, Bodhisattvas born in my country should not be able to hear, without any effort, whatever Dharmas they aspire to hear, may I not attain the Highest Enlightenment.

47. If, after my obtaining Buddhahood, all the Bodhisattvas in other lands by hearing my name should not instantly reach the stage of no turning back,[9] may I not attain the Highest Enlightenment.

48. If, after my obtaining Buddhahood, all the Bodhisattvas in other lands by hearing my name should not instantly realize the first, the second, and the third Recognition *(kṣāntī)* of the Dharma, and if they should ever turn back in the mastery of all the Buddha teachings, may I not attain the Highest Enlightenment.

These forty-eight separate vows were fulfilled by virtue of

[9] This is the stage where faith is firmly established and no retrogression ever takes place. *Avaivartika* in Sanskrit.

Dharmākara's loving and unselfish devotion to his work, and the country thus created is known as the Land of Bliss, Sukhāvatī, presided over by him now called Amitābha, Infinite Light, and also Amitāyus, Eternal Life—shortly, Amida in Japanese and Omitofu in Chinese. Ten kalpas have elapsed since the establishment of this miraculous kingdom.

The Sutra then proceeds to the description of the Land of Bliss, commonly designated Jōdo (*tsing-tu* in Chinese), meaning Land of Purity. The description is naturally filled with terms not of his world, being altogether beyond the ordinary human understanding.

The second part of the Sutra opens with Śākyamuni's confirmation of all that has been said before regarding the birth of all beings in the Pure Land of Amida as soon as they hear his Name with joy and trust. The Buddha tells Ānanda that all those destined to be born there are those who are definitely established in the true faith even while here, that all the Buddhas in the ten quarters numbering as many as the sands of the Ganga uniformly praise the power and virtue of Amida, both of which are indeed beyond comprehension, and that if we, hearing the Name Amida even once turn our thought toward him, he will assure us of our rebirth in his country.

The rest of the Sutra is largely devoted to the narration of the state of things as they are in this world compared with the Pure Land of Amida. The contrast is appalling and the reader would naturally turn away from those disgusting scenes taking place not only in his surroundings but in fact in his own heart day in day out. This depictment is no doubt an annotation added by a commentator, although it now forms an integral part of the Sutra itself.

After this Ānanda expresses his desire to see Amida's Pure Land, and the entire scene reveals itself at once before Ānanda and the whole congregation. The one statement which strikes us here most significantly is: "The four groups of beings on this side at once perceived all that was [on the other side], and those on the other side in turn saw this world in the same way." One may almost feel like making the remark that the Pure Land is the reflection of this world as this world is the reflection of the Pure Land and that if this be the case various inferences may be drawn from this, among which we can point out some theories going directly against the orthodox teaching of Shin.

After this the Sutra ends with the Buddha's usual exhortation to his assembly as to the continuance of the Buddhist teaching and the upholding of the Buddhist faith, especially as expounded in the present Sutra.

VII

The Gaṇḍavyūha

1

WHEN we come to the *Gaṇḍavyūha*[1] after the *Laṅkāvatāra,* or the *Vajracchedikā,* or the *Parinirvāṇa,* or even after the *Saddharma-Puṇḍarīka* and the *Sukhāvatīvyūha,* there is a complete change in the stage where the great religious drama of Mahāyāna Buddhism is enacted. We find here nothing cold, nothing gray or earth-colored, and nothing humanly mean; for everything one touches in the *Gaṇḍavyūha* shines out in an unsurpassable manner. We are no more in this world of limitation, obscurity, and adumbration; we are miraculously lifted up among the heavenly galaxies. The ethereal world is luminosity itself. The somberness of earthly Jetavana, the disreputableness of the dry-grass seat on which the Lion of the Śākya probably sat when preaching, a

[1] The *Gaṇḍavyūha,* or *Avataṁsaka,* comprehensively known as *Hua-yen-ching* in Chinese, represents a great school of Mahāyāna thought. Traditionally, the sūtra is believed to have been delivered by the Buddha while he was in deep meditation after the Enlightenment. In the sūtra the Buddha gives no personal discourses on any subject except giving the sanction, "Sādhu! Sādhu!" to the statements made by the attending Bodhisattvas such as Mañjuśrī or Samantabhadra, or emitting rays of supernatural light from the various parts of his body as required by the occasion. The Sanskrit *Gaṇḍavyūha* exclusively treats of the pilgrimage of Sudhana under the direction of the Bodhisattva Mañjuśrī. The young pilgrim-aspirant for Supreme Enlightenment visits one teacher after another, amounting to more than fifty in number. The object is to find out what constitutes the life of devotion as practiced by a Bodhisattva. The sūtra occupies more than one-fourth of the *Avataṁsaka* and is complete in itself, undoubtedly proving its independent origin.

group of shabbily dressed mendicants listening to a discourse on the unreality of an individual ego soul—all these have completely vanished here. When the Buddha enters into a certain kind of Samādhi, the pavilion where he is situated all of a sudden expands to the fullest limits of the universe; in other words, the universe itself is dissolved in the being of the Buddha. The universe is the Buddha, and the Buddha is the universe. And this is not mere expanse of emptiness, nor is it the shriveling-up of it into an atom; for the ground is paved with diamonds; the pillars, beams, railings, etc., are inlaid with all kinds of precious stones and gems sparkling brilliantly, and glittering with the reflection of one another.

Not only is the universe of the *Gaṇḍavyūha* not on this side of existence, but the audience surrounding the Buddha is not a mortal one. The Bodhisattvas, the Śrāvakas, and even the worldly lords who are assembling here are all spiritual beings. Though the Śrāvakas and lords and their followers do not fully comprehend the significance of the miracles going on about them, none of them are those whose minds are still under the bondage of ignorance and folly. If they were, they could not even be present at this extraordinary scene.

How does all this come about?

The compilation of the *Gaṇḍavyūha* was made possible owing to a definite change which took place in the mind of the Buddhist concerning life, the world, and especially the Buddha. Thus in the study of the *Gaṇḍavyūha,* what is most essential to know is that the Buddha is no more the one who is living in the world conceivable in terms of space and time. His consciousness is not that of an ordinary mind which must be regulated according to the senses and logic. Nor is it a product of poetical imagination which creates its own images and methods of dealing with particular objects. The Buddha of the *Gaṇḍavyūha* lives in a spiritual world which has its own rules.

In this spiritual world there are no time divisions such as the past, present, and future; for they have contracted themselves into a single moment of the present where life quivers in its true sense. The conception of time as an objective blank in which particular events as its contents succeed one after another has completely been discarded. The Buddha in the *Gaṇḍavyūha* thus knows no time continuity; the past and the future are both rolled up in this present moment of illumination, and this present moment is not something standing still with all its contents, for it ceaselessly moves on. Thus the past is the present, so is the future, but this present in which the past and the future are merged never remains the present; in other words, it is eternally present. And at the center of this eternal present the Buddha has fixed his abode which is no abode.

As with time, so with space. Space in the *Gaṇḍavyūha* is not an extension divided by mountains and forests, rivers and oceans, lights and shades, the visible and the invisible. Extension is here indeed, as there is no contraction of space into one single block of existence; but what we have here is an infinite mutual fusion or penetration of all things, each with its individuality yet with something universal in it. The general fusion thus taking place is the practical annihilation of space which is recognizable only through change and division and impenetrability. To illustrate this state of existence, the *Gaṇḍavyūha* makes everything it depicts transparent and luminous, for luminosity is the only possible earthly representation that conveys the idea of universal interpenetration, the ruling topic of the sūtra. A world of lights transcending distance, opacity, and ugliness of all sorts, is the world of the *Gaṇḍavyūha.*

With the annihilation of space and time, there evolves a realm of imagelessness or shadowlessness *(anābhāsa).* As long as there are lights and shades, the principle of individuation always overwhelms us human mortals. In the *Gaṇḍavyūha* there is no shadowiness; it is true there are rivers, flowers, trees, nets, banners, etc., in the land of purity, in the description of which the compiler taxes his human imagination to its utmost limits; but no shadows are visible here anywhere. The clouds themselves are luminous bodies inconceivable and inexpressible in number,[2] hanging all over the Jetavana of the *Gaṇḍavyūha*—which are described in its own terminology as "heavenly jewel palaces," "incense wood," "Sumeru," "musical instruments," "pearl nets," "heavenly figures," etc.

This universe of luminosity, this scene of interpretation, is

2 *Acintya* and *anabhilāpya* are numbers of high denominations.

known as the Dharmadhātu, in contrast to the Lokadhātu which is this world of particulars. In the Dharmadhātu there are space and time and individual beings as in the Lokadhātu, but they show none of their earthly characteristics of separateness and obduracy as are perceivable in the latter. For the Dharmadhātu is not a universe spatially or temporarily constructed like the Lokadhātu, and yet it is not utter blankness or mere void which is identifiable with absolute nonentity. The Dharmadhātu is a real existence and not separated from the Lokadhātu, only it is not the same as the latter, when we do not come up to the spiritual level where the Bodhisattvas are living. It is realizable when the solid outlines of individuality melt away and the feeling of finiteness no more oppresses us. The *Gaṇḍavyūha* is thus known under the title "The Entering into the Dharmadhātu" *(dharmadhātupraveśa).*

2

What then are some of the chief changes of thought that have taken place in Buddhism enabling it to evolve a universe to be known as Dharmadhātu? What are those feelings and ideas which have entered into the consciousness of the inhabitants of the Dharmadhātu? In other words, what are the qualifications of Tathāgata, Bodhisattva, and Śrāvaka?

When these are specified, we shall know how the Mahāyāna came to be differentiated from the Hīnayāna, that is, why some Buddhists became dissatisfied with the way Buddhism had so far taken in its development after the passing of the Buddha himself. This development had run steadily toward exclusive asceticism on the one hand and toward the elaboration of philosophical subleties on the other. This meant that Buddhism, instead of being a practical, social, everyday religion, had turned into a sort of mysticism which keeps it votaries on the giddy height of unapproachable abstractions making them refuse to descend among earthly entanglements. Such a religion may be all very well for the elite, for Arhats and Pratyekabuddhas, but it lacks vitality and democratic usefulness when it is kept from coming in contact with the concrete affairs of life. The Mahāyānists revolted against this aloofness and unconcernedness of the Śrāvaka ideal. Thus they could not help reviving and upholding the Bodhisattva ideal, which marked the career of the Buddha before his attainment of supreme enlightenment; they then endeavored to unfold to its furthest limits all that was to be found in the ideal. I have therefore selected the opening chapter of the *Gaṇḍavyūha,* where the Bodhisattva ideal is contrasted in strong color to the Śrāvaka ideal, to show what was in the consciousness of the Mahāyāna followers when they developed their own thoughts and aspirations.

The Zen followers in China have induced even the Buddha himself to take an active part in the common life of the masses. He no more sits on a high seat decorated with seven kinds of jewels, discoursing on such abstract subjects as Non-ego, Emptiness, or Mind-only. On the contrary, he takes up a spade in his hands, tills the ground, sows seeds, and garners the harvest. In outward appearances he cannot be distinguished from a commoner whom we meet on the farm, in the street, or in the office. He is just as hard-working a person as we are. The Buddha in his Chinese Zen life does not carry his *Gaṇḍavyūha* atmosphere ostentatiously about him but quietly within him. A Buddha alone discovers him.

The following points may then be noted in the reading of the *Gaṇḍavyūha:*

1. The one dominant feeling, we may almost assert, that runs through the text is an active sense of grand inscrutable mystery *(acintya),* going beyond the power of thinking and description. Everything one sees, hears, or observes in the Dharmadhātu is a mystery, because it is incomprehensible to the ordinary sense of logical measurement. Jetavana of so many square miles abruptly expands to the ends of the universe—does this not surpass human conception? A Bodhisattva comes from a world lying beyond even the furthest end of the universe—that is, beyond an ocean of worlds as innumerable as particles of atoms constituting a Buddha land—is this not a wonderful event? And let us remind you that this Bodhisattva is accompanied by his retinues as innumerable as the number of atoms constituting a Buddha land, and again that these visitors are coming from all the ten quarters, accompanied not only by their innumerable retinues but surrounded by luminous clouds, shining banners,

etc. Depict all this in your own minds, exercising all the power of imagination that you can command—is it not really a most miraculous sight altogether transcending human thought? All that the poor writer of the *Gaṇḍavyūha* can say is "inconceivable" *(acintya)* and "indescribable" *(anabhilāpya)*. The miracles performed are not of such local or partial nature as we encounter in most religious literature. Miracles so called are ordinarily a man's walking on water, a stick changing into a tree, a blind man being enabled to see, and so on. Not only are all such petty miracles as are recorded in the history of religion quite insignificant in scale and of no value when compared with those of the *Gaṇḍavyūha*, but they are fundamentally different from the latter; for the *Gaṇḍavyūha* miracles are possible only when the whole scheme of the universe as we conceive it is altered from its very basis.

2. We are impressed now with the spiritual powers of the Buddha who can achieve all these wonders by merely entering into a certain Samādhi. What are these powers? They are defined thus: (1) the sustaining and inspiring power *(adhiṣṭhāna)*[3] which is given to the Bodhisattva to achieve the aim of his life; (2) the power of working miracles *(vikurvita)*; (3) the power of ruling *(anubhāva)*; (4) the power of the original vow *(pūrva-praṇidhāna)*; (5) the power of goodness practiced in his former lives *(pūrvasukṛitakuśalamūla)*; (6) the power of receiving all good friends *(kalyāṇamitraparigraha)*; (7) the power of pure faith and knowledge *(śraddhāyajñānaviśuddhi)*; (8) the power of attaining a highly illuminating faith *(udārādhimuktyava-bhāsapratilambha)*; (9) the power of purifying the thought of the Bodhisattva *(bodhisattvādhyāśayapariśuddhi)*; and (10) the power of earnestly walking toward all-knowledge and original vows *(adhyāśayasarvajñatāpraṇidhānaprasthāna)*.

3. The fact that the transformation of the entire city of Jetavana was due to the miraculous power of the Samādhi attained by the Buddha makes one inquire into the nature of the Samādhi. According to the *Gaṇḍavyūha*, the miracle was effected by the strength of a great compassionate heart *(mahā-karuṇā)* which constitutes the very essence of the Samādhi; for

[3] This is an important conception in Mahāyāna Buddhism. For explanation see my *Studies in the Laṅkāvatāra Sūtra*, pp. 202 ff.

compassion is its body *(śarīra),* its source *(mukha),* its leader *(pūrvaṅgama),* and the means of expanding itself all over the universe. Without this great heart of love and compassion, the Buddha's Samādhi, however exalted it may be in every other way, will be of no avail in the enactment of the great spiritual drama so wonderfully described here. This is indeed what characteristically distinguishes the Mahāyāna from all that has preceded it in the history of Buddhism. Owing to its self-expanding and self-creating power, a great loving heart transforms this earthly world into one of splendor and mutual fusion, and this is where the Buddha is always abiding.

4. The *Gaṇḍavyūha* is in a sense the history of the inner religious consciousness of Samantabhadra the Bodhisattva, whose wisdom eye *(jñānacakṣus),* life of devotion *(caryā),* and original vows *(praṇidhāna)* make up its contents. Thus all the Bodhisattvas taking part in the establishment of the Dharmadhātu are born *(abhiniryāta)* of the life and vows of Samantabhadra. And Sudhana's chief object of pilgrimage which is told in such detail in the *Gaṇḍavyūha* was nothing else but the identifying of himself with Samantabhadra the Bodhisattva. When after visiting more than fifty teachers of all sorts he came to Samantabhadra, he was thoroughly instructed by the Bodhisattva as regards his life of devotion, his knowledge, his vows, his miraculous powers, etc.; and when Sudhana realized what all these Buddhist disciplines meant he found himself in complete identity not only with Samantabhadra, but with all the Buddhas. His body filled the universe to its ends, and his life of devotion *(caryā),* his enlightenment *(sambodhi),* his transformation bodies *(vikurvita),* his revolution of the Dharma wheel, his eloquence, his voice, his faith, his abode, his love and compassion, and his emancipation and mastery over the world were exactly those of Samantabhadra and all the Buddhas.

What most concerns us here is the idea of the vow *(praṇidhāna)* which is made by a Bodhisattva at the beginning of his career and which controls all his later life. His vows are concerned with enlightening, or emancipating, or saving all his fellow beings, which include not only sentient beings but the non-sentient. The reason he gives up everything that is ordinarily regarded as belonging to oneself is not to gain a word or a phrase of truth for himself—there is in fact no such thing as truth abstractly conceived, nor is there anything that is to be adhered to as ego substance, in the great ocean of Reality; what he wants to accomplish by his life of self-sacrifice is to lead all beings to final emancipation, to a state of happiness which is not of this world, to make the light of knowledge illuminate the whole universe, and to see all the Buddhas praised and adored by all beings. This is what mainly constitutes a life of devotion as practiced by Samantabhadra the Bodhisattva.

5. When I say that the Mahāyāna or Bodhisattva ideal is contrasted with the Hīnayāna or Arhat ideal in the former's being practical and intimately connected with our everyday earthly life, some may doubt this, seeing what a mysterious world the Dharmadhātu is where all kinds of apparent impossibilities are taking place as if they were the most ordinary things, such as carrying a bucket of water, or kindling a bundle of faggots. The Dharmadhātu which is the world of the *Gaṇḍavyūha* is assuredly a transcendental one standing in no connection with the hard facts of this life. But the objector must remember that the point from which we are to survey the world according to the *Gaṇḍavyūha* is not that of a mind immersed in the mire of individualization. In order to see life and the world in their proper bearing, the Mahāyāna expects us first to clear off all the obstacles that rise from our obstinacy in taking the world of relativity as the ultimate limit of reality. When the veil is lifted, the obstacles are swept away, and the self-nature of things presents itself in the aspect of Suchness; and it is then that the Mahāyāna is ready to take up the so-called real problems of life and solve them in accordance with the truth, i.e. *yathābhūtam*. Contradiction is so deep-seated in life that it can never be eradicated until life is surveyed from a point higher than itself. When this is done, the world of the *Gaṇḍavyūha* ceases to be a mystery, a realm devoid of form and corporeality, for it now overlaps this earthly world; no, it becomes that "Thou art it," and there is a perfect fusion of the two. The Dharmadhātu is the Lokadhātu, and its inhabitants—that is, all the Bodhisattvas, including the Buddhas—are ourselves, and their doings are our doings. They looked so

full of mystery, they were miracles, as long as they were observed from this earthly end, where we imagined that there was really something at the other end; but as soon as the dividing wall constructed by our imagination is removed, Samantabhadra's arms raised to save sentient beings become our own, which are now engaged in passing the salt to a friend at the table, and Maitreya's opening the Vairocana Tower for Sudhana is our ushering a caller into the parlor for a friendly chat. No more sitting on the summit of reality *(bhūtakoṭi)*, in the tranquility of absolute oneness, do we review a world of turmoil; but rather we see both the Bodhisattvas and the Buddhas shining in the sweat of their foreheads, in the tears shed for the mother who lost a child, in the fury of passions burning against injustice in its multifarious forms—in short, in their never-ending fight against all that goes under the name of evil. This again reminds us of P'ang's reputed verse:

> How wondrously supernatural!
> And how miraculous this!
> I draw water, I carry fuel!

Lin-chi's sermon on Mañjuśrī, Samantabhadra, and Avalokiteśvara may be considered also in this connection. "There are," he says, "some student-monks who look for Mañjuśrī at Wu-tai Shan,[4] but they have already taken the wrong road. There is no Mañjuśrī at Wu-tai Shan. Do you wish to know where he is? There is something this very moment at work in you, showing no tendency to waver, betraying no disposition to doubt—this is your living Mañjuśrī. The light of non-discrimination which flashes through every thought of yours—this is your Samantabhadra who remains true all the time. Every thought of yours which, knowing of itself how to break off the bondage, is emancipated at every moment—this is entering into the Samādhi of Avalokiteśvara. Each of them functions in harmonious mutuality and simultaneously, so that one is three, three is one. When this is understood, you are able to read the sūtras."

Commenting on Lin-chi's view of "No Mañjuśrī at Wu-tai Shan," a Zen master has this verse:

[4] The Wu-tai is the sacred abode of Mañjuśrī in China while the E-mei is consecrated to Samantabhadra and the P'u-t'o-lo to Avalokiteśvara.

Whenever there is a mountain well shaded in verdure,
There is a holy ground for your spiritual exercises;
What then is the use of climbing up, supported by the mountain staff,
Mañjusrī to worship on the Ch'ing-ling Peak?
Even when the golden-haired lion reveals itself in the clouds,
Indeed, rightly viewed, this is no auspicious sign.

3

Reference was made to the sense of mystery which envelops the whole text of the *Gaṇḍavyūha* as one of its striking characteristics. I want now to fathom this and point out where it originates—that is, what may be termed its fundamental spiritual insight. For the *Gaṇḍavyūha* has its own intuition of the world and the mind, from which so many miracles, mysteries, or inconceivabilities succeed one after another in a most wonderful manner—which to many may appear to be altogether too fantastic, too far beyond the bounds of common sense. But when we grasp the central fact of the spiritual experience gone through by the Bodhisattvas as narrated in the sūtra, all the rest of the scenes depicted here will suggest perfect naturalness, and there will be no more irrationalities in them. The main thing, therefore, for us to do if we desire to understand the *Gaṇḍavyūha,* is to take hold of its fundamental insight.

The fundamental insight of the *Gaṇḍavyūha* is known as Interpenetration. It is, philosophically speaking, a thought somewhat similar to the Hegelian conception of concrete-universals. Each individual reality, besides being itself, reflects in it something of the universal, and at the same time it is itself because of other individuals. A system of perfect relationship exists among individual existences and also between individuals and universals, between particular objects and general ideas. This perfect network of mutual relations has received at the hand of the Mahāyāna philosopher the technical name of Interpenetration.

When the Empress Tsê-t'ien of T'ang felt it difficult to grasp the meaning of Interpenetration, Fa-tsang, the great master of the Avataṁsaka school of Buddhism illustrated it in the following way. He had first a candle lighted, and then had mirrors placed encircling it on all sides. The central light reflected itself in every one of the mirrors, and every one of these reflected lights was reflected again in every mirror, so that there was a perfect interplay of lights, that is, of concrete-universals. This is said to have enlightened the mind of the Empress. It is necessary to have this kind of philosophy for the understanding of the *Gaṇḍavyūha* or the *Avataṁsaka*. The following extracts from the text before us will help us to have a glimpse into its deep intuition.

After describing the transformations that took place in Jetavana when the Buddha entered into a Samādhi known as Siṁhavijṛimbhita, the *Gaṇḍavyūha* goes on to say: "All this is due to the Buddha's miraculous *(acintya)* deeds of goodness, to his miraculous work of purity, to his miraculously mighty power; all this is because he has the miraculous power of transforming his one body and making it pervade the entire universe; it is because he has the miraculous power of making all the Buddhas, all the Buddha lands with their splendors, enter into his own body; it is because he has the miraculous power of manifesting all the images of the Dharmadhātu within one single particle of dust; it is because he has the miraculous power of revealing all the Buddhas of the past with their successive doings within a single pore of his skin; it is because he has the miraculous power of illuminating the entire universe with each one of the rays which emanate from his body; it is because he has the miraculous power of evolving clouds of transformation from a single pore of his skin and making them fill up all the Buddha lands; it is because he has the miraculous power of revealing in a single pore of his skin the whole history of all the worlds in the ten quarters from their first appearance until their final destruction. It is for these reasons that in this grove of Jetavana are revealed all the purities and splendors of the Buddha lands."

When all the Bodhisattvas with an inconceivable number of followers come from the ten quarters of the world and begin to get settled around the Buddha, the *Gaṇḍavyūha* explains for its readers who these Bodhisattvas are miraculously assembling here, accompanied generally by luminous clouds, and gives among others the following characterization of the Bodhisattvas:

"All these Bodhisattvas from the ten quarters of the world together with their retinues are born of the life and vows of Samantabhadra the Bodhisattva. By means of their pure wisdom-eye they see all the Buddhas of the past, present, and future, and also hear the ocean of the sūtras and the revolving of the Dharma wheel by all the Buddhas. They are all masters of the excellent Pāramitās; they approach and serve all the Tathāgatas who are performing miracles every minute; they are also able to expand their own bodies to the ends of the universe; they bring forth by means of their body of light all the religious assemblies conducted by the Buddhas; they reveal in each particle of dust all the worlds, singly and generally, with their different conditions and multitudes; and in these different worlds they choose the most opportune season to discipline all beings and to bring them to maturity; emitting a deep, full sound from every pore of the skin, which reverberates throughout the universe, they discourse on the teachings of all the Buddhas."

All such statements may sound too figurative, too fantastic to be seriously considered by the so-called rationally minded. From the realistic or rationalistic point of view, which upholds objective validity and sense measurement as the sole standard of truth, the *Gaṇḍavyūha* fares rather ill. But we must remember that there is another point of view, especially in matters spiritual, which pays no attention to the rationalistic interpretation of our inner experiences. The human body, ordinarily or from the sense point of view, occupies a limited area of space which can be measured, and continues to live also during a measurable period of time. And against this body there is the whole expanse of the universe, including all the mountains and oceans on earth and also all the starry heavens. How can this body of ours be made to take in the entire objectivity? How can our insignificant, ignominious "hair hole" or "pore of the skin" *(romakūpa)* be turned into a holy stage where all the Tathāgatas of the past, present, and future can congregate for their spiritual discourses? Obviously, this is an utter impossibility or the height of absurdity. But the strange fact is that when a door opens and a light shines from an unknown source into the dark chamber of consciousness, all time- and space-limitations dissolve away, and we make a Siṁhanāda (lion roar), "Before Abraham was I am," or "I alone am the honored one above and below all the heavens." The *Gaṇḍavyūha* is written always from this exalted point of view. If science surveys the objective world and philosophy unravels intricacies of logic, Buddhism dives into the very abyss of being, and tells us in the directest possible manner all it sees under the surface.

When we speak, as we sometimes do, of the philosophical background of the *Gaṇḍavyūha* or the Hegelian idea of concrete-universals, the reader may think that Buddhism is a system of philosophy, and the sūtras are attempts to expound it in their characteristic manner. If we have made him take this attitude toward the Mahāyāna, we must withdraw everything that was said in this connection and start afresh in our study of the sūtras. Whatever misunderstandings or misinterpretations Zen has incurred from its outside critics, its chief merit consists in clearing our consciousness of all the rubbish it has gathered in the way of philosophical explanations of existence. By its disclaiming the letter which is so apt to thwart the progress of the spirit, Zen has kept its central thought unspoiled. That is to say, it has succeeded in steadily upholding the value of experience and intuition in the understanding of Reality. The method of Zen differs from that of the *Gaṇḍavyūha,* but as both agree in spirit, the one will prove complementary to the other when we endeavor to study Buddhism comprehensively as it has developed in the Far East. The sūtras and Zen are not antagonistic, nor are they contradictory. What the sūtras express through the psychology and tradition of their compilers, Zen treats after its own fashion as conditioned by the intellectual equipment and psychological and racial peculiarities of its masters. Read the following Zen sermon[5] and compare it with the *Gaṇḍavyūha*:

"Here is a man who, even from the very beginning of things, has had no dwelling, nothing to depend on; above, not a fraction of tile is over his head; below, not an inch of earth supports his feet. Tell me where he gets his body at rest and

[5] Given by Hsiao-ch'un of Ling-ch'üan temple, perhaps of the eleventh century. *Hsü Chuan-têng Lu,* XX.

his life established for the twelve periods of the day. When you understand, he is known to be gone to India in the morning and to be back here in the evening."

4

Having acquainted ourselves with the general atmosphere in which the *Gaṇḍavyūha* moves, let us now proceed to see what are the constituents of the audience—that is, what are the particular characteristics of Bodhisattvahood as distinguished from those of Śrāvakahood. In other words, the question is concerned with the differentia of Mahāyāna Buddhism. When we know how the Bodhisattva is qualified in the *Gaṇḍavyūha*, we know also how Bodhisattvahood differentiates itself from Śrāvakahood and what are the Mahāyāna thoughts as they are presented in this sūtra against those of the Hīnayāna. For the opening chapter of the *Gaṇḍavyūha* emphatically sets up the Bodhisattvas against the Śrāvakas, giving reasons why the latter are unable to participate like the Bodhisattvas in the development of the grand spiritual life.

The Bodhisattvas numbering five hundred are attending the assembly which takes place under the supervision of the Buddha in Jetavana. The same number of the Śrāvakas are also found among the audience. Of the Srāvakas such names are mentioned as Maudgalyāyana, Mahākāśyapa, Revata, Subhūti, Aniruddha, Nandika, Kapphiṇa, Kātyāyana, Pūrṇa Maitrāyaṇīputra, etc., while Samantabhadra and Mañjuśrī stand out prominently as the two leaders of the five hundred Bodhisattvas. The Bodhisattvas are all said to have "issued from the life and vows of Samantabhadra," and qualified in the following way: (1) they are unattached in their conduct because they are able to expand themselves in all the Buddha lands; (2) they manifest innumerable bodies because they can go over wherever there are Buddhas; (3) they are in possession of an unimpeded and unspoiled eyesight because they can perceive the miraculous transformations of all the Buddhas; (4) they are able to visit anywhere without being bound to any one locality because they never neglect appearing in all places where the Buddhas attain to their enlightenment; (5) they are in possession of a limitless light because they can illumine the ocean of all the Buddha truths with the light of their knowledge; (6) they have an inexhaustible power of eloquence through eternity because their speech has no taint; (7) they abide in the highest wisdom which knows no limits like space because their conduct is pure and free from taints; (8) they have no fixed abode because they reveal themselves personally in accordance with the thoughts and desires of all beings; (9) they are free from obscurities because they know that there are really no beings, no soul substances in the world of beings; and finally (10) they are in possession of transcendental knowledge which is as vast as space because they illumine all the Dharmadhātus with their nets of light.

In another place where the Bodhisattvas visiting Jetavana from the ten quarters of the universe to contribute their share in the grand demonstration of the Buddha's spiritual powers are characterized, we find among other things the following statements: "All the Bodhisattvas know that all beings are like Māyā, that all the Buddhas are like shadows, that all existence with its rise and fall is like a dream, that all forms of karma are like images in a mirror, that the rising of all things is like a *fata morgana*, that all the worlds are mere transformations; further, the Bodhisattvas are all endowed with the ten powers, knowledge, dignity, and faith of the Tathāgata, which enable them to roar like lions; they have deeply delved into the ocean of inexhaustible eloquence, they have acquired the knowledge of how to explain the truths for all beings; they are complete masters of their conduct so that they move about in the world as freely as in space; they are in possession of all the miraculous powers belonging to a Bodhisattva; their strength and energy will crush the army of Māra; their knowledge power penetrates into the past, present, and future; knowing that all things are like space, they practice non-resistance, and are not attached to them; though they work indefatigably for others, they know that when things are observed from the point of view of all-knowledge, nobody knows whence they come; though they recognize an objective world, they know that its existence is something unobtainable; they enter into all the worlds by means of incorruptible knowledge; in all the worlds they reveal themselves with the utmost freedom; they are born in all the worlds, take all form; they transform a small area into an extended tract of land, and the latter again into a small area; all the Buddhas are revealed in one single moment of their thought; the powers of all the Buddhas are added on to them; they survey the entire universe in one glance and are not at all confused; they are able to visit all the worlds in one moment."

Against this characterization of the Bodhisattvas, what have we for that of the five hundred Śrāvakas? According to the *Gaṇḍavyūha,* "They are enlightened in the self-nature of truth and reason, they have an insight into the limit of reality, they have entered into the essence of things, they are out of the ocean of becoming, they abide where the Buddha merit is stored, they are released from the bondage of the Knots and Passions, they dwell in the house of non-attachment, they stay in the serenity of space, they have their desires, errors, and doubts wiped off by the Buddha, and they are rightly and faithfully devoted to the Buddha ocean."

When Śrāvakahood is compared with Bodhisattvahood as they are here particularized, we at once perceive how cold, aloof, and philosophical the one is, in great contrast to the spiritual activities and miraculous movements of the other. The Bodhisattva is always kept busy doing something for others, sometimes spreading himself all over the universe, sometimes appearing in one or another path of existence, sometimes destroying the army of evil ones, sometimes paying reverence and making offerings to the Buddhas of the past, present, and future. And in these movements he is perfectly at home, he goes on everywhere with the utmost ease and spontaneity as nothing impedes his maneuvering as a world savior. The Śrāvaka is, on the other hand, an intellectual recluse, his insight is altogether philosophical and has no religious fervor accompanying it; he is satisfied with what he has attained by himself, and has no desire stirred within himself to let others share also in his spiritual or rather metaphysical realization. To him the entire world of inconceivabilities is a closed book, and this world of inconceivabilities is the very place where all the Bodhisattvas belong and find the reason of their existence. However penetrating and perspicuous may be the intellect of the Śrāvaka, there is still a world altogether beyond his grasp.

This world, to use the *Gaṇḍavyūha* terminology, is where we find the Buddha's transformations *(vikurvita)*, orderly arrangements *(vyūha)*, superhuman virility *(vṛiṣabha)*, playful activities *(vikrīḍita)*, miracles *(pratihārya)*, sovereignty *(adhipateyatā)*, wonderful performances *(caritavikurvita)*, supreme power *(prabhāva)*, sustaining power *(adhiṣṭhāna)*, and land of purity *(kṣetra-pariśuddhi)*. And again here is where the Bodhisattvas have their realms, their assemblies, their entrances, their comings together, their visits, their transformations, their miracles, their groups, their quarters, their fine array of lion seats, their palatial residences, their resting abodes, their transports in Samādhi, their survey of the worlds, their energetic concentrations, their heroisms, their offerings to the Tathāgatas, their certifications, their maturities, their energies, their Dharmakāyas of purity, their knowledge bodies of perfection, their vow bodies in various manifestations, their material bodies in their perfected form, the fulfillment and purification of all their forms, the array of their boundless light images, the spreading out of their great nets of lights, and the bringing forth of their transformation clouds, the expansion of their bodies all over the ten quarters, the perfection of all their transformation deeds, etc.

5

What are the causes and conditions that have come to differentiate Bodhisattvahood so much from Śrāvakahood?

The *Gaṇḍavyūha* does not forget to point out what causes are contributive to this remarkable differentiation, to tell what are the conditions that make the Śrāvakas altogether blind to the various manifestations and transformations going on in a most wonderful way at the assembly of the Bodhisattvas in Jetavana. The *Gaṇḍavyūha* gives the following reasons:

Because the stock of merit is not the same (1); because the Śrāvakas have not seen, and disciplined themselves in, the virtues of the Buddha (2); because they have not approved the notion that the universe is filled with Buddha lands in all the ten quarters where there is a fine array of all Buddhas (3); because they have not given praise to the various wonderful manifestations put forward by the Buddhas (4); because they have not awakened the desire after supreme enlightenment attainable in the midst of transmigration (5); because they have not induced others to cherish the desire after supreme enlightenment (6); because they have not been able to continue the Tathāgata family (7); because they have not taken all beings under their protection (8); because they have not advised others to practice the Pāramitās of the Bodhisattva (9); because while yet in the transmigration of birth and death they have not persuaded others to seek for the most exalted wisdom-eye (10).

Further, because the Śrāvakas have not disciplined themselves in all the stock of merit from which issues all-knowledge (11); because they have not perfected all the stock of merit which makes the appearance of the Buddha possible (12); because they have not added to the enhancement of the Buddha land by seeking for the knowledge of transformation (13); because they have not entered into the realm which is surveyed by the Bodhisattva-eye (14); because they have not sought the stock of merit which produces an incomparable insight going beyond this world (15); because they have not made any of the vows constituting Bodhisattvahood (16); because they have not conformed themselves to all that is the product of the Tathāgata's sustaining power (17); because they have not realized that all things are like Māyā and the Bodhisattvas are like a dream (18); because they have not attained the most exhilarating excitements *(prativega-vivardhana)* of the Bodhisattva (19); in short, because they have not realized all these spiritual states belonging to the wisdom-eye of Samantabhadra to which the Śrāvakas and Pratyekabuddhas are strangers (20).

So, concludes the *Gaṇḍavyūha,* all these great *Śrāvakas* such as Śāriputra, etc., have no stock of merit, no wisdom-eye, no Samādhi, no emancipation, no power of transformation, no sovereignty, no energy, no mastery, no abode, no realm, which enable them to get into the assemblage of the Bodhisattvas and participate in the performance of the great spiritual drama that is going on in Jetavana. As they have sought their deliverance according to the vehicle and way of Śrāvakahood, what they have accomplished does not go beyond Śrāvakahood. They have indeed gained the knowledge whereby the truth is made manifest, they are abiding in the limit of reality *(bhūtakoṭi),* they are enjoying the serenity of the ultimate *(atyantaśānti)*; but they have no great compassionate all-embracing heart for all beings, for they are too intently occupied with their own doings *(ātmakārya)* and have no mind to accumulate the Bodhisattva knowledge and to discipline themselves in it. They have their own realization and emancipation, but they have no desire, make no vows to make others also find their resting abode in it. They do not thus understand what is really meant by the inconceivable power of the Tathāgata.

To sum up: the Śrāvakas are yet under the covering of too great a karma hindrance; they are unable to cherish such great vows as are made by the Bodhisattvas for the spiritual welfare of all beings; their insight is not clear and penetrating enough to see into all the secrets of life; they have not yet opened what is designated as the wisdom-eye *(jñānacakṣus)* in the *Gaṇḍavyūha,* wherewith a Bodhisattva takes in at a glance all the wonders and inconceivabilities of the spiritual realm to its deepest abyss. How superficial, compared to this, is the philosophical insight of the Śrāvakas!

6

The *Gaṇḍavyūha* gives us several parables to tell more graphically the conditions of Śrāvakahood under which its followers are still laboring. Let me quote one or two.

Along the river Gangā there are millions of millions of hungry ghosts *(preta)* all naked and tormented with hunger and thirst; they feel as if their bodies were burning; and their lives are threatened every minute by birds and beasts of prey. Thirst impels them to seek for water, but they cannot find it anywhere even though they are right close to the river. Some see the river, but for them there is no water, only the dried-up bed. Why? Because their karma hindrance lies too heavy on them. In the same way, these great learned philosophical Śrāvakas, even though they are in the midst of the large assembly of the Bodhisattvas, are not capable of recognizing the grand miracles of the Tathāgata. For they have relinquished all-knowledge *(sarvajñatā)* owing to the ignorance cataract covering their eyes; for they have never planted their stock of merit in the soil of all-knowledge.

In the Himālaya mountains many kinds of medicinal herbs are found, and they are distinguished by an experienced doctor each according to its specific qualities. But because they have no eye for them all these are not recognized by the hunters, nor by the herdsmen, who may frequent these regions. In the same way, the Bodhisattvas who have entered into a realm of transcendental knowledge and gained a spiritual power over form are able to see the Tathāgatas and their grand display of miracles. But the Śrāvakas, in the midst of these wonderful events, cannot see them, because they are satisfied only with their own deeds *(svakārya)*, and not at all concerned with the spiritual welfare of others.

To give another parable: here is a man in a large congregation of people. He happens to fall asleep, and in a dream he is suddenly transported to the summit of Mount Sumeru where Śakrendra has his magnificent palatial residence. There are a large number of mansions, pavilions, gardens, lakes, etc., each in its full splendor. There are also celestial beings incalculable in number, the grounds are strewn with heavenly flowers, the trees are decorated with beautiful robes, and the flowers are in full bloom. Most exquisite music is played among the trees, and the branches and leaves emit of their own accord pleasing sounds, and these go on in harmonious concert with the melodious singing of the celestial damsels. The dancers, innumerable and attired in resplendent garments, are enjoying themselves on the terrace. The man is now no more a bystander at these scenes, for he is one of the participants himself appareled in heavenly fashion, and going around among the inhabitants of Sudarśana as if he had belonged to them from the beginning.

These phenomena, however, have never come to be noticed by any other mortals who are congregated here, for what is perceived by the man is a vision only given to him. In a similar manner, the Bodhisattvas are able to see all the wonderful sights in the world taking place under the direction of the

Buddha's power. For they have been accumulating their stock of merit for ever so many kalpas, making vows based on all-knowledge which knows no bounds in time and space. For, again, they have studied all the virtues of the Buddhas, disciplining themselves in the way of Bodhisattvahood, and then perfecting themselves for the attainment of all-knowledge. In short, they have fulfilled all the vows of Samantabhadra and lived his life of devotion, whereas the Śrāvakas have none of the pure insight belonging to the Bodhisattvas.

7

From these quotations and delineations, we have now, I hope, a general background of the *Gaṇḍavyūha* more or less clearly outlined, and from them also we learn the following ideas which are really the contents of at least the opening chapter of the sūtra, while they also give us a further glimpse into the essence of the Mahāyāna teaching generally.

1. There is a world which is not of this world, though inseparable from it.

2. The world where we ordinarily move is characterized with limitations of all sorts. Each individual reality holds itself against others, which is indeed its self-nature *(svabhāva)*. But in the world of the *Gaṇḍavyūha* known as the Dharmadhātu, individual realities are enfolded in one great Reality, and this great Reality is found participated in by each individual one. Not only this, but each individual existence contains in itself all other individual existences as such. Thus there is a universal interpenetration, so called, in the Dharmadhātu.

3. These supernatural phenomena cannot take place in a world where darkness and obduracy prevail, because then a penetration would be impossible. If a penetration should take place in these conditions it would mean the general breaking-down of all individual realities, which is a chaos.

4. Therefore, the Dharmadhātu is a world of lights not accompanied by any form of shade. The essential nature of light is to intermingle without interfering or obstructing or destroying one another. One single light reflects in itself all other lights generally and individually.

5. This is not a philosophical interpretation of existence reached by cold logical reasoning, nor is it a symbolical representation of the imagination. It is a world of real spiritual experience.

6. Spiritual experience is like sense experience. It is direct, and tells us directly all that it has experienced without resorting to symbolism or ratiocination. The *Gaṇḍavyūha* is to be understood in this manner—that is, as a document recording one's actual spiritual life.

7. This realm of spirit belongs to the Bodhisattva and not to the Śrāvaka. The latter serenely abides in a world of intellectual intuition and monotony, supremely above the endlessly intermingling world of particulars and multiplicities. The Bodhisattva has a loving heart, and his is a life of devotion and self-sacrifice given up to a world of individualities.

8. A society of spiritual beings is approachable only by means of a great loving heart *(mahākaruṇā)*, a great friendly spirit *(mahāmaitrī)*, morality *(śīla)*, great vows *(praṇidhāna)*, miraculous powers *(abhijñā)*, purposelessness *(anabhisaṁskāra)*, perfect disinterestedness *(anāyūha)*, skillful means born of transcendental wisdom *(prajñopāya)*, and transformations *(nirmāṇa)*.[5]

9. As these attributes are lacking in Śrāvakahood, its devotees are not allowed to join the congregation of Buddhas and Bodhisattvas. Even when they are in it they are incapable of appreciating all that goes on in such assemblages. The Mahāyāna is more than mere Emptiness, a great social spirit is moving behind it.

10. Lastly, we must remember that there is a sustaining power *(adhiṣṭhāna)* behind all these spiritual phenomena that are going on in Jetavana, and also behind all those transformation-Bodhisattvas who have gathered around the Buddha. This power comes from the Buddha himself. He is the great center and source of illumination. He is the sun whose light reaches the darkest corners of the universe and yet leaves no shadow anywhere. The Buddha of the *Gaṇḍavyūha* is, therefore, called Mahāvairocana-Buddha, the Buddha of Great Illumination.

6 From Maitreya's instructions given to Sudhana. MMG, pp. 1414–5.

8

In conclusion, let me quote the verse uttered by one of the Bodhisattvas[7] in praise of the virtues of the Buddha, by which we can see in what relationship he generally stands to his devotees in the *Gaṇḍavyūha*:

"1. The great Muni, the best of the Śākya, is furnished with all the perfect virtues; and those who see him are purified in mind and turn toward the Mahāyāna.

"2. That the Tathāgatas appear in the world is to benefit all beings; out of a great compassionate heart they revolve the wheel of the Dharma.

"3. The Buddhas have gone through many a heart-rending experience for ages, for the sake of sentient beings; and how can all the world requite them for what it owes them?

"4. Rather suffer terribly in the evil paths of existence for ever so many kalpas, than seek emancipation somewhere else by abandoning the Buddha.

"5. Rather suffer all the pain that may befall all beings, than find comfort where there are no Buddhas to see.

"6. Rather abide in the evil paths of existence if the Buddhas can all the time be heard, than be born in the pleasant paths and never have the chance to hear them.

"7. Rather be born in the hells, however long one has to stay in each one of them, than be delivered therefrom by cutting oneself away from the Buddhas.

"8. Why? Because even though one may stay long in the evil paths, one's wisdom will ever be growing if only the Buddha is to be seen.

"9. When the Buddha, the Lord of the world, is to be seen somewhere, all pain will be eradicated; and one will enter into a realm of great wisdom which belongs to the Tathāgatas.

"10. When the Buddha, the peerless one, is to be seen somewhere, all the hindrances will be cleared away, and infinite bliss will be gained and the way of enlightenment perfected.

7 Dharmadhātu-tala-bheda-jñāna-abhijñā-rāja is his name; he comes from the upper part of the world to take part in the Jetavana assembly. MMG, p. 86.

"11. When the Buddhas are seen, they will cut asunder all the doubts cherished by all beings, and give satisfaction to each according to his aspirations worldly and super-worldly."

The above is given to illustrate the attitude which is generally assumed toward the Buddha by the Bodhisattvas who come to the community from every possible quarter of the world. . . .

9

In many Mahāyāna sūtras, reference is quite frequently made to "the raising of thought unattached to anything." One of the most famous of such phrases occurs in the *Vajracchedikā,* which is said to have awakened the mind of Hui-nêng, the Sixth Patriarch of Zen Buddhism in China, to a state of enlightenment, and which has ever since been utilized by Zen masters for the exposition of their teaching. The phrase runs in Chinese, *Ying wu so chu êrh sheng ch'i hsin,* the original Sanskrit of which is, *Na kvacit pratiṣṭhitaṁ cittam utpādayitavyam.*[8] Freely translated, it is, "Let your mind (or thought) take its rise without fixing it anywhere." *Citta* is generally rendered as "thought" but more frequently it is "mind" or "heart." The Chinese character *hsin* has a much wider connotation than "thought" or "mind," for it also means the "center or reason of being" and is one of the most significant and comprehensive terms in Chinese philosophy as well as in conventional everyday Chinese. In this case, "to set up one's mind without fixing it anywhere" means "to be perfect master of oneself." When we are dependent on anything, we cannot be perfectly free; and it is then that the idea of an ego-soul or of a creator known as God is generally found to be taking hold of us. For this reason, we cannot act without attaching ourselves to something—a state of dependence and slavery. To the question, "Where are you?" we have to say, "I am tied to a pole"; and to the question, "What are the sights or limits *(ching)* of your monastery?" "I move within the circle whose radius is the full length of the rope which is attached to

[8] Max Müller, p. 27. [Ch. 10c.]

the pole." As long as as this rope is not cut off, we cannot be free agents. The rope has its length which is measurable, and the circle described by it has its calculable limits. We are puppets dancing on somebody else's string. But a circle whose circumference knows no limits, because of its having no central pole, and its string must be said to be a very large one indeed, and this is where a Zen master locates his residence. The circle, the field *(ching* or *gocara),* whose range is infinity, and therefore whose center is nowhere fixed, is thus the fit site for the Bodhisattva to have his abode.

In the *Aṣṭasāhasrikā-Prajñāpāramitā*[9] we have: "The Tathāgata's thought is nowhere fixed, it is not fixed on things conditioned, nor it is fixed on things unconditioned; and it is therefore never put out of fixation."[10] By "thought not being fixed" is meant psychologically that consciousness rises from an unconscious source, because, according to Buddhism, there is no such psychological or metaphysical entity as that which is known as the ego-soul, and which is generally regarded as making up the basis of an individual being, and which is therefore the point of fixation for all its mental activities. But as this point of fixation is to be wiped off in order to reach the state of Buddhahood, the Mahāyāna sūtras, especially the *Prajñāpāramitās,* lay the entire stress of their teaching upon the doctrine of Emptiness. For it is by means of this alone that one can be cut off from a fixation and free for ever from the shackles of transmigration.

Buddhism being a practical spiritual training, whatever statements it makes are direct expressions of experience, and no interposition of intellectual or metaphysical interpretation is permitted here. It may sound quaint and unfamiliar to say that thought or mind is to be set up without any point of fixation behind it, like a cloud which floats away in the sky with no screws or nails attached to it. But when the sense is grasped the idea of no-fixation is altogether to the point. It is generally better to leave the original expressions as they are, and let the

9 Mitra, p. 37.

10 *Apratiṣṭitamānaso hi tathāgato 'rhan samyaksaṁbuddaḥ. Sa naiva saṁskṛite dhātau sthito nāpy asaṁskṛite dhātau sthito na ca tato vyutthitaḥ.*

reader experience them within himself. Their conversion into modern terminology may frequently be very desirable, but the intelligibility thus gained is generally the result of abstraction or intellectualization. This gain naturally means the loss of concrete visualization, a loss which may well outweigh the gain.

In the *Vimalakīrti* also, we have such phrases as "Bodhi has no abode, therefore it is not to be attained"; or "Depending on a source which has no abode, all things are established"; and in the *Śuraṅgama:* "Such Bodhisattvas make all the Buddha lands their abode, but they are not attached to this abode, which is neither attainable nor visible." Expressions of this sort are encountered everywhere in the Mahāyāna texts.

The *Prajñāpāramitā Sūtras,* again, which are disposed to be negative in their statements, give among others the following: "The truth as given out by the Tathāgata is unattainable, it knows no obstruction, its non-obstructibility resembles space as no traces *(pada)* are left; it is above all forms of contrast, it allows no opposition, it goes beyond birth and death, it has no passageway whereby one may approach it. This truth is realizable by one who follows the Tathāgata as he is in his Suchness *(tathatā).* For this Suchness is something uniform, something beyond going and coming, something eternally abiding *(sthititā),* above change and separateness and discrimination *(nirvikalpā),* absolutely one, betraying no traces of conscious striving, etc."[11] As the truth *(dharma)* of the Tathāgata cannot be defined in any positive way, the *Prajñāpāramitā* has a series of negations. The only affirmative way is to designate it *tathatā,* "state of being so," or "suchness," or "so-ness." To those who know, the term is expressive and satisfying, but from the logical point of view it may mean nothing, it may be said to be devoid of content. This is inevitable; terms of intuition are always so, and all the truths belonging to the religious consciousness, however intellectual they may appear, after all belong to this class of terminology. "What am I?" "Where am I?" or "Whither am I bound"—the questions are raised by the intellect, but the solution is not at all logical. If it is not a series of negations, it is simply enigmatical, defying the ordinary way of understanding.

11 Abridged, *Aṣṭasāhasrikā-prajñāpāramitā,* Ch. XVI, on "Tathatā."

10

Having viewed the principle of life that regulates the activities of Bodhisattvahood as it is conceived by compilers of the *Prajñāpāramitā Sūtras,* etc., let us proceed to see how it is described in the *Gaṇḍavyūha.* The Zen master does not use abstract terms such as the principle of life; he always makes use of events of daily life and the concrete objects with which he is surrounded and with which his monks are quite familiar. When he asks them whence they come or whither they go, he can tell at once by the answer he gets where their abode is, that is, what is that which prompts them to a definite set of actions. This method of training may be considered too difficult for ordinary minds to grasp what is really behind it.

Nor may the doctrine of no-fixation be easy to take hold of for those who are not used to this way of expressing their spiritual conditions. To have their minds set to working without anything behind them, without anything holding them to a definite intelligible center, may sound like jargon. When we state that the abode of the Bodhisattva is really no abode, that he is fixed where he is not fixed, that he wanders or floats like a cloud in the sky without anything at its back, the statements may seem to have no meaning whatever. But this is the way the Mahāyāna Buddhists have been trained in their religious life, to which no stereotyped rules of syllogism can be applied.

We are now perhaps ready to see what we can gather from the *Gaṇḍavyūha* on this subject: "Where is the abode of the Bodhisattva?" This it has been from the first our intention to find out, especially in contrast to the Zen way of handling the same idea. In the *Gaṇḍavyūha* the question "Where?" stands out before us in the form of the Tower known as Vairocana-vyūha-alaṅkāra-garbha—that is, the "tower which holds within itself an array of brilliantly shining ornaments." Sudhana, the young pilgrim, stands before it and describes it as he looks at it, knowing that it is the site of residence for the Bodhisattva Maitreya. The description is not of an objective sort, it is based on the reflections of the young aspirant after Bodhisattvahood, reflections taken from all his past experiences and whatever instructions he has gained in his long pilgrimage. When the Vairocana Tower is thus described as the Vihāra (abode or retreat) of Maitreya, the attributes enumerated here apply not only to Maitreya himself but to all the Bodhisattvas of the past, present, and future, including all the Zen masters also who have really attained spiritual enlightenment. In short, the Tower is the abode of all the spiritual leaders who have followed the steps of the Buddha. All that is said here is not Sudhana's own idea as to where the Bodhisattva should have his spiritual residence; it is in fact the Mahāyāna ideal.

11

"This Tower[12] is the abode where they are delighted to live who understand the meaning of Emptiness, Formlessness, and Will-lessness; who understand that all things are beyond discrimination, that the Dharmadhātu is devoid of separateness, that a world of beings is not attainable, that all things are unborn.

"This is the abode where they are delighted to live who are not attached to any world, who regard all the habitable worlds as no home to live in, who have no desire for any habitation, refuge, devotion, who have shaken off all thoughts of evil passions.

"This is the abode where they are delighted to live who understand that all things are without self-nature; who no more discriminate things in any form whatever; who are free from ideas and thoughts; who are neither attached to nor detached from ideas.

"This is the abode where they are delighted to live who have entered into the depths of Prajñā-pāramitā; who know how to penetrate into the Dharmadhātu which looks out in all directions; who have quieted all the fires of evil passions; who have destroyed by means of their superior knowledge all the wrong views, desires, and self-conceit; who live a playful life issuing from all the Dhyānas, Emancipations, Samādhis, Samāpattis,

[12] These quotations are based mainly on the palm-leaf manuscript kept by the Royal Asiatic Society, London. Folio 247b *et seq.*, corresponding to MMG, p. 1264 ff.

Miraculous Powers, and Knowledges; who produce all the Bodhisattvas' realm of Samādhis; who approach the footsteps of all the Buddhas.

"This is the abode of all those who make one kalpa (eon) enter into all kalpas and all kalpas into one kalpa; who make one kshetra (land) enter into all kshetras and all kshetras into one kshetra, and yet each without destroying its individuality; who make one dharma (thing) enter into all dharmas and all dharmas into one dharma, and yet each without being annihilated; who make one sattva (being) enter into all sattvas and all sattvas into one sattva, and yet each retaining its individuality; who understand that there is no duality between one Buddha and all Buddhas and between all Buddhas and one Buddha; who make all things enter into one thought-moment *(kṣaṇa);* who go to all lands by the raising of one thought; who manifest themselves wherever there are beings; who are always mindful of benefiting and gladdening the entire world; who keep themselves under perfect control.

"This is the abode of all those who, though they themselves have already attained emancipation, manifest themselves into this world for the sake of maturing all beings; who, while not attached to this earthly habitation, go about everywhere in the world in order to do homage to all the Tathāgatas; who, while not moving away from their own abode, go about everywhere in order to accept all the orderly disposition of things in all the Buddha lands; who, while following the footsteps of all the Tathāgatas, do not become attached to the idea of a Buddha; who, while depending upon good friends, do not become attached to the thought of a good friend; who, while living among the evil ones, are yet free from the enjoyment of desires and pleasures; who, while entering into all kinds of thoughts, are yet in their minds free from them; who, while endowed with the body after the manner of the world, yet have no dualistic individualistic thoughts; who, while endowed with the body belonging to the Lokadhātu, are not separated from the Dharmadhātu; who while desiring to live through all the time that is yet to come, are free from the thought of duration; who manifest themselves in all the worlds without moving a hair's breath from the place where they are.

"This is the abode of all those who preach the Dharma which rarely falls in one's way; who enjoy the Dharma which is difficult to understand, deep in meaning, non-dualistic, formless, having nothing in opposition, beyond obtainability; who abide in good will and compassion all-embracing; who are not immersed in the realm of all the Śrāvakas and Pratyekabuddhas; who have gone beyond the realm of all evil beings; who are not soiled by any worldly conditions; who are abiding where all the Bodhisattvas are, where all the Pāramitā virtues are amassed, where all the Buddhas are enjoying their comfortable habitations.

"This is the abode of all those who have severed themselves from all form and gone beyond the order of all the Śrāvakas; who are enjoying themselves where all things are unborn, and yet do not stay in the unbornness of things; who live among impurities, not penetrating into the absolute truth which is detached from greed, though they are in no way attached to objects of greed; who enjoy practicing compassion with a heart unattached to the defilement of morbidity; who dwell in the world where the chain of origination prevails, but absolutely free from being infatuated with things of the world; who practice the four Dhyānas but are not born according to the bliss they bring about; who practice the four immeasurables but are not born in the world of form because of their wish to mature all beings; who practice the four formless Samāpattis but are not born in the world of no-form because of their wish to embrace all beings with a great loving heart; who practice tranquilization *(śamatha)* and contemplation *(vipaśyana),* but for the sake of maturing all beings do not themselves realize knowledge and emancipation; who practice great indifference but are not indifferent to the affairs of the world; who enjoy Emptiness but do not give themselves up to wrong views of mere nothingness; who putting themselves in the realm of formlessness, are ever bent on instructing beings attached to form; who have no vows for their own sake but do not cut themselves off from the vows belonging to the Bodhisattva; who are masters of all karma- and passion-hindrances and yet show themselves for the sake of maturing all beings, as if subject to karma- and passion-hindrances; who thoroughly know what is meant by birth and death and yet show themselves as if subject to birth and transformation and death; who are themselves beyond all the paths of existence, but for the sake of disciplining all beings show themselves entering into the various paths; who practice compassion but are not given up to petty kindnesses; who practice loving kindness but are not given up to attachments; who are joyous in heart but ever grieved over the sight of suffering beings; who practice indifference but never cease benefiting others; who are disciplined in the nine successive Samāpattis, but are not horror-stricken with the idea of being born in the world of desire; who are detached from all efforts but do not live in the realization of the limit of reality *(bhūtakoṭi);* who are living in the triple emancipation but do not come in contact with the emancipation of Śrāvakahood; who view the world from the viewpoint of the four noble truths but do not live in the realization of the fruit of Arhatship; who perceive the deep significance of the doctrine of non-origination but do not take to absolute annihilation; who discipline themselves according to the eight noble paths but do not seek for an absolute deliverance; who have gone beyond the state of commonalty but do not fall into the state of Śrāvakahood and Pratyekabuddahood; who know well what is the destiny of the five grasping Skandhas but do not look for the absolute annihilation of the Skandhas; who have gone beyond the path of the four Māras[13] but do not make distinction between them; who go beyond the six Āyatanas but do not desire their absolute annihilation; who enjoy Suchness but do not remain in the limit of reality; who appear as if teaching all the vehicles *(yāna)* but by no means forsake the Mahāyāna. This is indeed the abode of beings endowed with such virtues."

12

Sudhana the youth then uttered the following gāthās:

"Here is the venerable compassionate Maitreya endowed with a great loving heart and undefiled knowledge and intent on benefiting the world. He who abides in the stage of Abhisheka is the best son of all the Victorious Ones; he is absorbed in the contemplation of the Buddha realm.

[13] The four Māras (evil ones) are: Skandha (aggregates), Kleśa (passion), Devaputra (son of a god), and Mṛtyu (death).

"This is the abode of all the sons of enlightenment, whose renown is far-reaching, who are established in the realm of supreme knowledge and emancipation, who walk around in the Dharmadhātu, unattached and companionless.

"This is the abode of those who have grown powerful in self-control, charity, morality, patience, and strenuousness; who are thoroughly equipped with the supernatural powers gained by means of Dhyāna; who are established in the transcendental wisdom and power of the vows; who are in possession of the Pāramitā virtues of the Mahāyāna.

"This is the abode of those whose intelligence knows no attachment; whose heart is broad, expansive, and unfettered as the sky expands; who know all that is moving in time and all that exists and becomes.

"This is the abode of those wise men endowed with transcendental wisdom, who enter into the reason of all things as unborn, examine into the original essence of things as by nature like space, which like a bird in the sky neither works nor is dependent on anything else.

"This is the abode of those who understand that greed, anger, and folly have no self-nature, and that the rise of falsehood is caused by imagination, and yet who do not discriminate as to detaching themselves from greed, anger, and folly, and who have thus reached a state of peace and quietude.

"This is the abode of those who are skillful in the use of transcendental wisdom, knowing what is meant by the triple emancipation, the doctrine of the twofold truth, the eightfold noble path, the Skandhas, Dhātus, Āyatanas, and the chain of origination, and yet not falling into the way of disquietude.

"This is the abode of those who have acquired perfect peace as they see into the realm of knowledge which is free from obstruction and in which all the Buddha lands and beings with their imaginations and discriminations are quiescent, observing that all things have no self-nature.

"This is the abode of those who go about everywhere in the Dharmadhātu, unattached, depending on nothing, with no habitation, burden-free, like the wind blowing in the air, leaving no track of their wanderings.

"This is the abode of those who are renowned on account of

their love and compassion, for when they see those suffering beings in the evil paths of existence they would descend into the midst of the sufferers and experience their sharp pain on themselves, shedding their light of sympathy on all unfortunate ones.

"This is the abode of those who are like the leader of a caravan; for they, observing how a company of wanderers is out of the track, destitute, and lost like men born blind in the wrong narrow path of transmigration, lead them to the highway of emancipation.

"This is the abode of those who are brave and unconquerable in rescuing and giving a friendly consolation to all those beings who are seen entrapped in the net of birth, old age, and grief and death—the threatening fate that befalls the Skandhas.

"This is the abode of those who, seeing people struggle under the bonds of the passions, give them, like the great kind physician, the wonderful medicine of immortal knowledge, and release them by means of great expanding love.

"This is the abode of those who, like the boatman, carry people on the boat of the immaculate Dharma across the ocean of birth and death where they are seen suffering all forms of grief and pain.

"This is the abode of those who, like the fisherman, lift all beings from the ocean of becoming and carry them over the waves of evil passions where they are seen drowning themselves, and who will arouse in them the desire for all-knowledge which is pure and free from sensualities.

"This is the abode of those who have reached where great vows are made and things are always viewed with love, and who, like the young king of Garuda, looking upon all beings immersed in the ocean of becoming, lift them up.

"This is the abode of those who are illuminators of the world, going about like the sun and the moon in the sky of the Dharmadhātu, and pouring the light of knowledge and the halo of vows into the homes of all beings.

"This is the abode of those who, being devoted to the salvation of the world, do not relax their efforts for nayutas of kalpas to bring one being to maturity, and would do so with the entire world as with one being.

"This is the abode of those whose determination is as hard

as Vajra; for in order to benefit beings in one country they put forward their untiring efforts until the end of time, and would do so also for all beings in all the ten quarters.

"This is the abode of those whose intelligence is as deep as the ocean; for they never feel exhausted in their minds even when nayutas of kalpas expire before they can preach all the truth clouds as declared by the Buddhas in the ten quarters, not to speak of their making an assembly at one sitting, unbewildered, imbibe all the truth.

"This is the abode of those who wander about, unattached, visiting an indescribable ocean of countries, entering into the ocean-like assemblies of the Buddhas, and making an ocean of offerings to all the Buddhas.

"This is the abode of those who have practiced all kinds of virtue by entering into the ocean of deeds from the midst of eternity, by persistently arousing the ocean of vows, and, in order to benefit all beings, by going about in the world for ever so many kalpas.

"This is the abode of those who are endowed with an eyesight that knows no obstructions; for they can penetratingly see into all the innumerable countries at the end of a hair, into all the limitless lands where are the Buddhas, beings, and kalpas, thus with nothing left to them which cannot clearly be perceived by them.

"This is the abode of those who come forth from the meritorious Pāramitās as they are able to perceive the great ocean of kalpas in one moment of thought, together with the appearance in it of all Buddhas, all worlds, and all beings, with a transcendental intelligence which defies every hindrance standing in its way.

"This is the abode of those who are altogether free from obstruction in any form, being able to arouse an innumerable number of vows which are equal in measure to the number of atoms to which all the worlds may be crushed, or to the number of drops to which the water of the great oceans may be analyzed.

"This is the abode of those Buddha sons who, establishing and practicing the various phases of Praṇidhānas (vows), Dhāraṇis, Samādhis, and also of Dhyānas, and of Vimokshas (emancipations), make them established also in every one of limitless kalpas.

"Here abide all classes of those Buddha sons who enjoy planning and establishing varieties of treatises, stories, dogmas, discourses, and also the useful arts and places of enjoyment belonging to the world.

"Here abide those who practice in a Māyā-like way deeds of unobstructed emancipation by means of miraculous powers, by contriving means of salvation based on transcendental wisdom, by appearing everywhere in the various paths of existence in the ten quarters of the world.

"Here abide those Bodhisattvas who, ever since their first awakening of the desire for enlightenment, have perfected all the deeds of the Dharma full of merit, and reveal themselves mysteriously all over the Dharmadhātu in their innumerable bodies of transformation.

"This is the abode of those who are hard to approach because of their supernatural wisdom which grasps the Buddha knowledge in one moment of thought and accomplishes illimitable karma all of which issues from their wisdom, while the wisdom of worldly thought ends nowhere but in complete madness.

"This is the abode, the immaculate shelter, of those who, being the owners of unimpeded intelligence, walk about in utmost freedom through the Dharmadhātu, and whose minds go even beyond the limits of intelligibility.

"This is the abode of those peerless ones who walk about everywhere and enjoy staying everywhere without ever leaving a track behind, as their knowledge rests on absolute oneness.

"This is the abode of those spotless ones who, seeing into the original nature of all things as quiet and homeless as the sky, live in a realm which may be likened unto the vastness of space.

"Here abide those compassionate ones whose loving hearts and intelligence, being deeply stirred as they observe all beings groaning with grief and pain, are ever contriving for the welfare of the world.

"Here abide those who make themselves visible like the sun and the moon everywhere where there are beings, and deliver them from the snare of transmigration by means of Samādhi and emancipation.

"Here abide those Buddha sons, who, following the footsteps of the Buddhas, manifest themselves in all countries through endless kalpas.

"Here abide all the Buddha sons who, in conformity with the dispositions of all beings, are seen manifesting themselves in their transformation bodies like clouds universally in all the ten quarters.

"Here abide those great beings who have entered the realm of all the Buddhas, and are never tired of enjoying it and walking in it for nayutas of kalpas.

"Here abide those who, knowing well what characterizes each one of the innumerable indescribable Samādhis, manifest the Buddha realm as they enter into it.

"Here abide those who hold in one thought moment all the kalpas, countries, and Buddha names, and whose all-comprehending intelligence can in one moment take in all kalpas beyond calculation.

"Here abide those who perceive in one thought all immeasurable kalpas, and who, while conforming themselves to the worldly way of thinking, are free from ideas and discriminations.

"Here abide those who have trained themselves in Samādhis perceiving in one thought moment all the past, present, and future, while themselves living in emancipation.

"Here abide those who, sitting cross-legged and without moving away from their seats, are able to manifest themselves simultaneously in all the paths of existence in all the lands.

"Here abide those great bulls who drink from the Dharma ocean of all the Buddhas and crossing over the water of knowledge attain to all the virtues that are perfect and indestructible.

"Here abide those who know with an unimpeded mind the number of all the lands, kalpas, Dharmas, and Buddha names.

"Here abide the Buddha sons who are familiar with the number of all the lands of the past, present, and future, and even also instantaneously think of their birth and disappearance.

"Here abide those who, disciplining themselves in the life of the Bodhisattva, are thoroughly conversant with the life and the vows of all the Buddhas, as well as the various dispositions of all beings.

"In one particle of dust is seen the entire ocean of lands, beings, and kalpas, numbering as many as all the particles of dust that are in existence, and this fusion takes place with no obstruction whatever.

"So with all the dust particles, all the lands, beings, and kalpas which are also seen here in fusion with all their multifariousness of appearances.

"Here in this abode the Bodhisattvas reflect, in accordance with the truth of no-birth, on the self-nature of all things, on all the lands, on the divisions of time, on kalpas, and on the enlightened ones, who are detached from the idea that there is such a thing as self-nature.

"While abiding here they also perceive that the principle of sameness prevails in all beings, in all things, in all the Buddhas, in all the lands, and in all the vows.

"Sitting firmly here, they are engaged in disciplining all beings, in paying homage to all the Buddhas, reflecting on the nature of things.

"For nayutas of kalpas they have been working for the perfection of the vows, knowledge, condition, mentality, conduct, the extent of which is indeed beyond description, beyond estimation.

"Before an immense amount of works accomplished by those irreproachable beings who are in enjoyment of their life of non-obstruction here, I bow and pay them my homage.

"O noble Maitreya, thou art the eldest son of the Buddha, thou livest a life of non-obstruction, thy immaculate knowledge goes beyond form; thinking of this I prostrate myself before thee."

13

Sudhana now asks the Bodhisattva Maitreya to open the Tower and allow him to enter. The Bodhisattva approaches and snaps his fingers, and lo! the doors open. How gladly Sudhana enters, when they close by themselves as mysteriously as they had opened before!

What a sight is now revealed before him!

The Tower is as wide and spacious as the sky itself. The ground is paved with asamkhyeyas[14] of precious stones of all kinds, and there are within the Tower asamkhyeyas of palaces, porches, windows, staircases, railings, and passages, all of

[14] Literally, innumerable.

which are made of the seven kinds of precious gems. There are again banners, canopies, strings, nets, and hangings of various shapes, also made of precious stones—asamkhyeyas in number. Asamkheyas of bells tinkle in the breeze, asamkhyeyas of flowers are showered, asamkhyeyas of wreaths are swinging, asamkhyeyas of incense burners stand everywhere, asamkhyeyas of golden flakes are scattered, asamkhyeyas of mirrors are shining, asamkhyeyas of lamps are burning, asamkhyeyas of robes are spread, asamkhyeyas of gem thrones covered with asamkhyeyas of tapestries are arranged in rows.

There are also asamkhyeyas of figures of various sorts, made of pure Jambūnada gold or of precious stones—figures of young maidens, of Bodhisattvas, etc.

Asamkhyeyas of beautiful birds are singing melodiously, asamkhyeyas of lotus flowers in several colors are in full bloom, asamkhyeyas of trees are planted in regular rows, asamkhyeyas of great mani jewels are emitting their exquisite rays of light—and all these asamkhyeyas of beautifully set-up decorations of precious stones fill the spacious Tower as far as it extends.

And within this Tower, spacious and exquisitely ornamented, there are also hundreds of thousands of asamkhyeyas of towers, each one of which is as exquisitely ornamented as the main Tower itself and as spacious as the sky. And all these towers beyond calculation in number stand not at all in one another's way; each preserves its individual existence in perfect harmony with all the rest; there is nothing here that bars one tower being fused with others individually and collectively; there is a state of perfect intermingling and yet of perfect orderliness. Sudhana the young pilgrim sees himself in all the towers as well as in each single tower, where all is contained in one and each contains all.

Finding himself in this wonderful sight and with his mind wandering from one mystery to another, his joy knows no bounds. He is free from all individualistic ideas, from all the hindrances, from all the bewilderments; for he is now in the midst of an emancipation which goes beyond all limitations.

Sustained by the power of the Bodhisattva Maitreya, Sudhana finds himself in each one of these towers simultaneously where he perceives an endless series of wonderful events taking place in regard to the Bodhisattva's life. That is to say, he sees how the Bodhisattva Maitreya first comes to rouse his devotional heart toward the realization of supreme enlightenment; he sees what is his name, who are his family and his friends, what good stock of merit he plants, what is his age, what Buddha land he is engaged in arraying, what discipline he undergoes, what vows he makes, what assemblies of Buddhas and Bodhisattvas he attends, and for how many kalpas he personally serves Buddhas and pays them homage—all these things in the life of the Bodhisattva Maitreya, Sudhana sees.

Sudhana sees how the Bodhisattva Maitreya for the first time attains the Samādhi called Maitra (compassion) and how after that the Bodhisattva comes to be known as Maitreya. He sees again by the Bodhisattva Maitreya what deeds are performed, what Pāramitās perfected, what Kshāntis gained, what stages of Bodhisattvahood attained, what Buddha land put in order, what Buddhist doctrines maintained. He sees again how Maitreya realizes the truth that all things are unborn, and when, where, and under what Tathāgata he is assured of supreme enlightenment.

Sudhana sees that in a certain tower the Bodhisattva is requested by a ruler of the world to lead all beings to the practice of the ten deeds of morality, that he is asked by a world protector to benefit and gladden all beings, that he is asked by Sakra to subjugate the pleasure-hunting instincts of all beings, by Brahma to praise the immeasurable merits of Dhyāna, by the god Yāma to praise the immeasurable merits of thoughtfulness, by the god of Tushita to eulogize the virtues of the Bodhisattva who becomes a Buddha in his next birth, by the god Nirmita to manifest himself in his transformation bodies for the sake of the heavenly beings, by the god Vaśavartin to preach Buddhism to his followers.

Sudhana sees that, becoming the king of evil ones, the Bodhisattva demonstrates the evanescence of all things, that for the sake of Asura he dives into the depths of the ocean of knowledge, and, seeing that all things are like a vision, teaches Asura and his army to put away all their pride, arrogance, and intoxication. Sudhana sees the realm of the dead displayed where the Bodhisattva radiating a great light is engaged in delivering all beings from the pain of the hells; he sees the Bodhisattva in the world of the hungry ghosts where he gives away all kinds of food and drink to relieve the inhabitants of their intense sufferings; he sees the Bodhisattva in the kingdom of beasts where he disciplines the creatures by varieties of means. He sees the Bodhisattva preaching the Dharma to the groups of beings in the heavens of the world protector, the Tushita, the Yāma, the Nirmita, the Vaśarvartin, and the Brahma Indra; to the groups of the Nāgas, the Yakshas and Rakshas, the Gandharvas, the Asuras, the Garuḍas, the Kinnaras, the Mahoragas, the Manushyas, and the Amanushyas. He sees the Bodhisattva preaching the Dharma to the groups of the Śrāvakas, Pratyekabuddhas, and of the Bodhisattvas from the first stage to the last. He sees the Bodhisattva eulogizing the merits of Bodhisattvahood in all stages, the fulfillment of all the Pāramitā virtues, the realization of all the Kshāntis, the attainment of all the great Samādhis, the deepness of the emancipation, the realm of the mysterious powers accruing from the Dhyānas and Samādhis, the Bodhisattva's life and deeds of devotion, and his vows. He also sees the Bodhisattva Maitreya, together with other Bodhisattvas of the same society, praising worldly business and all forms of craftsmanship which would increase the happiness of all beings. He sees the Bodhisattva Maitreya together with other Bodhisattvas who are to be Buddhas in another birth praising the Abhisheka (baptism) of all the Buddhas. He also sees the Bodhisattva Maitreya untiringly engaged in the performance of the various acts of devotion, in the practice of the Dhyānas and the four immeasurables, the Kṛitsnāyatanas, and the emancipations, in the displaying of the various mystic powers by the means gained in the Samādhis.

Sudhana sees the Bodhisattva Maitreya together with other Bodhisattvas enter into a Samādhi and issue from every single pore of their skin multitudes of transformation-bodies: clouds of heavenly beings, clouds of the Nāgas, Yakshas, Gandharvas, Asuras, Garuḍas, Kinnaras, Mahoragas, Śakras, Brahmas, Lokapālas, great sovereigns, minor lords, royal princes, state ministers, court dignitaries, wealthy householders, and lay disciples, clouds of Śrāvakas, Pratyekabuddhas, Bodhisattvas, and Tathāgatas, and clouds of all beings.

Sudhana now hears all the teachings and doctrines of the Buddha melodiously issuing from every single pore of the skin of all the Bodhisattvas—such teachings as concern the merits of Bodhicitta, charity, morality, patience, strenuousness, meditation, transcendental knowledge, the four forms of acceptance, the immeasurables, tranquilization *(samādhi)*, concentration *(samāpatti)*, miraculous powers, sciences *(vidyā)*, Dhāraṇis, intellectual perspicuity *(pratibhāna)*, truths *(satya)*, knowledges, Śamatha, Vipaśyana, emancipations, chain of origination, refuges *(pratiśaraṇa)*, utterances *(udhāna)*, subjects of memory, attendance *(upasthāna)*, right efforts, miracles, roots of strength *(indriyas)*, powers, the seven factors of enlightenment, the eightfold path of righteousness, the vehicle of Śrāvakahood, the vehicle of Pratyekabuddhahood, the vehicle of Bodhisattvahood, the stages of Bodhisattvahood, Kshāntis, deeds of devotion, and vows.

Sudhana sees the Buddhas surrounded each by his assemblies; he sees their various places of birth, their families, their forms, ages, kalpas, countries, names, discourses on the Dharma, ways of benefiting all beings, periods of continuation, etc., which vary according to different Buddhas.

Sudhana sees one especially high, spacious, and most exquisitely decorated tower, incomparably beautiful, among all the towers that are to be seen inside the Vairocana Tower. In this peerless tower, he sees all the tri-chiliocosm at one glance, containing hundreds of kotis of Tushita heavens. And in each one of these worlds he sees the Bodhisattva Maitreya's descent on earth and his birth, and Śakra, Brahma, and other celestial beings paying respect to the Bodhisattva, his walking seven steps, his surveying of the ten quarters, his lion roar, his child life in the court, the royal pavilion, and the pleasure ground, his renunciation for the sake of all-knowledge, his ascetic life, his accepting the milk, his visit to the ground of spiritual discipline, his subjugation of the army of the Evil One, his attainment of supreme enlightenment under the Bodhi tree, Brahma's request to revolve the Dharma wheel, the Buddha's ascent to the heavens to discourse on the Dharma; while his kalpa, his duration of life, his assemblies, the arraying of his country, the purification of lands, deeds of discipline, vows, the maturing of beings, the distribution of the ashes, the maintenance of the Dharma are seen to differ according to different Buddhas.

At this moment Sudhana finds himself to be with all those Buddhas who are performing the various works of Buddhahood among various assemblies. He is deeply impressed with these scenes which are never to be forgotten.

Then he hears all the bells large and small, all the jewel nets, all the musical instruments in all the towers preaching varieties of teachings in perfect melody and harmony beyond human conception. One voice is heard to be the teaching about the Bodhisattva's rousing the desire for enlightenment, another to be the teaching about the practice of the Pāramitās, another to be concerned with various vows, the states of Bodhisattvahood, the paying homage and making offerings to the Buddhas, the arraying of the Buddha lands, the differences of discourses to be given by different Buddhas—all these teachings in the form of heavenly music are heard proclaimed in their fullness.

Sudhana hears a voice, which says that certain Bodhisattvas are discoursing on such doctrines at such places, rousing the desire for enlightenment under the guidance of such good friends, listening to such Buddha's sermons in such assemblies of Bodhisattvas, in such kalpas, in such countries.

Sudhana hears another voice, saying that these Bodhisattvas on account of these merits awaken such desire, make such vows, plant a great stock of merit, and, after continuing deeds of Bodhisattvahood for a certain number of kalpas, attain supreme enlightenment, assume such names, live so long, complete the arraying of such countries, fulfill such vows, teach such beings, such Śrāvakas, and such Bodhisattvas, and after Nirvāṇa see the Dharma continuing to thrive for the benefit and happiness of all beings.

Sudhana hears another voice, saying that certain Bodhisattvas are at such places, practicing the six Pāramitās; that certain other Bodhisattvas at other places abandon the throne and all their precious possessions, even their own limbs, heads, and entire bodies ungrudgingly for the sake of the Dharma; that still other Bodhisattvas in other places, in order to guard the Dharma of all the Tathāgatas against corruption, become great teachers of the Dharma, strenuously engaged in its propagation and transmission, in erecting the Buddhist stupas and shrines, in producing Buddhist figures, and also in giving people what pleases them.

Sudhana hears another voice, saying that such Tathāgatas are in such places and in such kalpas and, after attaining supreme enlightenment, are living in such countries, in such assemblies, living so long, preaching such doctrines, fulfilling such vows, and teaching such innumerable beings.

Listening to these exquisitely melodious voices beyond human conception, Sudhana the young pilgrim is exceedingly gladdened in his heart. He attains innumerable Dhāraṇis, eloquences, deeds of devotion, vows, Pāramitās, miraculous powers, knowledges, sciences, emancipations, and Samādhis.

Sudhana sees again in all the mirrors figures and images of all sorts beyond calculation. That is, he sees representations of all the spiritual assemblages conducted by Buddhas, by Bodhisattvas, by Śrāvakas, by Pratyekabuddhas; he sees representations of lands of defilement, of lands of purity, of worlds with no Buddhas in them, of worlds large, middling, and small, of worlds with nets of Indra, of worlds irregularly shaped, of worlds even-surfaced, of worlds where there are the hells, the hungry ghosts, and all sorts of beasts, of worlds inhabited by celestial and human beings.

And in these worlds there are asamkhyeyas of Bodhisattvas walking, sitting, engaged in all kinds of work, doing charitable deeds out of a great compassionate heart, writing various treatises whereby to benefit the world, receiving them from the master, holding them for the future generations, copying them, reciting them, asking questions, answering them, or practicing confession three times a day and dedicating the merit to the attainment of enlightenment, or raising bows for the sake of all beings.

Sudhana sees all the pillars emitting all kinds of mani-jewel light: blue, yellow, red, white, crystal-colored, water-colored, rainbow-colored, colored like purified gold, and in all colors of light.

Sudhana sees figures of young maidens in Jambūnada gold and other figures made of precious stones. Some hold in their hands clouds of flowers, some clouds of draperies, banners, streamers, canopies, wreaths; some others hold incense of various kinds, precious nets of mani-jewels; some wear gold chains, necklaces of precious gems; some have on their arms varieties of ornaments; some are decorated with mani-gem crowns. Bending their bodies, they all gaze intently at the Buddhas.

Sudhana sees the scented water possessing eightfold merit issuing from the necklaces of pearl, long rays of bright light streaming from necklaces of lapis lazuli; he sees banners, nets, streamers, and canopies, all of which are made of various kinds of precious stones, most pleasing to the eye.

Sudhana sees the ponds planted with all kinds of lotus such as the Utpala, the Kumuda, the Puṇḍarīka, the Padma, each one of which bears innumerable flowers varying in magnitude; and within every flower are seen beautifully arrayed multitudes of figures, all with the body bent and hands folded in a most reverential attitude: men, women, young boys, young girls, Śakras, Brahmas, Lokapālas, Devas, Nāgas, Yakshas, Gandharvas, Asuras, Garuḍas, Kinnaras, Mahoragas, Śrāvakas, Pratyekabuddhas, and Bodhisattvas.

Sudhana sees the Tathāgatas, sitting cross-legged, who are fully arrayed with the thirty-two marks of great manhood.

Sudhana sees the ground perfectly paved with lapis lazuli, where at every step there are representations of wonderful things and personages, such as Buddha lands, Bodhisattvas, Tathāgatas, and towers in full array.

Sudhana sees in the jewel-made trees, branches, leaves, flowers, and fruits, the wonderful bust-representations of Buddhas, Bodhisattvas, Devas, Nāgas, Yakshas, Lokapālas, Cakravartins, kings of lesser importance, royal princes, state ministers, head officers, and of the four classes of Buddhists. Some of those representations are seen carrying flower wreaths in their hands, some jewel wreaths, some all kinds of ornamental articles. They are all in a most reverential attitude with the body bent forward and with the hands folded, intensely gazing at the Buddhas. Some praise the Buddhas, while others are in deep meditation. Their bodies in full array emit varieties of lights in different colors: gold, silver, coral, Tūshara, Indra blue, Vairocana jewel, Campaka, etc.

Sudhana sees in those crescent-representations in the towers asamkhyeyas of suns, moons, stars, constellations, and luminosities of all kinds, which illumine all the ten quarters.

Sudhana sees all the towers surrounded on all sides with walls which are ornamented at every step with all sorts of precious stones, and in each one of these stones the Bodhisattva Maitreya is seen reflected as he practiced in his past lives deeds of Bodhisattvahood. He is seen giving away his own head, eyes, limbs, lips, teeth, tongue, bones, marrow, etc. He is also seen giving away all his belongings such as wives, mistresses, maids, servants, towns, palaces, villages, countries, and even his own throne, to whomsoever needed them. He liberates those who are kept in prison, he releases those who are in bondage, he heals those who are afflicted with diseases, he leads back to the right path those who have gone astray. Becoming a boatman he helps people to cross the sea; becoming a charioteer he rescues people from disasters; becoming a great sage he discourses on various teachings; becoming a great sovereign he practices on himself the ten deeds of goodness and induces people to do the same; becoming a physician he heals all sorts of disease. To the parents he is a filial son, to friends a faithful companion. He becomes a Śrāvaka, a Pratyekabuddha, a Bodhisattva, a Tathāgata, thereby disciplining, educating, and teaching all beings. He becomes announcer of the Dharma in order to serve the cause of Buddhism by accepting, holding and reading it, by reflecting on it in the proper way, by erecting Caityas for the Buddhas, by making their images, by paying them homage not only by himself but making others do the same, by making them offerings, incense, and flowers, by repeating all these deeds of religious devotion without interruption.

Further, the Bodhisattva Maitreya is seen to be sitting on a lion throne giving to all beings sermons on the Dharma, instructing them in the ten deeds of goodness, in the threefold refuge, in the five precepts, and the eightfold Poshadha; and further, he teaches people to lead the life of a recluse, to listen to the Dharma, to accept and hold it, and to reflect on it in the right way. The Bodhisattva appears again represented as practicing the six Pāramitās and all other deeds of devotion for ever so many innumerable asamkhyeyas of kalpas; and all those good friends whom the Bodhisattva served in his past lives are seen as fully arrayed with multitudes of virtues. The Bodhisattva Maitreya is again seen himself as befriended by all the good friends.

Then those good friends said: "O Sudhana, thou art welcome! As thou seest all these wonderful things belonging to Bodhisattvahood, thou mayest not be fatigued!"

14

After this, the sūtra continues to explain how it came to pass that Sudhana the young pilgrim was permitted by the Bodhisattva Maitreya to be the witness of all these wonderful sights.

That Sudhana the young pilgrim should see all these and many other innumerable wonderful transformations in full array and beyond human conception, which were going on in each one of the towers, was because he had gained a power of memory which never allowed anything to slip off the mind, because he had gained a pure eye to survey all the ten quarters, because he had gained a knowledge which sees unobstructedly, because he had gained the Bodhisattva-knowledge, his sustaining power, and perfect mastery over things, because he had gained the far-reaching knowledge which belongs to those Bodhisattvas who have already entered on the first stage.

It is like the way of one who sees in his sleep all manner of things such as towns, villages, hamlets, mansions, parks, mountains, woods, rivers, lakes, dresses, provisions, and everything that is needed for a comfortable living. He may also see his own parents, brothers, relatives, great oceans, Mount Sumeru, all the celestial palaces, Jambudvīpa, etc.; he may also see his own body stretched out in size over hundreds of yojanas and the house wherein he lives and the garments which he wears and other things correspondingly grown up in magnitude. While his experience may have lasted just one day or one night, he will imagine it to have been a period of incalculable length, and that for ever so long he had been the recipient of all kinds of enjoyment and pleasurable excitement. When he is awakened, he realizes that all that appeared to him was in a dream though everything is perfectly remembered by him.

Similarly, Sudhana has been the witness of all these wonders *(vikurvita)* because of the sustaining powers of the Bodhisattva Maitreya, because of his knowledge that the triple world is like a dream, because of his having put an end to the limited knowledge shared by all beings, because of his attainment of an extensive, unobstructed understanding, because of his abiding in the unexcelled thought and spiritual state of Bodhisattvahood, because of his inconceivable knowledge whereby he can conform himself to the understandings of all beings.

When a man is about to die, he sees all that is going to happen to him after his death according to the life he lived. If he had been a doer of evil deeds, he will have a vision of a hell, or the realm of the hungry ghosts, or that of the beasts where all forms of pain are being suffered. He may see the demons armed with terrible weapons maltreating all those who have fallen into their hands. He may hear the wailing voices of lamentation or screams of pain. He may see the stream of alkaline, the boiling cauldron, the razor hill, the forest of thorns, the sword-leaved trees—all of which are meant to torment and harass the wicked. Whereas, those who had behaved properly may see the celestial palaces, celestial beings, celestial maidens, beautiful robes, exquisitely arrayed gardens and terraces, etc. Though they are not yet quite dead, they are able, because of their karma, to have such visions before them. Similarly, Sudhana has been able to see those wonderful scenes on account of his inconceivable Bodhisattva karma.

Again, like a spirit-seized man who can answer any question asked of him, Sudhana has been able to see those wonders and answer whatever questions have been asked of him because of his being sustained by the knowledge of the Bodhisattva Maitreya.

Again, like a man who, imagining himself to be a Nāga under the spell of the Nāgas, has entered into their palaces, and, spending a short time there, thinks he has passed many a year with them, Sudhana, because of his abiding in the knowledge belonging to Bodhisattvahood and also because of his being sustained by the power of the Bodhisattva Maitreya, has been able to see events of many a kalpa in the twinkling of an eye.

Again, like the Brahma palace called Vyūhagarbha surpassing anything of this world, where all the chiliocosm is seen comprehended and yet with all things in perfect order, all things in the Vairocana Tower were seen by Sudhana distributed in perfect scale so that all the differences did not at all interfere with one another.

Again, like a Bhikshu abiding in a Samāpatti called Kṛitsnāyatana, who, whether walking or sitting or standing or lying, sees all the world presented in the light of the Dhyāna in which he is, Sudhana too saw in a clear light all the wonderful scenes in the Tower.

Again, it is like a man's seeing the city of Ġandharvas in the sky, which is in full array with all kinds of ornamentation, without intermingling, without obstructing one another.

Again, it is like the Yakshas' abodes and the human worlds occupying the same space, and yet distinctly separate from one another so that one can see either of them according to one's karma.

Again, it is like the great ocean where one can see reflected everything that is in the chiliocosm.

Again, it is like the magician who because of his knowledge of the art can create all manner of things and make them do the same work.

Similarly, Sudhana, because of the sustaining power of the Bodhisattva Maitreya, because of his inconceivable power of Māyā knowledge, has been enabled to see all the wonderful transformations in the Tower.

15

At that time the Bodhisattva Maitreya, suspending his miraculous power, entered into the Tower, and snapping his fingers said this to Sudhana the young pilgrim:

"O son of a good family, arise! Such is the nature of all things appearing as they do in the accumulation and combination of conditions; such is the self-nature of things, which is not complete in itself, being like a dream, a vision, a reflection."

At that time Sudhana, hearing the sound of the fingers snapped rose from the Samādhi. Maitreya continued: "Seest thou now the wondrous transformations of the Bodhisattva, the outflowings of his power, the propagation of his vows and wisdom, the joy of his final beatitude, his deeds of devotion, the immeasurable array of the Buddha land, the unsurpassable vows of the Tathāgata, the inconceivable way of emancipation belonging to Bodhisattvahood, the pleasures of the Samādhi enjoyed by the Bodhisattva—these things seest thou and understandingly followest thou?"

Said Sudhana: "Yes, I do, O Venerable Sir, by the wondrous sustaining power of the good friend. But pray tell me, what is this emancipation?"

Maitreya: "This is known as the Vyūhagarbha in which the knowledge of all the triple chiliocosm is contained, retained, and never put out of memory. O son of a good family, in this emancipation there are more emancipations than can be described and enumerated, which can be attained only by the one-birth Bodhisattva."

Sudhana: "O Venerable Sir, pray tell me whither does all this go?"

Maitreya: "Where it comes from."

Sudhana: "Whence comes it?"

Maitreya: "It comes from the knowledge and the sustaining power of the Bodhisattva. It goes nowhere, it passes away nowhere, there is no accumulation, no increase, no standing still, no attachment, no dependence on the earth or in the sky.

"O son of a good family, it is like the Nāga-king's pouring forth the rain: it does not issue from his body, nor does it from his mind, nor is there any accumulation within him, but it comes from the mind power of the Nāga—this showering over the entire world. It goes beyond human comprehensibility.

"O son of a good family, it is the same with the arraying of things thou hast seen. It comes neither from within, nor from without, yet it is before thee, coming out of the wondrous power of the Bodhisattva, because of the merit of goodness thou hast accomplished.

"O son of a good family, it is like the art of a magician,

whose magical creations do not come from anywhere, nor do they pass away anywhere, yet they are seen as existing before people because of the spell of the mantram.

"Similarly, O son of a good family, the wonderful arraying of things thou hast seen comes from nowhere, passes away nowhere, stays nowhere accumulated, and it is there just because the Bodhisattva is to learn of his inconceivable Māyā knowledge, because of the all-sustaining and all-ruling power of the Bodhisattva's vows and knowledge."

Sudhana: "O Venerable Sir, pray tell me whence thou comest."

Maitreya: "The Bodhisattva comes as neither coming nor going; the Bodhisattva comes as neither moving nor staying, as neither dead nor born, as neither staying nor passing away, as neither departing nor rising, as neither hoping nor getting attached, as neither doing nor reaping the reward, as neither being born nor gone to annihilation, as neither eternal nor bound for death.

"And yet, O son of a good family, it is in this way that the Bodhisattva comes: he comes where an all-embracing love abides, because he desires to discipline all beings; he comes where there is a great compassionate heart, because he desires to protect all beings against sufferings; he comes where there are deeds of morality, because he desires to be born wherever he can be agreeable; he comes wherever there are great vows to fulfill because of the power of the original vows; he comes out of the miraculous powers because wherever he is sought after he manifests himself to please people; he comes where there is effortlessness because he is never away from the footsteps of all the Buddhas; he comes where there is neither giving nor taking because in his movements mental and physical there is no trace of striving; he comes out of the skillful means born of transcendental knowledge because he is ever in conformity with the mentalities of all beings; he comes where transformations are manifested because all that appears is like a reflection, like a transformed body.

"This being the case, O son of a good family, yet thou askest whence I come. As to that, I am here from my native country, Maladi. My object is to teach the Dharma to a young man called Gopālaka and all the other people living in my district each according to his or her fitness. It is also to get their parents, relatives, Brahmans, and others into the way of the Mahāyāna. . . ."

16

We are now in the position to ascertain where the Bodhisattva Maitreya, representing the entire family of Bodhisattvas, keeps his final abode and also what kind of abode this is. We notice the following points:

Since the Indian imagination is very much richer and more creative than the Chinese, the description of the Vairocana-alankāra-vyūha-garbha, which is the abode of Bodhisattvahood, may appear at first sight quite different from the simple and direct way in which the Chinese Zen master expresses himself. When the latter is asked where his abode is, he does not waste many words in describing it, he is not at all prolix, as we have already seen elsewhere. This is what most specifically characterizes Zen, while the *Gaṇḍavyūha* goes far beyond Zen; for it is not satisfied with merely pointing at the Tower, or entering into it with the snapping of the fingers, or exclaiming with a Japanese *haiku* poet:

> Oh! This is Yoshino!
> What more can I say?
> The mountain decked with cherry blossoms!

Every kind of imagery is resorted to in order to bring home to the reader's imagination the real nature of the Tower. This verbosity, however, helps him, in a way better than the Zen master, we might say, to get acquainted with the object of his curiosity, for we find this:

1. That Maitreya's Tower is no other than the Dharmadhātu itself;

2. That the Dharmadhātu is from one point of view different from the Lokadhātu which is this world of relativity and individuality, while from another point of view the Dharmadhātu is the Lokadhātu;

3. That the Dharmadhātu is not a vacuum filled with empty abstractions, but is brimful of concrete individual realities, as we can see from the use of the words *vyūha* and *alaṅkāra*;

4. That in the multiplicity of objects filling up the Dharmadhātu, however, there is perfect orderliness;

5. That this orderliness is decribed as: *Asya kūtāgāravyūhā anyonyā saṁbhinnā anyonyā maitrībhūtā anyonyā saṅkīrṇāḥ pratibhāsayogena 'bhāsam agamannekasminnārambaṇe yathā caikasminnārambaṇe tathā 'śeṣasarvārambaṇeṣu*;[15]

6. That in the Dharmadhātu, therefore, there is an interfusion of all individual objects, each of which, however, retaining all its individuality there is in it;

7. That there is not only a universal interfusion of things in such a way that in one object all the rest of the objects are reflected, but there is a reflection in each one of them of one personality known as Sudhana;

8. That the Dharmadhātu is, therefore, generally characterized as *anāvaraṇa*, "unobstructed," meaning that there is here a state of interpenetration of all objects in spite of their divisibility and mutual resistance;

9. That the Dharmadhātu is a world of radiance where not only each object of Alaṅkāra shines in its own light variously colored, but it does not refuse to take in or reflect the light of others as they are;

10. That all these wonderful phenomena, and indeed the Dharmadhātu itself, take their rise through the sustaining power of the Bodhisattva which is symbolized in the *Gaṇḍavyūha* by the "snapping of fingers";

11. That the sustaining power, Adhishṭhāna, while not expressly defined, is composed of the Bodhisattva's Pranidhāna (vow) and Jñāna (knowledge);

12. That when this Dharmadhātu, where such an exquisitely beautiful and altogether inconceivable spectacle takes place,

15 The Royal Asiatic Society MS, folio 270a. Freely rendered: "The objects are arrayed in such a way that their mutual separateness no more exists, as they are all fused, but each object thereby never losing its individuality, for the image of the Maitreya devotee is reflected in each one of the objects, and this not only in specific quarters but everywhere all over the Tower, so that there is a thoroughgoing mutual interreflection of images." (MMG, p. 1376.)

is psychologically described, the *Gaṇḍavyūha* has this: *Abhisyanditakāyacittaḥ sarvasaṃjñāgatavidhūtamānasaḥ sarvāvaraṇavivarjitacittaḥ sarvamohavigataḥ.*[16] And it was in this state of mind that Sudhana could remember all he saw and all he heard, that he could survey the world with a vision which knew no obstructions in whichever direction it moved, and that he could circulate in the Dharmadhātu with his body, nothing checking its perfectly free movements.

17

To a certain extent, let us hope, we have succeeded in delineating the inner nature and constitution of the Vairocana Tower both in terms of experience and from the point of view of intellectual clarification. After "What" comes "Whence" and "Whither." Without these, indeed, our inquiry into life will not be a complete one. Sudhana, therefore, naturally asks, after seeing all the wonders of the Tower, whence it comes and whither it passes. The Bodhisattva Maitreya answers that it comes from the Jñāna (knowledge) and the Adhishṭhāna (sustaining power) of the Bodhisattva. What is this Jñāna? What is this Adhishṭhāna?

Jñāna is a difficult term to translate, for "knowledge" or "intellection" does not cover its entire sense. It is something more fundamental. It is man's innate urge to discriminate, his constitutional inclination to dualism whereby subject and object, seer and the seen, are separated; it is that which makes a world of multiplicities possible. When, therefore, it is said that all the Vyūhas come forth from the midst of Jñāna, it has no other meaning than this, that the world evolves itself from the very constitution of our mind, that it is the content of our consciousness, that it is there simultaneously with the awakening of a mind which discriminates, that it comes and departs as mysteriously as our consciousness does. It is not proper in fact to ask whence is the world, or whither. The

16 R.A.S. MS, folio 270a; MMG, p. 1376. "Sudhana the young pilgrim felt as if both his body and mind completely melted away; he saw that all thoughts departed away from his consciousness; in his mind there were no impediments, and all intoxications vanished."

question itself issues from the very source of all mysteries and inconceivabilities, and to ask it is to defeat its own end. Its answer is possible only when we stand away from the conditions in which we are. That is to say, the question is answered only when it is no more asked. It is like fire's asking: "What am I?" "Whence do I come?" "Whither do I go?" "Why do I burn?" As long as fire is fire and keeps on burning these questions are unanswerable, because fire is to burn, just to burn, and not to reflect on itself; because the moment it reflects it is no more fire; because to know itself is to cease to be itself. Fire cannot transcend its own conditions, and its asking questions concerning itself is transcending them, which is to deny itself. The answer is possible when it contradicts itself. While standing still, we cannot leap. This contradiction is in the very essence of all intellectual questions as to the origin and the destiny of life. Hence Maitreya's statement: *na kvacid gato, nānugato, na rāśībhūto, na saṁcayabhūto, na kūṭastho, na bhāvastho, na deśastho, na pradeśasthaḥ.*[17] These negations, one may think, lead us nowhere, and naturally so, because the real answer lies where the question has not yet been asked.

Our next dealing will be with Adhishṭhāna. What does this mean? This is generally translated in Chinese as *shên-li* or *wei-li,* or *chia-chih-li.* It is "power," "will power," "spiritual power" belonging to a great personality, human or divine. As long as we remain on the plane of Jñāna, the world does not seem to be very real, as its Māyā-like existence in which it presents itself to Jñāna is too vapory; but when we come to the Adhishṭhāna aspect of Bodhisattvahood, we feel as if we have taken hold of something solid and altogether sustaining. This is where life really begins to have its meaning. To live ceases to be the mere blind assertion of a primordial urge, for Adhishṭhāna is another name for Praṇidhāna, or it is that spiritual power emanating from the Praṇidhāna which constitutes with Jñāna the essence of Bodhisattvahood. Adhishṭhāna is not mere power which likes to assert itself against others. Behind it there is always a Buddha or Bodhisattva, who is

17 MMG, p. 1413. "The Tower comes from nowhere, passes away nowhere; is neither a mass nor a collection; is neither static nor becoming; it is not to be located, nor is it to be located in a definite quarter."

endowed with a spiritual insight looking into the nature of things and at the same time with the will to sustain it. The will to sustain means the love and desire to save the world from its delusions and entanglements. Praṇidhāna is this will, love, and desire, called "inexhaustible" *(akṣaya)*.

Jñāna and Praṇidhāna are what constitutes Bodhisattvahood or Buddhahood, which is the same thing. By means of Jñāna we climb, as it were, and reach the summit of the thirty-three heavens; and sitting quietly we watch the underworld and its doings as if they were clouds moving underneath the feet; they are the whirling masses of commotion, but they do not touch one who is above them. The world of Jñāna is transparent, luminous, and eternally serene. But the Bodhisattva would not remain in this state of eternal contemplation above the world of particulars and hence of struggles and sufferings; for his heart aches at the sight. He is now determined to descend into the midst of the tempestuous masses of existence. His vows *(praṇidhāna)* are made, his power *(adhiṣṭhāna)* is added to all who look toward him, and every attempt *(upāya)* is made to lift up all those who are groping in the darkness and reduced to a state of utter subjugation. Praṇidhāna as an aspect of Adhishṭhāna is thus the descending ladder, or the connecting link between Bodhisattva and Sarvasattva (all beings). From this grows what is technically known as Nirmāṇakāya, or the transformation body, and in many Mahāyāna texts as Vikurvita or Vyūhavikurvita, an array of wonders.

18

That the Bodhisattva with all his penetrating and illuminating insight into the self-nature of things which is no self-nature should become himself entangled in the ever-ravelling intricacies of a world of particulars is a mystery of mysteries, and yet here opens the gate of inconceivable emancipation *(acintya-vimokṣa)* for him who is the embodiment of Jñāna and Praṇidhāna. And in this way we have to understand the contradiction between Maitreya's coming from nowhere and his being born in the province of Maladi.

This contradiction must have struck the reader as quite

inexplicable, though contradictions are generally of this nature; but in this case of Maitreya the contradiction comes too soon and in a glaring manner. At one moment, he says, he has no abode, and before we have hardly risen from this startling exclamation we are told that his native country *(jamnabhūmī)* is Maladi and that his mission is to teach Gopālaka, son of a wealthy household, in Buddhism. Is this not too sudden a descent from the Tushita heaven upon earthly business? Ordinarily, quite so. But when we realize what enters into the constitution of Bodhisattvahood we shall not think so. For he is born in Maladi as if born nowhere, as if coming nowhence. He is born, and yet unborn is he; he is before us, and yet he has not come from anywhere. He is with Sudhana in the Vairocana Tower as we are told in the *Gaṇḍavyūha,* but he has never left his abode in the Tushita heaven. So, says a Zen master, "The Bodhisattva's assemblage listening to the discourse of the Buddha at the Mount of Holy Vulture has never been dispersed; it is still going on, and the discourse is still reverberating in the Mount." This—what seems to be "too sudden a descent"—is in fact a prearranged order in the Bodhisattva's life of devotion *(bodhisattvacaryā).*

Where then is his real native country?[18]

"1. Wherever there is the awakening of the Bodhicitta there is the Bodhisattva's native land, because it belongs to the Bodhisattva family.

"2. Wherever there is deep-heartedness, there is the Bodhisattva's native land, because it is where the family of good friends rises.

"3. Wherever there is the experience of the Bhūmis, there is the Bodhisattva's native land, because it is where all the Pāramitās grow.

"4. Wherever the great vows are made, there is the Bodhisattva's native land, because it is where deeds of devotion are carried on.

"5. Wherever there is a great all-embracing love, there is the Bodhisattva's native land, because it is where the four ways of acceptance develop.

18 R.A.S. MS, folio 276b, *et seq.* Cf. MMG, p. 1415, *et seq.*

"6. Wherever there is the right way of viewing things, there is the Bodhisattva's native land, because it is where transcendental knowledge takes its rise.

"7. Wherever the Mahāyāna thrives well, there is the Bodhisattva's native land because it is where all the skillful means unfold.

"8. Wherever there is the training of all beings, there is the Bodhisattva's native land because it is where all the Buddhas are born.

"9. Wherever there are means born of transcendental knowledge,[19] there is the Bodhisattva's native land, because it is where the recognition obtains that all things are unborn.

"10. Wherever there is the practicing of all the Buddha teachings, there is the Bodhisattva's native land, because it is where all the Buddhas of the past, present and future are born."

Who then are his parents and relatives? What are his duties?

"Prajñā is his mother; Upāya (skillful means), his father; Dāna (charity), his wet nurse; Śīla (morality), his supporter; Kshānti (patience), his decoration; Vīrya (strenuousness), his nurse; Dhyāna, his cleaner; good friends, his instructors; all the factors of enlightenment, his companions; all the Bodhisattvas, his brothers; the Bodhicitta, his home; to conduct himself in accordance with the truth, his family manners; the Bhūmis, his residence; the Kshāntis, his family members; the vows, his family motto; to promote deeds of devotion, his family legacy; to make others accept the Mahāyāna, his family business; to be anointed after being bound for one more birth, his destiny as crown prince in the kingdom of the Dharma; and to arrive at the full knowledge of Tathāgatahood forms the foundation of his pure family relationship."[20]

19 *Prajñā-upāya.* When Upāya is used in its technical sense in Buddhism, it is the expression of the Buddha's or Bodhisattva's love for all beings. When the Buddha sees all the sufferings that are going on in the world owing to ignorance and egotism, he desires to deliver it and consequently contrives every means to carry out his intense desire. This is his Upāya. But as his desire has nothing to do with egotism or the clinging to the individualistic conception of reality, his Upāya is said to be born of his transcendental knowledge. See above where the philosophy of the Prajñāpāramitā was expounded.

20 Cf. MMG, pp. 1417 f.

What is that which makes up the definite basic mental attitude with which the Bodhisattva comes into our lives?

"The Bodhisattva does not detest anything in whatever world he may enter, for he knows *(parijñā)* that all things are like reflected images. He is not defiled in whatever path he may walk, for he knows that all is a transformation. He feels no fatigue whatever in his endeavor to mature all beings, for he knows that there is nothing to be designated as an ego-soul. He is never tired of receiving all beings, for he is essentially love and compassion. He has no fear in going through all kalpas, for he understands *(adhimukta)* that birth-and-death, is like a dream. He is never tired of being repeatedly reborn for he understands that all the Skandhas are like a vision. He does not destroy any path of existence, for he knows that all the Dhātus and Āyatanas are the Dharmadhātu. He has no perverted view of the paths, for he knows that all thoughts are like a mirage. He is not defiled even when he is in the realm of evil beings, for he knows that all bodies are mere appearances. He is never enticed by any of the evil passions, for he has become a perfect master over things revealed. He goes anywhere with perfect freedom, for he has full control over all appearances."[21]

19[22]

That the realization of supreme enlightenment *(anuttara-samyaksaṁbodhi)* is the end of the Buddhist life, Mahāyāna and Hīnayāna, is a well-known fact to all Buddhist students; for what constitutes Buddahood is the enlightenment itself, which the Buddha attained under the Bodhi tree by the River Nairañjanā about twenty-five centuries ago. All the teachings of Buddhism which are taught in the East at present uniformly find their source of inspiration in this truth which is at once historical and metaphysical. If not for this enlightenment there would be no Buddhas, no Buddhism, no Śrāvakas, no Pratyeka-

21 Cf. MMG, pp. 1419–20.

22 [Numbers 19–23 deal with the desire for enlightenment as defined in the *Gaṇḍavyūha Sūtra*.]

buddhas, no Arhats, no Bodhisattvas. Enlightenment is the basis of all Buddhist philosophy as well as all Buddhist activity, moral and spiritual.

The early Buddhists sought enlightenment for their own sakes, for their own spiritual welfare, and evidently had no thought for others and for the world at large. Even when they thought of them, they required of each individual Buddhist to make his own effort for salvation—that is, for enlightenment; because, according to them, ignorance which prevents them from getting enlightened and karma which keeps them bound to transmigration are based on the notion of individual realities.

It was otherwise with the Mahāyānists. Their wish for enlightenment was first of all for the sake of the world. Just because they desired the enlightenment and emancipation of all the world they strove first to enlighten themselves, to emancipate themselves, to make themselves free from the bondage of all the karma- and the knowledge-hindrances. Being thus prepared they could go out into the world and proclaim the Buddha dharmas to their fellow beings.

For this reason the Mahāyānists put great stress upon the significance of a compassionate heart *(mahākaruṇā)*. Whatever Mahāyāna texts we may turn over, we never fail to notice terms belonging to the category of love *(karuṇā)* and compassion *(anukampana)* which are directed toward all beings *(sarvasattva* or *jagat)* in such a way as to give them refuge *(paritrāṇa)*, protection *(saṅgraha)*, inspiration *(paricodana)*, maturity *(paripāka)*, discipline *(vinaya)*, purification *(pariśuddhi)*, etc.

The idea of the Bodhisattva, a being *(sattva)* who seeks enlightenment *(bodhi)*, as I said elsewhere, thus came to take root in Buddhism, and a sort of secular Buddhism came to replace the old school of ascetic and exclusive monasticism. The householder was made more of than the homeless mendicant, the teaching of the Buddha was to be practiced outside a community of the elite, and this democratic social tendency brought about many great changes in Buddhist thought. One of them was to analyze in a practical way the process of enlightenment.

The doctors of the Hīnayāna busied themselves with many subtle problems regarding the world of form *(rūpaloka),* the doctrine of the non-existence of a soul substance *(anātmya),* the personality of the Buddha, the analysis of the mind, etc. They tended to be too metaphysical, too scholastic, too rationalistic, with the result that practical questions concerning the attainment of enlightenment and its effective application in the realm of our daily lives were neglected. The Mahāyānists' chief concern was with life itself.

When the actual process of enlightenment was examined, the Mahāyāna found that it consisted of two definite steps. In the beginning it was necessary to create for the sake of others an urgent longing for enlightenment, and then the attainment of the final goal itself would be possible. The longing was just as important and full of meaning as the attainment itself, for the latter was impossible without the former; indeed the latter determined the former in every way; that is, the time, strength, efficacy, etc., of enlightenment entirely depended upon the quality of the initiative will power raised for the attainment of the final object. The motive determined the course, character, and power of the conduct. The desire for enlightenment intensely stirred meant, indeed, that the greater and more difficult part of the work was already achieved. In one sense, to begin was fulfillment.

However this is, the Mahāyānists are fully conscious of the value of the initial cherishing of the desire for the realization of enlightenment. While there still remain much in the spiritual exercises which follow the first awakening, the course the Bodhisattva has now to take is fully and clearly defined. The task is arduous, no doubt, but he is no more in the darkness of doubt and ignorance. Therefore, in the Mahāyāna texts this first stirring of the desire for enlightenment is considered a great event in the life of a Buddhist, and receives special mention in them.

The idea of the Bodhisattva as a being who on the one hand seeks after enlightenment and, on the other, out of his compassionate heart intensely desires to lead the whole universe to the enjoyment of spiritual welfare has been persistently alive among all the Mahāyāna followers. *"Jyō gu bo dai, ge ke shu jō*"[23] has thus come to be the normative principle of the Buddhist life in the Far East. In all the Zen monasteries the following "Four Great Vows" are heard chanted on every occasion, after a service, after a lecture, after a meal, and after the sūtra reading:

All beings, however limitless, I vow to carry across;
My evil passions, however inexhaustible, I vow to destroy;
The Dharma teachings, however innumerable, I vow to study;
The Buddha way, however peerless, I vow to attain.

It is not known exactly when these "vows" came to be formulated and incorporated into the life of the Zen monk; but there is no doubt that the spirit pervading them is the spirit of the Mahāyāna and as such that of Zen, and that ever since the introduction of Buddhism into China and Japan the principle of the "Vows" has influenced the cultural life of the East in all its branches.

In the *Gaṇḍavyūha,* these two aspects of the Buddhist life are described, first, as raising the desire for supreme enlightenment, and, secondly, practicing the life of the Bodhisattva—that is, the Bodhisattva Samantabhadra. Sudhana the young pilgrim had his first awakening of the desire *(cittotpāda)* under the direction of Mañjuśrī, and his later pilgrimage consisted wholly in inquiries into living the life of enlightenment *(bodhicaryā).* So says Mañjuśrī to his disciple when he sends Sudhana off on his long, arduous "Pilgrim's Progress": "Well done, well done, indeed, O son of a good family! Having awakened the desire for supreme enlightenment,[24] thou now wishest to seek for the life of the Bodhisattva. O son of a good family, it is a rare thing to see beings whose desire is raised to supreme enlightenment; but it is a still rarer thing to see beings who, having awakened the desire for supreme enlightenment, proceed to seek for the life of the Bodhisattva. Therefore, O son of a good family, if thou wishest to attain the knowledge which is possessed by the All-Knowing One, be ever assiduous to get associated with good friends *(kalyāṇamitra)*. . . ."

23 *"Chang Ch'iu p'u ti, hsia hua chuang chêng."* Literally, "Above, [I] seek for Bodhi (enlightenment); below, [I] convert all beings (*sarvasattva*)."

24 *Annuttarāyai samyaksaṁbodhaye cittam utpādya*. Idzumi, p. 154.

In the *Prajñāpāramitā,* the second aspect of the Buddhist life after the awakening of the desire for enlightenment consists in practicing Prajñāpāramitā. In the *Gaṇḍavyūha* this practice is deeply associated with the life of the Bodhisattva known as Samantabhadra, and the Bodhicaryā, the life of enlightenment, is identified with the Bhadracaryā, the life of Bhadra, that is, Samantabhadra. Samantabhadra thus stands contrasted to Mañjuśrī in the *Gaṇḍavyūha*; the idea of personality we may say has entered here. In the *Prajñāpāramitā Sūtras* Prajñā remains impersonal throughout. One of the sūtras[25] gives the following:

"There are only a few people in this world who can clearly perceive what the Buddha, Dharma, and Samgha are and faithfully follow them. . . . Fewer are those who can raise their minds to supreme enlightenment.[26] . . . Fewer still are those who practice Prajñāpāramitā. . . . Fewer and fewer still are those who, most steadfastly practicing Prajñāpāramitā and finally reaching the stage of No-turning-back, abide in the state of Bodhisattvahood. . . ."

The usual Sanskrit phrase for "the desire for enlightenment" is *bodhicittotpāda,* which is the abbreviation of *anuttarāyāṁ samyaksaṁbodhau cittasya utpādaḥ*—that is, "to have a mind raised to supreme enlightenment." To translate the phrase by "to awaken the idea of enlightenment" would be incorrect and misleading, as will be explained later. For it is equivalent to *anuttarāṁ samyaksaṁbodhim ākāṅkṣamāṇa,* "longing for supreme enlightenment,"[27] or to *anuttarāyāṁ samyaksaṁbodhau praṇidhānaṁ parigṛihya,* "cherishing an intense desire for supreme enlightenment."[28] In the *Gaṇḍavyūha* we have such expressions as these, which convey the same idea: *vipula-kṛipa-karaṇa-mānasa, paryeṣase 'nuttamāṁ bodhim,* "raising a far-reaching compassion, thou seekest for supreme enlightenment";[29] *ye bodhiṃ prārthayante,* "those who desire enlightenment."[30]

25 *Aṣṭasāhasrikā,* edited by Rājendralāla Mitra, pp. 60 ff.

26 Tebhyo 'py alpebho 'lpatarakās te ye 'nuttarāyāṁ samyaksaṁbodhau cittānyutpādayanti.

27 *Saddharma-puṇḍarīka,* edited by Kern and Nanjo, p. 414.

28 *Ibid.,* p. 43.

29 Idzumi, p. 152.

30 *Ibid.,* p. 154.

Anuttarāyāṁ samyaksaṁbodhau cittasya utpādaḥ, the abbreviated form of which, as already referred to, is *bodhicittotpādam,* is also equivalent to *anuttarāyāṁ samyaksaṁbodhau praṇidadhanti.*[31] *Praṇidadhāti* means "to give one's entire attention to something," that is, "to resolve firmly to accomplish the work." The Bodhisattva's Praṇidhāna is his intense determination to carry out his plan of universal salvation. Of course, it is necessary here to have an adequate knowledge or a full intellectual grasp of the work he intends to accomplish, but a Praṇidhāna is far more than this, it is the will to do. Mere intellectuality has no backing of the will power; mere idealism can never be an efficient executive agency. The Cittotpāda is a form of Praṇidhāna. "To conceive an idea" or "to awaken a thought" is one thing, and to carry it out in action is quite another, especially when it is carried out with intensity and fervency.

For *anuttarāyāṁ samyaksaṁbodhau cittasya utpādaḥ,* the Chinese translators generally have a phrase which literally means "to raise supreme-enlightenment-mind." This is, however, not an exact translation. The original literal sense is "to have a mind raised to enlightenment" and not "to raise enlightenment-mind." If the latter, we may think that there is a special mental quality to be called "enlightenment-mind," and that by means of this faculty one's mind opens up to enlightenment, or that this mind itself is enlightenment. But the sense is really "cherishing the desire for enlightenment." It is a sort of conversion, the turning toward enlightenment of the mind which was formerly engaged in something worldly, or the awakening of a new spiritual aspiration which has been dormant, or a new orientation of one's mental activities in a way hitherto undreamed of, or the finding of a new center of energy which opens up an entirely fresh spiritual vista. We can say that here a glimpse of enlightenment has been caught which helps one to determine one's future course of conduct, and that here a Bodhisattva enters upon the stage of aspiration.

[31] This expression is used by Maitreya when he praises Sudhana's determination to pursue the course of Bodhisattvahood. *Durlabhāḥ kulaputrās te sattvaḥ sarvaloke ye 'nuttarāyāṁ samyaksaṁbodhau praṇidadhanti.* Idzumi MS, p. 1321.

There is another misunderstanding as regards the abbreviated form of *anuttarāyāṁ samyaksaṁbodhau cittasya utpādam,* by which I mean the usual interpretation by scholars of the compound *bodhicittotpāda* in Sanskrit. When this is carelessly taken, as is frequently done, it may seem to mean "to awaken the thought of enlightenment." But this is wrong, because the compound simply means "to cherish the desire for enlightenment," that is, "to cherish a spiritual aspiration for the attainment of supreme enlightenment." *Citta* here is not "thought," but "desire," and *bodhicittotpādam* is after all the shortening of *anuttarāyāṁ samyaksaṁbodhau*[32] *cittasya utpādaḥ.*

"To awaken or raise the thought of enlightenment" means, if it means anything definite, to have the conception of enlightenment, or to find out what enlightenment means. But *citta* as we have it suggests no such intellectual content, for it is used in its conative sense. *Cittotpāda* is a volitional movement definitely made toward the realization of enlightenment. Where the intellect in concerned, the Mahāyānists use such words as *jñāna, mati, buddhi, vijñāna,* etc. *Citta,* or *cittāśya,* or *adhyāśaya,* on the other hand, has generally a conative force, and the Chinese translators have very properly adopted *hsin* for it. Whether *citta* is derived from the root *ci,* "to collect," or *cit,* "to perceive," the Mahāyāna usage is decidedly not intellectual, but affective and volitional. The Citta is a disposition, predilection or characteristic attitude of mind.

The Bodhicittotpāda is, therefore, a new spiritual excitement which shifts one's center of energy. It is the becoming conscious of a new religious aspiration which brings about a cataclysm in one's mental organization. A man who has been a stranger to the religious life now cherishes an intense desire for enlightenment, or all-knowledge *(sarvajñatā),* and the whole course of his future life is thereby determined—this is the Bodhicittotpāda.

By way of a note I wish to add the following. Since the *Out-*

32 The locative is not always adhered to. Sometimes it is in the dative, for instance, *anuttarāyai samyaksaṁbodhaye cittam utpādya* (Idzumi copy of *Gaṇḍavyūha,* p. 154). Further, the form *bodha* alone is frequently used for *sambodhi* and in the *dative.* Examples: *Bodhāya cittam utpadyate* (Rahder—*Daśabhūmika,* p. 11, R); *bodhāya cittam utpādya (Aṣṭasāhasrikā,* pp. 62, 63, 71, 93, etc.); *bodhāya cittam utpadyate* (*Gaṇḍavyūha,* p. 169, etc.).

lines of Mahāyāna Buddhism was published in 1907, my views of the Mahāyāna have changed in some details, and there are many points in it upon which I would now express myself differently, especially in connection with the explanation of some Sanskrit terms. For instance, in treating of the Bodhicitta, I defined it to be "intelligence-heart," adding that theoretically the Bodhi or Bodhicitta is in every sentient being and constitutes its essential nature, only it is in most cases found enveloped in ignorance and egotism. Thus the Bodhicitta is understood to be a form of the Tathāgatagarbha or Ālayavijñāna. In some respects, this way of interpreting the Citta is not incorrect, seeing that supreme enlightenment is the perfection of the Citta, that is, that the Citta when fully developed leads up to enlightenment. But now I find that it is not legitimate from the historical point of view to consider Bodhicitta in the same manner as we do such compounds as *ātmagrahacitta, ātmaparanānātvacitta, bodhimārgavipravāsacitta,* etc. For, as I propose in this article, *bodhicitta* is the abbreviation of *anuttarāyāṃ samyaksaṁbodhau cittasya utpādaḥ,* and is synonymously used with *sarvajñatācitta,* so *bodhicittotpāda* = *sarvajñatācittotpāda.*[33] Bodhi is what makes up the essence of Buddhahood, so is Sarvajñatā, all-knowledge. It is true that later this historical connection between the compound *bodhicitta* and the phrase *anuttarāyāṁ samyaksaṁbodhau cittasya utpādaḥ* was altogether forgotten so that the Bodhicitta came to be treated as having an independent technical value. This was natural, and it is

[33] In the *Gaṇḍavyūha* where Maitreya describes the desire for enlightenment as one of the most wonderful things a Buddhist can experience in his spiritual career, the compound *bodhicitta* frequently changes into *sarvajñatā,* p. 1332 *et passim.* In the Chinese translations, *fa p'u t'i hsin* seems to be used both for *bodhicitta* and *sarvajñatācitta. Fa p'u t'i hsin* is misleading, as I said before, although we have in the sūtras, e.g. in the *Aṣṭasāhasrikā* (p. 61), such phrases as *bodhicittam utpādayanti* or *bodhicittam upabṛinhayanti.* That the latter means "to raise or to strengthen the desire for enlightenment" is evident from the context, and the compound is used no doubt to avoid the repetition of the longer phrase. While this is so in the *Prajñāpāramitā,* the *Gaṇḍavyūha,* etc., the later writers of the Buddhist texts have come to treat the desire for enlightenment as if it were a specific faculty of the mind whereby we can testify to the truth of enlightenment. As was said above, this is not altogether wrong, only that it ignores the historical significance of the term. As to rendering it by "the thought of enlightenment," the original sense is here altogether missed.

not necessarily incorrect so to treat the compound. But it will be well to remember what I have explained here.

In the *Tathāgata-guhyaka* or the *Guhyasamāja Tantra*, I find the Bodhicitta described in a more abstract and highly technical manner. The text must date much later than the *Gaṇḍavyūha*. It is mixed with a great deal of Tantrism, which must be regarded as a degeneration of pure Mahāyāna Buddhism. The treatment of the Bodhicitta deviates from that in the *Gaṇḍavyūha* as we shall see further on. Below are the definitions of the Citta as given by the different Buddhas who constitute the great mystic Vajra assemblage:[34]

Vairocana: "To perceive a being as devoid of efficiency in itself is said not to perceive it; if a being is perceived as not a being, it is said to be unattainable."[35]

Another statement by Vairocana: "The Bodhicitta is free from all becoming, is neither attached to nor detached from the Skandhas, Dhātus, and Āyatanas; seeing into the egolessness and sameness of all things, it is my own Mind from the first unborn, and of the nature of Śūnyatā."

Akshobhya: "[The Bodhicitta sees that] these existences are unborn, that they are neither individual objects nor that which constitutes their being; the Citta is like the sky and has no ego-substance; and this is where the principle of enlightenment is firmly established."

Ratnaketu: "[The Bodhicitta sees that] all individual objects are unborn, they are devoid of forms of individuality, they are born of the egolessness of things; and this is where the principle of enlightenment is firmly established."

Amitāyus: "Individual objects being unborn, there is neither becoming nor perceiving; as the term sky is used [though it has no reality], so is the Citta said to be something existent."

Amoghasiddhi: "Individual objects are by nature illuminating, they are as pure as the sky; when there is no [something to be designated] as enlightenment or realization, there is the principle of enlightenment firmly established."

[34] [Ed. B. Bhattacharyya, GOS, LIII, Baroda, 1931, pp. 11–13.]

[35] This verse requires a full explanation as it is too abstractedly and technically expressed.

20

To cherish the desire for enlightenment is no ordinary event in the life of the Mahāyāna Buddhist, for this is the definite step he takes toward the goal as distinguished from the life of the so-called Hīnayāna follower. Enlightenment is not a mere personal affair which does not concern the community at large; its background is laid in the universe itself. When I am enlightened, the whole Dharmadhātu is enlightened; in fact the reason of my enlightenment is the reason of the Dharmadhātu, the two are most intimately bound up with each other. Therefore, that I have been able to conceive a great longing for enlightenment means that the entire world wishes to be liberated from ignorance and evil passions. This is the meaning of the following statement made by Sāgaramegha, one of the teachers whom Sudhana visited in his long spiritual pilgrimage: "It is indeed well for you that you have already awakened the desire for enlightenment; this is an impossibility for those who have not accumulated enough stock of merit in their past lives." "A stock of merit" so called has value only when it concerns the welfare of the world generally. Unless a man is able to survey the entire field of relationships in which he stands—that is, unless his spiritual outlook extends to its furthest end—his *"merit" (kuśala)* is not real "merit," and no accumulation of such will result in the awakening of the desire for enlightenment. Hence the utmost importance of this awakening.

Sāgaramegha continues to praise Sudhana's cherishing the desire which is only possible to those who have the following qualities:

1. That their meritorious deeds are of universal character and illuminating;

2. That their attainment of the Samādhi is full of the light of knowledge which is derived from walking the path of righteousness;

3. That they are able to produce the great ocean of merits;

4. That they are never tired of amassing all kinds of purities;

5. That they are ever ready to associate with good friends and attend upon them with reverence;

6. That they are not accumulators of wealth and never hesitate to give up their lives for a good cause;

7. That they are free from the spirit of arrogance and like the great earth treat others impartially;

8. That their hearts being filled with love and compassion they are always thinking of the welfare of others;

9. That they are always friendly disposed toward all beings in the various paths of existence;

10. That they are ever desirous of being admitted into the community of Buddhas.

Sāgaramegha now concludes that only to those souls who are endowed with these aspirations, affections, and dispositions is vouchsafed the privilege of cherishing the desire for enlightenment. For this desire for enlightenment is really aroused from:

1. A great loving heart *(mahākaruṇācitta)* which is desirous of protecting all beings;

2. A great compassionate heart *(mahāmaitrīcitta)* which ever wishes for the welfare of all beings;

3. The desire to make others happy *(sukhacitta)*, which comes from seeing them suffer all forms of pain;

4. The desire to benefit others *(hitacitta)*, and to deliver them from evils and wrong deeds;

5. A sympathetic heart *(dayācitta)* which desires to protect all beings from tormenting thoughts;

6. An unimpeded heart *(asaṁgacitta)* which wishes to see all the impediments removed for others;

7. A large heart *(vipulacitta)* which fills the whole universe;

8. An endless heart *(anantacitta)* which is like space;

9. A spotless heart *(vimalacitta)* which sees all the Buddhas;

10. A pure heart *(viśuddhacitta)* which is in conformity with the wisdom of the past, present, and future;

11. A wisdom heart *(jñānacitta)* by which one can enter the great ocean of all-knowledge.

The further quotations from the *Daśabhūmika*[36] will throw more light on the preliminary steps leading to the desire for

36 Rahder edition, p. 11, R.

enlightenment, on the reasons why enlightenment is desired, on the constituent elements of enlightenment, and on the effect of enlightenment. Both the *Daśabhūmika* and the *Gaṇḍavyūha* belong in the Chinese Tripitaka to the Mahāyāna collection known as the *Kegon-gyō*.[37]

What are the preliminary conditions that lead to the cherishing of the desire for supreme enlightenment? They are:

1. The stock of merit *(kuśalamūla)* is well filled;
2. Deeds of goodness *(caraṇa)* are well practiced;
3. The necessary moral provisions *(sambhāra)* are well stored up;
4. The Buddhas have been respectfully served *(paryupāsita)*;
5. Works of purity *(śukladharma)* are well accomplished;
6. There are good friends *(kalyāṇamitra)* kindly disposed;
7. The heart is thoroughly cleansed *(viśuddhāśaya)*;
8. Broad-mindedness *(vipulādhyāśaya)* is firmly secured;
9. A deep sincere faith *(adhimukti)* is established;
10. There is the presence of a compassionate heart *(karuṇā)*.

According to the *Daśabhūmika*, these ten things are needed for the awakening of the desire for enlightenment. To have this desire is in itself a great Buddhist experience, which does not take place without some spiritual preparation. It sprouts from a seed deeply laid in the ground and well nourished. One of the ideas requiring special notice in the enumeration here cited is the reference to good friends. Their

[37] The Sanskrit title of the *Kegon-gyō* is *Avataṁsaka*, as we gather from the *Mahāvyutpatti* and also from the *Chih-yüan Lu*, a catalogue of the Chinese Tripitaka compiled in A.D. 1285–1287, but it is *Gaṇḍavyūha* according to Fa-tsang's commentary on the sixty-fascicle *Kegon-gyō*. *Avataṁsaka* means "a garland," and *gaṇḍa* is "a flower of ordinary kind," and *vyūha* "an orderly arrangement" or "array." From this, *Kegon* more exactly corresponds to *Gaṇḍavyūha* than to *Avataṁsaka*. *Ke (hua)* is a flower, and *gon (yen)* or *shōgon (chüang-yen)* in Chinese is equivalent to *vyūha*. When the contents of the Chinese *Kegon*, either of sixty or eighty fascicles, are examined, we find that there were in the beginning many independent sūtras which were later compiled into one encyclopedic collection, as the subject matters treated in them are all classifiable under one head, and they came to be known as the *Avataṁsaka* or *Kegon*. It will be better to restrict the use of *Avataṁsaka* to the whole collection of the *Kegon* and *Gaṇḍavyūha* to the Sanskrit text as an independent one, though it constitutes the last chapter of the sixty- and eighty-fascicle *Kegon*. The forty-fascicle *Kegon* corresponds to the *Gaṇḍavyūha*.

good will and assistance are powerful instruments in the cultivation of the Buddhist aspiration. The *Gaṇḍavyūha* is emphatic in this respect.

All the sūtras belonging to Kegon literature have a deliberate penchant for decimal enumeration, and even when there is apparently no intrinsic need for filling up the required formula the author or compiler scrupulously proceeds to count up a complete series of ten. Thus in the above recapitulation ideas belonging to one category are divided into so many heads, evidently for no other purpose than to keep up the form. "Stock of merit," "deeds of goodness," "moral provisions," and "work of purity" may be gathered up under the one head of moral conduct. If this is possible, the conditions necessary for awakening the desire for enlightenment may be summarized thus: (1) moral conduct, (2) the friendly disposition of the Buddhas and good friends, and (3) a heart pure, true, loving and all-embracing. When these three conditions are perfectly fulfilled, the Bodhicitta is said to raise its head and to be ready for further evolution.

The question next is, Why is the desire for supreme enlightenment so necessary in the life of a devout Mahāyānist? Or simply, What has the Buddhist enlightenment to do with our life? The *Daśabhūmika*[38] gives the following reasons:

1. For the realization of Buddha knowledge *(jñāna)*;

2. For the attainment of the ten powers *(daśabala)*;

3. For the attainment of great fearlessness *(mahāvaiśāradya)*;

4. For the attainment of the truth of sameness which constitutes Buddhahood *(samatabuddhadharma)*;

5. For protecting and securing the whole world *(sarvajagatparitrāṇa)*;

6. For the purification of a pitying and compassionate heart *(kṛipākaruṇā)*;

7. For the attainment of a knowledge which leaves nothing unknown *(aśeṣajñāna)* in the ten quarters of the world;

8. For the purification of all the Buddha lands so that a state of non-attachment *(asaṁga)* will prevail;

9. For the perception of the past, present, and future in one moment *(kṣaṇabodha)*;

38 Rahder, p. 11, S.

10. For the revolving of the great wheel of the Dharma (*dharmacakrapravartana*) in the spirit of fearlessness.

From this, we can partly see what are the elements of supreme enlightenment, for the reasons given for its realization are already found involved in it as its own constituents. Then what are these constituents? They are:

1. The knowledge which belongs to Buddhahood, and which sees into everything that is in space and time—the knowledge which goes beyond the realm of relativity and individuation because it penetrates into every corner of the universe and surveys eternity at one glance;

2. The will power that knocks down every possible obstruction lying athwart its way when it wishes to reach its ultimate end, which is the deliverance of the whole world from the bondage of birth-and-death;

3. An all-embracing love or compassion which, in combination with knowledge and will power, never ceases from devising all means to promote the spiritual welfare of every sentient being.

In order to clarify further the nature of enlightenment as conceived by the Mahāyānists, the following is taken again from the *Daśabhūmika*,[39] according to which the desire for enlightenment comprises in it the following elements:

1. A great compassionate heart which is the chief factor of the desire;

2. Knowledge born of transcendental wisdom which is the ruling element;

3. Skillful means which works as a protecting agent;

4. The deepest heart which gives it a support.

And, further, the Bodhicitta is:

5. Of the same measure with the Tathāgata power;

6. Endowed with the power to discern the power and intelligence of all beings (*sattvabalabuddhi*);

7. Directed toward the knowledge of non-obstruction (*asambhinnajñāna*);

8. In conformity with spontaneous knowledge (*svayambhūjñāna*);

9. Capable of instructing all beings in the truths of Buddhism according to knowledge born of transcendental wisdom;

39 *Ibid.*, p. 11, T.

10. Extending to the limits of the Dharmadhātu which is as wide as space itself.

In these qualifications too one can see what is meant by cherishing the desire for enlightenment. The cherishing of the desire at once stamps a man as a Bodhisattva and thus distinguishes him from the other followers of Buddhism; for he holds a great compassionate heart for all beings, and also has perspicuity of spiritual insight which sees into the nature of existence, and further the power of controlling love with wisdom and tempering wisdom with love so that he is able to adapt himself to the ever-changing conditions of existence.

Since the desire for enlightenment is composed of all these attributes as here described, the Bodhisattva is capable of producing the following results at the moment this desire asserts itself in the depths of his being.[40]

1. He passes beyond the stage of an ordinary being;
2. He enters into the rank of Bodhisattvahood;
3. He is born in the family of Tathāgatas;
4. He is irreproachable and faultless in his family honor;
5. He stands away from all worldly courses;
6. He enters into a supra-worldly life;
7. He is established in things belonging to Bodhisattvahood;
8. He abides in the abode of the Bodhisattva;
9. He is impartially ushered into the Tathāgata groups of the past, present, and future;
10. He is ultimately destined for supreme enlightenment.

When he thus takes his abode in these things, he is said to have gained the first stage of a Bodhisattva known as Joy *(pramuditā)*, because he is now immovable in his faith.

These passages from the *Daśabhūmika* defining the source, nature, scope and outcome of the Bodhicitta or the desire for enlightenment are explicit enough. We can realize of what a weighty significance this aspiration is for the Mahāyānists. It is almost like the realization itself. When it is sufficiently strongly awakened, the Buddhist's course afterward determines itself. If the Bodhicittotpāda or Bodhicitta were

40 *Ibid.*, pp. 11–12, U.

no more than mere thinking of enlightenment even as something of the utmost importance in the life of a Buddhist, the Citta as "thought" could by no means achieve so much as is described above. The Citta is not an idea, is not mere thinking, it is an intense desire or aspiration which causes an entire rearrangement or reconstruction of all the former experiences made by the Buddhist. The Citta is the reason of one's being, it is the original will that constitutes the foundation of one's personality. Otherwise, the meaning of the forceful manner in which the editor of the *Gaṇḍavyhūya* endeavors to describe the nature of the Bodhicitta becomes incomprehensible, as will be seen in the following pages.

21

When the young Buddhist pilgrim Sudhana calls upon the Bodhisattva Maitreya for instruction, the latter first praises Sudhana for his strong determination to search for the final truth of Buddhism; and before he opens his magnificent Vairocana Tower for the young man's observation and contemplation, he eulogizes the virtues of the Bodhicitta, urged by which indeed the young pilgrim has until now visited one teacher after another until he comes to Maitreya. If not for this ardent desire for enlightenment, Sudhana would never have undertaken his arduous task of pilgrimaging among the seers and philosophers, the wise men and women, who probably represent to a certain extent historical personages of the day. The *Gaṇḍavyūha* is indeed the record of those intellectual and spiritual struggles which take place around the question, "What is the life of a Bodhisattva?," that is to say, "What is the meaning of human life?" The awakening of the Bodhicitta is the key to this eternal riddle, hence Maitreya's most extended and exhaustive characterization of the Bodhicitta, "the desire for enlightenment."

"Well done," said Maitreya to Sudhana, "well done, O son of a good family! Already you have awakened the desire for supreme enlightenment, in order to benefit the world, to lead it to happiness, to rescue all beings from sufferings, and to acquire all the truths of Buddhism. O son of a good family, you have many advantages, you enjoy the life of a human being, you live in the world of living beings, you live at the time when a Tathāgata has appeared, you have interviewed the good friend Mañjuśrī. You are indeed a good vessel of truth, you are well nourished with stocks of merit, well supported by works of purity, you are already well cleansed in the understanding, great in intuition, you are already well protected by all the Buddhas, well guarded by good friends, for the reason that you have already sincerely awakened the desire for supreme enlightenment."

22

Evidently Maitreya exhausted his power of speech in order to extol the importance of the Bodhicitta in the career of a Bodhisattva, for without this being duly impressed on the mind of the young Buddhist pilgrim Sudhana, he could not have been led into the interior of the Tower of Vairocana. The Tower harbors all the secrets that belong to the spiritual life of the highest Buddhist. If the novice were not quite fully prepared for the initiation, the secrets would have no signification whatever. They may even be grossly misunderstood, and the result will be calamitous indeed. For this reason Maitreya left not a stone unturned to show Sudhana what the Bodhicitta really meant. The following points may be gathered concerning the Bodhicitta:

1. The Bodhicitta rises from a great compassionate heart, without which there will be no Buddhism. This emphasis on Mahākaruṇā is characteristic of the Mahāyāna. We can say that the whole panorama of its teachings revolves on this pivot. The philosophy of Interpenetration so pictorially depicted in the *Gaṇḍavyūha* is in fact no more than the outburst of this life energy. As long as we tarry on the plane of intellection, such Buddhist doctrines as Emptiness *(śūnyatā)*, Egolessness *(anātmya)*, etc., may sound so abstract and devoid of spiritual force as not to excite anyone to fanatic enthusiasm. The main point is to remember that all the Buddhist teachings are the outcome of a warm heart cherished toward all sentient beings and not of a cold intellect which tries to unveil the secrets

of existence by logic. That is to say, Buddhism is personal experience and not impersonal philosophy.

2. The raising of the Bodhicitta is not an event of one day, for it requires a long preparation, not of one life but of many lives. The Citta will remain dormant in those souls where there is no stock of merit ever accumulated. Moral merit must be stored up in order to germinate later into the great overshadowing tree of the Bodhicitta. The doctrine of karma may not be a very scientific statement of facts, but all Buddhists, Mahāyāna and Hīnayāna, believe in its working in the moral realm of our lives. Broadly stated, as long as we are all historical beings we cannot escape the karma that preceded us, whatever this may mean. Wherever there is the notion of time, there is a continuity of karma. When this is admitted, the Bodhicitta could not grow from the soil where no nourishing stock of goodness had ever been secured.

3. If the Bodhicitta comes out of a stock of merit, it cannot fail to be productive of all the good things that belong to the Buddhas and Bodhisattvas and other great beings. At the same time it must also be the great crusher of evils, for nothing can withstand the terrible blow inflicted by the thunderbolt of the Citta-Indra.

4. The intrinsic nobility of the Bodhicitta can never be defamed even when it is found among defilements of every description, whether they belong to knowledge or deeds or passions. The great ocean of transmigration drowns every body that goes into it. Especially the philosophers, who are satisfied with interpretations and not with facts themselves, are utterly unable to extricate themselves from the bondage of birth and death, because they never cut asunder the invisible tie of karma and knowledge that securely keeps them down to the earth of dualities because of their intellectualism. Therefore, the awakening of the Bodhicitta which takes place in the depths of one's being is a great religious event.

5. For this reason again the Bodhicitta is beyond the assault of Māra the Evil One, who represents the principle of dualism in Buddhism. It is he who is always looking for his chance to throw himself against the solid stronghold of Prajñā and Karuṇā. Before the awakening of the Bodhicitta the soul is

inclined toward the dualism of being and non-being, and is thus necessarily outside the pale of the sustaining power of all the Buddhas, Bodhisattvas, and good friends. The awakening, however, marks a decisive turning away from the old line of thought. The Bodhisattva has now an open highway before him, which is well guarded by the moral influence of all his good protectors. He walks on straightway, his footsteps are firm, and the Evil One has no chance to tempt him away from his steady progress toward perfect enlightenment.

6. The Bodhicitta means, as was explained in the beginning of this article, the awakening of the desire for supreme enlightenment which was attained by the Buddha, enabling him to become the leader of the religious movement known as Buddhism. Supreme enlightenment is no other than all-knowledge, *sarvajñatā*, to which reference is constantly made in all the Mahāyāna texts. All-knowledge is what constitutes the essence of Buddhahood. It does not mean that the Buddha knows every individual thing, but that he has grasped the fundamental principle of existence and that he has penetrated deep down into the center of his own being. When the Bodhicitta is aroused, the Bodhisattva's hold on all-knowledge is definite and firm.

7. The rise of the Bodhicitta marks the beginning of the career of a Bodhisattva. Before this, the idea of a Bodhisattva was no more than an abstraction. We are perhaps all Bodhisattvas, but the notion has not been brought home to our consciousness, the image has not been vivid enough to make us feel and live the fact. The Citta is aroused and the fact becomes a personal event. The Bodhisattva is now quivering with life. The Bodhisattva and the Bodhicitta are inseparable; where the one is there the other is. The Citta indeed is the key that opens all the secret doors of Buddhism.

8. The Bodhicitta is the first stage of the Bodhisattva's life of devotion and vow. The chief object of Sudhana's quest as far as the *Gaṇḍavyūha* is concerned consists in finding out what is the Bodhisattva's life of devotion and vow. It was through Maitreya that the young Buddhist pilgrim came to realize within himself all that he had been searching for among the various teachers, philosophers, gods, etc. The final con-

firmation comes from Samantabhadra, but without Maitreya's instruction in the Bodhicitta and his admission into the Tower of Vairocana, Sudhana could not expect to start really on his career of Bodhisattvahood. The life of devotion and vows which stamps a Buddhist as Mahāyānist and not as Hīnayānist is impossible without first arousing the Bodhicitta.

9. The *Gaṇḍavyūha* describes the Bodhisattva as one who never becomes tired of living a life of devotion in order to benefit all beings spiritually as well as materially. His life lasts till the end of the world spatially and temporarily. If he cannot finish his work in one life or in many lives, he is ready to be reborn a countless number of times when time itself comes to an end. Nor is his field of action confined to this world of ours. As there are innumerable worlds filling up an infinite expanse of space, he will manifest himself there, until he can reach every being that has any value at all to be delivered from ignorance and egotism. Not to know what exhaustion means characterizes Bodhisattvahood born of the Bodhicitta.

10. Lastly, the notion of Bodhicitta is one of those marks which label the Mahāyāna as distinct from the Hīnayāna. The exclusiveness of the monastic organization is a death to Buddhism. As long as this system rules, Buddhism limits its usefulness to a specific group of ascetics. Nor is this the last word one can say about the Hīnayāna; the weightiest objection is that it stops the growth of the spiritual germ nursed in the depths of every sentient being, which consists in the arousing of the Bodhicitta. The Citta has its desire never to be nipped by the cold frost of intellectual enlightenment. This desire is too deep-seated, and the enlightenment itself must yield to its dictates. The Bodhisattva's untiring activities are the outcome of this desire, and this is what keeps the spirit of the Mahāyāna very much alive in the Far East in spite of its worn-out institutionalism.

In short, the Bodhicitta is more than love, it contains something of a philosophical insight. It is a concrete unified embodiment of Prajñā and Karuṇā. In the Citta they really begin to work. What this means was explained in our exposition of the *Prajñāpāramitā*. The latter makes no explicit references to the Bodhicitta, but the study or practice of the deep Prajñāpāramitā is really the awakening of the Citta and the beginning of the Bodhisattva's life of devotion and vows *(praṇidhānacaryā).* If the Mahāyāna has anything to contribute to the deepening of the religious consciousness, it is no other than our realization of the Citta as Prajñā and Karuṇā.

23

As I started this paper with an introductory quotation from the *Daśabhūmika,* it may not be out of place to conclude it with another quotation from the same sūtra, which, as was stated before, belongs to the same *Avataṁsaka* group of Mahāyāna literature as the *Gaṇḍavyūha* itself. The following[41] is from the final gāthās attached to the tenth stage of Bodhisattvahood known as Dharmamegha (law-cloud), in which Vajragarbha, the leading Bodhisattva of the *Daśabhūmika* assembly, tells all the other Bodhisattvas gathered in the heavenly palace called Paranirmita-vaśavartin, about the desire for enlightenment:

Listen to the most distinguished, most excellent deeds of the Bodhisattvas,
Who enjoy peace and self-control, and whose hearts are quiet and tamed,
Who are like the passage in the sky, who resemble the air,
Who are free from crudities and defilements, abiding in the knowledge of the path.

They have accumulated hundreds of thousands of stocks of merit for kotis of kalpas,
They have paid homage to hundreds of thousands of the Buddhas and great Rishis,
They have also paid homage to an unlimited number of the Arhats and Pratyekabuddhas,
And in order to benefit all the world the Bodhicitta is produced [in them].

[In the Bodhisattvas] who have disciplined themselves in moral austerities, who have perfected the virtue of patience,
Who are shy [of evil-doings] but active in blissful deeds, who have merit and knowledge ever increasing,

41 "The Gāthā Portion of the *Daśabhūmika,*" Final Gāthās, 1–14. *The Eastern Buddhist,* VI–1, 1932. [Ed. R. Kondō, 1936, pp. 207 *et seq.*]

Who are broad in intellectual understanding with a heart filled with Buddha knowledge,
[In them] the Bodhicitta is produced which is equal to [the owner of] the ten powers.

Homage has been offered to all the Buddhas of the past, present and future,
All the lands have been purified extending as far as space extends,
And seeing that all things partake of the nature of sameness,
The Bodhicitta is produced [in the Bodhisattvas] in order to liberate the entire world.

[In the Bodhisattvas] who are the owners of joy and good understanding, who are delighted in practicing charity,
Who are ever striving to benefit the whole world,
Who find pleasure in the virtues of the Buddha, who are strenuous in guarding beings [from evils],
[In them] the Bodhicitta is produced in order to accomplish works of beneficence for the triple world.

[In the Bodhisattvas] who have ceased from evil doings, ever strenuous in pure morality,
Who are delighted in disciplining themselves in austerities, with all their senses under perfect control,
Who take refuge in the Buddha and who are wholeheartedly devoted to deeds of enlightenment,
[In them] the Bodhicitta is produced in order to carry out works of beneficence for the triple world.

[In the Bodhisattvas] who are sympathetic for all that is good and share in the delights of patience,
Who understand the taste of meritorious deeds and are averse to arrogant spirit,
Who are fixed in religious thought, and in disposition gentle and happy,
[In them] the Bodhicitta is produced so that the whole world may be regulated beneficially.

The Bodhisattva lions carry out their deeds of purity, courageously enduring hardships,
Nobly rising for the interest of all beings,
They continually achieve what is meritorious, subduing the army of the passions:
In such minds the Bodhicitta is instantly produced.

Their minds are in the state of perfect tranquillity, they have dispelled the darkness of ignorance,

Their minds are drained of intoxication, they have forsaken paths of defilement,
They are happy with the pleasure of tranquillity, released from the bondage of transmigration:
In such minds the Bodhicitta is instantly produced.

Their thoughts are as pure as the sky, they know what is meant by transcendental and relative knowledge.
They have subdued Māra the Evil One, they have ejected the threatening passions,
They have taken refuge in the words of the Buddha, they have attained to the meaning of Suchness:
In such minds the Bodhicitta is instantly produced.

In order to bring about the weal of the triple world, they stand firmly in knowledge,
In order to remove the wrappage of contention, they are furnished with knowledge and power;
They praise the virtues of the Sugata, and are delighted with his mind:
In such minds the Bodhicitta is instantly produced.

They desire the happiness of the triple world, fulfilling the requirements of the Bodhi,
Determined in their minds to carry out their plans, the Bodhisattvas will practice deeds however difficult,
Striving for ever to do what is good:
In such minds the Bodhicitta is instantly produced.

Desirous of the virtues of one who has the ten powers, delighted with deeds of enlightenment
They are victorious over the ocean veiled with contention, they have severed the bonds of self-conceit,
Following the way of goodness, they are desirous of attaining to the meaning of the Dharma:
In such minds the Bodhicitta is instantly produced.

Let them practice such deeds of enlightenment full of merits as are recounted here,
Let them attain the wonderful powers, who are in possession of the Buddha words and vows,
Let them attain the Bodhicitta, who are cleansed in the triple virtue,
Let them be the Bodhisattvas who are cleansed in the triple refuge.

VIII

The Basis of Buddhist Philosophy

1

BUDDHIST philosophy is based on the experience Buddha had about twenty-five centuries ago. To understand, therefore, what Buddhist philosophy is, it is necessary to know what that experience was which Buddha had after six years' hard thinking and ascetic austerities and exercises in meditation.

We generally think that philosophy is a matter of pure intellect, and, therefore, that the best philosophy comes out of a mind most richly endowed with intellectual acumen and dialectical subtleties. But this is not the case. It is true that those who are poorly equipped with intellectual powers cannot be good philosophers. Intellect, however, is not the whole thing. There must be a deep power of imagination, there must be a strong, inflexible willpower, there must be a keen insight into the nature of man, and finally there must be an actual seeing of the truth as synthesized in the whole being of the man himself.

I wish to emphasize this idea of "seeing." It is not enough to "know" as the term is ordinarily understood. Knowledge unless it is accompanied by a personal experience is superficial and no kind of philosophy can be built upon such a shaky foundation. There are, however, I suppose many systems of thought not backed by real experiences, but such are never inspiring. They may be fine to look at but their power to move the readers is nil. Whatever knowledge the philosopher may have, it must come out of his experience, and this experience is seeing. Buddha has always emphasized this. He couples knowing *(ñāṇa, jñāna)* with seeing *(passa, paśya),* for without seeing, knowing has no depths, cannot understand the realities of life. Therefore, the first item of the Eightfold Noble Path is *sammādiṭṭhi,* right seeing, and *sammāsankappa,* right knowing, comes next. Seeing is experiencing, seeing things in their state of suchness *(tathatā)* or is-ness. Buddha's whole philosophy comes from this "seeing," this experiencing.

The experience which forms the basis of Buddhist philosophy is called "enlightenment-experience," for it is this experience of enlightenment which Buddha had after six years of hard thinking and profound reflection, and everything he taught afterward is the unfolding of this inner perception he then had.

What then was this enlightenment-experience?

2

Roughly speaking, we can say that there are two ways of approaching this question: What is the enlightenment-experience Buddha had? One is objective and the other subjective. The objective approach is to find out the first rationalized statements ascribed to Buddha after the experience and understood as forming the basis of his teaching. That is, what did he first teach? What was the main thesis he continued to preach throughout his life? This will be to discover what characteristically constitutes the Buddhist teaching as distinguished from that of the rest of the Indian thinkers. The second approach, called subjective, is to examine Buddha's utterances reflecting his immediate feelings after the experience of enlightenment. The first approach is metaphysical whereas the second is psychological or existential. Let us start with the first.

What is universally recognized as Buddhist thought regardless of its varieties of interpretation is the doctrine of *anattā* or *anātman,* that is, the doctrine of non-ego. Its argument begins with the idea: (1) that all things are transient as they are composites *(skandha* or *khandha)* and go on disintegrating all the time, that there is nothing permanent; and (2) that there is therefore nothing worth clinging to in this world where every one of us is made to undergo all kinds of sorrow and suffering. How do we escape from them? Or, how do we conquer them? For we cannot go on like this. We must somehow find the way out of this torture. It was this feeling of fear and insecurity individually and collectively that made Buddha leave his home and wander about for six long years seeking for a way out not only for himself but for the whole world. He finally discovered it by hitting upon the idea of non-ego *(anattā)*. The formula runs thus:[1]

"All composite things *(sankhāra)* are impermanent. When a man by wisdom *(paññā) realizes* [this], he heeds not [this world of] sorrow; this is the path to purity.

"All composite things are sorrowful. When a man by widsom realizes [this], he heeds not [this world of] sorrow; this is the path to purity.

"All things *(dhammā)* are egoless. When a man by wisdom realizes [this], he heeds not [this world of] sorrow; this is the path to purity."

The one thing I wish to call to the readers' attention is the term "wisdom," *paññā*, or *prajñā* in Sanskrit. This is a very important term throughout Buddhist philosophy. There is no English equivalent for it. "Transcendental wisdom" is too heavy, besides it does not exactly hit the mark. But temporarily let "wisdom" do. We know that seeing is very much emphasized in Buddhism, but we must not fail also to notice that seeing is not just an ordinary seeing by means of relative knowledge; it is the seeing by means of a *prajñā*-eye which is a special kind of intuition enabling us to penetrate right into the bedrock of Reality itself. I have elsewhere[2] given a somewhat detailed account of *prajñā* and its role in Buddhist teachings, especially in Zen Buddhism.

The doctrine of non-ego not only repudiates the idea of an ego-substance but points out the illusiveness of the ego-idea itself. As long as we are in this world of particular existences

[1] *The Dhammapada*, translated by S. Radhakrishnan (Oxford University Press, 1951), verses 277–9, pp. 146–7. I do not, however, always follow him in my quotations in this book.

[2] *Studies in Zen* (London: Rider and Company, 1955), pp. 85–128.

we cannot avoid cherishing the idea of an individual ego. But this by no means warrants the substantiality of the ego. Modern psychology has in fact done away with an ego-entity. It is simply a workable hypothesis by which we carry on our practical business. The problem of the ego must be carried on to the field of metaphysics. To really understand what Buddha meant by saying that there is no *ātman*, we must leave psychology behind. Because it is not enough just to state that there is no *ātman* if we wish really to reach the end of sorrow and to be thus at peace with ourselves and with the world at large. We must have something positive in order to see ourselves safely in the harbor and securely anchored. Mere psychology cannot give us this. We must go out to a broader field of Reality where *prajñā*-intuition comes into play.

As long as we wander in the domain of the senses and intellect, the idea of an individual ego besets us, and makes us eternally pursue the shadow of the ego. But the ego is something always eluding our grasp; when we think we have caught it, it is found to be no more than a slough left by the snake while the real ego is somewhere else. The human ego snake is covered with an infinity of sloughs; the catcher will before long find himself all exhausted. The ego must be caught not from outside but from within. This is the work of *prajñā*. The wonder *prajñā* performs is to catch the actor in the midst of his action; he is not made to stop acting in order to be seen as actor. The actor is the acting, and the acting is the actor, and out of this unification or identification *prajñā* is awakened. The ego does not go out of himself in order to see himself. He stays within himself and sees himself as reflected in himself. But as soon as a split takes place between the ego as actor and the ego as seer or spectator, *prajñā* is dichotomized, and all is lost.

Eckhart expresses the same experience in terms of Christian theology. He talks about Father, Son, Holy Ghost, and love. They sound unfamiliar to Buddhist ears but when they are read with a certain insight we will find that "the love with which he [God] loves himself" is the same as the *prajñā*-intuition that sees into the ego itself. Eckhart tells us: "In giving us his love God has given us his Holy Ghost so that we can love him with the love wherewith he loves himself. We love God with his own love; awareness of it deifies us."[3] The Father loving the Son and the Son loving the Father—this mutual love, that is, love loving itself is, in Zen terminology, one mirror reflecting another with no shadow between them. Eckhart calls this "the play going on in the Father-nature. Play and audience are the same." He continues:

"This play was played eternally before all natures. As it is written in the Book of Wisdom, 'Prior to creatures, in the eternal now, I have played before the Father in an eternal stillness.' The Son has eternally been playing before the Father as the Father has before his Son. The playing of the twain is the Holy Ghost in whom they both disport themselves and he disports himself in both. Sport and players are the same. Their nature proceeding in itself. 'God is a fountain flowing into itself,' as St. Dionysius says."

Prajñā-intuition comes out of itself and returns to itself. The self or ego that has been constantly eluding our rationalized scrutiny is at last caught when it comes under *prajñā*-intuition which is no other than the self.

Buddhists generally talk about the egolessness *(anattā* or *anātmya)* of all things, but they forget that the egolessness of things cannot really be understood until they are seen with the eye of *prajñā*-intuition. The psychological annihilation of an ego-substance is not enough, for this still leaves the light of *prajñā*-eye under a coverage. Eckhart says, "God is a light shining itself in silent stillness." (Evans, p. 146.) As long as our intellectually analytic eye is hotly pursuing the shadow of Reality by dichotomizing it, there will be no silent stillness of absolute identity where *prajñā* sees itself reflected in itself. Eckhart is in accord with the Buddhist experience when he proceeds: "The Word of the Father is none other than his understanding of himself. The understanding of the Father understands that he understands, and that his understanding understands is the same as that he is who is understanding. That is, the light from the light." *(Ibid.*, p. 146.)

The psychological analysis that cannot go further or deeper

[3] Evans, pp. 147 ff.

than the egolessness of the psychological ego fails to see into the egolessness of all things *(dharma)*, which appears to the eye of *prajñā*-intuition not as something sheerly of privative value but as something filled with infinite possibilities. It is only when the *prajñā*-eye surveys the nature of all things *(sarvadharmā* or *sabbe dhammā)* that their egolessness displays positive constructive energies by first dispelling the clouds of Māyā, by demolishing every structure of illusion, and thus finally by creating a world of altogether new values based on *prajñā* (wisdom) and *karuṇā* (love). The enlightenment-experience therefore means going beyond the world of psychology, the opening of the *prajñā*-eye, and seeing into the realm of Ultimate Reality, and landing on the other shore of the stream of *samsāra*, where all things are viewed in their state of suchness, in the way of purity. This is when a man finds his mind freed from everything *(sabbattha vimuttamānasa)*,[4] not confounded by the notions of birth-and-death, of constant change, of before, behind, and middle. He is the "conqueror" to whom *The Dhammapada* (179) gives this qualification:

> He whose conquest nobody can conquer again,
> Into whose conquest nobody in this world can enter—
> By what track can you trace him,
> The awakened, of infinite range, the trackless?

Such an awakened one is an absolute conqueror and nobody can follow his tracks as he leaves none. If he leaves some, this will be turned into the means whereby he can be defeated. The realm where he lives has no limiting boundaries, it is like a circle whose circumference is infinite, therefore with no center to which a path can lead. This is the one Zen describes as a man of *anābhogacaryā* ("an effortless, purposeless, useless man").[5] This corresponds to Eckhart's man of freedom who is defined as "one who clings to nothing and to whom nothing clings" (Evans, p. 146). While these statements are apt to suggest the doctrine of doing-nothing-ness we must remember that Buddhists are great adherents of what is known as the teaching of *karuṇā* and *praṇidhāna*.

[4] *The Dhammapada*, verse 348, p. 167.
[5] *Studies in the Lankāvatāra Sūtra*, pp. 223 ff.

3

When "the egolessness of all things seen with *prajñā*,"[6] which makes us transcend sorrows and sufferings and leads to "the path of purity," is understood in the sense herein elucidated, we find the way to the understanding of the lines known as "hymn of victory."

The hymn is traditionally ascribed to Buddha, who uttered it at the time of his enlightenment. It expresses more of the subjective aspect of his experience which facilitates our examination of the content of the enlightenment. While the egolessness of things is Buddha's metaphysical interpretation of the experience as he reflected upon it, the hymn of victory echoes his immediate reaction, and we are able to have a glimpse into the inner aspect of Buddha's mind more directly than through the conceptualization which came later. We can now proceed to what I have called the second approach. The hymn runs as follows:

> Looking for the maker of this tabernacle
> I ran to no avail
> Through a round of many births;
> And wearisome is birth again and again.
> But now, maker of the tabernacle, thou hast been seen;
> Thou shalt not rear this tabernacle again.
> All thy rafters are broken,
> Thy ridge-pole is shattered;
> The mind approaching the Eternal,
> Has attained to the extinction of all desires.[7]

This is Irving Babbitt's translation, the lines of which were rearranged according to the original Pali. Incidentally, I wish to remark that there is one point in it which is unsatisfactory from my point of view. This is the phrase, "the mind approaching the Eternal." The original is "*visankhāragataṃ cittaṃ.*" This means "the mind released from its binding conditions." "Approaching the Eternal" is the translator's own idea read into the line. Henry Warren, author of *Buddhism in Trans-*

[6] "*Sabbe dhammā anattā, ti yadā paññāya passati.*"

[7] *The Dhammapada*, pp. 153–4. (Published by Oxford University Press, 1936.)

lations, translates it "this mind has demolition reached," which points to nihilism or negativism, while Babbitt's translation has something of positive assertion. The difference so conspicuous in these two translations shows that each interprets the meaning according to his own philosophy. In this respect my understanding, which is given below, also reflects my own thought as regards the significance of Buddhist teaching generally.

The most essential thing here is the experience that Buddha had of being released from the bondage in which he had been kept so long. The utmost consciousness that filled his mind at the time of enlightenment was that he was no longer the slave to what he calls "the maker of the tabernacle," or "the builder of this house," that is, *gahakāraka.* He now feels himself to be a free agent, master of himself, not subject to anything external; he no longer submits himself to dictation from whatever source it may come. The *gahakāraka* is discovered, the one who was thought to be behind all his mental and physical activities, and who, as long as he, that is, Buddha, was ignorant, made him a slave to this autocrat, and employed Buddha—in fact anybody who is ignorant of the *gahakāraka*—to achieve the latter's egocentric impulses, desires, cravings. Buddha was an abject creature utterly under the control of this tyrant, and it was this sense of absolute helplessness that made Buddha most miserable, unhappy, and given over to all kinds of fears, dejection, and moroseness. But Buddha now discovers who this *gahakāraka* is; not only does he know him, but he has actually seen him face to face, taken hold of him at work. The monster, the house-builder, the constructor of the prison house, being known, being seen, being caught, ceases at last to weave his entrapping network around Buddha. This means what the phrase *"visankhāragataṃ cittaṃ"* means, the mind freed from the bondage of its primary disposition *(sankhāra).*

We must however remember that the *gahakāraka* is not dead, he is still alive, for he will be living as long as this physical existence continues. Only he has ceased to be my master; on the contrary, I am his master, I can use him as I wish, he is ready now to obey my command. "Being free from the tyranny of its binding conditions" does not mean that the conditions no longer exist. As long as we are relative existences we are to that extent conditioned, but the knowledge that we are so conditioned transcends the conditions and thus we are above them. The sense of freedom arises from this, and freedom never means lawlessness, wantonness, or libertinism. Those who understand freedom in this latter sense and act accordingly are making themselves slaves to their egotistic passions. They are no longer masters of themselves but most despicable slaves of the *gahakāraka.*

The seeing of the *gahakāraka* therefore does not mean the "seeing of the last of all desire," nor is it "the extinction of all desires." It only means that all the desires and passions we are in possession of, as human beings, are now under the control of one who has caught the *gahakāraka* working out his own limited understanding of freedom. The enlightenment-experience does not annihilate anything; it sees into the working of the *gahakāraka* from a higher point of understanding, which is to say, by means of *prajñā,* and arranges it where it properly belongs. By enlightenment Buddha sees all things in their proper order, as they should be, which means that Buddha's insight has reached the deepest depths of Reality.

As I have said before, the seeing plays the most important role in Buddhist epistemology, for seeing is at the basis of knowing. Knowing is impossible without seeing; all knowledge has its origin in seeing. Knowing and seeing are thus found generally united in Buddha's teaching. Buddhist philosophy therefore ultimately points to seeing reality as it is. Seeing is experiencing enlightenment. The *Dharma*[8] is predicated as *ehipassika,* the *Dharma* is something "you come and see." It is for this reason that *sammādiṭṭhi* is placed at the beginning of the Eightfold Noble Path.

What is the *gahakāraka*?

The *gahakāraka* detected is our relative, empirical ego, and the mind freed from its binding conditions *(sankhāra)* is the absolute ego,[9] *Ātman,* as it is elucidated in the *Nirvāṇa Sūtra.*

[8] *Dhamma* in Pali. It has a multiple meaning and it is difficult to render it uniformly. Here is stands for Truth, Reality, Norm.

[9] The term is not a happy one. It still suggests something concrete and substantial which exists as such, separate from our ordinary psychological self. Buddhists call it "emptiness" *(śūnyatā)* or "unattainable" *(anupalabdha).*

The denial of *Ātman* as maintained by earlier Buddhists refers to *Ātman* as the relative ego and not to the absolute ego, the ego after enlightenment-experience.

Enlightenment consists in seeing into the meaning of life as the interplay of the relative ego with the absolute ego. In other words, enlightenment is seeing the absolute ego as reflected in the relative ego and acting through it.

Or we may express the idea in this way: the absolute ego creates the relative ego in order to see itself reflected in it, that is, in the relative ego. The absolute ego, as long as it remains absolute, has no means whereby to assert itself, to manifest itself, to work out all its possibilities. It requires a *gahakāraka* to execute its biddings. While the *gahakāraka* is not to build his tabernacle according to his own design, he is an efficient agent to actualize whatever lies quiescently in the *Ātman* in the sense of the *Nirvāṇa Sūtra*.

4

The question now is: Why does the absolute *Ātman* want to see itself reflected in the empirical *Ātman?* Why does it want to work out its infinite possibilities through the empirical *Ātman?* Why does it not remain content with itself instead of going out to a world of multitudes, thereby risking itself to come under the domination of *sankhāra*? This is making itself, as it were, a willing slave of the *gahakāraka*.

This is a great mystery which cannot be solved on the plane of intellection. The intellect raises the question, but fails to give it a satisfactory solution. This is in the nature of the intellect. The function of the intellect consists in leading the mind to a higher field of consciousness by proposing all sorts of questions which are beyond itself. The mystery is solved by living it, by seeing into its working, by actually experiencing the significance of life, or by tasting the value of living.[10]

Tasting, seeing, experiencing, living—all these demonstrate that there is something common to enlightenment-experience

[10] "O taste and see that the Lord is good; blessed is the man that trusteth in him." (Psalms, 34:8.)

and our sense-experience; the one takes place in our innermost being, the other on the periphery of our consciousness. Personal experience is thus seen to be the foundation of Buddhist philosophy. In this sense Buddhism is radical empiricism or experientialism, whatever dialectic later developed to probe the meaning of enlightenment-experience.

Buddhist philosophy has long been wrongly regarded as nihilistic and not offering anything constructive. But those who really try to understand it and are not superficially led to misconstrue such terms as demolition, annihilation, extinction, breaking up, cessation, or quiescence, or without thirst, cutting off lust and hatred, will readily see that Buddha never taught a religion of "eternal death."

"Eternal death," which is sometimes regarded as the outcome of the Buddhist idea of egolessness, is a strange notion making no sense whatever. "Death" can mean something only when it is contrasted to birth, for it is a relative term. Eternal death is squaring a circle. Death never takes place unless there is a birth. Where there is birth there is death; where there is death there is birth; birth and death go together. We can never have just one of them, leaving out the other. Where there is eternal death there must be continuous birth. Where eternal death is maintained there must be a never-ceasing birth. Those who talk about total annihilation or extinction as if such things were possible are those who have never faced facts of experience.

Life is a never-ending concatenation of births and deaths. What Buddhist philosophy teaches is to see into the meaning of life as it flows on. When Buddhists declare that all things are impermanent, subject to conditions, and that there is nothing in this world of *samsāra* (birth-and-death) which can give us the hope for absolute security, they mean that as long as we take this world of transiency as something worth clinging to we are sure to lead a life of frustration. To transcend this negativistic attitude toward life we must make use of *prajñā* which is the way of purity. We must see things with the eye of *prajñā*, not to deny them as rubbish but to understand them from an aspect closed to ordinary observers. The latter see nothing but the impermanence or transiency or changeability of things and are unable to see eternity itself that goes along with time-serialism which can never be demolished. The demolition is on our side and not on the side of time. Buddha's enlightenment-experience clearly points to this. The ridgepole smashed and the rafters torn down all belong to time-serialism and not to eternity which suffers no kind of demolition. To imagine that when serialism is transcended eternity goes out of sight as if it were something relatively coexistent with time is altogether an erroneous way to interpret Buddha's utterance. It really requires the *prajñā*-eye to see into the "*sankhāra*-freed mind," which is in fact no other than Eckhart's eye: "The eye wherein I see God is the same eye wherein God sees me: my eye and God's eye are one eye, one vision, one knowing, one love." Time is eternity and eternity is time. In other words, zero is infinity and infinity is zero. The way of purity opens when the eye sees inwardly as well as outwardly—and this simultaneously. The *prajñā* seeing is one act, one glimpse, one *cittakṣaṇa* which is no *cittakṣaṇa*. Unless this truth is seen with *prajñā*-intuition, the "hymn of victory" will never yield its full meaning. Those who read it otherwise cannot go beyond negativism or nihilism.

The following from Eckhart will shed much light:

"Renewal befalls all creatures under God; but for God there is no renewal, only all eternity. What is eternity?—It is characteristic of eternity that in it youth and being are the same, for eternity would not be eternal could it newly become and were not always."[11]

"Renewal" means "becoming" which is "transiency." What is eternal never knows "renewal," never grows old, remains forever "youthful," and transcends "demolition" or "annihilation" of all kinds. Enlightenment is to know what this "eternity" is, and this knowing consists in "knowing eternity-wise his [God's] is-ness free from becoming, and his nameless nothingness."[12] Eckhart is quite definite in giving us what kind of God he has in mind in this matter of knowing and not knowing:

"Know'st thou of him anything? He is no such thing, and in

[11] Evans, p. 246.

[12] Pfeiffer, p. 319. "*Du mit ime verstandest ewicliche sine ungewordene istikeit under sine ungenanten nihtheit.*"

that thou dost know of him anything at all thou art in ignorance, and ignorance leads to the condition of the brute; for in creatures what is ignorant is brutish. If thou wouldst not be brutish then, know nothing of the unuttered God.—"What then shall I do?"—Thou shalt lose thy thy-ness and dissolve in his his-ness: thy thine shall be his mine, so utterly one mine that thou in him shalt know eternalwise his is-ness, free from becoming: his nameless nothingness."[13]

Eckhart's God of nameless nothingness is in Buddhist terms no other than the egolessness of all things, the *sankhāra*-free mind, and the cessation of all cravings.

5

In this connection I think it is opportune to say a few words about the negative statements liberally used in Buddhist and other texts dealing with problems of ultimate reality. I may also touch a little on the frequency of paradoxical propositions used to express a certain experience popularly known as mystic.

Considering all in all, there are two sources of knowledge, or two kinds of experience, or "two births of man" as Eckhart has it, or two forms of truth *(satya)* according to the upholders of the "Emptiness" doctrine *(śūnyavāda)*. Unless this is recognized we can never solve the problem of logical contradiction which when expressed in words characterizes all religious experiences. The contradiction so puzzling to the ordinary way of thinking comes from the fact that we have to use language to communicate our inner experience which in its very nature transcends linguistics. But as we have so far no means of communication except the one resorted to by followers of Zen Buddhism, the conflicts go on between rationalists and so-called mystics. Language developed first for the use of the first kind of knowledge which was highly utilitarian, and for this reason it came to assert itself over all human affairs and experiences. Its overwhelming authority is such that we have almost come to accept everything language commands. Our thoughts have now to be molded according to its dictates, our acts are to be regulated by

[13] Evans, p. 246.

the rules it came to formulate for its own effective operation. This is not all. What is worse is that language has now come even to suppress the truth of new experiences, and that when they actually take place, it will condemn them as "illogical" or "unthinkable" and therefore as false, and finally that as such it will try to put aside anything new as of no human value

The Sūnyatā school distinguishes two forms of truth *(satya):* (1) *samvṛiti* of the relative world and (2) *paramārtha* of the transcendental realm of *prajñā*-intuition. When Buddha speaks of his enlightenment in the *Saddharmapuṇḍarīka Sūtra* ("Lotus Gospel"), he describes his experience as something which cannot be comprehended by any of his followers because their understanding can never rise up to the level of Buddha's. It is another Buddha who understands a Buddha, Buddhas have their own world into which no beings of ordinary caliber of mentality can have a glimpse. Language belongs to this world of relativity, and when Buddha tries to express himself by this means his hearers are naturally barred from entering his inner life. While in the *Lankāvatāra Sūtra* we are told of many other Buddha countries where Buddha activities are carried on by means other than mere language, for instance, by moving hands or legs, by smiling, by coughing, by sneezing, etc. Evidently Buddhas can understand one another by whatever means they may employ in conveying their inner acts, because they all know what they are through their experience. But where there are no such corresponding experiences, no amount of technique one may resort to will be possible to awaken them in others.

In Aśvaghoṣa's *Awakening of Faith* reference is made to two aspects of *Tathatā* (Suchness"), one of which is altogether beyond speaking or writing, because it does not fall into the categories of communicability. Language here has no use whatever. But Aśvaghoṣa continues: if we did not appeal to language there is no way to make others acquainted with the absolute; therefore language is resorted to in order to serve as a wedge in getting out of the one already in use; it is like a poisonous medicine to counteract another. It is a most dangerous weapon and its user has to be cautioned in every way not to hurt himself. The *Lankāvatāra* is decisive in this respect:

. . . word-discrimination cannot express the highest reality, for external objects with their multitudinous individual marks are non-existent, and only appear before us as something revealed out of Mind itself. Therefore, Mahāmati, you must try to keep yourself away from the various forms of word-discrimination.[14]

Word-discrimination belongs to the *samvṛiti,* to things of the relative world, and is not meant for communicating anything that goes beyond this world of numbers and multiplicities. For here language ceases to be supreme and must realize that it has its limitations. Two of the three kinds of knowledge distinguished by Eckhart are of the *samvṛiti,* where the third corresponds to the *paramārtha.* To quote Eckhart:

These three things stand for three kinds of knowledge. The first is sensible. The eye sees from afar what is outside it. The second is rational and is a great deal higher. The third corresponds to an exalted power of the soul, a power so high and noble it is able to see God face to face in his own self. This power has naught in common with naught, it knows no yesterday or day before, no morrow or day after (for in eternity there is no yesterday or morrow) : therein it is the present now; the happenings of the thousand years ago, a thousand years to come, are there in the present and the antipodes the same as here.[15]

The first two kinds apply to the world of senses and the intellect, where language has its utmost usefulness. But when we try to use it in the realm where "the exalted power of the soul" has its sway it miserably fails to convey the activities going on there to those whose "power" has never been "heightened" or enhanced to the level indicated by Eckhart. But as we are forced to make use of language inasmuch as we are creatures of the sense-intellect, we contradict ourselves, as we see in Eckhart's statements just quoted. In this respect Eckhart and all other thinkers of Eckhart's pattern go on disregarding rules of logic or linguistics. The point is that linguists or logicians are to abandon their limited way of studying facts of experience so that they can analyze the facts themselves and make language amenable to what they discover there. As long as they take up

[14] *Lankāvatāra Sūtra,* translated by D. T. Suzuki (London: George Routledge and Sons, Ltd., 1932), p. 77.
[15] Evans, p. 228.

language first and try to adjust all human experiences to the requirements of language instead of the opposite, they will have their problems unsolved.

Eckhart further writes:

> The just man serves neither God nor creature: he is free; and the more he is just the more he is free and the more he is freedom itself. Nothing created is free. While there is aught above me, excepting God himself, it must constrain me, however [great]; even love and knowledge, so far as it is creature and not actually God, confines me with its limits.[16]

Let us first see what linguistics would say about this statement. Its reasoning may run something like this: "When Eckhart expresses himself as 'a free man' he is irresistible and wonderful, but he still recognizes God as he confesses 'excepting God.' Why, we may ask, has he to make the exception of God instead of asserting his absolute freedom above all things small and great? If he has to consider God, he cannot be so free as he claims to be?" These objections hold good indeed so far as our logical analysis does not extend beyond language and its values. But one who has an Eckhartian experience will very well understand what he really means. And what he means is this: a man is free only when he is in God, with God, for God, and this is not the condition of freedom for when he is in God he is freedom itself: he is free when he realizes that he is actually himself by forswearing that he is in God and absolutely free. Says Eckhart:

> I was thinking lately: that *I am a man* belongs to other men in common with myself; I see and hear and eat and drink like any other animal; but that *I am* belongs to no one but myself, not to man nor angel, no, nor yet to God excepting in so far as I am one with him.[17]

In the latter part of the same sermon, Eckhart adds: "*Ego,* the word 'I,' is proper to none but to God himself in his sameness." This "I" is evidently referred to in another sermon entitled "The Castle of the Soul" as "a spark," "a spiritual light."

> From time to time I tell of the one power in the soul which alone is free. Sometimes I have called it the tabernacle of the soul; some-

16 *Ibid.*, p. 204.
17 *Ibid.*, p. 204.

times a spiritual light, anon I say it is a spark. But now I say: it is neither this nor that. Yet it is somewhat: somewhat more exalted over this and that than the heavens are above the earth. . . . It is of all names free, of all forms void: exempt and free as God is in himself.[18]

Our language is the product of a world of numbers and individuals of yesterdays and todays and tomorrows, and is most usefully applicable to this world *(loka)*. But our experiences have it that our world extends beyond that *(loka)*, that there is another called by Buddhists a "transcendental world" *(loka-uttara)* and that when language is forced to be used for things of this world, *lokottara,* it becomes warped and assumes all kinds of crookedness: oxymora, paradoxes, contradictions, contortions, absurdities, oddities, ambiguities, and irrationalities. Language itself is not to be blamed for it. It is we ourselves who, ignorant of its proper functions, try to apply it to that for which it was never intended. More than this, we make fools of ourselves by denying the reality of a transcendental world *(lokottara)*.

Let us see how impossible it is to bring a transcendental world or an "inner power" onto the level of linguistic manageability.

There is something, transcending the soul's created nature, not accessible to creature, non-existent; no angel has gotten it for his is a clear[19] nature, and clear and overt things have no concern with this. It is akin to Deity, intrinsically one, having naught in common with naught. Many a priest finds it a baffling thing. It is one; rather unnamed than named, rather unknown than known. If thou couldst naught thyself an instant, less than an instant, I should say, all that this is in itself would belong to thee. But while thou dost mind thyself at all thou knowest no more of God than my mouth does of colour or my eye of taste: so little thou knowest, thou discernest, what God is.[20]

What "a baffling thing" this "something" or "somewhat" is! But it is no doubt a light and if you can get a glimpse into it even "less than an instant" you will be master of yourself. Plato describes the light in the following words: It is "a light which is not in this world; not in the world and not out of

18 *Ibid.*, p. 37.

19 *"Ein luter wesen"* in German. *Luter* means "intellectually or analytically clear and distinct," opposed to what may be called "metaphysically indefinite."

20 Evans, pp. 204–5.

the world; not in time nor in eternity; it has neither in nor out."[21] Linguistically considered, how could a thing be said to be "neither in the world nor in out-of-the-world"? Nothing can be more absurd than this. But, as Eckhart says (Evans, p. 227), when we transcend time *(zit)*, body *(liplicheit)*, and multiplicity *(manicvaltikeit)*,[22] we reach God, and these three things are the very principle of linguistics. No wonder that when things of the *lokottara* try to find their expression through language, the latter shows every trace of its shortcomings.

6

It is now time to come back to the original topic and see if we cannot get once more into the subjective approach to Buddha's experience of enlightenment. The experience cannot merely be designated as a kind of feeling and thus done away with as if this designation exhausted all the contents of enlightenment. For, as I understand it, the enlightenment cannot be said to be devoid of any noetic elements which yield to a certain extent to a linguistic and intellectual treatment. The feeling of enlightenment has something profoundly fundamental and gives one a sense of absolute certainty and finality which is lacking in the ordinary kind of feeling we generally have. A feeling may occasionally give one the sense of exaltation and self-assurance, but this will after a while pass away and may leave no permanent effect on the being of one who has the experience. The enlightenment feeling on the other hand affects the whole personality, influencing his attitude toward life and the world not only morally and spiritually but in his metaphysical interpretation of existence as a whole. Buddha's experience was not just a matter of feeling which moves on the periphery of consciousness, but something awakened in the deepest recesses of a human being. In this sense only is his utterance recorded in the *Vinaya* and the *Majjhima Nikāya* and elsewhere to be understood. In the *gāthā* already quoted above from *The Dhammapada* (vv. 153, 154), something similar to the one below is noticeable, but the positive and dynamic aspect

21 Quoted by Eckhart, Evans, p. 205.
22 Pfeiffer, p. 296.

comes forward more strongly and conspicuously in the following:[23]

> I have conquered and I know all,
> I am enlightened quite by myself and have none as teacher.
> There is no one that is the same as I in the whole world where there are many deities.
> I am the one who is really worth,
> I am the most supreme teacher.
> I am the only one who is fully enlightened.
> I am tranquilized.
> I am now in Nirvana.[24]

This victory song is expressive of the supreme moment of the enlightenment-experience which Buddha had. In the first verse depicting the discovery of the *gahakāraka* (house builder) and the demolition of his handiwork, we see the negative aspect of Buddha's experience, while in the second one dealing with the exalted feeling of victory, the realization of the highest knowledge *(prajñā)* and the consciousness of one's own value as he is, we see its positive aspect coming out in full view.

The consciousness of conquest such as was awakened in the mind of Buddha at the time of enlightenment cannot be regarded as the product of a self-conceit which is often cherished by minds tarnished with schizophrenia and the wielders of political or military powers. With him however whose ego-centered desires have been shattered to pieces the consciousness of victory rises from the deepest sources of being. So the feeling of conquest is not the outcome of a struggle of powers belonging to the low level of existence. The enlightenment-experience is the manifestation of a higher power, a higher insight, a higher unification. It is beyond the sphere of relative consciousness

23 *The Vinaya*, I, p. 8. *The Majjhima Nikāya* (translated by Lord Chalmers, published by Oxford University Press), 26, p. 12.

24 It will be interesting to note that we have another *gāthā* in *The Dhammapada*, v. 353, which also echoes the same sentiment as the one here quoted from another source. It is possible that they are from one and the same original source. *The Dhammapada* one runs thus:

> I have conquered all, I know all, in all conditions of life I am free from taint. I have left all, and through the destruction of thirst I am free. Having by myself attained specific knowledge, to whom can I point as my teacher?

which is the battleground for forces belonging to the same order. One force may temporarily proclaim its victory over another, but his kind of victory is sure before long to be superseded by another. This is in the nature of our relative consciousness. Enlightenment is the experience a man can have only when a higher realm of unification is revealed, that is, when the most fundamental basis of identification is reached.

The enlightenment-experience, therefore, is the one which we can have only when we have climbed up to the highest peak from which we can survey the whole field of Reality. Or we can say that it is the experience which is attained only when we have touched the very bedrock which sustains the entire system of multiple worlds. Here is the consciousness of intensive quantity to which nothing more could be added. All is fulfilled, satisfied; everything here appears to it such as it is; in short, it is a state of absolute Suchness, of absolute Emptiness which is absolute fullness.

Buddhist philosophy, therefore, is the philosophy of Suchness, or philosophy of Emptiness, or philosophy of Self-identity. It starts from the absolute present which is pure experience, an experience in which there is yet no differentiation of subject and object, and yet which is not a state of sheer nothingness. The experience is variously designated: in Japanese it is *sono-mama;* in Chinese it is *chih mo,* sometimes *tzu-jan fa-erh* (Japanese: *jinen hōni);* there are many technical names for it, each denoting its specific features or characters as it is viewed in various relationships.

In fact, this Suchness, or "is-ness" *(isticheit)* in Eckhart's terminology, defies all characterization or denotation. No words can express what it is, but as words are the only instrument given us human beings to communicate our thought, we have to use words, with this caution: Nothing is available for our purpose; to say "not available" *(anupalabdha* in Sanskrit and *pu k'o tê* in Chinese) is not to the point either. Nothing is acceptable. To say it is, is already negating itself. Suchness transcends everything, it has no moorings. No concepts can reach it, no understanding can grasp it. Therefore, it is called pure experience.

In pure experience there is no division between "ought" and "is," between form and matter or content, and therefore there is no judgment in it yet. There is the Christ who says "I am before Abraham was," or God who has not yet uttered his fiat. This is Buddha who, according to *The Dhammapada* (179), is the *anantagocara* ("one whose limits are infinite"), the *apada* ("the pathless"), whose conquest can never be conquered again and into whose conquest nobody in this world can enter, and who is where there is no track leading to it. If it were a Zen master, he would demand that you show your face, however ugly it might be, which you have even before your birth into this world of mutiplicities.

The Buddhist philosophy of Suchness thus starts with what is most primarily given to our consciousness—which I have called pure experience. But, in point of fact, to say "pure experience" is to commit oneself to something already posited somewhere, and thus it ceases to be pure. *The Dhammapada* reflects this thought when it designates the starting point of Buddhist philosophy as trackless *(apada),* unboundable *(anantagocara),* abodeless *(aniketa),* empty *(suñña),* formless *(animitta),* delivered *(vimokkha).* In psychological terms, it is described thus: sorrowless *(vippamutta),* released on all sides *(sabbaganthappahīna),* fearless *(asantāsin),* without craving *(vītataṇha).* These psychological terms are apt to be very much misunderstood because they point to negativism when superficially and linguistically interpreted. But I will not dwell upon this here.

One thing that must be noted in this connection is that pure experience is not pure passivity. In fact there is nothing we can call pure passivity. This does not make sense and does not lead us anywhere. As long as passivity is also an experience, there must be one who experiences passivity. This one, this experiencer, is an actor. Not only is he an actor, but he is a knower, for he is conscious of experiencing. Pure experience is not an abstraction or a state of passivity. It is very much active, and creative. Eckhart voices this idea when he states: "In this sense thy unkowing is not a defect but thy chief perfection, and suffering thy highest activity. Kill thy activities and still thy faculties if thou wouldst realize this birth in thee."[25]

[25] Evans, p. 14. "This birth" in this sermon means "the newborn Being" or "the child of man turned into the child of God." It also means "hearing of the Word" which is revealed to "one who knows aright in unknowing."

Another thing I should like to emphasize in this *gāthā* of conquest is that Buddha calls himself "all-conqueror" and also "all-knower," showing that his victory is absolute and that his knowledge is not at all fragmentary. He is omniscient as well as omnipotent. His experience has something noetic and at the same time something conative or affective, reflecting the nature of Reality itself which consists in *prajñā* and *karuṇā*. As regards *prajñā,* which is sometimes translated as "transcendental wisdom," I have written about it elsewhere. Therefore I shall speak here about *karuṇā*. *Karuṇā* corresponds to love. It is like the sands on the Ganges: they are trampled by all kinds of beings: by elephants, by lions, by assess, by human beings, but they do not make any complaints. They are again soiled by all kinds of filth scattered by all kinds of animals, but they just suffer them all and never utter a word of ill-will. Eckhart would declare the sands on the Ganges to be "just" *(gerecht),* because "the just have no will at all: whatever God wishes it is all one to them, however great the discomfort may be."[26]

> The just are so firmly devoted to justice and so wholly selfless that whatever they do, they regard neither the pains of hell nor the joys of heaven. . . . To the just person, nothing is so hard to bear or so painful as anything opposed to justice, that is to say, as not feeling impartially the same about everything that happens.[27]

"Justice" savors a great deal of legalism contrary to the idea of love. But when, as Eckhart interprets it, justice is considered from the affective point of view as meaning "impartiality," "sameness," "universality," or "all embracing," it begins to approach the Buddhist idea of *karuṇā*. I may add that Mahāyāna Buddhism further developed the idea of *karuṇā* into that of *praṇidhāna* or *pūrvapraṇidhāna* and made each one of the Bodhisattvas an incarnation of a certain number of *praṇidhāna,* for example, Amitābha has forty-eight *praṇidhāna,* Samantabhadra has ten, and Kṣitigarbha also has ten. *Praṇidhāna* is generally translated as "vow" or "fervent wish" or "prayer," or simply "the will," but these English terms do not convey the full meaning of the Sanskrit as it is used in the Mahāyāna. Roughly speaking, we may interpret *praṇidhāna* as love specified

26 Blakney, p. 179.
27 *Ibid.*

or itemized or particularized and made applicable to each practical situation in which we may find ourselves in the course of an individual life. Amitābha has his Pure Land where he wants to be born; Mañjuśrī is the Bodhisattva of *prajñā* and whoever comes to him will be rewarded with an amount of transcendental wisdom.

This being the case, we will see that "the destruction of desires or cravings" *(taṇhānam khayam)* so much emphasized in the teaching of earlier Buddhism is not to be understood negativistically. The Buddhist training consists in transforming *tṛiṣṇā (taṇhā)* into *karuṇā,* ego-centered love into something universal, eros into agape.

When Jōshu (778–897) was asked, "Could Buddha cherish any desires *(kleśa)*?" he answered, "Yes, he decidedly has." The questioner demanded, "How could that be?" The master replied, "His desire is to save the whole universe."

One day Jōshu had another visitor who asked, "I hear so much of the stone bridge reputed to be on one of the sites in your monastery grounds. But as I see it, it is no more than an old log. How is that?"

The master said, "You see the log and don't see the stone bridge."

"What is the stone bridge, then?" the visitor demanded.

The master's answer was, "It permits horses to pass and also asses to pass."

Someone's *praṇidhāna* is too rickety for safe crossing whereas the other's is strong and broad, allowing anything to pass over it safely. Let *taṇhā* be destroyed but we must not forget that it has another root which reaches the very ground of being. The enlightenment-experience must realize that, though ordinarily Buddhists are more or less neglectful in bringing out the *karuṇā* aspect of the experience. This is due to their being too anxious and therefore too much in a hurry to destroy all the obstacles lying on the way to enlightenment, for they know that when this is accomplished what is to come therefrom is left to itself as it knows full well how to take care of it. When the devastating fire is extinguished the forest will not wait for any external help but will resume its biological functions by itself. When a man is shot by a poisonous arrow the first thing to do is to remove it before it is embedded too deeply into the flesh. When this is done the body will heal the wound by its own power of vitality. So with human passions, the first work is to destroy their root of ignorance and egoism. When this is thoroughly accomplished, the Buddha nature which consists in *prajñā* and *karuṇā* will start its native operation. The principle of Suchness is not static, it is full of dynamic forces.

IX

Meister Eckhart[1] and Buddhism

1

IN THE following pages I attempt to call the reader's attention to the closeness of Meister Eckhart's way of thinking to that of Mahāyāna Buddhism, especially of Zen Buddhism. The attempt is only a tentative and sketchy one, far from being systematic and exhaustive. But I hope the reader will find something in it which evokes his curiosity enough to undertake further studies of this fascinating topic.

When I first read—which was more than a half century ago—a little book containing a few of Meister Eckhart's sermons, they impressed me profoundly, for I never expected that any Christian thinker ancient or modern could or would cherish such daring thoughts as expressed in those sermons. While I do not

[1] There are two English translations of Eckhart, one British and the other American. The British, in two volumes, is by C. de B. Evans, published by John M. Watkins, London, 1924. The American translation is by Raymond B. Blakney, published by Harper & Brothers, New York, 1941. Neither of them is a complete translation of all of Eckhart's known works in German. Franz Pfeiffer published in 1857 a collection of Eckhart's works, chiefly in the High German dialect of Strassburg of the fourteenth century. This edition was reprinted in 1914. Blakney's and Evans' translations are mainly based on the Pfeiffer edition. In the present book, "Blakney" refers to the Blakney translation and "Evans" to the Evans, Vol. I, while "Pfeiffer" means his German edition of 1914. [Pfeiffer could not always clearly distinguish between Eckhart's works and those of his school. For the present state of our knowledge see J. M. Clark, *Meister Eckhart*, London, Thomas Nelson & Sons, 1957.]

remember which sermons made up the contents of the little book, the ideas expounded there closely approached Buddhist thoughts, so closely indeed, that one could stamp them almost definitely as coming out of Buddhist speculations. As far as I can judge, Eckhart seems to be an extraordinary "Christian."

While refraining from going into details we can say at least this: Eckhart's Christianity is unique and has many points which make us hesitate to classify him as belonging to the type we generally associate with rationalized modernism or with conservative traditionalism. He stands on his own experiences which emerged from a rich, deep, religious personality. He attempts to reconcile them with the historical type of Christianity modeled after legends and mythology. He tries to give an "esoteric" or inner meaning to them, and by so doing he enters fields which were not touched by most of his historical predecessors.

First, let me give you the views Eckhart has on time and creation. These are treated in his sermon delivered on the commemoration day for St. Germaine. He quotes a sentence from Ecclesiasticus: "In his days he pleased God and was found just." Taking up first the phrase "In his days," he interprets it according to his own understanding:

> . . . there are more days than one. There is the soul's day and God's day. A day, whether six or seven ago, or more than six thousand years ago, is just as near to the present as yesterday. Why? Because all time is contained in the present Now-moment. Time comes of the revolution of the heavens and day began with the first revolution. The soul's day falls within this time and consists of the natural light in which things are seen. God's day, however, is the complete day, comprising both day and night. It is the real Now-moment, which for the soul is eternity's day, on which the Father begets his only begotten Son and the soul is reborn in God.[2]

The soul's day and God's day are different. In her natural day the soul knows all things above time and place; nothing is far or near. And that is why I say, this day all things are of equal rank. To talk about the world as being made by God to-morrow, yesterday, would be talking nonsense. God makes the world and all things in this present now. Time gone a thousand years ago is now as present and as near to God as this very instant. The soul who is in this present now, in her the Father bears his one-begotten Son and in that same

2 Blakney, p. 212.

birth the soul is born back into God. It is one birth; as fast as she is reborn into God the Father is begetting his only Son in her.[3]

God the Father and the Son have nothing to do with time. Generation is not in time, but at the end and limit of time. In the past and future movements of things, your heart flits about; it is in vain that you attempt to know eternal things; in divine things, you should be occupied intellectually. . . .[4]

Again, God loves for his own sake, acts for his own sake: that means that he loves for the sake of love and acts for the sake of action. It cannot be doubted that God would never have begot his Son in eternity if [his idea of] creation were other than [his act of] creation. Thus God created the word so that he might keep on creating. The past and future are both far from God and alien to his way.[5]

From these passages we see that the Biblical story of Creation is thoroughly contradicted; it has not even a symbolic meaning in Eckhart, and further, his God is not at all like the God conceived by most Christians. God is not in time mathematically enumerable. His creativity is not historical, not accidental, not at all measurable. It goes on continuously without cessation with no beginning, with no end. It is not an event of yesterday or today or tomorrow, it comes out of timelessness, of nothingness, of Absolute Void. God's work is always done in an absolute present, in a timeless "now which is time and place in itself." God's work is sheer love, utterly free from all forms of chronology and teleology. The idea of God creating the world out of nothing, in an absolute present, and therefore altogether beyond the control of a serial time conception will not sound strange to Buddhist ears. Perhaps they may find it acceptable as reflecting their doctrine of Emptiness (*śūnyatā*).

2

Below are further quotations from Eckhart giving his views on "being," "life," "work," etc.:

Being is God. . . . God and being are the same—or God has being from another and thus himself is not God. . . . Everything

[3] Evans, p. 209.
[4] Blakney, p. 292.
[5] *Ibid.*, p. 62.

that is has the fact of its being through being and from being. Therefore, if being is something different from God, a thing has its being from something other than God. Besides, there is nothing prior to being, because that which confers being creates and is a creator. To create is to give being out of nothing.[6]

Eckhart is quite frequently metaphysical and makes one wonder how his audience took to his sermons—an audience which is supposed to have been very unscholarly, being ignorant of Latin and all the theologies written in it. This problem of being and God's creating the world out of nothing must have puzzled them very much indeed. Even the scholars might have found Eckhart beyond their understanding especially when we know that they were not richly equipped with the experiences which Eckhart had. Mere thinking or logical reasoning will never succeed in clearing up problems of deep religious significance. Eckhart's experiences are deeply, basically, abundantly rooted in God as Being which is at once being and not-being: he sees in the "meanest" thing among God's creatures all the glories of his is-ness *(isticheit)*. The Buddhist enlightenment is nothing more than this experience of is-ness or suchness *(tathatā)*, which in itself has all the possible values *(guṇa)* we humans can conceive.

God's characteristic is being. The philosopher says one creature is able to give another life. For in being, mere being, lies all that is at all. Being is the first name. Defect means lack of being. Our whole life ought to be being. So far as our life is being, so far it is in God. So far as our life is feeble but taking is as being, it excels anything life can ever boast. I have no doubt of this, that if the soul had the remotest notion of what being means she would never waver from it for an instant. The most trivial thing perceived in God, a flower for example as espied in God, would be a thing more perfect than the universe. The vilest thing present in God as being is better than angelic knowledge.[7]

This passage may sound too abstract to most readers. The sermon is said to have been given on the commemoration day of the "blessed martyrs who were slain with the swords." Eckhart begins with his ideas about death and suffering which come to an end like everything else that belongs to this world.

[6] *Ibid.*, p. 278.
[7] Evans, p. 206.

He then proceeds to tell us that "it behooves us to emulate the dead in dispassion *(niht betrüeben)* towards good and ill and pain of every kind," and he quotes St. Gregory: "No one gets so much of God as the man who is thoroughly dead," because "death gives them [martyrs] being,—they lost their life and found their being." Eckhart's allusion to the flower as espied in God reminds us of Nansen's interview with Rikko in which the Zen master also brings out a flower in the monastery courtyard.

It is when I encounter such statements as these that I grow firmly convinced that the Christian experiences are not after all different from those of the Buddhist. Terminology is all that divides us and stirs us up to a wasteful dissipation of energy. We must however weigh the matter carefully and see whether there is really anything that alienates us from one another and whether there is any basis for our spiritual edification and for the advancement of a world culture.

> When God made man, he put into the soul his equal, his active, everlasting masterpiece. It was so great a work that it could not be otherwise than the soul and the soul could not be otherwise than the work of God. God's nature, his being, and the Godhead all depend on his work in the soul. Blessed, blessed be God that he does work in the soul and that he loves his work! That work is love and love is God. God loves himself and his own nature, being and Godhead, and in the love he has for himself he loves all creatures, not as creatures but as God. The love God bears himself contains his love for the whole world.[8]

Eckhart's statement regarding God's self-love which "contains his love for the whole world" corresponds in a way to the Buddhist idea of universal enlightenment. When Buddha attained the enlightenment, it is recorded, he perceived that all beings non-sentient as well as sentient were already in the enlightenment itself. The idea of enlightenment may make Buddhists appear in some respects more impersonal and metaphysical than Christians. Buddhism thus may be considered more scientific and rational than Christianity which is heavily laden with all sorts of mythological paraphernalia. The movement is now therefore going on among Christians to denude the

[8] Blakney, pp. 224–5.

religion of this unnecessary historical appendix. While it is difficult to predict how far it will succeed, there are in every religion some elements which may be called irrational. They are generally connected with the human craving for love. The Buddhist doctrine of enlightenment is not after all such a cold system of metaphysics as it appears to some people. Love enters also into the enlightenment experience as one of its constituents, for otherwise it could not embrace the totality of existence. The enlightenment does not mean to run away from the world, and to sit cross-legged at the peak of the mountain, to look down calmly upon a bomb-struck mass of humanity. It has more tears than we imagine.

> Thou shalt know him [God] without image, without semblance and without means.—"But for me to know God thus, with nothing between, I must be all but he, he all but me."—I say, God must be very I, I very God, so consummately one that this he and this I are one "is," in this is-ness working one work eternally; but so long as this he and this I, to wit, God and the soul, are not one single here, one single now, then I cannot work with nor be one with that he.[9]

> What is life? God's being is my life, but if it is so, then what is God's must be mine and what is mine God's. God's is-ness is my is-ness, and neither more nor less. The just live eternally with God, on a par with God, neither deeper nor higher. All their work is done by God and God's by them.[10]

Going over these quotations, we feel that it was natural that orthodox Christians of his day accused Eckhart as a "heretic" and that he defended himself. Perhaps it is due to our psychological peculiarities that there are always two opposing tendencies in the human way of thinking and feeling; extrovert and introvert, outer and inner, objective and subjective, exoteric and esoteric, traditional and mystical. The opposition between these two tendencies or temperaments is often too deep and strong for any form of reconciliation. This is what makes Eckhart complain about his opponents not being able to grasp his point. He would remonstrate: "Could you see with my heart you would understand my words, but it is true, for the truth itself has said it."[11]

[9] Evans, p. 247.
[10] Blakney, p. 180.
[11] Evans, p. 38.

Augustine is however tougher than Eckhart: "What is it to me though any comprehend not this!"[12]

3

One of Eckhart's heresies was his pantheistic tendency. He seemed to put man and God on an equal footing: "The Father begets his Son in me and I am there in the same Son and not another."[13] While it is dangerous to criticize Eckhart summarily as a pantheist by picking one or two passages at random from his sermons, there is no doubt that his sermons contain many thoughts approaching pantheism. But unless the critics are a set of ignorant misinterpreters with perhaps an evil intention to condemn him in every way as a heretic, a fair-minded judge will notice that Eckhart everywhere in his sermons is quite careful to emphasize the distinction between the creature and the creator as in the following:

> "Between the only begotten Son and the soul there is no distinction." This is true. For how could anything white be distinct from or divided from whiteness? Again, matter and form are one in being; living and working. Yet matter is not, on this account, form, or conversely. So in the proposition. A holy soul is one with God, according to John 17:21. That they all may be one in us, even as we are one. Still the creature is not the creator, nor is the just man God.[14]

> God and Godhead are as different as earth is from heaven. Moreover I declare: the outward and the inward man are as different, too, as earth and heaven. God is higher, many thousand miles. Yet God comes and goes. But to resume my argument: God enjoys himself in all things. The sun sheds his light upon all creatures, and anything he sheds his beams upon absorbs them, yet he loses nothing of his brightness.[15]

From this we can see most decidedly that Eckhart was far from being a pantheist. In this respect Mahāyāna Buddhism is

[12] Quoted by Eckhart, Blakney, p. 305.

[13] *Cf.* Blakney, p. 214: "The soul that lives in the present Now-moment is the soul in which the Father begets his only begotten Son and in that birth the soul is born again into God. It is one birth, as fast as she is reborn into God the Father is begetting his only Son in her." (The last sentence is from Evans, p. 209.)

[14] *Ibid.*, "The Defense," p. 303.

[15] Evans, pp. 142–3.

also frequently and erroneously stamped as pantheistic, ignoring altogether a world of particulars. Some critics seem to be ready and simple-minded enough to imagine that all doctrines that are not transcendentally or exclusively monotheistic are pantheistic and that they are for this reason perilous to the advancement of spiritual culture.

It is true that Eckhart insists on finding something of a Godlike nature in each one of us, otherwise the birth of God's only Son in the soul would be impossible and his creatures would forever be something utterly alienated from him. As long as God is love, as creator, he can never be outside the creatures. But this cannot be understood as meaning the oneness of one with the other in every possible sense. Eckhart distinguishes between the inner man and the outer man and what one sees and hears is not the same as the other. In a sense therefore we can say that we are not living in an identical world and that the God one conceives for oneself is not at all to be subsumed under the same category as the God for another. Eckhart's God is neither transcendental nor pantheistic.

God goes and comes, he works, he is active, he becomes all the time, but Godhead remains immovable, imperturbable, inaccessible. The difference between God and Godhead is that between heaven and earth and yet Godhead cannot be himself without going out of himself, that is, he is he because he is not he. This "contradiction" is comprehended only by the inner man, and not by the outer man, because the latter sees the world through the senses and intellect and consequently fails to experience the profound depths of Godhead.

Whatever influence Eckhart might have received from the Jewish (Maimonides), Arabic (Avicenna), and Neoplatonic sources, there is no doubt that he had his original views based on his own experiences, theological and otherwise, and that they were singularly Mahāyānistic. Coomaraswamy is quite right when he says:

> Eckhart presents an astonishingly close parallel to Indian modes of thought; some whole passages and many single sentences read like a direct translation from Sanskrit. . . . It is not of course suggested that any Indian elements whatever are actually present in Eckhart's writing, though there are some Oriental factors in the

European tradition, derived from neo-Platonic and Arabic sources. But what is proved by analogies is not the influence of one system of thought upon another, but the coherence of the metaphysical tradition in the world and at all times.[16]

4

It is now necessary to examine Eckhart's close kinship with Mahāyāna Buddhism and especially with Zen Buddhism in regard to the doctrine of Emptiness.

The Buddhist doctrine of Emptiness is unhappily greatly misunderstood in the West. The word "emptiness" or "void" seems to frighten people away, whereas when they use it among themselves, they do not seem to object to it. While some Indian thought is described as nihilistic, Eckhart has never been accused of this, though he is not sparing in the use of words with negative implications, such as "desert," "stillness," "silence," nothingness." Perhaps when these terms are used among Western thinkers, they are understood in connection with their historical background. But as soon as these thinkers are made to plunge into a strange, unfamiliar system or atmosphere, they lose their balance and condemn it as negativistic or anarchistic or upholding escapist egoism.

According to Eckhart,

> I have read many writings both of heathen philosophers and sages, of the Old and the New Testaments, and I have earnestly and with all diligence sought the best and the highest virtue whereby man may come most closely to God and wherein he may once more become like the original image as he was in God when there was yet no distinction between God and himself before God produced creatures. And having dived into the basis of things to the best of my ability I find that it is no other than absolute detachment (*abgeschiedenheit*) from everything that is created. It was in this sense when our Lord said to Martha: "One thing is needed," which is to say: He who would be untouched and pure needs just one thing, detachment.[17]

16 *The Transformation of Nature in Art,* p. 201.

17 Blakney, "About Disinterest," p. 82. The translator prefers "disinterest" to "detachment" for *abgeschiedenheit*. I really do not know which is better. The German word seems to correspond to the Sanskrit *anabhiniveśa* or *asaṅga* (*mushūjaku* in Japanese and *wu chih chu* in Chinese), meaning "not attached," "not clinging to." [May I rather suggest *viveka*? E. C.]

What then is the content of absolute detachment? It cannot be designated "as this or that," as Eckhart says. It is pure nothing *(bloss niht),* it is the highest point at which God can work in us as he pleases.

Perfect detachment is without regard, without either lowliness or loftiness to creatures; it has no mind to be below nor yet to be above; it is minded to be master of itself, loving none and hating none, having neither likeness nor unlikeness, neither this nor that, to any creature; the only thing it desires to be is to be one and the same. For to be either this or that is to want something. He who is this or that is somebody; but detachment wants altogether nothing. It leaves all things unmolested.[18]

While Buddhist emphasis is on the emptiness of all "composite things" *(skandha)* and is therefore metaphysical, Eckhart here insists on the psychological significance of "pure nothingness" so that God can take hold of the soul without any resistance on the part of the individual. But from the practical point of view the emptying of the soul making it selfless can never be thoroughly realized unless we have an ontological understanding of the nature of things, that is, the nothingness of creaturely objects. For the created have no reality; all creatures are pure nothing, for "all things were made by him [God] and without him was not anything made" (John, 1:3). Further, "If without God a creature has any being however small, then God is not the cause of all things. Besides, a creature will not be created, for creation is the receiving of being from nothing."[19] What could this mean? How could any being come from nothing or non-being? Psychology herein inevitably turns to metaphysics. We here encounter the problem of Godhead.

This problem was evidently not touched upon frequently by Eckhart, for he warns his readers repeatedly, saying: "Now listen: I am going to say something I have never said before." Then he proceeds: "When God created the heavens, the earth, and creatures, he did not work; he had nothing to do; he made no effort." He then proceeds to say something about Godhead, but he does not forget to state: "For yet again I say a thing I never said before: God and Godhead are different as earth is from

18 Evans, with a little change, pp. 341–2.
19 Blakney, pp. 298–9.

heaven." Though he often fails to make a clear distinction between the two and would use "God" where really "Godhead" is meant, his attempt to make a distinction is noteworthy. With him God is still a something as long as there is any trace of movement or work or of doing something. When we come to the Godhead, we for the first time find that it is the unmoved, a nothing where there is no path *(apada)* to reach. It is absolute nothingness; therefore it is the ground of being from where all beings come.

> While I subsisted in the ground, in the bottom, in the river and fount of Godhead, no one asked me where I was going or what I was doing: there was no one to ask me. When I was flowing all creatures spake God. If I am asked, Brother Eckhart, when went ye out of your house? Then I must have been in. Even so do all creatures speak God. And why do they not speak the Godhead? Everything in the Godhead is one, and of that there is nothing to be said. God works, the Godhead does no work, there is nothing to do; in it is no activity. It never envisaged any work. God and Godhead are as different as active and inactive. On my return to God, where I am formless, my breaking through will be far nobler than my emanation. I alone take all creatures out of their sense into my mind and make them one in me. When I go back into the ground, into the depths, into the well-spring of the Godhead, no one will ask me whence I came or whither I went. No one missed me: God passes away.[20]

What would Christians think of "the divine core of pure (or absolute) stillness," or of "the simple core which is the still desert onto which no distinctions ever creep"? Eckhart is in perfect accord with the Buddhist doctrine of *śūnyatā* when he advances the notion of Godhead as "pure nothingness" *(ein bloss niht)*.

The notion of Godhead transcends psychology. Eckhart tells us that he has made frequent references in his sermons to "a light in the soul that is uncreated" and that "this light is not satisfied by the simple still, motionless essence of the divine being that neither gives nor takes. It is more interested in knowing where this essence came from."[21] This "where" is where "the Father, the Son, and the Holy Ghost" have not yet made their

[20] Evans, p. 143.
[21] Blakney, p. 247.

distinctions. To come in touch with this source and to know what it is, that is to say, "to see my own face even before I was born" I must plunge into "the vast emptiness of the Absolute Tao."

"To see one's face which one has even prior to his birth" is ascribed to Hui-nêng (Yeno, died 713), the sixth patriarch of Zen Buddhism in China. This corresponds to Eckhart's statement which he quotes as by "an authority": "Blessed are the pure in heart who leave everything to God now as they did before ever they existed."[22] Those who have not tasted wine in the cellar[23] may put in a question here: "How could we talk about a man's purity of heart prior to his existence? How could we also talk about seeing our own face before we were born?" Eckhart quotes St. Augustine: "There is a heavenly door for the soul into the divine nature—where somethings are reduced to nothing."[24] Evidently we have to wait for the heavenly door to open by our repeated or ceaseless knocking at it when I am "ignorant with knowing, loveless with loving, dark with light."[25] Everything comes out of this basic experience and it is only when this is comprehended that we really enter into the realm of emptiness where the Godhead keeps our discriminatory mind altogether "emptied out to nothingness."[26]

5

What is the Absolute Tao?

Before we go on to the Zen conception of the "Absolute Tao" or Godhead who sets itself up on "pure nothingness," it may be appropriate to comment on the Taoist conception of it as expounded by Lao-tzu. He was one of the early thinkers of China on philosophical subjects and the theme of the *Tao Tê Ching* ascribed to him is *Tao*.

Tao literally means "way" or "road" or "passage," and in more than one sense corresponds to the Sanskrit *Dharma*. It

22 *Ibid.*, p. 89.

23 *Ibid.*, p. 216.

24 *Ibid.*, p. 89.

25 "*Von erkennen kennelos und von minne minnelos und von liehte vinster.*" Pfeiffer, p. 491.

26 Blakney, p. 88.

is one of the key terms in the history of Chinese thought. While Taoism derives its name from this term, Confucius also uses it extensively. With the latter however it has a more moralistic than metaphysical connotation. It is Taoists who use it in the sense of "truth," "ultimate reality," "logos," etc. Lao-tzu defines it in his *Tao Tê Ching* as follows:

> The Way is like an empty vessel
> That yet may be drawn from
> Without ever needing to be filled.
> It is bottomless: the very progenitor of
> all things in the world. . . .
> It is like a deep pool that never dries
> I do not know whose child it could be.
> It looks as if it were prior to God.[27]

There is another and more detailed characterization of Tao in Chapter XIV:

> When you look at it you cannot see it;
> It is called formless.
> When you listen to it you cannot hear it;
> It is called soundless.
> When you try to seize it you cannot hold it;
> It is called subtle.
> No one can measure these three to their
> ultimate ends,
> Therefore they are fused to one.
>
> It is up, but it is not brightened;
> It is down, but it is not obscured.
> It stretches endlessly,
> And no name is to be given.
> It returns to nothingness.
> It is called formless form, shapeless shape.
> It is called the intangible.
> You face it but you cannot see its front.
> You follow it but you cannot see its back.
> Holding on to the Ancient Way (*Tao*)
> You control beings of today.
> Thus you know the beginning of things,
> Which is the essence of the Way (*Tao-chi*).

[27] Translated by Arthur Waley. (From his *The Way and Its Power*, published 1934 by George Allen and Unwin Ltd. The succeeding quotations from *Tao Tê Ching* are all my rendering.) Chapter IV. God here is distinguished from Godhead as by Eckhart. The last two lines are my own version.

When these quotations are compared with Ekhart's, we see points common to both. Lao-tzu is expressing in his classical Chinese way what the medieval Dominican preacher would talk about in his German vernacular. Lao-tzu is poetical and concrete, full of imageries, whereas Eckhart the theologian is more conceptual. He would say:

"God has no before nor after."

"God is neither this nor that."

"God is perfect simplicity."

"Prior to creatures, in the eternal now, I have played before the Father in his eternal stillness."[28]

For comparison I will give another definition for Tao from *Tao Tê Ching*, Chapter XXV:

> There is something in a state of fusion,
> It is born prior to heaven and earth.
> How still! How lonely!
> It stands by itself unchanging,
> It moves about everywhere unfailingly.
> Let us have it as mother [of all things]
>   under the heavens.
> I do not know its name,
> But if needed call it Great.
> The Great walks on,
> Walks on to the farthest end,
> And then returns.
> Therefore the Tao is great,
> Heaven is great,
> Earth is great,
> The ruler is great.
> Within the realm there are four greats
> And the ruler is one of them.
> Man is earth when conforming to earth,
> He is heaven when conforming to heaven,
> He is Tao when conforming to Tao.
> Let him thus conform himself to the suchness
>   (*tzu jan*) of things.

R. B. Blakney remarks in his preface to the *Tao Tê Ching* translation that Lao-tzu's book fascinated him for many years and that he finally could not help producing his own translation in spite of the fact that there are already a large number of such translations available. He suspects that every foreigner

[28] Evans, p. 148.

who at all knows the Chinese language and can read Lao-tzu in the original would feel the same as this new translator did. This remark or confession on the part of the translator is highly significant. In my view the fascination he feels about Lao-tzu is not just due to the Old Philosopher's contribution to "the literature of mysticism," but partly to the language in which it is expressed. It may be better to say that the charm one feels about Chinese literature comes quite frequently from visually going over those unwieldy ideogrammatic characters with which thoughts or feelings are made communicative. The Chinese books are best perused in large type printed from the wooden blocks.

Besides this visual appeal of the ideograms there is an element in the Chinese language which, while rare in others, especially in Indo-European languages, expresses more directly and concretely what our ordinary conceptualized words fail to communicate. For instance, read the *Tao Tê Ching*, Chapter XX, in the original and compare it with any of the translations you have at hand and see that the translations invariably lack that rich, graphic, emotional flavor which we after more than two thousand five hundred years can appreciate with deep satisfaction. Arthur Waley is a great Chinese scholar and one of the best interpreters of Chinese life. His English translation of Lao-tzu is a fine piece of work in many senses, but he cannot go beyond the limitations of the language to which he is born.

6

The following story may not have historicity but it is widely circulated among Zen followers, who are occasionally quite disrespectful of facts. It is worth our consideration as illustrating the way in which the Zen teachers handle the problem of "Emptiness" or "absolute nothingness" or the "still desert" lying beyond "this and that" and prior to "before and after." The story and comments are taken from a Chinese Zen textbook[29] of the Sung dynasty of the eleventh century. The text

29 It is entitled *Hekigan-shu* or *Hekigan-roku*, meaning "Blue Rock Collection" or "Blue Rock Records."

is studied very much in Japan and some of the stories are used as *kō-an* (problems given to Zen students for solution).

Bodhidharma, who is the first Zen patriarch in China, came from India in the sixth century. The Emperor Wu of the Liang dynasty invited him to his court. The Emperor Wu, a good pious Buddhist studying the various Mahāyāna *Sūtras* and practicing the Buddhist virtues of charity and humility, asked the teacher from India: "The *Sūtras* refer so much to the highest and holiest truth, but what is it, my Reverend Master?"

Bodhidharma answered, "A vast emptiness and no holiness in it."

The Emperor: "Who are you then who stand before me if there is nothing holy, nothing high in the vast emptiness of ultimate truth?"

Bodhidharma: "I do not know, your Majesty."

The Emperor failed to understand the meaning of this answer and Bodhidharma left him to find a retreat in the North.

When Bodhidharma's express purpose of coming to China was to elucidate the teaching of "vast emptiness" *(śūnyatā)*, why did he answer "I do not know" to the Emperor's all-important and to-the-very-point question? It is evident, however, that Bodhidharma's answer could not have been one of an agnostic who believes in the unknowability of ultimate truth. Bodhidharma's unknowability must be altogether of a different sort. It is really what Eckhart would like to see us all have—"transformed knowledge, not ignorance which comes from lack of knowing; it is by knowing that we get to this unknowing. Then we know by divine knowing, then our ignorance is ennobled and adorned with supernatural knowledge."[30] It was this kind of unknowing which is transcendental, divine, and supernatural that he wished his imperial friend to realize.

From our ordinary relative point of view Bodhidharma may seem too abrupt and unacceptable. But the fact is that the knowledge or "I do not know" which is gained only by "sinking into oblivion and ignorance"[31] is something quite abrupt or

30 Evans, p. 13.

31 *"Hie muoz komen in ein vergezzen und in ein nihtwizzen."* Pfeiffer, p. 14. Evans, p. 13.

discrete or discontinuous in the human system of knowability, for we can get it only by leaping or plunging into the silent valley of Absolute Emptiness. There is no continuity between this and the knowledge we highly value in the realm of relativity where our senses and intellect move.

The Zen teachers are all unknowing knowers or knowing unknowers. Therefore their "I do not know" does not really mean our "I do not know." We must not take their answers in the way we generally do at the level of relative knowledge. Therefore, their comments which are quoted below do not follow the line we ordinarily do. They have this unique way. Yengo (1063–1135) gives his evaluation of the *mondo* ("question and answer") which took place between Bodhidharma and the Emperor Wu of the Liang dynasty in the following words:[32]

> Bodhidharma came to this country, via the southern route, seeing that there was something in Chinese mentality which responds readily to the teaching of Mahāyāna Buddhism. He was full of expectations, he wanted to lead our countrymen to the doctrine of "Mind-alone" which cannot be transmitted by letters or by means of word of mouth. The Mind could only be immediately taken hold of whereby we attain to the perception of the Buddha nature, that is, to the realization of Buddhahood. When the Nature is attained, we shall be absolutely free from all bondage and will not be led astray because of linguistic complications. For here Reality itself is revealed in its nakedness with no kinds of veil on it. In this frame of mind Bodhidharma approached the Emperor. He also thus instructed his disciples. We see that Bodhidharma's [emptied mind] had no premeditated measures, no calculating plans. He just acted in the freest manner possible, cutting everything asunder that would obstruct his seeing directly into the Nature in its entire nakedness. Here was neither good nor evil, neither right nor wrong, neither gain nor loss. . . .
>
> The Emperor Wu was a good student of Buddhist philosophy and wished to have the first principle elucidated by the great teacher from India. The first principle consists in the identity of being and non-being beyond which the philosophers fail to go. The Emperor wondered if this blockage could somehow he broken down by Bodhidharma. Hence his question. Bodhidharma knew that whatever answers he might give would be frustrating.
>
> "What is Reality? What is Godhead?"
>
> "Vast emptiness and no distinctions whatever (neither Father nor Son nor Holy Ghost)."

[32] Yengo is given here in a modernized fashion, for the original Chinese would require a detailed interpretation.

No philosopher however well trained in his profession could ever be expected to jump out of this trap, except Bodhidharma himself who knew perfectly well how to cut all limitations down by one blow of a sword.

Most people nowadays fail to get into the ultimate signification of Bodhidharma's pronouncement and would simply cry out, "vast emptiness" as if they really experienced it. But all to no purpose! As my old master remarks, "When a man truly understands Bodhidharma, he for the first time finds himself at home quietly sitting by the fireside." Unfortunately, the Emperor Wu happened to be one of those who could not rise above the limitations of linguistics. His views failed to penetrate the screen of *meum* and *tuum* (you and me). Hence his second question: "Who are you who face me?" Bodhidharma's blunt retort, "I do not know," only helped make the august inquirer blankly stare.

Later, when he learned more about Bodhidharma and realized how stupid he was to have missed the rare opportunity of going deeper into the mystery of Reality, he was greatly upset. Hearing of Bodhidharma's death after some years he erected a memorial stele for him and inscribed on it: "Alas! I saw him, I met him, I interviewed him, and failed to recognize him. How sad! It is all past now. Alas, history is irrevocable!" He concluded his eulogy thus:

> "As long as the mind tarries on the plane of
> relativity,
> It forever remains in the dark.
> But the moment it loses itself in the Emptiness,
> It ascends the throne of Enlightenment."

After finishing the story of the Emperor Wu, Yengo the commentator puts this remark: "Tell me by the way where Bodhidharma could be located." This is expressly addressed to the readers and the commentator expects us to give him an answer. Shall we take up his challenge?

There is another commentator on this episode, who lived some years prior to the one already referred to. This one, called Seccho (980–1052), was a great literary talent and his comments are put in a versified form full of poetic fantasies. Alluding to the Emperor Wu's attempt to send a special envoy for Bodhidharma, who after the interview crossed the Yang-tzu Chiang and found a retreat somewhere in the North, the commentator goes on:

> "You [the Emperor Wu] may order all your
> subjects to fetch him [Bodhidharma],

But he will never show himself up again!
We are left alone for ages to come
Vainly thinking of the irrevocable past.
But stop! let us not think of the past!
The cool refreshing breeze sweeps all over the
earth,
Never knowing when to suspend its work."

Seccho (the master commentator) now turns around and surveying the entire congregation (as he was reciting his versified comments), asks: "O Brethren, is not our Patriarch[33] to be discovered among us at this very moment?"

After this interruption, Seccho continues, "Yes, yes, he is here! Let him come up and wash the feet for me!"

It would have been quite an exciting event if Eckhart appeared to be present at this session which took place in the Flowery Kingdom in the first half of the eleventh century! But who can tell if Eckhart is not watching me writing this in the most modern and most mechanized city of New York?

7

A few more remarks about "Emptiness."

Relativity is an aspect[34] of Reality and not Reality itself. Relativity is possible somewhere between two or more things, for this is the way that makes one get related to another.

A similar argument applies to movement. Movement is possible in time; without the concept of time there cannot be a movement of any sort. For a movement means an object going out of itself and becoming something else which is not itself. Without the background of time this becoming is unthinkable.

Therefore, Buddhist philosophy states that all these concepts, movement and relativity, must have their field of operation, and this field is designated by Buddhist philosophers as Emptiness *(śūnyatā)*.

When Buddha talks about all things being transient, impermanent, and constantly changing, and therefore teaches that

[33] Bodhidharma.

[34] *Sō* in Japanese, *hsiang* in Chinese, *lakṣaṇa* in Sanskrit.

there is nothing in this world which is absolutely dependable and worth clinging to as the ultimate seat of security, he means that we must look somewhere else for things permanent *(jō)*, bliss-imparting *(raku)*, autonomous *(ga)*, and absolutely free from defilements *(jō)*. According to the *Nirvana Sūtra* (of the Mahāyāna school) these four *(jō-raku-ga-jō)* are the qualities of Nirvana, and Nirvana is attained when we have knowledge, when the mind is freed from thirst *(taṇhā)*, cravings *(āsava)*, and conditionality *(sankhāra)*. While Nirvana is often thought to be a negativistic idea the Mahāyāna followers have quite a different interpretation. For they include autonomy *(ga, ātman)* as one of its qualities *(guṇa)*, and autonomy is free will, something dynamic. Nirvana is another name for the Emptiness.

The term "emptiness is apt to be misunderstood for various reasons. The hare or rabbit has no horns, the turtle has no hair growing on its back. This is one form of emptiness. The Buddhist *śūnyatā* does not mean absence.

A fire has been burning until now and there is no more of it. This is another kind of emptiness. Buddhist *śūnyatā* does not mean extinction.

The wall screens the room: on this side there is a table, and on the other side there is nothing, space is unoccupied. Buddhist *śūnyatā* does not mean vacancy.

Absence, extinction, and unoccupancy—these are not the Buddhist conception of emptiness. Buddhists' Emptiness is not on the plane of relativity. It is Absolute Emptiness transcending all forms of mutual relationship, of subject and object, birth and death, God and the world, something and nothing, yes and no, affirmation and negation. In Buddhist Emptiness there is no time, no space, no becoming, no-thing-ness; it is what makes all these things possible; it is a zero full of infinite possibilities, it is a void of inexhaustible contents.

Pure experience is the mind seeing itself as reflected in itself, it is an act of self-identification, a state of suchness. This is possible only when the mind is *śūnyatā* itself, that is, when the mind is devoid of all its possible contents except itself. But to say "except itself" is apt to be misunderstood again. For it may be questioned, what is this "itself"? We may have to answer in the same way as St. Augustine did: "When you ask, I do not know; but when you do not, I know."

The following dialogue which took place between two Zen masters of the T'ang dynasty will help show us what methodology was adopted by Zen for communicating the idea of "itself."

One master called Isan (771–853) was working with his disciples in the garden, picking tea leaves. He said to one of the disciples in the garden called Kyōzan, who also was a master: "We have been picking the tea leaves all day; I hear your voice only and do not see your form. Show me your primeval form." Kyōzan shook the tea bushes. Isan said, "You just got the action, but not the body." Kyōzan then said, "What would be your answer?" Isan remained quiet for a while. Thereupon Kyōzan said, "You have got the body, but not the action." Isan's conclusion was, "I save you from twenty blows of my stick."

As far as Zen philosophy is concerned this may be all right, as these two masters know what each is seeking to reveal. But the business of philosophers of our modern epoch is to recognize or to probe the background of experience on which these Zen masters stand and try to elucidate it to the best of their capacity. The masters are not simply engaged in mystifying the bystanders.

To say "empty" is already denying itself. But you cannot remain silent. How to communicate the silence without going out of it is the crux. It is for this reason that Zen avoids as much as possible resorting to linguistics and strives to make us go underneath words, as it were to dig out what is there. Eckhart is doing this all the time in his sermons. He picks out some innocent words from the Bible and lets them disclose an "inner act" which he experiences in his unconscious consciousness. His thought is not at all in the words. He turns them into instruments for his own purposes. In a similar way the Zen master makes use of anything about himself including his own person, trees, stones, sticks, etc. He may then shout, beat, or kick. The main thing is to discover what is behind all these actions. In order to demonstrate that Reality is "Emptiness," the Zen master may stand still with his hands folded over his chest. When he is asked a further question, he may shake the tea plant or walk away without a word, or give you a blow of a stick.

Sometimes the master is more poetic and compares the

mind of "emptiness" to the moon, calling it the mind-moon or the moon of suchness. An ancient master of Zen philosophy sings of this moon:

> The mind-moon is solitary and perfect:
> The light swallows the ten thousand things.
> It is not that the light illuminates objects,
> Nor are objects in existence.
> Both light and objects are gone,
> And what is it that remains?

The master leaves the question unanswered. When it is answered the moon will no longer be there. Reality is differentiated and Emptiness vanishes into an emptiness. We ought not to lose sight of the original moon, primeval mind-moon, and the master wants us to go back to this, for it is where we have started first. Emptiness is not a vacancy, it holds in it infinite rays of light and swallows all the multiplicities there are in this world.

Buddhist philosophy is the philosophy of "Emptiness," it is the philosophy of self-identity. Self-identity is to be distinguished from mere identity. In an identity we have two objects for identification; in self-identity there is just one object or subject, one only, and this one identifies itself by going out of itself. Self-identity thus involves a movement. And we see that self-identity is the mind going out of itself in order to see itself reflected in itself. Self-identity is the logic of pure experience or of "Emptiness." In self-identity there are no contradictions whatever. Buddhists call this suchness.

I once talked with a group of lovers of the arts on the Buddhist teaching of "Emptiness" and Suchness, trying to show how the teaching is related to the arts. The following is part of my talk.

To speak the truth, I am not qualified to say anything at all about the arts, because I have no artistic instincts, no artistic education, and have not had many opportunities to appreciate good works of art. All that I can say is more or less conceptual.

Take the case of painting. I often hear Chinese or Japanese art critics declare that Oriental art consists in depicting spirit and not form. For they say that when the spirit is understood the form creates itself; the main thing is to get into the spirit of an object which the painter chooses for his subject. The West, on the other hand, emphasizes form, endeavors to reach the spirit by means of form. The East is just the opposite: the spirit is all in all. And it thinks that when the artist grasps the spirit, his work reveals something more than colors and lines can convey. A real artist is a creator and not a copyist. He has visited God's workshop and has learned the secrets of creation—creating something out of nothing.

With such a painter every stroke of his brush is the work of creation, and it cannot be retraced because it never permits a repetition. God cannot cancel his fiat; it is final, irrevocable, it is an ultimatum. The painter cannot reproduce his own work. When even a single stroke of his brush is absolute, how can the whole structure or composition be reproduced, since this is the synthesis of all his strokes, every one of which has been directed toward the whole?

In the same way every minute of human life as long as it is an expression of its inner self is original, divine, creative, and cannot be retrieved. Each individual life thus is a great work of art. Whether or not one makes it a fine inimitable masterpiece depends upon one's consciousness of the working of *śūnyatā* within oneself.

How does the painter get into the spirit of the plant, for instance, if he wants to paint a hibiscus as Mokkei (Mu-chi) of the thirteenth century did in his famous picture, which is now preserved as a national treasure at Daitokuji temple in Kyoto? The secret is to become the plant itself. But now can a human being turn himself into a plant? Inasmuch as he aspires to paint a plant or an animal, there must be in him something which corresponds to it in one way or another. If so, he ought to be able to become the object he desires to paint.

The discipline consists in studying the plant inwardly with his mind thoroughly purified of its subjective, self-centered contents. This means to keep the mind in unison with the "Emptiness" or Suchness, whereby one who stands against the object ceases to be the one outside that object but transforms himself into the object itself. This identification enables the painter to feel the pulsation of one and the same life animating both him and the object. This is what is meant when it is said that the subject is lost in the object, and that when the painter begins his work it is not he but the object itself that is working and it is then that his brush, as well as his arm and his fingers, become obedient servants to the spirit of the object. The object makes its own picture. The spirit sees itself as reflected in itself. This is also a case of self-identity.

It is said that Henri Matisse looked at an object which he intended to paint for weeks, even for months, until its spirit began to move him, to urge him, even to threaten him, to give it an expression.

A writer on modern art, I am told, says that the artist's idea of a straight line is different from that of the mathematician, for the former conceives a straight line as fusing with a curve. I do not know whether this quotation is quite correct, but the remark is most illuminating. For a straight line that remains always straight is a dead line and the curve that cannot be anything else is another dead line. If they are at all living lines, and this ought to be the case with every artistic production, a straight line is curved and a curve is straight; besides there ought to be what is known as "dimensional tension" in every line. Every living line is not just on one plane, it is suffused with blood, it is tridimensional.

I am also told that color with the artist is not just red or blue, it is more than perceptual, it is charged with emotion. This means that color is a living thing with the artist. When he sees red it works out its own world; the artist bestows a heart on the color. The red does not stop just at being one of the seven colors as decomposed through the prism. As a living thing it calls out all other colors and combines them in accordance with its inner promptings. Red with the artist is not a mere physical or psychological event, it is endowed with a spirit.

These views are remakably Oriental. There is another striking statement made by a Western artist. According to him, when he is thoroughly absorbed in a visual perception of any kind, he feels within himself certain possibilities out of the visual representation which urge him to give them an expression. The artist's life is that of the creator. God did not make the world just for the sake of making something.

He had a certain inner urge, he wanted to see himself reflected in his creation. That is what is meant when the Bible speaks about God's making man after his own likeness. It is not man alone that is God's image, the whole world is his image, even the meanest flea as Eckhart would say shares God's is-ness in its is-ness. And because of this is-ness the whole world moves on. So with the artist. It is due to his is-ness being imbued into his works that they are alive with his spirit. The artist himself may not be conscious of all this proceeding, but Zen knows and is also prepared to impart the knowledge to those who would approach it in the proper spirit. The is-ness of a thing is not just being so, but it contains in it infinite possibilities which Buddhists call *tê* in Chinese, *toku* in Japanese, and *guṇa* in Sanskrit. This is where lies "the mystery of being," which is "the inexhaustibility of the Emptiness."

The following story of Rakan Osho (Lohan Hoshang), of Shōshu, China, who lived in the ninth century, is given here to illustrate how Zen transforms one's view of life and makes one truly see into the is-ness of things. The verse relates his own experience.

> It was in the seventh year of Hsien-t'ung [868 A.D.] that I for the first time took up the study of the Tao [that is, Zen].
>
> Wherever I went I met words and did not understand them.
> A lump of doubt inside the mind was like a willow-basket.
> For three years, residing in the woods by the stream, I was altogether unhappy.
> When unexpectedly I happened to meet the Dharmarāja [Zen master] sitting on the rug,
> I advanced towards him earnestly asking him to dissolve my doubt.
> The master rose from the rug on which he sat deeply absorbed in meditation;
> He then baring his arm gave me a blow with his fist on my chest.
> This all of a sudden exploded my lump of doubt completely to pieces.
> Raising my head I for the first time perceived that the sun was circular.
> Since then I have been the happiest man in the world, with no fears, no worries;

Day in day out, I pass my time in a most lively way.
Only I notice my inside filled with a sense of fullness and satisfaction;
I do not go out any longer, hither and thither, with my begging bowl for food.[35]

What is of the most significant interest in his verse story of Rakan Osho's experience is that "he for the first time perceived that the sun was round." Everybody knows and sees the sun and the Osho also must have seen it all his life. Why then does he specifically refer to it as circular as if he saw it really for the first time? We all think we are living, we really eat, sleep, walk, talk. But are we really? If we were, we would never be talking about "dread," "insecurity," "fear," "frustration," "courage to be," "looking into the vacant," "facing death."

[35] *The Transmission of the Lamp (Dentoroku),* fas. XI.

Bibliographical Note

1. *Sources of the selections, listed by chapter*

I. *Essays in Zen Buddhism,* Third Series (London, Luzac and Co., 1934; reprinted London, Rider and Co., 1953, 1958). Pp. 234–78, 283–319.

II. *Essays in Zen Buddhism,* Second Series (London, Luzac and Co., 1933; reprinted London, Rider and Co., 1950, 1958). Pp. 294–303.

III. *Essays in Zen Buddhism,* Second Series. Pp. 322–26

IV. *Essays in Zen Buddhism,* Second Series. Pp. 315–20.

V. *Studies in the Lankāvatāra Sūtra* (London, G. Routledge and Sons, Ltd., 1930, reprinted 1957). Pp. 90–101, 104–05.

VI. "The Shin Sect of Buddhism" (in *The Eastern Buddhist,* VII [1939]; reprinted in *A Miscellany on the Shin Teaching of Buddhism,* Kyoto, Shinshu Otaniha Shumusho, 1949). Pp. 227–46.

VII. *Essays in Zen Buddhism,* Third Series Pp. 78–103, 112–15, 117–48, 155–61, 164–180, 205–14.

VIII. *Mysticism: Christian and Buddhist* (New York, Harper and Brothers; London, Allen and Unwin, 1957). "The Basis of Buddhist Philosophy," pp. 36–74. I have omitted pp. 57–66, which Suzuki himself (p. 67) described as "these lengthy excursions."

IX. *Mysticism: Christian and Buddhist.* "Meister Eckhart and Buddhism," pp. 3–35. Originally I had intended to give only the passages relating to Mahayana philosophy, but in the end I had not the heart to tear apart an almost perfect work of art, which is therefore presented here in its entirety.

2. *Other writings of Suzuki on the Indian Mahayana, in order of original publication*

1. *Outlines of Mahayana Buddhism* (London, Luzac and Co., 1907; Chicago, The Open Court Publishing Co., 1908).
2. Articles in *The Eastern Buddhist* (founded in 1921):
   a. "The Avatamsaka Sutra, Kegon-kyo (Epitomized)," I (1920–21), 1–12; 147–55 (chs. 4–5); 237–42 (chs. 6–7); 282–90 (ch. 8).
   b. "The Buddha in Mahāyāna Buddhism," I (1920–21), 109–22.
   c. "Notes on the Avatamsaka Sutra," I (1921–22), 233–36.
   d. "The Psychological School of Mahāyāna Buddhism," II (1922), 105–28 (on Yogācāra).
   e. "Enlightenment and Ignorance," III (1924), 1–31.
   f. "The Lankāvatāra Sūtra," IV (1928), 199–298 (reprinted, with modifications, in *Studies in the Lankāvatāra Sūtra*, pp. 90–236); V (1929), 1–79 (reprinted in *Studies in the Lankāvatāra Sūtra*, pp. 3–85).
   g. "Mahāyāna and Hīnayāna Buddhism, or the Bodhisattva-Ideal and the Śrāvaka-Ideal as Distinguished in the Opening Chapter of the Gaṇḍavyūha," VI (1932), 1–22 (reprinted in *Essays in Zen Buddhism*, Third Series, pp. 78–103).
3. *The Lankāvatāra Sūtra* (London, G. Routledge and Son, 1933; reprinted in 1956, 1959), translated by D. T. Suzuki.
4. *An index to the Lankāvatāra Sūtra* (Kyoto, The Eastern Buddhist Society, 1933; Kyoto, The Sanskrit Buddhist Text Publishing Society, 1934).
5. *The Gaṇḍavyūha Sūtra* (Kyoto, The Sanskrit Buddhist Text Publishing Society, 1934–36), critically edited by D. T. Suzuki in collaboration with H. Idzumi.
6. "The *Vajracchedikā*," in *Manual of Zen Buddhism* (Kyoto, The Eastern Buddhist Society, 1935; reprinted London, Rider and Co., 1950, 1956, and New York, Grove Press, 1960), pp. 43–56.
7. Introduction to B. L. Suzuki, *Mahayana Buddhism* (London, The Buddhist Lodge, 1938; reprinted London, David Marlow Ltd. 1948, and London, G. Allen and Unwin, 1959), pp. xii–xxxiv.

Glossary

Dr. Suzuki habitually uses Sanskrit technical terms without giving their English equivalents. This must bewilder the non-reader of Sanskrit and this *Glossary* is designed to meet his needs. The English renderings are usually Dr. Suzuki's own, and pages references are added where he gives more than one rendering. Where he gives none, I have inserted my own in brackets, and all other additions in brackets are also my own. The Sanskrit spelling in the *Glossary* has everywhere been normalized, i.e., brought into conformity with that familiar to scholars all over the world (thus "Abhisheka" on page 177 appears as *abhiṣeka*).

abhāva-svabhāva, lacking in self-substance

Abhidharma, [The "Higher Dharma," a series of philosophical texts composed after 200 B.C.]

abhiṣeka, 177 [consecration]

ābhoga, effort

acintya, the Unthinkable, incomprehensible, inconceivable, miraculous, 157

adhiṣṭhāna, sustaining and inspiring power, 152; sustaining power, 163 etc.; divine power, cf. 132; expl. 200 sq.

ākāsa, void space; cf. 95

alakṣaṇa, devoid of individualizing marks, (114)

ālaya-vijñāna, store-consciousness

Amitābha, Infinite Light [a Buddha]

Amitāyus, Eternal Life [a Buddha]

anabhilāpya, indescribable

anābhogacaryā, the effortless life, effortlessness, cf. 232

anātman, non-ego

anātmya, egolessness

anattā, (Pali), not-self

anujāta, to be born after, 44 "brothers"

animitta, no-form, formlessness

anukampā, sympathy

anupalabdha, unattainable, not available, (246)

anupalambha, unattainable, non-attainment

anutpattika-dharma-kṣānti, acceptance of all things as unborn

anuttara-samyak-saṃbodhi, supreme enlightenment

apraṇihita, no-desire
apratiṣṭhita, not-abiding
Arhat, [the ideal saint of the Hīnayāna]
asaṃga, no clinging, non-attachment
asaṃga-citta, an unimpeded heart
asaṃkhyeya, innumerable
asaṃskṛta, unconditioned
aśleṣa, non-attachment
astitva, being
ātman, self
atyanta-vivikta, absolutely solitary
avidyā, ignorance
avinivartanīya, no turning back
avaivartika, no turning back; cf. 144
āyatana, [the 12 sense-fields, i.e., the six sense-organs and six sense-objects]

bhikṣu, monk
bhūmi, stage
bhūtakoṭi, reality limit; def. 94; summit of reality, 155; limit of reality, 165
bodhi, enlightment
bodhi-caryā, (living the) life of enlightenment
bodhicitta, [the desire for the supreme enlightenment]
Bodhisattva, celestial, 23
bodhisattva-caryā, the life of a Bodhisattva, a Bodhisattva's life of devotion
buddha-kṣetra, Buddha land
buddhatā, Buddha-nature

cakravartin, [a world-ruler or universal monarch]
caryā, life (of devotion)
citta, mind, thought, heart, cf. 170; desire, 210; cf. 210 and 219
citta-kṣaṇa, [thought-moment]
citta-mātra, Mind itself; Mind-only
cittotpāda, desire for supreme enlightenment; cf. 208 sq.

dhāraṇī, [a magical formula which condenses the truth into a few syllables]
dharma, ideas, 63; existence, 67; thing, 68, 175; truth, 172; cf. 235 n. 8, *sarva-dharma,* the universe; *sarva-dharmā,* all things
dharma-dhātu, spiritual realm; cf. 149-50
dharma-kāya, Dharma-body; Being-body; cf. 136

dharma-rāja, king of Dharma
dharmatā, the nature of ultimate reality, essence (39); Truth (43)
dhātu, (18) [the six sense-organs, six sense-objects, and six sense-consciousnesses]
dhyāna, meditation or trance

Gaṇḍavyūha [A Mahāyāna scripture. See now: L. O. Gomez, *Selected Verses from the Gaṇḍavyūha,* 1967, Yale doctoral dissertation.]
garuḍa, [a celestial bird]
gocara, experience, field, 171
guṇa, values, qualities, cf. 275

Hīna-yāna, the lesser vehicle
Hṛdaya Sūtra, Heart Sutra

Jambudvīpa, [the Buddhist name for the Indian sub-continent]
jñāna, knowledge, cf. 199
jñāna-cakṣus, wisdom-eye

kalpa, eon
kalyāṇa-mitra, good friend
karuṇā, compassion, love; compassionate heart, 215; cf. 248
kleśa, evil passions
koan, [a Zen device designed to awaken the mind]
koṭi, a high number
kṛtsnāyatana, ["all-bases," a meditational device]
kṣaṇa, thought-moment
kṣānti, patience
kuśala-mūla, stock of merit

lakṣaṇa, (characteristic) mark; aspect, 269; *sva-lakṣana,* self-character
lokapāla, [World-guardian, one for each quarter]
lokottara, transcendental
mahā-karuṇā(-citta), great love, a great compassionate heart, a great loving heart
mahā-maitrī(-citta), a great friendly spirit, 168; a great compassionate heart, 214
Mahāvairocana-Buddha, The Buddha of Great Illumination
Mahāyāna, [the great vehicle]
Māra, the Tempter, cf. 177
māyā, illusion, vision, 74
maitra, compassion
maitrī, friendliness

mokṣa, liberation
muni, [a silent sage]

Nāga, [a Serpent or Dragon]
nāstitva, non-being
nayuta or *niyuta,* a high number
nimitta, appearance, form, 91
nirmāṇa-kāya, transformation body
nirodha, cessation
niṣyanda, outpourings

pāram, the other shore
paramārtha, the transcendental realm of *prajñā*-intuition, cf. 240 sq.
pāramitā, perfections or virtues of perfection; (six) o.e., charity, morality, patience, strenuousness, meditation, wisdom
parāvṛtti, turning up, turning back, 58; turning over, 59; revulsion, 124, 128
pariṇāmana, turning over
parinirvāṇa, [final Nirvana]
poṣadha, eightfold [Uposatha vows, rules regulating the conduct of monks on days of the full and new moon]
prajñā, wisdom, intuition, 76; transcendental or intuitive knowledge, 132; highest knowledge, 245; cf. 229
Prajñāpāramitā, The Perfection of Wisdom
prakṛti, primary nature, 45; original nature, 92
pramuditā, Joy [the first stage (*bhūmi*) of a Bodhisattva]
praṇidhāna, (original) vow (s) ; cf. 209; def. 248-9; desire, 80
praṇidhāna-caryā, life of devotion and vows
pratiṣṭhita, established, abiding
pratyātma-gocara, state of inner realization
pratyātmāryajñāna, [the holy cognition which has been achieved inwardly by oneself]
Pratyekabuddha, [Single Buddha]
preta, hungry ghost
pūrva-praṇidhāna, (the power of the) original vow

roshi, [The ideal saint of Zen]
rūpam, form
rūpa-kāya, physical body

Sadāprarudita, Ever-Weeping (a Bodhisattva)
samādhi, tranquilization
samāpatti, concentration

samatā, sameness
śamatha, tranquilization
saṃbodhi, enlightenment, awakening, 58
saṃga, attachment
saṃjñā, thought [perception]
saṃsāra, birth-and-death
saṃskāra, conformations, 101 etc.; composite things, 229; primary disposition, 234; binding conditions, 235; conditionality, 270
saṃskṛta, conditioned
saṃvṛti, relative world, cf. 240
sarvajñatā, all-knowledge
sattva, being
siddha, [the ideal saint of the Tantras]
śīla, morality
siṃhanāda, lion roar
skandha, (five), aggregates; composites; composite things
śrāvaka, Disciple [follower of the Hīnayāna]
Sukhāvatī, Land of Happiness
Sumeru, [a mythical mountain at the centre of the world]
śūnyatā, emptiness, Void
svabhāva, self-nature, cf. 49
svasiddhānta, [one's own achievement]
svayambhū-jñāna, spontaneous knowledge

tathatā, suchness; is-ness 228; cf. 172
Tathāgata, [epithet of the Buddha]
tathāgata-garbha, the "Womb of Tathagatahood" [the embryonic Tathagata]
Theravāda, ["The teaching of the Elders," at present confined to Southern Buddhism]
tri-kāya, triple body
tṛṣṇā, ego-centred love

upāya, (skillful) means, device, contrivance, attempt, 201; cf. 203 n. 19
upāyakauśalya, skillful means

Vajracchedikā, The Diamond Sutra
vāsanā, memory, def. 125-6
vedanā, sensation [feeling]
vijñāna, consciousness
vikalpa, discrimination
vimokṣa, emancipation
vipaśyana, contemplation

virāgatā, detachment
vīrya, strenuousness, energy
vivikta, transcendental, 93
vivikta-vihāra, the detached life; cf. 99
vyūha, [array]
vyūha-vikurvita, an array of wonders

yāna, vehicle
yathābhūtam, (the essence of things) as they are, 40; in accordance with the truth, 154
yathāvatta, suchness

71 72 73 12 11 10 9 8 7 6 5 4 3

Revised January, 1970

harper torchbooks

American Studies: General

HENRY ADAMS Degradation of the Democratic Dogma. ‡ *Introduction by Charles Hirschfeld.* TB/1450

LOUIS D. BRANDEIS: Other People's Money, *and How the Bankers Use It. Ed. with Intro, by Richard M. Abrams* TB/3081

HENRY STEELE COMMAGER, Ed.: The Struggle for Racial Equality TB/1300

CARL N. DEGLER: Out of Our Past: *The Forces that Shaped Modern America* CN/2

CARL N. DEGLER, Ed.: Pivotal Interpretations of American History Vol. I TB/1240; Vol. II TB/1241

A. S. EISENSTADT, Ed.: The Craft of American History: *Selected Essays* Vol. I TB/1255; Vol. II TB/1256

LAWRENCE H. FUCHS, Ed.: American Ethnic Politics TB/1368

MARCUS LEE HANSEN: The Atlantic Migration: 1607-1860. *Edited by Arthur M. Schlesinger. Introduction by Oscar Handlin* TB/1052

MARCUS LEE HANSEN: The Immigrant in American History. *Edited with a Foreword by Arthur M. Schlesinger* TB/1120

ROBERT L. HEILBRONER: The Limits of American Capitalism TB/1305

JOHN HIGHAM, Ed.: The Reconstruction of American History TB/1068

ROBERT H. JACKSON: The Supreme Court in the American System of Government TB/1106

JOHN F. KENNEDY: A Nation of Immigrants. *Illus. Revised and Enlarged. Introduction by Robert F. Kennedy* TB/1118

LEONARD W. LEVY, Ed.: American Constitutional Law: *Historical Essays* TB/1285

LEONARD W. LEVY, Ed.: Judicial Review and the Supreme Court TB/1296

LEONARD W. LEVY: The Law of the Commonwealth and Chief Justice Shaw: *The Evolution of American Law, 1830-1860* TB/1309

GORDON K. LEWIS: Puerto Rico: *Freedom and Power in the Caribbean. Abridged edition* TB/1371

HENRY F. MAY: Protestant Churches and Industrial America TB/1334

RICHARD B. MORRIS: Fair Trial: *Fourteen Who Stood Accused, from Anne Hutchinson to Alger Hiss* TB/1335

GUNNAR MYRDAL: An American Dilemma: *The Negro Problem and Modern Democracy. Introduction by the Author.* Vol. I TB/1443; Vol. II TB/1444

GILBERT OSOFSKY, Ed.: The Burden of Race: *A Documentary History of Negro-White Relations in America* TB/1405

CONYERS READ, Ed.: The Constitution Reconsidered. *Revised Edition. Preface by Richard B. Morris* TB/1384

ARNOLD ROSE: The Negro in America: *The Condensed Version of Gunnar Myrdal's* An American Dilemma. *Second Edition* TB/3048

JOHN E. SMITH: Themes in American Philosophy: *Purpose, Experience and Community* TB/1466

WILLIAM R. TAYLOR: Cavalier and Yankee: *The Old South and American National Character* TB/1474

American Studies: Colonial

BERNARD BAILYN: The New England Merchants in the Seventeenth Century TB/1149

ROBERT E. BROWN: Middle-Class Democracy and Revolution in Massachusetts, 1691–1780. *New Introduction by Author* TB/1413

JOSEPH CHARLES: The Origins of the American Party System TB/1049

HENRY STEELE COMMAGER & ELMO GIORDANETTI, Eds.: Was America a Mistake? *An Eighteenth Century Controversy* TB/1329

WESLEY FRANK CRAVEN: The Colonies in Transition: 1660-1712† TB/3084

CHARLES GIBSON: Spain in America † TB/3077

CHARLES GIBSON, Ed.: The Spanish Tradition in America + HR/1351

LAWRENCE HENRY GIPSON: The Coming of the Revolution: 1763-1775. † *Illus.* TB/3007

JACK P. GREENE, Ed.: Great Britain and the American Colonies: 1606-1763. + *Introduction by the Author* HR/1477

AUBREY C. LAND, Ed.: Bases of the Plantation Society + HR/1429

JOHN LANKFORD, Ed.: Captain John Smith's America: *Selections* from his Writings ‡ TB/3078

LEONARD W. LEVY: Freedom of Speech and Press in Early American History: *Legacy of Suppression* TB/1109

† The New American Nation Series, edited by Henry Steele Commager and Richard B. Morris.
‡ American Perspectives series, edited by Bernard Wishy and William E. Leuchtenburg.
a History of Europe series, edited by J. H. Plumb.
§ The Library of Religion and Culture, edited by Benjamin Nelson.
‖ Researches in the Social, Cultural, and Behavioral Sciences, edited by Benjamin Nelson.
Σ Harper Modern Science Series, edited by James A. Newman.
° Not for sale in Canada.
+ Documentary History of the United States series, edited by Richard B. Morris.
# Documentary History of Western Civilization series, edited by Eugene C. Black and Leonard W. Levy.
Λ The Economic History of the United States series, edited by Henry David et al.
¶ European Perspectives series, edited by Eugene C. Black.
** Contemporary Essays series, edited by Leonard W. Levy.
* The Stratum Series, edited by John Hale.

PERRY MILLER: Errand Into the Wilderness TB/1139

PERRY MILLER & T. H. JOHNSON, Eds.: The Puritans: *A Sourcebook of Their Writings* Vol. I TB/1093; Vol. II TB/1094

EDMUND S. MORGAN: The Puritan Family: *Religion and Domestic Relations in Seventeenth Century New England* TB/1227

RICHARD B. MORRIS: Government and Labor in Early America TB/1244

WALLACE NOTESTEIN: The English People on the Eve of Colonization: 1603-1630. † *Illus.* TB/3006

FRANCIS PARKMAN: The Seven Years War: *A Narrative Taken from* Montcalm and Wolfe, The Conspiracy of Pontiac, *and* A Half-Century of Conflict. *Edited by John H. McCallum* TB/3083

LOUIS B. WRIGHT: The Cultural Life of the American Colonies: 1607-1763. † *Illus.* TB/3005

YVES F. ZOLTVANY, Ed.: The French Tradition in America + HR/1425

American Studies: The Revolution to 1860

JOHN R. ALDEN: The American Revolution: 1775-1783. † *Illus.* TB/3011

MAX BELOFF, Ed.: The Debate on the American Revolution, 1761-1783: *A Sourcebook* TB/1225

RAY A. BILLINGTON: The Far Western Frontier: 1830-1860. † *Illus.* TB/3012

STUART BRUCHEY: The Roots of American Economic Growth, 1607-1861: *An Essay in Social Causation. New Introduction by the Author.* TB/1350

WHITNEY R. CROSS: The Burned-Over District: *The Social and Intellectual History of Enthusiastic Religion in Western New York, 1800-1850* TB/1242

NOBLE E. CUNNINGHAM, JR., Ed.: The Early Republic, 1789-1828 + HR/1394

GEORGE DANGERFIELD: The Awakening of American Nationalism, 1815-1828. † *Illus.* TB/3061

CLEMENT EATON: The Freedom-of-Thought Struggle in the Old South. *Revised and Enlarged. Illus.* TB/1150

CLEMENT EATON: The Growth of Southern Civilization, 1790-1860. † *Illus.* TB/3040

ROBERT H. FERRELL, Ed.: Foundations of American Diplomacy, 1775-1872 + HR/1393

LOUIS FILLER: The Crusade against Slavery: 1830-1860. † *Illus.* TB/3029

DAVID H. FISCHER: The Revolution of American Conservatism: *The Federalist Party in the Era of Jeffersonian Democracy* TB/1449

WILLIAM W. FREEHLING, Ed.: The Nullification Era: *A Documentary Record* ‡ TB/3079

WILLIM W. FREEHLING: Prelude to Civil War: *The Nullification Controversy in South Carolina, 1816-1836* TB/1359

PAUL W. GATES: The Farmer's Age: *Agriculture, 1815-1860* Δ TB/1398

FELIX GILBERT: The Beginnings of American Foreign Policy: *To the Farewell Address* TB/1200

ALEXANDER HAMILTON: The Reports of Alexander Hamilton. ‡ *Edited by Jacob E. Cooke* TB/3060

THOMAS JEFFERSON: Notes on the State of Virginia. ‡ *Edited by Thomas P. Abernethy* TB/3052

FORREST MCDONALD, Ed.: Confederation and Constitution, 1781-1789 + HR/1396

BERNARD MAYO: Myths and Men: *Patrick Henry, George Washington, Thomas Jefferson* TB/1108

JOHN C. MILLER: Alexander Hamilton and the Growth of the New Nation TB/3057

JOHN C. MILLER: The Federalist Era: 1789-1801. † *Illus.* TB/3027

RICHARD B. MORRIS, Ed.: Alexander Hamilton and the Founding of the Nation. *New Introduction by the Editor* TB/1448

RICHARD B. MORRIS: The American Revolution Reconsidered TB/1363

CURTIS P. NETTELS: The Emergence of a National Economy, 1775-1815 Δ TB/1438

DOUGLASS C. NORTH & ROBERT PAUL THOMAS, Eds.: *The Growth of the American Economy to 1860* + HR/1352

R. B. NYE: The Cultural Life of the New Nation: 1776-1830. † *Illus.* TB/3026

GILBERT OSOFSKY, Ed.: Puttin' On Ole Massa: *The Slave Narratives of Henry Bibb, William Wells Brown, and Solomon Northup* ‡ TB/1432

JAMES PARTON: The Presidency of Andrew Jackson. *From Volume III of the* Life of Andrew Jackson. *Ed. with Intro. by Robert V. Remini* TB/3080

FRANCIS S. PHILBRICK: The Rise of the West, 1754-1830. † *Illus.* TB/3067

MARSHALL SMELSER: The Democratic Republic, 1801-1815 † TB/1406

TIMOTHY L. SMITH: Revivalism and Social Reform: *American Protestantism on the Eve of the Civil War* TB/1229

JACK M. SOSIN, Ed.: The Opening of the West + HR/1424

GEORGE ROGERS TAYLOR: The Transportation Revolution, 1815-1860 Δ TB/1347

A. F. TYLER: Freedom's Ferment: *Phases of American Social History from the Revolution to the Outbreak of the Civil War. Illus.* TB/1074

GLYNDON G. VAN DEUSEN: The Jacksonian Era: 1828-1848. † *Illus.* TB/3028

LOUIS B. WRIGHT: Culture on the Moving Frontier TB/1053

American Studies: The Civil War to 1900

W. R. BROCK: An American Crisis: *Congress and Reconstruction, 1865-67* ° TB/1283

T. C. COCHRAN & WILLIAM MILLER: The Age of Enterprise: *A Social History of Industrial America* TB/1054

W. A. DUNNING: Reconstruction, Political and Economic: 1865-1877 TB/1073

HAROLD U. FAULKNER: Politics, Reform and Expansion: 1890-1900. † *Illus.* TB/3020

GEORGE M. FREDRICKSON: The Inner Civil War: *Northern Intellectuals and the Crisis of the Union* TB/1358

JOHN A. GARRATY: The New Commonwealth, 1877-1890 † TB/1410

JOHN A. GARRATY, Ed.: The Transformation of American Society, 1870-1890 + HR/1395

WILLIAM R. HUTCHISON, Ed.: American Protestant Thought: *The Liberal Era* ‡ TB/1385

HELEN HUNT JACKSON: A Century of Dishonor: *The Early Crusade for Indian Reform.* † *Edited by Andrew F. Rolle* TB/3063

ALBERT D. KIRWAN: Revolt of the Rednecks: *Mississippi Politics, 1876-1925* TB/1199

WILLIAM G. MCLOUGHLIN, Ed.: The American Evangelicals, 1800-1900: An Anthology ‡ TB/1382

ARTHUR MANN: Yankee Reforms in the Urban Age: *Social Reform in Boston, 1800-1900* TB/1247

ARNOLD M. PAUL: Conservative Crisis and the Rule of Law: *Attitudes of Bar and Bench, 1887-1895. New Introduction by Author* TB/1415

JAMES S. PIKE: The Prostrate State: *South Carolina under Negro Government.* ‡ *Intro. by Robert F. Durden* TB/3085

WHITELAW REID: After the War: *A Tour of the Southern States, 1865-1866.* ‡ *Edited by C. Vann Woodward* TB/3066

FRED A. SHANNON: The Farmer's Last Frontier: ....*Agriculture, 1860-1897* TB/1348

VERNON LANE WHARTON: The Negro in Mississippi, 1865-1890 TB/1178

American Studies: The Twentieth Century

RICHARD M. ABRAMS, Ed.: The Issues of the Populist and Progressive Eras, 1892-1912 + HR/1428

RAY STANNARD BAKER: Following the Color Line: *American Negro Citizenship in Progressive Era.* ‡ *Edited by Dewey W. Grantham, Jr. Illus.* TB/3053

RANDOLPH S. BOURNE: War and the Intellectuals: *Collected Essays, 1915-1919.* ‡ *Edited by Carl Resek* TB/3043

A. RUSSELL BUCHANAN: The United States and World War II. † *Illus.* Vol. I TB/3044; Vol. II TB/3045

THOMAS C. COCHRAN: The American Business System: *A Historical Perspective, 1900-1955* TB/1080

FOSTER RHEA DULLES: America's Rise to World Power: 1898-1954. † *Illus.* TB/3021

JEAN-BAPTISTE DUROSELLE: From Wilson to Roosevelt: *Foreign Policy of the United States, 1913-1945. Trans. by Nancy Lyman Roelker* TB/1370

HAROLD U. FAULKNER: The Decline of Laissez Faire, 1897-1917 TB/1397

JOHN D. HICKS: Republican Ascendancy: 1921-1933. † *Illus.* TB/3041

ROBERT HUNTER: Poverty: *Social Conscience in the Progressive Era.* ‡ *Edited by Peter d'A. Jones* TB/3065

WILLIAM E. LEUCHTENBURG: Franklin D. Roosevelt and the New Deal: 1932-1940. † *Illus.* TB/3025

WILLIAM E. LEUCHTENBURG, Ed.: The New Deal: *A Documentary History* + HR/1354

ARTHUR S. LINK: Woodrow Wilson and the Progressive Era: 1910-1917. † *Illus.* TB/3023

BROADUS MITCHELL: Depression Decade: *From New Era through New Deal, 1929-1941* Λ TB/1439

GEORGE E. MOWRY: The Era of Theodore Roosevelt and the Birth of Modern America: 1900-1912. † *Illus.* TB/3022

WILLIAM PRESTON, JR.: Aliens and Dissenters: *Federal Suppression of Radicals, 1903-1933* TB/1287

WALTER RAUSCHENBUSCH: Christianity and the Social Crisis. ‡ *Edited by Robert D. Cross* TB/3059

GEORGE SOULE: Prosperity Decade: *From War to Depression, 1917-1929* Δ TB/1349

GEORGE B. TINDALL, Ed.: A Populist Reader: *Selections from the Works of American Populist Leaders* TB/3069

TWELVE SOUTHERNERS: I'll Take My Stand: *The South and the Agrarian Tradition. Intro. by Louis D. Rubin, Jr.; Biographical Essays by Virginia Rock* TB/1072

Art, Art History, Aesthetics

CREIGHTON GILBERT, Ed.: Renaissance Art ** *Illus.* TB/1465

EMILE MALE: The Gothic Image: *Religious Art in France of the Thirteenth Century.* § *190* illus. TB/344

MILLARD MEISS: Painting in Florence and Siena After the Black Death: *The Arts, Religion and Society in the Mid-Fourteenth Century. 169 illus.* TB/1148

ERWIN PANOFSKY: Renaissance and Renascences in Western Art. *Illus.* TB/1447

ERWIN PANOFSKY: Studies in Iconology: *Humanistic Themes in the Art of the Renaissance. 180 illus.* TB/1077

JEAN SEZNEC: The Survival of the Pagan Gods: *The Mythological Tradition and Its Place in Renaissance Humanism and Art. 108 illus.* TB/2004

OTTO VON SIMSON: The Gothic Cathedral: *Origins of Gothic Architecture and the Medieval Concept of Order. 58 illus.* TB/2018

HEINRICH ZIMMER: Myths and Symbols in Indian Art and Civilization. *70 illus.* TB/2005

Asian Studies

WOLFGANG FRANKE: China and the West: *The Cultural Encounter, 13th to 20th Centuries. Trans. by R. A. Wilson* TB/1326

L. CARRINGTON GOODRICH: A Short History of the Chinese People. *Illus.* TB/3015

DAN N. JACOBS, Ed.: The New Communist Manifesto and Related Documents. *3rd revised edn.* TB/1078

DAN N. JACOBS & HANS H. BAERWALD, Eds.: Chinese Communism: *Selected Documents* TB/3031

BENJAMIN I. SCHWARTZ: Chinese Communism and the Rise of Mao TB/1308

BENJAMIN I. SCHWARTZ: In Search of Wealth and Power: *Yen Fu and the West* TB/1422

Economics & Economic History

C. E. BLACK: The Dynamics of Modernization: *A Study in Comparative History* TB/1321

STUART BRUCHEY: The Roots of American Economic Growth, 1607-1861: *An Essay in Social Causation. New Introduction by the Author.* TB/1350

GILBERT BURCK & EDITORS OF *Fortune:* The Computer Age: *And its Potential for Management* TB/1179

JOHN ELLIOTT CAIRNES: The Slave Power. ‡ *Edited with Introduction by Harold D. Woodman* TB/1433

SHEPARD B. CLOUGH, THOMAS MOODIE & CAROL MOODIE, Eds.: Economic History of Europe: *Twentieth Century #* HR/1388

THOMAS C.COCHRAN: The American Business System: *A Historical Perspective, 1900-1955* TB/1180

ROBERT A. DAHL & CHARLES E. LINDBLOM: Politics, Economics, and Welfare: *Planning and Politico-Economic Systems Resolved into Basic Social Processes* TB/3037

PETER F. DRUCKER: The New Society: *The Anatomy of Industrial Order* TB/1082

HAROLD U. FAULKNER: The Decline of Laissez Faire, 1897-1917 Δ TB/1397

PAUL W. GATES: The Farmer's Age: *Agriculture, 1815-1860* Λ TB/1398

WILLIAM GREENLEAF, Ed.: American Economic Development Since 1860 + HR/1353

J. L. & BARBARA HAMMOND: The Rise of Modern Industry. || *Introduction by R. M. Hartwell* TB/1417

ROBERT L. HEILBRONER: The Future as History: *The Historic Currents of Our Time and the Direction in Which They Are Taking America* TB/1386

ROBERT L. HEILBRONER: The Great Ascent: *The Struggle for Economic Development in Our Time* TB/3030

FRANK H. KNIGHT: The Economic Organization TB/1214

DAVID S. LANDES: Bankers and Pashas: *International Finance and Economic Imperialism in Egypt. New Preface by the Author* TB/1412

ROBERT LATOUCHE: The Birth of Western Economy: *Economic Aspects of the Dark Ages* TB/1290

ABBA P. LERNER: Everbody's Business: *A Reexamination of Current Assumptions in Economics and Public Policy* TB/3051

W. ARTHUR LEWIS: Economic Survey, 1919-1939 TB/1446

W. ARTHUR LEWIS: The Principles of Economic Planning. *New Introduction by the Author*° TB/1436

ROBERT GREEN MC CLOSKEY: American Conservatism in the Age of Enterprise TB/1137

PAUL MANTOUX: The Industrial Revolution in the Eighteenth Century: *An Outline of the Beginnings of the Modern Factory System in England*° TB/1079

WILLIAM MILLER, Ed.: Men in Business: *Essays on the Historical Role of the Entrepreneur* TB/1081

GUNNAR MYRDAL: An International Economy. *New Introduction by the Author* TB/1445

HERBERT A. SIMON: The Shape of Automation: *For Men and Management* TB/1245

PERRIN STRYER: The Character of the Executive: *Eleven Studies in Managerial Qualities* TB/1041

RICHARD S. WECKSTEIN, Ed.: Expansion of World Trade and the Growth of National Economies ** TB/1373

Education

JACQUES BARZUN: The House of Intellect TB/1051

RICHARD M. JONES, Ed.: Contemporary Educational Psychology: *Selected Readings* ** TB/1292

CLARK KERR: The Uses of the University TB/1264

Historiography and History of Ideas

HERSCHEL BAKER: The Image of Man: *A Study of the Idea of Human Dignity in Classical Antiquity, the Middle Ages, and the Renaissance* TB/1047

J. BRONOWSKI & BRUCE MAZLISH: The Western Intellectual Tradition: *From Leonardo to Hegel* TB/3001

EDMUND BURKE: On Revolution. Ed. by Robert A. Smith TB/1401

WILHELM DILTHEY: Pattern and Meaning in History: *Thoughts on History and Society.*° *Edited with an Intro. by H. P. Rickman* TB/1075

ALEXANDER GRAY: The Socialist Tradition: *Moses to Lenin* ° TB/1375

J. H. HEXTER: More's Utopia: *The Biography of an Idea. Epilogue by the Author* TB/1195

H. STUART HUGHES: History as Art and as Science: *Twin Vistas on the Past* TB/1207

ARTHUR O. LOVEJOY: The Great Chain of Being: *A Study of the History of an Idea* TB/1009

JOSE ORTEGA Y GASSET: The Modern Theme. *Introduction by Jose Ferrater Mora* TB/1038

RICHARD H. POPKIN: The History of Scepticism from Erasmus to Descartes. *Revised Edition* TB/1391

G. J. RENIER: History: *Its Purpose and Method* TB/1209

MASSIMO SALVADORI, Ed.: Modern Socialism # HR/1374

GEORG SIMMEL et al.: Essays on Sociology, Philosophy and Aesthetics. *Edited by Kurt H. Wolff* TB/1234

BRUNO SNELL: The Discovery of the Mind: *The Greek Origins of European Thought* TB/1018

W. WARREN WAGER, ed.: European Intellectual History Since Darwin and Marx TB/1297

W. H. WALSH: Philosophy of History: In Intro-*duction* TB/1020

History: General

HANS KOHN: The Age of Nationalism: *The First Era of Global History* TB/1380

BERNARD LEWIS: The Arabs in History TB/1029

BERNARD LEWIS: The Middle East and the West ° TB/1274

History: Ancient

A. ANDREWS: The Greek Tyrants TB/1103

ERNST LUDWIG EHRLICH: A Concise History of Israel: *From the Earliest Times to the Destruction of the Temple in A.D. 70* ° TB/128

ADOLF ERMAN, Ed.: The Ancient Egyptians: *A Sourcebook of their Writings. New Introduction by William Kelly Simpson* TB/1233

THEODOR H. GASTER: Thespis: *Ritual Myth and Drama in the Ancient Near East* TB/1281

MICHAEL GRANT: Ancient History ° TB/1190

A. H. M. JONES, Ed.: A History of Rome through the Fifgth Century # *Vol. I: The Republic* HR/1364
Vol. II The Empire: HR/1460

SAMUEL NOAH KRAMER: Sumerian Mythology TB/1055

NAPHTALI LEWIS & MEYER REINHOLD, Eds.: Roman Civilization *Vol. I: The Republic* TB/1231
Vol. II: The Empire TB/1232

History: Medieval

MARSHALL W. BALDWIN, Ed.: Christianity Through the 13th Century # HR/1468

MARC BLOCH: Land and Work in Medieval Europe. *Translated by J. E. Anderson* TB/1452

HELEN CAM: England Before Elizabeth TB/1026

NORMAN COHN: The Pursuit of the Millennium: *Revolutionary Messianism in Medieval and Reformation Europe* TB/1037

G. G. COULTON: Medieval Village, Manor, and Monastery HR/1022

HEINRICH FICHTENAU: The Carolingian Empire: *The Age of Charlemagne. Translated with an Introduction by Peter Munz* TB/1142

GALBERT OF BRUGES: The Murder of Charles the Good: *A Contemporary Record of Revolutionary Change in 12th Century Flanders. Translated with an Introduction by James Bruce Ross* TB/1311

F. L. GANSHOF: Feudalism TB/1058

F. L. GANSHOF: The Middle Ages: *A History of International Relations. Translated by Rêmy Hall* TB/1411

W. O. HASSALL, Ed.: Medieval England: *As Viewed by Contemporaries* TB/1205

DENYS HAY: The Medieval Centuries ° TB/1192

DAVID HERLIHY, Ed.: Medieval Culture and Socitey # HR/1340

J. M. HUSSEY: The Byzantine World TB/1057
ROBERT LATOUCHE: The Birth of Western Economy: *Economic Aspects of the Dark Ages* ° TB/1290
HENRY CHARLES LEA: The Inquisition of the Middle Ages. || *Introduction by Walter Ullmann* TB/1456
FERDINARD LOT: The End of the Ancient World and the Beginnings of the Middle Ages. *Introduction by Glanville Downey* TB/1044
H. R. LOYN: The Norman Conquest TB/1457
ACHILLE LUCHAIRE: Social France at the time of Philip Augustus. *Intro. by John W. Baldwin* TB/1314
GUIBERT DE NOGENT: Self and Society in Medieval France: *The Memoirs of Guibert de Nogent.* || Edited by John F. Benton TB/1471
MARSILIUS OF PADUA: The Defender of Peace. *The* Defensor Pacis. *Translated with an Introduction by Alan Gewirth* TB/1310
CHARLES PETET-DUTAILLIS: The Feudal Monarchy in France and England: *From the Tenth to the Thirteenth Century* ° TB/1165
STEVEN RUNCIMAN: A History of the Crusades Vol. I: *The First Crusade and the Foundation of the Kingdom of Jerusalem. Illus.* TB/1143
Vol. II: *The Kingdom of Jerusalem and the Frankish East 1100-1187. Illus.* TB/1243
Vol. III: *The Kingdom of Acre and the Later Crusades. Illus.* TB/1298
J. M. WALLACE-HADRILL: The Barbarian West: *The Early Middle Ages, A.D. 400-1000* TB/1061

History: Renaissance & Reformation

JACOB BURCKHARDT: The Civilization of the Renaissance in Italy. *Introduction by Benjamin Nelson and Charles Trinkaus. Illus.* Vol. I TB/40; Vol. II TB/41
JOHN CALVIN & JACOPO SADOLETO: A Reformation Debate. *Edited by John C. Olin* TB/1239
FEDERICO CHABOD: Machiavelli and the Renaissance TB/1193
THOMAS CROMWELL: Thomas Cromwell on Church and Commonwealth,: *Selected Letters 1523-1540.* ¶ *Ed. with an Intro. by Arthur J. Slavin* TB/1462
R. TREVOR DAVIES: The Golden Century of Spain, 1501-1621 ° TB/1194
J. H. ELLIOTT: Europe Divided, 1559-1598 a ° TB/1414
G. R. ELTON: Reformation Europe, 1517-1559 ° a TB/1270
DESIDERIUS ERASMUS: Christian Humanism and the Reformation: *Selected Writings. Edited and Translated by John C. Olin* TB/1166
DESIDERIUS ERASMUS: Erasmus and His Age: *Selected Letters. Edited with an Introduction by Hans J. Hillerbrand. Translated by Marcus A. Haworth* TB/1461
WALLACE K. FERGUSON et al.: Facets of the Renaissance TB/1098
WALLACE K. FERGUSON et al.: The Renaissance: *Six Essays. Illus.* TB/1084
FRANCESCO GUICCIARDINI: History of Florence. *Translated with an Introduction and Notes by Mario Domandi* TB/1470
WERNER L. GUNDERSHEIMER, Ed.: French Humanism, 1470-1600. * *Illus.* TB/1473
MARIE BOAS HALL, Ed.: Nature and Nature's Laws: *Documents of the Scientific Revolution #* HR/1420
HANS J. HILLERBRAND, Ed., The Protestant Reformation # HR/1342
JOHAN HUIZINGA: Erasmus and the Age of Reformation. *Illus.* TB/19
JOEL HURSTFIELD: The Elizabethan Nation TB/1312
JOEL HURSTFIELD, Ed.: The Reformation Crisis TB/1267
PAUL OSKAR KRISTELLER: Renaissance Thought: *The Classic, Scholastic, and Humanist Strains* TB/1048
PAUL OSKAR KRISTELLER: Renaissance Thought II: *Papers on Humanism and the Arts* TB/1163
PAUL O. KRISTELLER & PHILIP P. WIENER, Eds.: Renaissance Essays TB/1392
DAVID LITTLE: Religion, Order and Law: *A Study in Pre-Revolutionary England.* § *Preface by R. Bellah* TB/1418
NICCOLO MACHIAVELLI: History of Florence and of the Affairs of Italy: *From the Earliest Times to the Death of Lorenzo the Magnificent. Introduction by Felix Gilbert* TB/1027
ALFRED VON MARTIN: Sociology of the Renaissance. ° *Introduction by W. K. Ferguson* TB/1099
GARRETT MATTINGLY et al.: Renaissance Profiles. *Edited by J. H. Plumb* TB/1162
J. E. NEALE: The Age of Catherine de Medici ° TB/1085
J. H. PARRY: The Establishment of the European Hegemony: 1415-1715: *Trade and Exploration in the Age of the Renaissance* TB/1045
J. H. PARRY, Ed.: The European Reconnaissance: *Selected Documents #* HR/1345
BUONACCORSO PITTI & GREGORIO DATI: Two Memoirs of Renaissance Florence: *The Diaries of Buonaccorso Pitti and Gregorio Dati. Edited with Intro. by Gene Brucker. Trans. by Julia Martines* TB/1333
J. H. PLUMB: The Italian Renaissance: *A Concise Survey of Its History and Culture* TB/1161
A. F. POLLARD: Henry VIII. *Introduction by A. G. Dickens.* ° TB/1249
RICHARD H. POPKIN: The History of Scepticism from Erasmus to Descartes TB/139
PAOLO ROSSI: Philosophy, Technology, and the Arts, in the Early Modern Era 1400-1700. || *Edited by Benjamin Nelson. Translated by Salvator Attanasio* TB/1458
FERDINAND SCHEVILL: The Medici. *Illus.* TB/1010
FERDINAND SCHEVILL: Medieval and Renaissance Florence. *Illus. Vol. I: Medieval Florence* TB/1090
Vol. II: The Coming of Humanism and the Age of the Medici TB/1091
R. H. TAWNEY: The Agrarian Problem in the Sixteenth Century. *Intro. by Lawrence Stone* TB/1315
H. R. TREVOR-ROPER: The European Witch-craze of the Sixteenth and Seventeenth Centuries and Other Essays ° TB/1416
VESPASIANO: Rennaissance Princes, Popes, and *XVth Century: The Vespasiano Memoirs. Introduction by Myron P. Gilmore. Illus.* TB/1111

History: Modern European

RENE ALBRECHT-CARRIE, Ed.: The Concert of Europe # HR/1341
MAX BELOFF: The Age of Absolutism, 1660-1815 TB/1062
OTTO VON BISMARCK: Reflections and Reminiscences. *Ed. with Intro. by Theodore S. Hamerow* ¶ TB/1357
EUGENE C. BLACK, Ed.: British Politics in the Nineteenth Century # HR/1427

EUGENE C. BLACK, Ed.: European Political History, 1815-1870: *Aspects of Liberalism* ¶ TB/1331

ASA BRIGGS: The Making of Modern England, 1783-1867: *The Age of Improvement* ° TB/1203

D. W. BROGAN: The Development of Modern France ° Vol. I: *From the Fall of the Empire to the Dreyfus Affair* TB/1184 Vol. II: *The Shadow of War, World War I, Between the Two Wars* TB/1185

ALAN BULLOCK: Hitler, A Study in Tyranny. ° *Revised Edition. Illus.* TB/1123

EDMUND BURKE: On Revolution. *Ed. by Robert A. Smith* TB/1401

E. R. CARR: International Relations Between the Two World Wars. 1919-1939 ° TB/1279

E. H. CARR: The Twenty Years' Crisis, 1919-1939: *An Introduction to the Study of International Relations* ° TB/1122

GORDON A. CRAIG: From Bismarck to Adenauer: *Aspects of German Statecraft. Revised Edition* TB/1171

LESTER G. CROCKER, Ed.: The Age of Enlightenment # HR/1423

DENIS DIDEROT: The Encyclopedia: *Selections. Edited and Translated with Introduction by Stephen Gendzier* TB/1299

JACQUES DROZ: Europe between Revolutions, 1815-1848. ° *a Trans. by Robert Baldick* TB/1346

JOHANN GOTTLIEB FICHTE: Addresses to the German Nation. *Ed. with Intro. by George A. Kelly* ¶ TB/1366

FRANKLIN L. FORD: Robe and Sword: *The Re-Louis XIV* TB/1217

ROBERT & ELBORG FORSTER, Eds.: European Society in the Eighteenth Century # HR/1404

C. C. GILLISPIE: Genesis and Geology: *The Decades before Darwin* § TB/51

ALBERT GOODWIN, Ed.: The European Nobility in the Enghteenth Century TB/1313

ALBERT GOODWIN: The French Revolution TB/1064

ALBERT GUERARD: France in the Classical Age: *The Life and Death of an Ideal* TB/1183

JOHN B. HALSTED, Ed.: Romanticism # HR/1387

J. H. HEXTER: Reappraisals in History: *New Views on History and Society in Early Modern Europe* ° TB/1100

STANLEY HOFFMANN et al.: In Search of France: *The Economy, Society and Political System In the Twentieth Century* TB/1219

H. STUART HUGHES: The Obstructed Path: *French Social Thought in the Years of Desperation* TB/1451

JOHAN HUIZINGA: Dutch Civilisation in the 17th Century and Other Essays TB/1453

LIONAL KOCHAN: The Struggle for Germany: *1914-45* TB/1304

HANS KOHN: The Mind of Germany: *The Education of a Nation* TB/1204

HANS KOHN, Ed.: The Mind of Modern Russia: *Historical and Political Thought of Russia's Great Age* TB/1065

WALTER LAQUEUR & GEORGE L. MOSSE, Eds.: Education and Social Structure in the 20th Century. ° *Volume 6 of the Journal* of Contemporary History TB/1339

WALTER LAQUEUR & GEORGE L. MOSSE, Ed.: International Fascism, 1920-1945. ° *Volume 1 of the* Journal of Contemporary History TB/1276

WALTER LAQUEUR & GEORGE L. MOSSE, Eds.: Literature and Politics in the 20th Century. ° *Volume 5 of the* Journal of Contemporary History. TB/1328

WALTER LAQUEUR & GEORGE L. MOSSE, Eds.: The New History: *Trends in Historical Research and Writing Since World War II.* ° *Volume 4 of the* Journal of Contemporary History TB/1327

WALTER LAQUEUR & GEORGE L. MOSSE, Eds.: 1914: *The Coming of the First World War.* ° *Volume3 of the* Journal of Contemporary *History* TB/1306

C. A. MACARTNEY, Ed.: The Habsburg and Hohenzollern Dynasties in the Seventeenth and Eighteenth Centuries # HR/1400

JOHN MCMANNERS: European History, 1789-1914: *Men, Machines and Freedom* TB/1419

PAUL MANTOUX: The Industrial Revolution in the Eighteenth Century: *An Outline of the Beginnings of the Modern Factory System in England* TB/1079

FRANK E. MANUEL: The Prophets of Paris: *Turgot, Condorcet, Saint-Simon, Fourier, and Comte* TB/1218

KINGSLEY MARTIN: French Liberal Thought in the Eighteenth Century: *A Study of Political Ideas from Bayle to Condorcet* TB/1114

NAPOLEON III: Napoleonic Ideas: *Des Idées Napoléoniennes, par le Prince Napoléon-Louis Bonaparte. Ed. by Brison D. Gooch* ¶ TB/1336

FRANZ NEUMANN: Behemoth: *The Structure and Practice of National Socialism, 1933-1944* TB/1289

DAVID OGG: Europe of the Ancien Régime, 1715-1783 ° *a* TB/1271

GEORGE RUDE: Revolutionary Europe, 1783-1815 ° *a* TB/1272

MASSIMO SALVADORI, Ed.: Modern Socialism # TB/1374

HUGH SETON-WATSON: Eastern Europe Between the Wars, 1918-1941 TB/1330

DENIS MACK SMITH, Ed.: The Making of Italy, 1796-1870 # HR/1356

ALBERT SOREL: Europe Under the Old Regime. *Translated by Francis H. Herrick* TB/1121

ROLAND N. STROMBERG, Ed.: Realism, Naturalism, and Symbolism: *Modes of Thought and Expression in Europe, 1848-1914* # HR/1355

A. J. P. TAYLOR: From Napoleon to Lenin: *Historical Essays* ° TB/1268

A. J. P. TAYLOR: The Habsburg Monarchy, 1809-1918: *A History of the Austrian Empire and Austria-Hungary* ° TB/1187

J. M. THOMPSON: European History, 1494-1789 TB/1431

DAVID THOMSON, Ed.: France: Empire and Republic, 1850-1940 # HR/1387

ALEXIS DE TOCQUEVILLE & GUSTAVE DE BEAUMONT: Tocqueville and Beaumont on Social Reform. *Ed. and trans. with Intro. by Seymour Drescher* TB/1343

G. M. TREVELYAN: British History in the Nineteenth Century and After: 1792-1919 ° TB/1251

H. R. TREVOR-ROPER: Historical Essays TB/1269

W. WARREN WAGAR, Ed.: Science, Faith, and MAN: *European Thought Since 1914* # HR/1362

MACK WALKER, Ed.: Metternich's Europe, 1813-1848 # HR/1361

ELIZABETH WISKEMANN: Europe of the Dictators, 1919-1945 ° *a* TB/1273

JOHN B. WOLF: France: 1814-1919: *The Rise of a Liberal-Democratic Society* TB/3019

Literature & Literary Criticism

JACQUES BARZUN: The House of Intellect TB/1051

W. J. BATE: From Classic to Romantic: *Premises of Taste in Eighteenth Century England* TB/1036

VAN WYCK BROOKS: Van Wyck Brooks: The Early Years: *A Selection from his Works, 1908-1921 Ed. with Intro. by Claire Sprague* TB/3082

ERNST R. CURTIUS: European Literature and the Latin Middle Ages. *Trans. by Willard Trask* TB/2015

RICHMOND LATTIMORE, Translator: The Odyssey of Homer TB/1389

JOHN STUART MILL: On Bentham and Coleridge. *Introduction by F. R. Leavis* TB/1070

SAMUEL PEPYS: The Diary of Samual Pepys. ° *Edited by O. F. Morshead. 60 illus. by Ernest Shepard* TB/1007

ROBERT PREYER, Ed.: Victorian Literature ** TB/1302

ALBION W. TOURGEE: A Fool's Errand: *A Novel of the South during Reconstruction. Intro. by George Fredrickson* TB/3074

BASIL WILEY: Nineteenth Century Studies: *Coleridge to Matthew Arnold* ° TB/1261

RAYMOND WILLIAMS: Culture and Society, 1780-1950 ° TB/1252

Philosophy

HENRI BERGSON: Time and Free Will: *An Essay on the Immediate Data of Consciousness* ° TB/1021

LUDWIG BINSWANGER: Being-in-the-World: *Selected Papers. Trans. with Intro. by Jacob Needleman* TB/1365

H. J. BLACKHAM: Six Existentialist Thinkers: *Kierkegaard, Nietzsche, Jaspers, Marcel, Heidegger, Sartre* ° TB/1002

J. M. BOCHENSKI: The Methods of Contemporary Thought. *Trans. by Peter Caws* TB/1377

CRANE BRINTON: Nietzsche. *Preface, Bibliography, and Epilogue by the Author* TB/1197

ERNST CASSIRER: Rousseau, Kant and Goethe. *Intro. by Peter Gay* TB/1092

FREDERICK COPLESTON, S. J.: Medieval Philosophy TB/376

F. M. CORNFORD: From Religion to Philosophy: *A Study in the Origins of Western Speculation* § TB/20

WILFRID DESAN: The Tragic Finale: *An Essay on the Philosophy of Jean-Paul Sartre* TB/1030

MARVIN FARBER: The Aims of Phenomenology: *The Motives, Methods, and Impact of Husserl's Thought* TB/1291

MARVIN FARBER: Basic Issues of Philosophy: *Experience, Reality, and Human Values* TB/1344

MARVIN FARBER: Phenomenology and Existence: *Towards a Philosophy within Nature* TB/1295

PAUL FRIEDLANDER: Plato: *An Introduction* TB/2017

MICHAEL GELVEN: A Commentary on Heidegger's "Being and Time" TB/1464

J. GLENN GRAY: Hegel and Greek Thought TB/1409

W. K. C. GUTHRIE: The Greek Philosophers: *From Thales to Aristotle* ° TB/1008

G. W. F. HEGEL: On Art, Religion Philosophy: *Introductory Lectures to the Realm of Absolute Spirit. || Edited with an Introduction by J. Glenn Gray* TB/1463

G. W. F. HEGEL: Phenomenology of Mind. ° || *Introduction by George Lichtheim* TB/1303

MARTIN HEIDEGGER: Discourse on Thinking. *Translated with a Preface by John M. Anderson and E. Hans Freund. Introduction by John M. Anderson* TB/1459

F. H. HEINEMANN: Existentialism and the Modern Predicament TB/28

WERER HEISENBERG: Physics and Philosophy: *The Revolution in Modern Science. Intro. by F. S. C. Northrop* TB/549

EDMUND HUSSERL: Phenomenology and the Crisis of Philosophy. § *Translated with an Introduction by Quentin Lauer* TB/1170

IMMANUEL KANT: Groundwork of the Metaphysic of Morals. *Translated and Analyzed by H. J. Paton* TB/1159

IMMANUEL KANT: Lectures on Ethics. § *Introduction by Lewis White Beck* TB/105

WALTER KAUFMANN, Ed.: Religion From Tolstoy to Camus: *Basic Writings on Religious Truth and Morals* TB/123

QUENTIN LAUER: Phenomenology: *Its Genesis and Prospect. Preface by Aron Gurwitsch* TB/1169

MAURICE MANDELBAUM: The Problem of Historical Knowledge: *An Answer to Relativism* TB/1338

GEORGE A. MORGAN: What Nietzsche Means TB/1198

H. J. PATON: The Categorical Imperative: *A Study in Kant's Moral Philosophy* TB/1325

MICHAEL POLANYI: Personal Knowledge: *Towards a Post-Critical Philosophy* TB/1158

KARL R. POPPER: Conjectures and Refutations: *The Growth of Scientific Knowledge* TB/1376

WILLARD VAN ORMAN QUINE: Elementary Logic *Revised Edition* TB/577

WILLARD VAN ORMAN QUINE: From a Logical Point of View: *Logico-Philosophical Essays* TB/566

JOHN E. SMITH: Themes in American Philosophy: *Purpose, Experience and Community* TB/1466

MORTON WHITE: Foundations of Historical Knowledge TB/1440

WILHELM WINDELBAND: A History of Philosophy
Vol. I: Greek, Roman, Medieval TB/38
Vol. II: Renaissance, Enlightenment, Modern TB/39

LUDWIG WITTGENSTEIN: The Blue and Brown Books ° TB/1211

LUDWIG WITTGENSTEIN: Notebooks, 1914-1916 TB/1441

Political Science & Government

C. E. BLACK: The Dynamics of Modernization: *A Study in Comparative History* TB/1321

KENNETH E. BOULDING: Conflict and Defense: *A General Theory of Action* TB/3024

DENIS W. BROGAN: Politics in America. *New Introduction by the Author* TB/1469

CRANE BRINTON: English Political Thought in the Nineteenth Century TB/1071

ROBERT CONQUEST: Power and Policy in the USSR: *The Study of Soviet Dynastics* ° TB/1307

ROBERT A. DAHL & CHARLES E. LINDBLOM: Politics, Economics, and Welfare: *Planning and Politico-Economic Systems Resolved into Basic Social Processes* TB/1277

HANS KOHN: Political Ideologies of the 20th Century TB/1277

ROY C. MACRIDIS, Ed.: Political Parties: *Contemporary Trends and Ideas* ** TB/1322

ROBERT GREEN MC CLOSKEY: American Conservatism in the Age of Enterprise, 1865-1910 TB/1137

MARSILIUS OF PADUA: The Defender of Peace. *The* Defensor Pacis. *Translated with an Introduction by Alan Gewirth* TB/1310

KINGSLEY MARTIN: French Liberal Thought in the Eighteenth Century: *A Study of Political Ideas from Bayle to Condorcet* TB/1114

BARRINGTON MOORE, JR.: Political Power and Social Theory: *Seven Studies* || TB/1221
BARRINGTON MOORE, JR.: Soviet Politics—The Dilemma of Power: *The Role of Ideas in Social Change* || TB/1222
BARRINGTON MOORE, JR.: Terror and Progress—USSR: *Some Sources of Change and Stability*
JOHN B. MORRALL: Political Thought in Medieval Times TB/1076
KARL R. POPPER: The Open Society and Its Enemies *Vol. I: The Spell of Plato* TB/1101 *Vol. II: The High Tide of Prophecy: Hegel, Marx, and the Aftermath* TB/1102
CONYERS READ, Ed.: The Constitution Reconsidered. *Revised Edition, Preface by Richard B. Morris* TB/1384
JOHN P. ROCHE, Ed.: Origins of American Political Thought: *Selected Readings* TB/1301
JOHN P. ROCHE, Ed.: American Political Thought: *From Jefferson to Progressivism* TB/1332
HENRI DE SAINT-SIMON: Social Organization, The Science of Man, and Other Writings. || *Edited and Translated with an Introduction by Felix Markham* TB/1152
CHARLES SCHOTTLAND, Ed.: The Welfare State ** TB/1323
JOSEPH A. SCHUMPETER: Capitalism, Socialism and Democracy TB/3008
PETER WOLL, Ed.: Public Administration and Policy: *Selected Essays* TB/1284

Psychology

ALFRED ADLER: The Individual Psychology of Alfred Adler: *A Systematic Presentation in Selections from His Writings. Edited by Heinz L. & Rowena R. Ansbacher* TB/1154
ALFRED ADLER: Problems of Neurosis: *A Book of Case Histories. Introduction by Heinz L. Ansbacher* TB/1145
LUDWIG BINSWANGER: Being-in-the-World: *Selected Papers. || Trans. with Intro. by Jacob Needleman* TB/1365
ARTHUR BURTON & ROBERT E. HARRIS: Clinical Studies of Personality Vol. I TB/3075 Vol. II TB/3076
HADLEY CANTRIL: The Invasion from Mars: *A Study in the Psychology of Panic* || TB/1282
MIRCEA ELIADE: Cosmos and History: *The Myth of the Eternal Return* § TB/2050
MIRCEA ELIADE: Myth and Reality TB/1369
MIRCEA ELIADE: Myths, Dreams and Mysteries: *The Encounter Between Contemporary Faiths and Archaic Realities* § TB/1320
MIRCEA ELIADE: Rites and Symbols of Initiation: *The Mysteries of Birth and Rebirth* § TB/1236
HERBERT FINGARETTE: The Self in Transformation: *Psychoanalysis, Philosophy and the Life of the Spirit* || TB/1177
SIGMUND FREUD: On Creativity and the Unconscious: *Papers on the Psychology of Art, Literature, Love, Religion. § Intro. by Benjamin Nelson* TB/45
J. GLENN GRAY: The Warriors: *Reflections on Men in Battle. Introduction by Hannah Arendt* TB/1294
WILLIAM JAMES: Psychology: *The Briefer Course. Edited with an Intro. by Gordon Allport* TB/1034
C. G. JUNG: Psychological Reflections. *Ed. by J. Jacobi* TB/2001
KARL MENNINGER, M.D.: Theory of Psychoanalytic Technique TB/1144
JOHN H. SCHAAR: Escape from Authority: *The Perspectives of Erich Fromm* TB/1155
MUZAFER SHERIF: The Psychology of Social Norms. *Introduction by Gardner Murphy* TB/3072
HELLMUT WILHELM: Change: *Eight Lectures on the* I Ching TB/2019

Religion: Ancient and Classical, Biblical and Judaic Traditions

W. F. ALBRIGHT: The Biblical Period from Abraham to Ezra TB/102
SALO W. BARON: Modern Nationalism and Religion TB/818
C. K. BARRETT, Ed.: The New Testament Background: *Selected Documents* TB/86
MARTIN BUBER: Eclipse of God: *Studies in the Relation Between Religion and Philosophy* TB/12
MARTIN BUBER: Hasidism and Modern Man. *Edited and Translated by Maurice Friedman* TB/839
MARTIN BUBER: The Knowledge of Man. *Edited with an Introduction by Maurice Friedman. Translated by Maurice Friedman and Ronald Gregor Smith* TB/135
MARTIN BUBER: Moses. *The Revelation and the Covenant* TB/837
MARTIN BUBER: The Origin and Meaning of Hasidism. *Edited and Translated by Maurice Friedman* TB/835
MARTIN BUBER: The Prophetic Faith TB/73
MARTIN BUBER: Two Types of Faith: *Interpenetration of Judaism and Christianity* ° TB/75
MALCOLM L. DIAMOND: Martin Buber: *Jewish Existentialist* TB/840
M. S. ENSLIN: Christian Beginnings TB/5
M. S. ENSLIN: The Literature of the Christian Movement TB/6
ERNST LUDWIG EHRLICH: A Concise History of Israel: *From the Earliest Times to the Destruction of the Temple in A.D. 70* ° TB/128
HENRI FRANKFORT: Ancient Egyptian Religion: *An Interpretation* TB/77
MAURICE S. FRIEDMAN: Martin Buber: *The Life of Dialogue* TB/64
ABRAHAM HESCHEL: The Earth Is the Lord's & The Sabbath. *Two Essays* TB/828
ABRAHAM HESCHEL: God in Search of Man: *A Philosophy of Judaism* TB/807
ABRAHAM HESCHEL: Man Is not Alone: *A Philosophy of Religion* TB/838
ABRAHAM HESCHEL: The Prophets: *An Introduction* TB/1421
T. J. MEEK: Hebrew Origins TB/69
JAMES MUILENBURG: The Way of Israel: *Biblical Faith and Ethics* TB/133
H. J. ROSE: Religion in Greece and Rome TB/55
H. H. ROWLEY: The Growth of the Old Testament TB/107
D. WINTON THOMAS, Ed.: Documents from Old Testament Times TB/85

Religion: General Christianity

ROLAND H. BAINTON: Christendom: *A Short History of Christianity and Its Impact on Western Civilization. Illus.* Vol. I TB/131; Vol. II TB/132
JOHN T. MCNEILL: Modern Christian Movements. *Revised Edition* TB/1402
ERNST TROELTSCH: The Social Teaching of the Christian Churches. *Intro. by H. Richard Niebuhr* Vol. TB/71; Vol. II TB/72

Religion: Early Christianity Through Reformation

ANSELM OF CANTERBURY: Truth, Freedom, and Evil: *Three Philosophical Dialogues. Edited and Translated by Jasper Hopkins and Herbert Richardson* TB/317

MARSHALL W. BALDWIN, Ed.: Christianity through the 13th Century # HR/1468

W. D. DAVIES: Paul and Rabbinic Judaism: *Some Rabbinic Elements in Pauline Theology. Revised Edition* ° TB/146

ADOLF DEISSMAN: Paul: *A Study in Social and Religious History* TB/15

JOHANNES ECKHART: Meister Eckhart: *A Modern Translation by R. Blakney* TB/8

EDGAR J. GOODSPEED: A Life of Jesus TB/1

ROBERT M. GRANT: Gnosticism and Early Christianity TB/136

WILLIAM HALLER: The Rise of Puritanism TB/22

GERHART B. LADNER: The Idea of Reform: *Its Impact on the Christian Thought and Action in the Age of the Fathers* TB/149

ARTHUR DARBY NOCK: Early Gentile Christianity and Its Hellenistic Background TB/111

ARTHUR DARBY NOCK: St. Paul ° TR/104

ORIGEN: On First Principles. *Edited by G. W. Butterworth. Introduction by Henri de Lubac* TB/311

GORDON RUPP: Luther's Progress to the Diet of Worms ° TB/120

Religion: The Protestant Tradition

KARL BARTH: Church Dogmatics: *A Selection. Intro. by H. Gollwitzer. Ed. by G. W. Bromiley* TB/95

KARL BARTH: Dogmatics in Outline TB/56

KARL BARTH: The Word of God and the Word of Man TB/13

HERBERT BRAUN, et al.: God and Christ: *Existence and Province. Volume 5 of* Journal for Theology and the Church, *edited by Robert W. Funk and Gerhard Ebeling* TB/255

WHITNEY R. CROSS: The Burned-Over District: *The Social and Intellectual History of Enthusiastic Religion in Western New York, 1800-1850* TB/1242

NELS F. S. FERRE: Swedish Contributions to Modern Theology. *New Chapter by William A. Johnson* TB/147

WILLIAM R. HUTCHISON, Ed.: American Protestant Thought: *The Liberal Era* ‡ TB/1385

ERNST KASEMANN, et al.: Distinctive Protestant and Catholic Themes Reconsidered. *Volume 3 of* Journal for Theology and the Church, *edited by Robert W. Funk and Gerhard Ebeling* TB/253

SOREN KIERKEGAARD: On Authority and Revelation: *The Book on Adler, or a Cycle of Ethico-Religious Essays. Introduction by F. Sontag* TB/139

SOREN KIERKEGAARD: Crisis in the Life of an Actress, *and Other Essays on Drama. Translated with an Introduction by Stephen Crites* TB/145

SOREN KIERKEGAARD: Edifying Discourses. *Edited with an Intro. by Paul Holmer* TB/32

SOREN KIERKEGAARD: The Journals of Kierkegaard. ° *Edited with an Intro. by Alexander Dru* TB/52

SOREN KIERKEGAARD: The Point of View for My Work as an Author: *A Report to History.* § *Preface by Benjamin Nelson* TB/88

SOREN KIERKEGAARD: The Present Age. § *Translated and edited by Alexander Dru. Introduction by Walter Kaufmann* TB/94

SOREN KIERKEGAARD: Purity of Heart. *Trans. by Douglas Steere* TB/4

SOREN KIERKEGAARD: Repetition: *An Essay in Experimental Psychology* § TB/117

SOREN KIERKEGAARD: Works of Love: *Some Christian Reflections in the Form of Discourses* TB/122

WILLIAM G. MCLOUGHLIN, Ed.: The American Evangelicals: 1800-1900: *An Anthology* TB/1382

WOLFHART PANNENBERG, et al.: History and Hermeneutic. *Volume 4 of* Journal for Theology and the Church, *edited by Robert W. Funk and Gerhard Ebeling* TB/254

JAMES M. ROBINSON, et al.: The Bultmann School of Biblical Interpretation: New Directions? *Volume 1 of* Journal for Theology and the Church, *edited by Robert W. Funk and Gerhard Ebeling* TB/251

F. SCHLEIERMACHER: The Christian Faith. *Introduction by Richard R. Niebuhr.* Vol. I TB/108; Vol. II TB/109

F. SCHLEIERMACHER: On Religion: *Speeches to Its Cultured Despisers. Intro. by Rudolf Otto* TB/36

TIMOTHY L. SMITH: Revivalism and Social Reform: *American Protestantism on the Eve of the Civil War* TB/1229

PAUL TILLICH: Dynamics of Faith TB/42

PAUL TILLICH: Morality and Beyond TB/142

EVELYN UNDERHILL: Worship TB/10

Religion: The Roman & Eastern Christian Traditions

A. ROBERT CAPONIGRI, Ed.: Modern Catholic Thinkers II: *The Church and the Political Order* TB/307

G. P. FEDOTOV: The Russian Religious Mind: *Kievan Christianity, the tenth to the thirteenth Centuries* TB/370

GABRIEL MARCEL: Being and Having: *An Existential Diary. Introduction by James Collins* TB/310

GABRIEL MARCEL: Homo Viator: *Introduction to a Metaphysic of Hope* TB/397

Religion: Oriental Religions

TOR ANDRAE: Mohammed: *The Man and His Faith* § TB/62

EDWARD CONZE: Buddhism: *Its Essence and Development.* ° *Foreword by Arthur Waley* TB/58

EDWARD CONZE: Buddhist Meditation TB/1442

EDWARD CONZE et al, Editors: Buddhist Texts through the Ages TB/113

ANANDA COOMARASWAMY: Buddha and the Gospel of Buddhism TB/119

H. G. CREEL: Confucius and the Chinese Way TB/63

FRANKLIN EDGERTON, Trans. & Ed.: The Bhagavad Gita TB/115

SWAMI NIKHILANANDA, Trans. & Ed.: The Upanishads TB/114

D. T. SUZUKI: On Indian Mahayana Buddhism. ° *Ed. with Intro. by Edward Conze.* TB/1403

Religion: Philosophy, Culture, and Society

NICOLAS BERDYAEV: The Destiny of Man TB/61

RUDOLF BULTMANN: History and Eschatology: *The Presence of Eternity* ° TB/91

RUDOLF BULTMANN AND FIVE CRITICS: Kerygma and Myth: *A Theological Debate* TB/80

RUDOLF BULTMANN and KARL KUNDSIN: Form Criticism: *Two Essays on New Testament Research. Trans. by F. C. Grant* TB/96

WILLIAM A. CLEBSCH & CHARLES R. JAEKLE: Pastoral Care in Historical Perspective: *An Essay with Exhibits* TB/148

FREDERICK FERRE: Language, Logic and God. *New Preface by the Author* TB/1407

LUDWIG FEUERBACH: The Essence of Christianity. *§ Introduction by Karl Barth. Foreword by H. Richard Niebuhr* TB/11

C. C. GILLISPIE: Genesis and Geology: *The Decades before Darwin §* TB/51

ADOLF HARNACK: What Is Christianity? § *Introduction by Rudolf Bultmann* TB/17

KYLE HASELDEN: The Racial Problem in Christian Perspective TB/116

MARTIN HEIDEGGER: Discourse on Thinking. *Translated with a Preface by John M. Anderson and E. Hans Freund. Introduction by John M. Anderson* TB/1459

IMMANUEL KANT: Religion Within the Limits of Reason Alone. § *Introduction by Theodore M. Greene and John Silber* TB/FG

WALTER KAUFMANN, Ed.: Religion from Tolstoy to Camus: *Basic Writings on Religious Truth and Morals. Enlarged Edition* TB/123

JOHN MACQUARRIE: An Existentialist Theology: *A Comparison of Heidegger and Bultmann. ° Foreword by Rudolf Bultmann* TB/125

H. RICHARD NIERUHR: Christ and Culture TB/3

H. RICHARD NIEBUHR: The Kingdom of God in America TB/49

ANDERS NYGREN: Agape and Eros. *Translated by Philip S. Watson °* TB/1430

JOHN H. RANDALL, JR.: The Meaning of Religion for Man. *Revised with New Intro. by the Author* TB/1379

WALTER RAUSCHENBUSCHS Christianity and the Social Crisis. ‡ *Edited by Robert D. Cross* TB/3059

JOACHIM WACH: Understanding and Believing. *Ed. with Intro. by Joseph M. Kitagawa* TB/1399

Science and Mathematics

JOHN TYLER BONNER: The Ideas of Biology. Σ *Illus.* TB/570

W. E. LE GROS CLARK: The Antecedents of Man: *An Introduction to the Evolution of the Primates. ° Illus.* TB/559

ROBERT E. COKER: Streams, Lakes, Ponds. *Illus.* TB/586

ROBERT E. COKER: This Great and Wide Sea: *An Introduction to Oceanography and Marine Biology. Illus.* TB/551

W. H. DOWDESWELL: Animal Ecology. *61 illus.* TB/543

C. V. DURELL: Readable Relativity. *Foreword by Freeman J. Dyson* TB/530

GEORGE GAMOW: Biography of Physics. Σ *Illus.* TB/567

F. K. HARE: The Restless Atmosphere TB/560

S. KORNER: The Philosophy of Mathematics: *An Introduction* TB/547

J. R. PIERCE: Symbols, Signals and Noise: *The Nature and Process of Communication* Σ TB/574

WILLARD VAN ORMAN QUINE: Mathematical Logic TB/558

Science: History

MARIE BOAS: The Scientific Renaissance, 1450-1630 ° TB/583

W. DAMPIER, Ed.: Readings in the Literature of *Science. Illus.* TB/512

STEPHEN TOULMIN & JUNE GOODFIELD: The Architecture of Matter: *The Physics, Chemistry and Physiology of Matter, Both Animate and Inanimate, as it has Evolved since the Beginnings of Science* TB/584

STEPHEN TOULMIN & JUNE GOODFIELD: The Discovery of Time TB/585

STEPHEN TOULMIN & JUNE GOODFIELD: The Fabric of the Heavens: *The Development of Astronomy and Dynamics* TB/579

Science: Philosophy

J. M. BOCHENSKI: The Methods of Contemporary Thought. *Tr. by Peter Caws* TB/1377

J. BRONOWSKI: Science and Human Values. *Revised and Enlarged. Illus.* TB/505

WERNER HEISENBERG: Physics and Philosophy: *The Revolution in Modern Science. Introduction by F. S. C. Northrop* TB/549

KARL R. POPPER: Conjectures and Refutations: *The Growth of Scientific Knowledge* TB/1376

KARL R. POPPER: The Logic of Scientific Discovery TB/576

STEPHEN TOULMIN: Foresight and Understanding: *An Enquiry into the Aims of Science. Foreword by Jacques Barzun* TB/564

STEPHEN TOULMIN: The Philosophy of Science: *An Introduction* TB/513

Sociology and Anthropology

REINHARD BENDIX: Work and Authority in Industry: *Ideologies of Management in the Course of Industrialization* TB/3035

BERNARD BERELSON, Ed., The Behavioral Sciences Today TB/1127

JOSEPH B. CASAGRANDE, Ed.: In the Company of Man: *Twenty Portraits of Anthropological Informants. Illus.* TB/3047

KENNETH B. CLARK: Dark Ghetto: *Dilemmas of Social Power. Foreword by Gunnar Myrdal* TB/1317

KENNETH CLARK & JEANNETTE HOPKINS: A Relevant War Against Poverty: *A Study of Community Action Programs and Observable Social Change* TB/1480

W. E. LE GROS CLARK: The Antecedents of Man: *An Introduction to the Evolution of the Primates. ° Illus.* TB/559

LEWIS COSER, Ed.: Political Sociology TB/1293

ROSE L. COSER, Ed.: Life Cycle and Achievement in America ** TB/1434

ALLISON DAVIS & JOHN DOLLARD: Children of Bondage: *The Personality Development of Negro Youth in the Urban South* || TB/3049

ST. CLAIR DRAKE & HORACE R. CAYTON: Black Metropolis: *A Study of Negro Life in a Northern City. Introduction by Everett C. Hughes. Tables, maps, charts, and graphs* Vol. I TB/1086; Vol. II TB/1087

PETER E. DRUCKER: The New Society: *The Anatomy of Industrial Order* TB/1082

CORA DU BOIS: The People of Alor. *With a Preface by the Author* Vol. I *Illus.* TB/1042; Vol. II TB/1043

EMILE DURKHEIM et al.: Essays on Sociology and Philosophy: *with Appraisals of Durkheim's Life and Thought.* || *Edited by Kurt H. Wolff* TB/1151

LEON FESTINGER, HENRY W. RIECKEN, STANLEY SCHACHTER: When Prophecy Fails: *A Social and Psychological Study of a Modern Group that Predicted the Destruction of the World* || TB/1132

CHARLES Y. GLOCK & RODNEY STARK: Christian Beliefs and Anti-Semitism. *Introduction by the Authors* TB/1454

ALVIN W. GOULDNER: The Hellenic World TB/1479

ALVIN W. GOULDNER: Wildcat Strike: *A Study in Worker-Management Relationships* || TB/1176

CESAR GRANA: Modernity and Its Discontents: *French Society and the French Man of Letters in the Nineteenth Century* TB/1318

L. S. B. LEAKEY: Adam's Ancestors: *The Evolution of Man and His Culture. Illus.* TB/1019

KURT LEWIN: Field Theory in Social Science: *Selectcd Theoretical Papers.* || *Edited by Dorwin Cartwright* TB/1135

RITCHIE P. LOWRY: Who's Running This Town? *Community Leadership and Social Change* TB/1383

R. M. MACIVER: Social Causation TB/1153

GARY T. MARX: Protest and Prejudice: *A Study of Belief in the Black Community* TB/1435

ROBERT K. MERTON, LEONARD BROOM, LEONARD S. COTTRELL, JR., Editors: Sociology Today: *Problems and Prospects* || Vol. I TB/1173; Vol. II TB/1174

GILBERT OSOFSKY, Ed.: The Burden of Race: A Documentary History of Negro-White Relations in America TB/1405

GILBERT OSOFSKY: Harlem: The Making of a Ghetto: *Negro New York 1890-1930* TB/1381

TALCOTT PARSONS & EDWARD A. SHILS, Editors: Toward a General Theory of Action: *Theoretical Foundations for the Social Sciences* TB/1083

PHILIP RIEFF: The Triumph of the Therapeutic: *Uses of Faith After Freud* TB/1360

JOHN H. ROHRER & MUNRO S. EDMONSON, Eds.: The Eighth Generation Grows Up: *Cultures and Personalities of New Orleans Negroes* || TB/3050

ARNOLD ROSE: The Negro in America: *The Condensed Version of Gunnar Myrdal's* An American Dilemma. *Second Edition* TB/3048

GEORGE ROSEN: Madness in Society: *Chapters in the Historical Sociology of Mental Illness.* || *Preface by Benjamin Nelson* TB/1337

PHILIP SELZNICK: TVA and the Grass Roots: *A Study in the Sociology of Formal Organization* TB/1230

PITIRIM A. SOROKIN: Contemporary Sociological Theories: *Through the First Quarter of the Twentieth Century* TB/3046

MAURICE R. STEIN: The Eclipse of Community: *An Interpretation of American Studies* TB/1128

WILLIAM I. THOMAS: The Unadjusted Girl: *With Cases and Standpoint for Behavior Analysis. Intro. by Michael Parenti* TB/1319

EDWARD A. TIRYAKIAN, Ed.: Sociological Theory, Values and Sociocultural Change: *Essays in Honor of Pitirim A. Sorokin* ° TB/1316

FERDINAND TONNIES: Community and Society: *Gemeinschaft und Gesellschaft. Translated and Edited by Charles P. Loomis* TB/1116

SAMUEL E. WALLACE: Skid Row as a Way of Life TB/1367

W. LLOYD WARNER and Associates: Democracy in Jonesville: *A Study in Quality and Inequality* || TB/1129

W. LLOYD WARNER: Social Class in America: *The Evaluation of Status* TB/1013

FLORIAN ZNANIECKI: The Social Role of the Man of Knowledge. *Introduction by Lewis A. Coser* TB/1372